ENGLISH DRAMA TO 1660

(EXCLUDING SHAKESPEARE)

AMERICAN LITERATURE, ENGLISH LITERATURE, AND WORLD LITERATURES IN ENGLISH: AN INFORMATION GUIDE SERIES

Series Editor: Theodore Grieder, Curator, Division of Special Collections, Fales Library, New York University, New York, New York

Associate Editor: Duane DeVries, Assistant Professor, Polytechnic Institute of New York, Brooklyn, New York

Other books on English Literature in this series:

ENGLISH DRAMA, 1660-1800–*Edited by Frederick M. Link**

ENGLISH DRAMA AND THEATRE, 1800-1900–*Edited by L. W. Conolly and J. P. Wearing**

BRITISH DRAMA, 1900-1950–*Edited by E. H. Mikhail**

CONTEMPORARY DRAMA IN AMERICA AND ENGLAND, 1950-1970–*Edited by Richard H. Harris***

THE BRITISH LITERARY JOURNAL TO 1900–*Edited by Robert B. White, Jr.**

ENGLISH-CANADIAN LITERATURE TO 1900–*Edited by R. G. Moyles*

ENGLISH PROSE, PROSE FICTION, AND CRITICISM TO 1660–*Edited by S. K. Heninger, Jr.*

OLD AND MIDDLE ENGLISH POETRY TO 1500–*Edited by Walter M. Beale**

ENGLISH POETRY, 1500-1660–*Edited by S. K. Heninger, Jr.***

ENGLISH POETRY, 1660-1800–*Edited by Christopher Cohane***

ENGLISH POETRY IN THE NINETEENTH CENTURY–*Edited by Donald Reiman***

BRITISH POETRY, 1900-1950–*Edited by Emily Ann Anderson***

CONTEMPORARY POETRY IN AMERICA AND ENGLAND, 1950-1970–*Edited by Calvin Skaggs***

*in press
**in preparation

The above series is part of the
GALE INFORMATION GUIDE LIBRARY

The Library consists of a number of separate series of guides covering major areas in the social sciences, humanities, and current affairs.

General Editor: Paul Wasserman, Professor and former Dean, School of Library and Information Services, University of Maryland

ENGLISH DRAMA TO 1660

(EXCLUDING SHAKESPEARE)

A GUIDE TO INFORMATION SOURCES

Volume 5 in the American Literature, English Literature, and World Literatures in English Information Guide Series

Frieda Elaine Penninger

Professor of English and Chairman of the Department of English
Westhampton College, University of Richmond

Gale Research Company
Book Tower, Detroit, Michigan 48226

Library of Congress Cataloging in Publication Data

Penninger, Frieda Elaine
English drama to 1660 (excluding Shakespeare).

(American literature, English literature, and world literatures in English; v. 5) (Gale information guide library)
1. English drama--Bibliography. 2. English drama--History and criticism--Bibliography. I. Title.
Z2014.D7P46 016.822'008 73-16988
ISBN 0-8103-1223-9

VITA

Frieda Elaine Penninger was born in Marion, North Carolina, and received the AB degree from the Woman's College of the University of North Carolina, the MA and PhD degrees from Duke University. She has taught in the public schools, at Flora Macdonald College, at the University of Tennessee, and at the Woman's College of the University of North Carolina, and is now Professor of English and Chairman of the Department of English at Westhampton College, the University of Richmond, Virginia. Her fields of interest are Medieval and Renaissance drama, Chaucer, and Caxton.

To the memory of Bascomb Whitfield Young and Edna Jennie Cox Young and to the memory of Fred Hoyle Penninger

CONTENTS

Contents

FORE-FOREWORD

Dibdin, T.F. THE LIBRARY COMPANION; OR, THE YOUNG MAN'S GUIDE, AND OLD MAN'S COMFORT, IN THE CHOICE OF A LIBRARY. Part II. Second Edition. London: Printed for Harding, Triphook, and Lepard, Finsbury-Square; and J. Major, Fleet-Street, MDCCCXXV.

In recommending an edition of Beaumont and Fletcher, Dibdin advises: "[P]rocure the edition of Mr. Weber, 1812, 8vo., fourteen vols. This edition might have been better; but in this life we must swallow much of bitter with a little that is sweet" (p. 828).

FOREWORD

This is an annotated bibliography of primary and secondary materials for the study of English drama to 1660. A persistent problem in its compilation has been to choose out of the enormous amounts of material, primary and secondary, the body of items which could be included within the compass of a reasonably sized, annotated bibliography. In making choices I have kept in mind one primary group of users--undergraduate and graduate students who seek direction towards editions and discussions which will enable them to initiate and pursue a study of a given area of the drama. If the needs of these users can be provided for, the bibliography will readily lend itself to the use of others who wish for any reason to explore English drama to 1660 and the scholarship related to it.

No criteria for inclusion or exclusion except utility for the potential user can be consistently applied if the goal of that basic utility is to be even approximately met. However, certain broad guidelines have been followed.

1) Periodical articles are often among the most valuable studies of sharply focused problems, but they cannot, by their length, provide broad in-depth studies. Some periodical materials must have a place here. Most, however, are omitted with the expectation that the student will seek out, in the notes and bibliographies of the studies here mentioned, the periodical materials relevant to his specific topic.

2) As length is no guide to value, neither is age. I have stressed materials published in the last two decades, again with the expectation that these will lead the user back to earlier relevant materials. Some early studies contain basic factual information. Others reveal essential perceptions or introduce germinal ideas. Some are the products of remarkably original minds, whether whimsical or profound. Some are essentially characteristic of their period. I have tried to include at least representative samplings of these. Perhaps it is unnecessary to remark that some titles will have appeared between the assembling of these materials and the user's securing the BIBLIOGRAPHY. In addition, I have tried to describe books which I have actually examined; some titles, however, I have mentioned without viewing; most of these are quite recent.

3) National origin is no guide to quality; but assuming that most users will be English-speaking, I have omitted books in foreign languages unless these make some special demand for inclusion.

4) Accessibility is again no measure of quality. Unless the volume is readily accessible, however, it will be used only by the advanced or specialized student. The books here included are in general those which can be found in a reasonably well-stocked university library.

5) Unpublished dissertations and theses are omitted. The various printed guides to and abstracts of dissertations will enable the specialized student to discover those he must review.

6) Shakespeare bibliography is a subject in itself. I have made no attempt to review Shakespeare materials. The user will remember, however, that studies of Shakespeare will almost inevitably include information about other Renaissance drama, dramatists, and stagecraft. In some instances, Shakespeare items are inescapable. If its topic is the assumption that Marlowe wrote the Shakespeare plays, for example, a book may deal as much with the former as with the latter.

7) Editions of Medieval and Renaissance texts have recently multiplied in number and kind. Editions of single plays or of small groups of plays are in general omitted, but the user is reminded that many of these contain valuable commentaries. Some single-play volumes appear in serial editions of plays by various authors. I have provided notices of several such series, mostly current ones, at the end of Part 1, Section 2: Editions. Collected editions fall into three general categories--period, genre, and author. Some representative examples of the first two are included in Part 1, Section 2. Editions designed basically as textbooks for survey courses are generally omitted. Under individual authors, one or more kinds of editions are to be found: a few instances of collected editions contemporary with the author himself or the early collected editions; some examples of editions representative of the evolution of editorial work on an author; and recent editions, either a recognized standard edition of a given author or several editions if the apparatus provided, controversy over text or canon, or the like, make it necessary to mention several.

8) Even the group of authors included is selective. A major author who wrote a few plays but had little impact on the drama and whose reputation rests largely on work in other genres--Milton, for example--must give way to a dramatist of small output but large dramatic significance, like Thomas Kyd, or one of large output, like Massinger or Middleton.

One must choose between including as many titles as possible or mentioning fewer titles but repeating them under every category to which they belong. I have kept cross-references to a minimum. The user ought to search in various categories for likely materials, remembering that any general book will mention the major authors and probably the minor ones as well.

While I have kept in mind an audience composed primarily of college and university students and the libraries which serve them, the materials nevertheless vary considerably in range and depth. A few are useful primarily to the freshman writing a term paper or being introduced to the serious study of a play. A few are intended chiefly for the advanced student or scholar. Some, like the collections of reprinted materials, are most useful to small libraries which lack extensive periodical and specialized holdings or to individuals who wish to have in one cover a few basic discussions of certain topics.

The choice of an item for inclusion does not necessarily imply that it offers an accepted or even a viable argument. Psychological biography affords an example of one type of study which, in given instances, may or may not be sound or acceptable. Arguments about authorship and canon often cannot be settled definitely. Even the editing of texts is sometimes controversial and presents problems which must be answered differently for different users. Whether spelling and punctuation are modernized, whether all textual variants are noted, how extensive a glossary is needed are in part matters of editorial judgment and in part of audience. The materials here included have been chosen, not because I necessarily agree with their methods or conclusions or because they have met general approval, but because I think the user of this BIBLIOGRAPHY ought to be aware of them.

That this should be a bibliography without flaw is my fond dream, but it is, I know all too well, a dream which has issued through the gates of ivory and not of horn. If the volume is to serve its potential audience, it must come into print, and the delays required to pursue perfection would finally not serve that end. I have tried to make it accurate; I hope I have succeeded at least to the point that the user will not find such errors as will seriously impede his discovery of the book itself. For clarity's sake a few matters might be kept in mind: This is not a bibliography designed to provide definitive descriptions of a class of books. It aims at pointing to books useful to the study of the drama and at describing them in such a way as to help the user choose those he needs. I have, in general, described books which I have held in hand. The user may discover that the book carries a different imprint from the one I have shown. For example, Edmund Creeth's TUDOR PLAYS: AN ANTHOLOGY OF EARLY ENGLISH DRAMA, copyrighted by Doubleday in 1966, can be found in a Doubleday Anchor paperback edition and also in the Norton Library. To seek out all such possible multiple printings would delay the appearance of this BIBLIOGRAPHY and would not, finally, be of particular help to the user who wishes to know what plays Creeth edited and in what fashion. Certain users may need to check the total publishing history of a given title, but the purpose in compiling this list is more general. Again, I have occasionally noted that volumes are in paperback, especially if they seem to me books that the user might well want to purchase. I have made no final search for paperback publications, however. Availability of both paperback and hardback editions and reprints may be rather easily traced for a given title through BOOKS IN PRINT and PAPERBOUND BOOKS IN PRINT (see Part 1, Section 3 B: Availability and Prices--Current Prices of Readily Available Books).

It should also be noted that, when a book does not show the author's full name, place of publication, date of publication, or the like, I have relied on attributions in library catalogs, or in the Library of Congress or British Museum printed catalogs.

In citing book titles I have tried to leave every author his own choices in spelling: Shakespeare, Shakspere, etc.; Medieval, Mediaeval. Capitilization and punctuation on titlepages often have more motive in art than in letters, however, and I have generally altered these to a standard pattern where necessary.

Much that might have been, perhaps much that should have been, included has been omitted because of space limitations. Such limits are a problem but not, in the end, an evil; a bibliography may be more readily usable by the fact of its being selective and manageable in bulk. Omissions which are the result of oversight or ignorance, however, are the compiler's nightmare and are, alas, far from impossible. For the remedy of such lapses I can only trust that the complex net of bibliographies spun out of bibliographies will enable the user to catch the here-omitted. In any case, this BIBLIOGRAPHY should be used as a tool for beginning to locate one's interests and materials. It is not for nothing that bibliographies are called tools; they exist to aid in the accomplishment of a project. Even if a perfect one could be achieved it would not replace the student's own thoughtful effort.

More pleasant than to think of the errors or inadequacies which may lurk here is to thank the people who have helped to make them fewer. The libraries in which I have sought materials are that of my own school, the University of Richmond, and those of Duke University, the University of North Carolina at Chapel Hill, and the University of Virginia. The staff of the University of Richmond's Boatwright Library has gone many second miles for me in the pursuit of details and in ordering materials; their unfailing courtesy and interest have been of great help. The Reference Departments at Duke and UNC have given generously of their time and have saved time for me through their knowledgeability. Space and memory will not allow me to name the names of all who have answered my queries, but I must name two, Miss Mary Whitfield Canada and Miss Florence Blakely of the Duke Reference Department, who, from the time when I first commenced to pursue the arcane ways of scholarship, have come to my aid beyond any call of duty or friendship. The University of Virginia, as the editions in the BIBLIOGRAPHY itself will recall, has been particularly active in the field of Renaissance drama, and its collection has proved useful. That I came to it last in my search has spared its staff some of my questions, but such as I asked received prompt attention.

The University of Richmond has given me generous support, in the tangible forms of a semester's sabbatical leave in the fall of 1973 and two research grants. Both the time and the money have been of the greatest use.

Dr. Theodore Grieder, the general editor of this series, has provided sane and kindly aid and has encouraged the hope that the job could be done. Dr. Duane DeVries, the associate editor, has read the manuscript with uncommon vigilance.

Finally, I should like to thank my mother, who has put up with more than I hope she will remember.

Frieda Elaine Penninger

Richmond, Virginia

A NOTE ON CROSS-REFERENCING

This study is organized in two basic parts, each divided into sections. Part 1 contains numbered and lettered subdivisions. In Part 2, the subdivisions are not numbered, coming regularly in the order: Bibliographies (if any), Editions, Concordances (if any), and Secondary Works. Cross-references in Part 1 to materials in Part 2 or in Part 2 to materials in Part 1 begin with notice of the part; indication of part is omitted when reference and cross-reference fall within the same part. Similarly, cross-references to another section or subdivision carry an indication of section or subdivision when these are not within the section or subdivision at hand, except that cross-references to subdivisions under individual authors in Part 2 will not note "Secondary Works" and the like when the location is self-evident.

Part 1

GENERAL WORKS

1. BIBLIOGRAPHIES

Like anything else, bibliographies fall into mixed and overlapping categories. In general, however, the bibliographies listed here are grouped as follows:

1) Bibliographies of bibliographies.

2) General literary bibliographies (with some entries which are more general than literary but which include literary material and specifically sections helpful in the discovery of materials concerned with drama). There are subsections of bibliographies of microform indexes and of bibliographies concerned with old books.

3) Bibliographies of drama, including some period bibliographies.

One piece of advice may be in order: the usefulness of bibliographical tools depends very greatly on the user's familiarity with the organization and intent of the bibliography; careful examination of prefatory materials, indexes, and the general format of the book will enable the user to save time in the long run.

See also Section 9: Playlists, Records of Early Publication, Etc., for certain bibliographies of plays per se.

Note: Persons who prepare bibliographies are in the nature of things compilers or editors rather than authors. This fact being evident, I have omitted comp., or ed. after the names of persons responsible for the bibliographies shown here except for those who are general editors. In other sections of the present bibliography, compilers of bibliographies are so labeled, however.

A. BIBLIOGRAPHIES OF BIBLIOGRAPHIES

Besterman, Theodore. A WORLD BIBLIOGRAPHY OF BIBLIOGRAPHIES AND OF BIBLIOGRAPHICAL CATALOGUES, CALENDARS, ABSTRACTS, DIGESTS, INDEXES, AND THE LIKE. 4th ed. 5 vols. Lausanne: Societas Bibliographica, 1965-66.

Since the publication of the first edition in 1939-40, Besterman has been a basic guide to bibliographies. The fourth edition is intended to be inclusive through 1963, with a limited number of later publications also included. Volume V is the INDEX.

BIBLIOGRAPHIC INDEX. A CUMULATIVE BIBLIOGRAPHY OF BIBLIOGRAPHIES. New York: H.W. Wilson, 1937--.

The first cumulative issue of the INDEX, for 1937-42, appeared in 1945, edited by Dorothy Charles and Bea Joseph. The imprint varies over the years, the 1973 volume, for 1972, being edited by Marga Franck, with the assistance of Ann Massie Case. The INDEX lists books and articles containing bibliographies as well as volumes devoted solely to bibliography. The cumulations of early issues are bound in various year groups; cumulations are now annual.

Gray, Richard A. A GUIDE TO BOOK REVIEW CITATIONS: A BIBLIOGRAPHY OF SOURCES. Columbus: Ohio State University Press, 1968.

Gray defines "a book review citing source" as a source "which cites reviews from more than one periodical. Such sources may be book review indexes per se, periodical indexes, serial bibliographies, monographic bibliographies and specialized tools." Gray further specifies that the GUIDE is designed as a supplement to "all the standard tools . . . traditionally . . . used to locate review references" (p. [1]).

Gray, Richard A., with Dorothy Villmow. SERIAL BIBLIOGRAPHIES IN THE HUMANITIES AND SOCIAL SCIENCES. Ann Arbor, Mich.: Pierian Press, 1969.

The declared purpose is "to identify and to designate the salient characteristics of those serial bibliographies . . . of primary utility to humanists and social scientists." Gray and Villmow include "concealed bibliographies," that is, bibliographies appearing within periodicals and the like, as well as those published in separate covers (see p. i for a general statement of editorial principles).

Howard-Hill, T[revor] H[oward]. INDEX TO BRITISH LITERARY BIBLIOGRAPHY. Oxford: Clarendon Press, 1969--.

Two of the proposed three volumes are now in print. Volume I, 1969, is BIBLIOGRAPHY OF BRITISH LITERARY BIBLIOGRAPHIES. It carries a description of the entire INDEX as designed to include any English-language "books, substantial parts of books, and periodical articles . . . published in the English-speaking Commonwealth and the United States after 1890, on the bibliographical and textual examination of English manuscripts, books, printing and publishing." It also includes "any other books" which have appeared "in English in Great Britain or by British authors abroad," from the time the printing press was introduced into England, with the exception of materials on the subjects of "modern . . . printing and publishing" which are of secondary interest to bibliographical or literary studies (see 1, [xi]). Volume II, 1971, is SHAKESPEARIAN BIB-

LIOGRAPHY AND TEXTUAL CRITICISM: A BIBLIOGRAPHY. Volume III, forthcoming, is to contain a BIBLIOGRAPHY OF BRITISH BIBLIOGRAPHY AND TEXTUAL CRITICISM and will index the whole set.

Pownall, David E. "English-American-Commonwealth Serial Bibliographies." RENAISSANCE QUARTERLY, 4 (Winter, 1969), 75-105.

Excellent survey of serial bibliographies.

Walford, A.J. GUIDE TO REFERENCE MATERIAL. 2nd ed. Vol. 3: GENERALITIES, LANGUAGE, THE ARTS AND LITERATURE. London: Library Association, 1970.

Useful general guide, clearly arranged.

Winchell, Constance M. GUIDE TO REFERENCE BOOKS. 8th ed. Chicago: American Library Association, 1967. Supplements to the 8th ed.: Eugene P. Sheehy, FIRST SUPPLEMENT, 1965-1966, published 1968; Eugene P. Sheehy, with the assistance of Rita G. Keckeissen, SECOND SUPPLEMENT, 1967-1968, published 1970; Eugene P. Sheehy, with the assistance of Rita G. Keckeissen and Eileen McIlvaine, THIRD SUPPLEMENT, 1969-1970, published 1972.

Clearly organized, well annotated, but by its breadth of coverage and one-volume size, limited to basic books in a given discipline.

B. GENERAL LITERARY BIBLIOGRAPHIES

Altick, Richard D., and Andrew Wright. SELECTIVE BIBLIOGRAPHY FOR THE STUDY OF ENGLISH AND AMERICAN LITERATURE. 5th ed. New York: Macmillan; London: Collier Macmillan, Publishers, 1975.

Described in the "Preface" as "highly selective; many items . . . have been rejected as being obsolete, or untrustworthy, or simply not valuable enough for the student to bother with." Paperback publication is one of the ways in which the volume fulfills its aim "to keep in mind the needs of today's scholars" (p. vii).

Baer, Eleanora A. TITLES IN SERIES; A HANDBOOK FOR LIBRARIANS AND STUDENTS. 2nd ed. 2 vols. New York and London: Scarecrow Press, 1964. SUPPLEMENTS, 1967, 1971.

Among the many thousands of titles entered in Baer one may find lists of the titles included in such important series as the MALONE SOCIETY REPRINTS and the Stratford-upon-Avon Studies.

Bateson, F[rederick] W., ed. THE CAMBRIDGE BIBLIOGRAPHY OF ENGLISH LITERATURE. 4 vols. New York: Macmillan; Cambridge: At the University Press, 1941. Vol. V: SUPPLEMENT: A.D. 600-1900. Ed. George Watson. Cambridge: At the University Press, 1957.

The CBEL has long been a standard tool. Volume I covers the years 600-1660. Volume IV is the INDEX. One may still find the 1941, 1957 volumes serviceable; however, they have been superseded in many ways by a new edition:

Watson, George, ed. THE NEW CAMBRIDGE BIBLIOGRAPHY OF ENGLISH LITERATURE. Vol. 1. (See below.)

______. A GUIDE TO ENGLISH LITERATURE. 2nd ed. Chicago: Aldine Publishing Co., 1968.

Compiled, as the "Preface" indicates, for persons "entering, or re-entering, the serious study of English literature" (p. [v]). Not generally designed as a guide to doing "original research . . . though a special section on literary scholarship makes some attempt to provide the researcher with some of the indispensable equipment." Bateson enters both primary and secondary material.

Bohn, Henry G. THE BIBLIOGRAPHER'S MANUAL OF ENGLISH LITERATURE CONTAINING AN ACCOUNT OF RARE, CURIOUS, AND USEFUL BOOKS, PUBLISHED IN OR RELATING TO GREAT BRITAIN AND IRELAND, FROM THE INVENTION OF PRINTING; WITH BIBLIOGRAPHICAL AND CRITICAL NOTICES, COLLATIONS OF THE RARER ARTICLES, AND THE PRICES AT WHICH THEY HAVE BEEN SOLD. BY WILLIAM THOMAS LOWNDES. New edition, revised, corrected and enlarged; with an appendix relating to the books of literary and scientific societies. 4 vols. London: George Bell & Sons, [1857-1864?].

In addition to the material indicated by the title, volume 4 contains an appendix listing various groups--the Roxburghe Club, the Percy Society, the Shakespeare Society, and the like, with their publications. The "Notice to the Tenth Part" describes this appendix as containing "a complete list of all the books printed by the Literary and Scientific Societies of Great Britain, with such particulars respecting them as are likely to be useful to the scholar and collector" (Vol. 4, p. [iii]). Although now more than a century old, the Lowndes-Bohn MANUAL has both antiquarian and contemporary interest. It may also be bound in six volumes and six volumes in eleven parts.

Bond, Donald F. A REFERENCE GUIDE TO ENGLISH STUDIES. 2nd ed. Chicago and London: University of Chicago, 1971.

Descended from Tom Peete Cross's BIBLIOGRAPHICAL GUIDE TO ENGLISH STUDIES (10 editions, from 1919 to 1951, the original title being A LIST OF BOOKS AND ARTICLES, CHIEFLY BIBLIOGRAPHICAL), Bond's GUIDE is "designed primarily for the use of the graduate student . . . to clear the way through the enormous number of publications which he faces" (p. ix).

BOOK REVIEW INDEX. Detroit: Gale Research Co., 1965--.

Issued monthly, cumulated annually. The editors have changed through the years. The "Preface" to the first cumulation describes the INDEX as "a current guide to current reviews of current books" (p. [iii]).

BRITISH MUSEUM CATALOGUES.

The British Museum has issued a number of catalogs of various parts of its enormous collection. Available in many libraries is the basic catalog:

British Museum. GENERAL CATALOGUE OF PRINTED BOOKS TO 1955. Compact Edition. 27 vols. New York: Readex Microprint Corp., 1967. With a TEN-YEAR SUPPLEMENT, 1956-1965. 5 vols. New York: Readex Microprint Corp., 1969. The card catalogs in major libraries will reveal their holdings of additional specialized catalogs of this important collection.

Cole, George Watson. "A Survey of the Bibliography of English Literature, 1475-1640, with Especial Reference to the Work of the Bibliographical Society of London." THE PAPERS OF THE BIBLIOGRAPHICAL SOCIETY OF AMERICA, 23 (1929), Part II, pp. [i]-[iv], 1-95.

Cole surveys not only the work but the personalities of an important group of bibliographers, including a number whose work involves drama. This article should be consulted for identification and frank evaluation of many bibliographers of earlier times. The reader may well be astonished at how fascinating the account is.

Farrar, Clarissa P., and Austin P. Evans. BIBLIOGRAPHY OF ENGLISH TRANSLATIONS FROM MEDIEVAL SOURCES. New York: Columbia University Press, [1948].

Headings include groups such as "Mystery and miracle plays," individual authors such as "Medwall, Henry," and individual topics such as "Harrowing of hell."

Fisher, John H., general ed. THE MEDIEVAL LITERATURE OF WESTERN EUROPE. A REVIEW OF RESEARCH, MAINLY 1930-1960. New York: Published for the Modern Language Association of America by the New York University Press; London: University of London Press, 1966.

Robert W. Ackerman has edited "Middle English Literature to 1400," of which pages 101-6 deal with drama.

Frye, Roland Mushat. "The New Xerox Library of British Renaissance Books at the University of Pennsylvania." THE LIBRARY CHRONICLE (University of Pennsylvania), 34 (1968), 3-6.

Formerly unobtainable materials may now be secured in Xerox books. Frye describes such a collection, in this case of all the materials in the Pollard and Redgrave SHORT-TITLE CATALOGUE (see main entry in Section 9: Playlists, Records of Early Publication, Etc.).

Gable, J. Harris. BIBLIOGRAPHY OF ROBIN HOOD. University of Nebraska Studies in Language, Literature and Criticism, No. 17. Lincoln: University of Nebraska Press, 1939.

> Intended as an exhaustive bibliography of all kinds of Robin Hood material. See the index for references to plays.

[Ghosh, Jyotish C., et al]. ANNALS OF ENGLISH LITERATURE, 1475-1925; THE PRINCIPAL PUBLICATIONS OF EACH YEAR, TOGETHER WITH AN ALPHABETICAL INDEX OF AUTHORS WITH THEIR WORKS. Rev. ed. Oxford: Clarendon Press, 1961.

> A chronological list arranged alphabetically by author under the year. The 1961 revision of the original 1935 edition carries the list through 1950. The "Preface to the Second Edition" attributes the "main work of revision" to "the late Dr. R.W. Chapman" (p. [iii]).

[Great Britain: British Council]. ENGLISH LITERATURE FROM THE 16TH CENTURY TO THE PRESENT. A SELECT LIST OF EDITIONS. Rev. ed. London: Published for the British Council by Longmans, Green & Co., 1965.

> The "Prefatory Note" indicates the intention to include "the best edition or editions" and also "other sound and useful low-priced editions currently available" as well as "the best secondary works currently available" and secondary works considered to be "of particular value" which are out of print but obtainable "in libraries or secondhand booksellers' catalogues" (p. vii). The entries are brief, without annotation.

Hartung, Albert E., general ed. A MANUAL OF THE WRITINGS IN MIDDLE ENGLISH, 1050-1500. New Haven: Connecticut Academy of Arts and Sciences, 1967--.

> The revision of the Wells MANUAL (see Wells, John Edwin), now under the general editorship of Albert E. Hartung, is appearing at intervals. Hartung advises me by letter, of February 5, 1974, that Volume 5 is to contain a chapter on drama and should appear in 1974 or 1975. (Hartung succeeds J. Burke Severs as editor.)

INDEX TO BOOK REVIEWS IN THE HUMANITIES, AN. Vol. I--(March 31, 1960--).

> Quarterly, published by Phillip Thomson, now in Williamston, Michigan.

Library of Congress.

> Like the British Museum, the Library of Congress has issued a number of catalogs of its massive holdings. See:
>
> > The Association of Research Libraries. A CATALOG OF BOOKS REPRESENTED BY LIBRARY OF CONGRESS

PRINTED CARDS, ISSUED TO JULY 31, 1942. 167 vols. Ann Arbor, Mich.: Edwards Brothers, 1942-46.

This publication was followed by supplementary volumes and by a catalog for 1948-52, then by:

THE LIBRARY OF CONGRESS CATALOGS. THE NATIONAL UNION CATALOG, 1952-1955 IMPRINTS. AN AUTHOR LIST REPRESENTING LIBRARY OF CONGRESS PRINTED CARDS AND TITLES REPORTED BY OTHER AMERICAN LIBRARIES. Compiled by the Library of Congress under the Auspices of the Committee on Resources of American Libraries of the American Library Association. 30 vols. Ann Arbor, Mich.: J.W. Edwards, 1961.

With some variations in imprint, publication of catalogs continues. There are catalogs in addition to the AUTHOR LIST.

Two other publications of great value from the Library of Congress are:

THE NATIONAL UNION CATALOG OF MANUSCRIPT COLLECTIONS.

Ten volumes of the catalog have been issued from 1969 through 1973. The imprint varies from volume to volume, some copies reading Ann Arbor, Mich.: J.W. Edwards; some, Hamden, Conn.: The Shoe String Press; and some, Washington: The Library of Congress. The "Preface" to the 1973 volume, page iii, signed L. Quincey Mumford, states: "This publication is the 10th in a continuing series designed to bring under bibliographic control manuscript collections housed permanently in American repositories that are regularly open to scholars. . . . [I]t brings the total number of collections described to 29,356, representing holdings in 850 repositories." Indexes are issued from time to time.

THE NATIONAL UNION CATALOG. PRE-1956 IMPRINTS. A CUMULATIVE AUTHOR LIST REPRESENTING LIBRARY OF CONGRESS PRINTED CARDS AND TITLES REPORTED BY OTHER AMERICAN LIBRARIES. Compiled and edited with the cooperation of the Library of Congress and National Union Catalog Subcommittee of the Resources Committee of the Resources and Technical Services Division, American Library Association. London: Mansell, 1968--.

By early 1974 publication had reached Volume 318, through LAVANDERO (omitting 53-56, to contain BIBLE). Publication of the remainder should be achieved without undue delay. Entries show one or more of the libraries holding each item. Notice, however, that only PRE-1956 IMPRINTS are included.

(LONDON) TIMES INDEX. 1790--.

The London TIMES is indexed at regular intervals. These indexes will reveal reviews of current productions of Medieval and Renaissance plays when these attract major interest. Various imprints; reprints.

Lowndes, William Thomas.

See Bohn, Henry G., above.

Modern Humanities Research Association. ANNUAL BIBLIOGRAPHY OF ENGLISH LANGUAGE AND LITERATURE. 1921--.

The imprint varies over the years. The title page of the first volume reads: BIBLIOGRAPHY OF ENGLISH LANGUAGE AND LITERATURE, 1920. Compiled by Members of the Modern Humanities Research Association. Cambridge: Bowes & Bowes, 1921. The word ANNUAL and the volume number begin to appear on the title page with Volume 4 for 1923 (published 1924). The "Preface" states: "The countries represented . . . are as follows: Australia, British Isles, Canada, Czecho-Slovakia, Denmark, France, Germany, Holland, India, Italy, Portugal, Rumania, Serbia, Spain (including works in Catalan), Sweden, Switzerland, and the United States of America. Both books and articles are included in the list; the aim has been to include all serious contributions to the subject" (Vol. 1, p. ii). Volume 45 appeared with the title page: ANNUAL BIBLIOGRAPHY OF ENGLISH LANGUAGE AND LITERATURE FOR 1970, Volume 45. Editor, John Horden; American Editor, James B. Misenheimer, Jr. Modern Humanities Research Association, 1972. The broad coverage announced in the first volume remains the aim of the series. The early issues are available in a reprint: London: Wm. Dawson & Sons, 1964. This is, of course, the publication familiarly known as the MHRA ANNUAL BIBLIOGRAPHY.

Modern Language Association of America. ANNUAL BIBLIOGRAPHY. 1921--.

Beginning in 1922 (for 1921) the Modern Language Association of America has issued an annual bibliography in one of the issues of PMLA (PUBLICATIONS OF THE MODERN LANGUAGE ASSOCIATION OF AMERICA). Through 1956 (for 1955) this was the MLA AMERICAN BIBLIOGRAPHY OF BOOKS AND ARTICLES ON THE MODERN LANGUAGES AND LITERATURES. In 1957 (for 1956) it became the MLA INTERNATIONAL BIBLIOGRAPHY OF BOOKS AND ARTICLES ON THE MODERN LANGUAGES AND LITERATURES. Publication continues to date. Kraus Reprint Corporation has issued clothbound reprints of the 1921-70 editions, grouping several years together according to overall length. Coverage is not limited to literatures or scholarship in English or of British Commonwealth and United States origin. Beginning with 1969, the date on spine and cover corresponds to the date of publication of materials indexed.

NATIONAL UNION CATALOG.

See Library of Congress, above.

NEW YORK TIMES INDEX. 1913--.

These indexes appear regularly and provide a guide to reviews of current productions.

Northrup, Clark Sutherland, with contributions by Joseph Quincy Adams and Andrew Keogh. A REGISTER OF BIBLIOGRAPHIES OF THE ENGLISH LANGUAGE AND LITERATURE. 1925; reprint ed. New York: Hafner, 1962.

Two major divisions, "General" and "Individual Authors and Topics." Light annotation. Although old, still useful for its coverage of early work.

Ogden, Margaret S., Charles E. Palmer, and Richard L. McKelvey. A BIBLIOGRAPHY OF MIDDLE ENGLISH TEXTS. Ann Arbor: University of Michigan Press, 1954.

Designed for use with the MIDDLE ENGLISH DICTIONARY, the list is usable in itself.

Palmer, Henrietta R. LIST OF ENGLISH EDITIONS AND TRANSLATIONS OF GREEK AND LATIN CLASSICS PRINTED BEFORE 1641. With an Introduction by Victor Scholderer. London: Printed for the Bibliographical Society by Blades, East & Blades, 1911.

Arranged alphabetically by author, with full bibliographical descriptions. Useful for determining which classical works were available to Renaissance dramatists and in what form.

Pownall, David E. "English-American-Commonwealth Serial Bibliographies."

See Section 1 A: Bibliographies of Bibliographies. Pownall evaluates a number of serial bibliographies relevant to studies in English literature.

PROGRESS OF MEDIEVAL AND RENAISSANCE STUDIES IN THE UNITED STATES AND CANADA. Boulder, Colo.: American Council of Learned Societies, Committee on Mediaeval Latin, Mediaeval Academy of America, 1923-60.

This periodic review of progress has ceased publication.

PUBLICATIONS OF THE MODERN LANGUAGE ASSOCIATION OF AMERICA.

See Modern Language Association of America.

Spargo, John Webster. A BIBLIOGRAPHICAL MANUAL FOR STUDENTS OF THE LANGUAGE AND LITERATURE OF ENGLAND AND THE UNITED STATES. A SHORT-TITLE LIST. 3rd ed. New York: Hendricks House, 1956.

See pages 167-77 for "The Drama and The Theatre." No annotation.

STUDIES IN PHILOLOGY.

Volumes 14-66, 1917-69, printed an annual bibliography of Renaissance literature, highly regarded by its users. Unhappily, Volume 66 (May, 1969) carries with the bibliography, "Literature of the Renaissance in 1968," the notice that the expense of printing the bibliography together with the fact of the duplication of substantial parts of the information in other sources would make the 1968 bibliography "the last. Plans are being made for an annual Texts and Studies number, which in 1970 will supplant the annual bibliography." These numbers are now appearing.

Tanner, Thomas. BIBLIOTHECA BRITANNICO-HIBERNICA: SIVE, DE SCRIPTORIBUS, QUI IN ANGLIA, SCOTIA, ET HIBERNIA AD SAECULI XVII INITIUM FLORUERENT, LITERARUM ORDINE JUXTA FAMILIARUM NOMINA DISPOSITIS COMMENTARIUS. Londini: Excudit Guilielmus Bowyer, Impensis Societatis ad Literas Promovendas Institutae, Anno Domini MDCCXLVIII.

Alphabetical list. Entries in Latin.

Watson, George, ed. THE NEW CAMBRIDGE BIBLIOGRAPHY OF ENGLISH LITERATURE. 5 vols. Cambridge and New York: Cambridge University Press, 1971--.

Volume I, for the years 600-1660, appeared in 1974. Volume V, GENERAL INDEX, is yet to be published. The NCBEL is a revision of the original CAMBRIDGE BIBLIOGRAPHY OF ENGLISH LITERATURE (see Bateson, F[rederick] W., ed.). The revision not only brings the material up to date but revises the format in several ways.

Watt, Robert. BIBLIOTHECA BRITANNICA; OR A GENERAL INDEX TO BRITISH AND FOREIGN LITERATURE. IN TWO PARTS: AUTHORS AND SUBJECTS. 4 vols. Edinburgh: Printed for Archibald Constable, Edinburgh, and for Longman, Hurst, Rees, Orme, Brown, & Green, London, and for Hurst, Robinson & Co., London, 1824.

See relevant authors and such subjects as "Drama," "Dramatist," "Play," "Player." But notice the age of the volume.

Wells, John Edwin. A MANUAL OF THE WRITINGS IN MIDDLE ENGLISH,

1050-1400. New Haven: Connecticut Academy of Arts and Sciences, 1916, with 9 SUPPLEMENTS, 1919-51.

See Chapter XIV, "Dramatic Pieces." Wells provides descriptions of manuscripts, summaries of contents, and secondary bibliography. For the revision of Wells, see Hartung, Albert E., general ed.

Williams, Harry F. AN INDEX OF MEDIAEVAL STUDIES PUBLISHED IN FESTSCHRIFTEN, 1865-1946, WITH SPECIAL REFERENCE TO ROMANIC MATERIALS. Berkeley and Los Angeles: University of California Press, 1951.

Because articles in collections are easily overlooked, such an index as this is particularly needed. Some bibliographies, for example the PUBLICATIONS OF THE MODERN LANGUAGE ASSOCIATION ANNUAL BIBLIOGRAPHY, enter Festschriften by volume title and by article and can be used to bring the Williams list up to date. Williams notes that he proposes to list "all material found in Festschrift volumes dealing with the art, customs, history, language, literature, and science of Western Europe from about the fifth century to the first years of the sixteenth" (p. vii).

YEAR'S WORK IN ENGLISH STUDIES, THE.

Issued annually since 1921, the first volume has on the title page: THE YEAR'S WORK IN ENGLISH STUDIES, 1919-20. Ed. for the English Association by Sir Sidney Lee. London: Humphrey Milford, 1921. The 1972 title page reads: Volume 51, 1970. Ed. Geoffrey Harlow and Val M. Bonnell, Elizabeth M. Brennan, James Redmond. London: Published for the English Association by John Murray, 1972. Rather full discussion of the items indexed.

Note: See also the publications of such groups as the Oxford Bibliographical Society, the Bibliographical Society of America, and the Bibliographical Society of the University of Virginia for discussions of bibliographical problems and for the publication of special bibliographies.

i. Microform Indexes

We have now passed from the relatively new and yet relatively simple day of micro<u>films</u> to one of multiple kinds of microforms which reproduce materials in greatly reduced size and which make available otherwise rare materials or materials which have not been produced in regular printed form, such as theses and dissertations. The cataloguing of microform reproductions has become a complex problem in itself. A few catalogs and guides to microforms are shown here. Certain libraries maintain lists of available microform collections.

Diaz, A[lbert] J[ames]. GUIDE TO MICROFORMS IN PRINT. Dayton, Ohio: The National Cash Register Co., 1961--.

The GUIDE is self-described as "an annual, cumulative guide . . .

to books, journals, and other materials . . . available on microfilm and other microforms from United States publishers" (1973 ed., p. iv). The editor further points out that the GUIDE "is not a union list of microfilms--it is essentially a listing of microform publications offered for sale on a regular basis."

LIBRARY OF CONGRESS CATALOGS, THE. NATIONAL REGISTER OF MICROFORM MASTERS. Compiled by the Library of Congress with the Cooperations of the American Library Association and the Association of Research Libraries. Washington: The Library of Congress, 1965--.

The "Preface" of the 1966 edition states: "The NATIONAL REGISTER . . . provides a new bibliographical record devoted to the listing of titles for which master negatives exist and which are retained as file or master negatives of library materials which have been filmed. The REGISTER is being published in order to avoid the duplication of costly master negatives and to make known which library materials have been transferred to microforms" (p. iii). The 1972 edition points out that it "does not supersede the previous issues" (p. ii). It states further: "It is emphasized that the NATIONAL REGISTER . . . is concerned only with master microfilms, that is, only with those that may not be used by a reader but are retained solely for the purpose of making other copies" (p. viii).

Philadelphia Bibliographical Center and Union Library Catalogue. UNION LIST OF MICROFILMS. Revised, Enlarged and Cumulated Edition, 1951. Ann Arbor, Mich.: J.W. Edwards, 1951.

The cumulation includes all entries from the 1942 edition and from Supplements 1-5, 1943-47. The "Introduction" is signed "Eleanor Este Campion, Editor." See next item.

______. UNION LIST OF MICROFILMS, CUMULATION 1949-1959. 2 vols. Ann Arbor, Mich.: J.W. Edwards, 1961.

The "Introduction," signed "Eleanor Este Campion, Editor," announces that for various reasons the CUMULATION 1949-1959 is "the final publication of the UNION LIST OF MICROFILMS by the Philadelphia Bibliographical Center and Union Library Catalogue."

UNIVERSITY MICROFILMS.

University Microfilms, Inc., a Subsidiary of Xerox Corporation, is printing on microfilm all the materials in both the Pollard and Redgrave SHORT-TITLE CATALOGUE and the Wing SHORT-TITLE CATALOGUE (see Section 9: Playlists, Records of Early Publication, Etc., for main entries of both catalogues). University Microfilms periodically issues guides to the materials currently available, using STC (SHORT-TITLE CATALOGUE) numbers and a helpful system of cross-indexing. Once this project is completed--and an enormous lot has been done--it will make available in reliable texts (reliable, that is, in representing what the early printers printed) all the books printed in England, Scotland, Ireland, Wales, and "British America" and all the books printed in English elsewhere from the beginning of printing through 1700 which have survived and which could be located by three vigorous researchers and their assistants. The prospect rather staggers the imagination.

Note: For bibliographies of microform related specifically to drama, see Angotti, Vincent L., and Bergquist, G. William, in Section 1 C: Bibliographies of Drama.

ii. Old Books

Old books, because they are rare or fine or simply because they are old, command attention and are, in terms of dollars and cents, generally valuable. When these books are in manuscript form their value is particularly great, since every manuscript is in a real sense unique. Rare materials should not be worn away by casual use. Microform copies make many of these materials available in quite literal reproductions, as do facsimile copies and Xerox books. Students whose interest in old materials can be met by such copies should use them. Those whose interest is largely visual should examine the display exhibits which are frequently provided by libraries with rare book holdings and which allow perusal of the materials without wear upon them. Scholars whose projects demand direct access to rare materials may find that they need to secure advanced permission to use each library's holdings. Cost has now made the collection of really rare old books feasible only for large budgets.

There are various catalogs and bibliographies of manuscripts and rare printed books offering full bibliographical descriptions which are often useful in themselves as well as providing guides to locations of materials. Auction sales catalogs are not merely ephemera, since the auction catalog for the sale of a major collection is likely to be prepared by experts and to carry detailed descriptions. Such catalogs and bibliographies are, however, so numerous as to be inappropriate for entry here. Records of them can be found in the printed or card catalogs of the holdings of major libraries; the various catalogs issued by the Library of Congress and the British Museum, for example, list these items. Another useful list, available in printed form and to be found on the shelves of many libraries, is:

Harvard University Library. WIDENER LIBRARY SHELFLIST NUMBER 7: BIBLIOGRAPHY AND BIBLIOGRAPHY PERIODICALS. Cambridge, Mass.: Harvard University Library, 1966.

See such headings as "Booksellers, Publishers, and Auction Catalogues," "Personal Library Catalogues," "Catalogues of Manuscripts."

Listed below are a few books on old books, many of them now collectors' items themselves and of as much historic as immediate interest. See Cole, George

Watson, Section 1 B: General Literary Bibliographies, for evaluations of some of these bibliographers.

Brydges, Samuel Egerton. CENSURA LITERARIA. CONTAINING TITLES, ABSTRACTS, AND OPINIONS OF OLD ENGLISH BOOKS, WITH ORIGINAL DISQUISITIONS, ARTICLES OF BIOGRAPHY, AND OTHER LITERARY ANTIQUITIES. 10 vols. London: Printed by T. Bensley for Longman, Hurst, Rees, and Orme, and J. White, 1805-9.

> The title varies somewhat from volume to volume, but in whatever form, it suffices to describe this miscellaneous collection of information. Diligent use of the index is recommended.

______. RESTITUTA; OR TITLES, EXTRACTS, AND CHARACTERS OF OLD BOOKS IN ENGLISH LITERATURE, REVIVED. 4 vols. London: Printed by T. Bensley for Longman, Hurst, Rees, Orme, and Brown, 1814-16.

> To be used in the same general way as CENSURA LITERARIA, above.

Brydges, Sir [Samuel] Egerton, and Joseph Haslewood. THE BRITISH BIBLIOGRAPHER. 4 vols. London: R. Triphook, 1810-14.

> Volume I was prepared by Brydges; Volumes II-IV, by Brydges and Haslewood. The contents are curious and miscellaneous, but the user may find a great deal through the various indexes and tables of contents. Memoirs of authors and samples of their works are offered. (Brydges varies the form of his own name from time to time, but these Brydgeses are the same man.)

Collier, J[ohn] Payne. A BIBLIOGRAPHICAL AND CRITICAL ACCOUNT OF THE RAREST BOOKS IN THE ENGLISH LANGUAGE, ALPHABETICALLY ARRANGED, WHICH DURING THE LAST FIFTY YEARS HAVE COME UNDER THE OBSERVATION OF J. PAYNE COLLIER, F.S.A. 4 vols. New York: David G. Francis, Charles Scribner & Co., 1866.

> Collier's work is to be used with great caution. In addition to being rather more creative than behooves a good bibliographer, however, Collier did examine a great many old books.

Corser, Thomas, and James Crossley. COLLECTANEA ANGLO-POETICA: OR A BIBLIOGRAPHICAL AND DESCRIPTIVE CATALOGUE OF A PORTION OF A COLLECTION OF EARLY ENGLISH POETRY, WITH OCCASIONAL EXTRACTS AND REMARKS BIOGRAPHICAL AND CRITICAL. Printed in the REMAINS HISTORICAL & LITERARY CONNECTED WITH THE PALATINE COUNTIES OF LANCASTER AND CHESTER, vols. 52, 55, 71, 73, and 77. Manchester: The Chetham Society, 1860-83.

> Also to be found in eleven parts rather than five volumes. See Cole, George Watson, pages 36-38, 75, under Section 1 B: General Literary Bibliographies, on the more than usually complex history of this publication.

Gray, G[eorge] J. A GENERAL INDEX TO HAZLITT'S HANDBOOK AND HIS BIBLIOGRAPHICAL COLLECTIONS (1867-1889). Ed. W[illiam] Carew Hazlitt. London: Bernard Quaritch, 1893.

This provides the index for Hazlitt's series of bibliographies, below.

Hazlitt, W[illiam] Carew. HAND-BOOK TO THE POPULAR, POETICAL, AND DRAMATIC LITERATURE OF GREAT BRITAIN, FROM THE INVENTION OF PRINTING TO THE RESTORATION. London: John Russell Smith, 1867.

Hazlitt arranges his notes alphabetically by author, or by title for anonymous works. He was a knowledgeable and diligent bibliographer and can still be consulted with profit. This and the next five items make a set.

_____. COLLECTIONS AND NOTES, 1867-1876. London: Reeves and Turner, 1876.

_____. SECOND SERIES OF BIBLIOGRAPHICAL COLLECTIONS AND NOTES ON EARLY ENGLISH LITERATURE, 1474-1700. London: Bernard Quaritch, 1882.

_____. THIRD AND FINAL SERIES OF BIBLIOGRAPHICAL COLLECTIONS AND NOTES ON EARLY ENGLISH LITERATURE, 1474-1700. London: Bernard Quaritch, 1887.

_____. SUPPLEMENTS TO THE THIRD AND FINAL SERIES OF BIBLIOGRAPHICAL COLLECTIONS AND NOTES, 1474-1700. London: Bernard Quaritch, 1889.

_____. BIBLIOGRAPHICAL COLLECTIONS AND NOTES (1474-1700), THIRD AND FINAL SERIES, SECOND SUPPLEMENT. London: Bernard Quaritch, 1892.

Ricci, Seymour de, with the assistance of W.J. Wilson. CENSUS OF MEDIEVAL AND RENAISSANCE MANUSCRIPTS IN THE UNITED STATES AND CANADA. 3 vols. New York: H.W. Wilson, 1935-40; reprint ed. New York: Kraus Reprint, 1961. Supplement: C.U. Faye and W.H. Bond. SUPPLEMENT TO THE CENSUS OF MEDIEVAL AND RENAISSANCE MANUSCRIPTS IN THE UNITED STATES AND CANADA. New York: Bibliographical Society of America, 1962.

Reliable survey by reputable bibliographers.

C. BIBLIOGRAPHIES OF DRAMA

Angotti, Vincent L. AN ANNOTATED BIBLIOGRAPHY AND SUBJECT INDEX TO THE MICROFILM COLLECTION, SOURCE MATERIALS IN THE FIELD OF THEATRE. Ann Arbor, Mich.: Xerox Education Division, University Microfilms Library Services, 1967.

The "Preface" describes the collection as "eighty books, periodicals, manuscripts, journals, and diaries" of "selected primary and secondary sources of historical and critical importance," many of which microfilm makes "accessible for the first time to a larger number of libraries and students of theatre" (p. iii). A good many of the materials are out of the immediate field of English drama to 1660. They are in various languages, but the rather full annotations in the BIBLIOGRAPHY are in English. The BIBLIOGRAPHY can be used independently of the collection. (See p. 88.)

ANNUAL MAGAZINE SUBJECT-INDEX . . . : A SUBJECT-INDEX TO A SELECTED LIST OF AMERICAN AND ENGLISH PERIODICALS AND SOCIETY PUBLICATIONS NOT ELSEWHERE INDEXED, COMPILED BY FREDERICK WINTHROP FAXON, INCLUDING AS PART II THE DRAMATIC INDEX. Boston: Boston Book Co., 1909-49.

The fuller title of Part II is: THE DRAMATIC INDEX . . . COVERING ARTICLES AND ILLUSTRATIONS CONCERNING THE STAGE AND ITS PLAYERS IN THE PERIODICALS OF AMERICA AND ENGLAND; WITH A RECORD OF BOOKS ON THE DRAMA AND OF TEXTS OF PLAYS PUBLISHED DURING [YEAR]. Ed. Frederick Winthrop Faxon. Compiled with the Co-operation of Twenty-Four Librarians.

The imprint for this annual varies somewhat over the years. When publication ended with the INDEX for 1949, the whole was cumulated with the title:

CUMULATED DRAMATIC INDEX, 1909-1949: A CUMULATION OF THE F.W. FAXON COMPANY'S DRAMATIC INDEX, EDITED BY FREDERICK WINTHROP FAXON, 1909-1935; MARY E. BATES, 1936-1944; ANNE C. SUTHERLAND [AND OTHERS], 1942-1949; CUMULATED BY G.K. HALL & CO. 2 vols. Boston, Mass.: G.K. Hall & Co., 1965.

The periodicals indexed range from ACADEMY to the YALE REVIEW, with CHILD LIFE, LADIES' HOME JOURNAL, LIFE, PHOTOPLAY MAGAZINE, and much else, between. A large part of what one finds is not related to English drama to 1660.

Arnott, James Fullarton, and John William Robinson. ENGLISH THEATRICAL LITERATURE, 1559-1900, A BIBLIOGRAPHY, INCORPORATING ROBERT W. LOWE'S "A BIBLIOGRAPHICAL ACCOUNT OF ENGLISH THEATRICAL LITERATURE" PUBLISHED IN 1888. London: Society for Theatre Research, 1970.

More inclusive than Lowe's in general coverage as well as time span (see Lowe, Robert W.), this bibliography has as its main headings: "Bibliography," "Government Regulation of the Theatre," "The Morality of the Theatre," "General History," "The London Theatre," "The Theatre Out of London," "A National Theatre," "Opera," "Irregular Forms: Pantomime, Music Hall, Etc.," "Societies," "The Amateur Theatre," "Biography," "Theory and Criticism," "Periodicals." It is an enormously useful tool.

Baker, Blanch M. DRAMATIC BIBLIOGRAPHY: AN ANNOTATED LIST OF BOOKS ON THE HISTORY AND CRITICISM OF THE DRAMA AND THE STAGE AND ON THE ALLIED ARTS OF THE THEATRE. New York: H.W. Wilson, 1933.

Limited in general to books in English, including translations but omitting Shakespeare materials, the bibliography has four major sections: "Drama and Theatre," "Production and Stagecraft," "Pageantry, Religious Drama and Entertainment," and "Anthologies, Bibliographies and Directories." In addition there are a "List of Current Periodicals Containing Material on the Drama, Theatre, Production, Costume, Etc." and a "Directory of Publishers and Play Brokers." Baker provides rather full annotations.

_____. THEATRE AND ALLIED ARTS: A GUIDE TO BOOKS DEALING WITH THE HISTORY, CRITICISM, AND TECHNIC OF THE DRAMA AND THEATRE AND RELATED ARTS AND CRAFTS. New York: H.W. Wilson, 1952.

The bibliography is designed for "professional and amateur artists and craftsmen, actors, drama students, and librarians, . . . the playgoer and general reader." It contains materials deemed useful "in the history, theory, criticism, technic, and production of drama and other forms of stage entertainment, exclusive of the motion picture, radio, television and grand opera" (p. [v]). There is a section on "Early, Elizabethan, and Jacobean Drama." Entries are fully annotated.

Bates, Katharine Lee, and Lydia Boker Godfrey. ENGLISH DRAMA: A WORKING BASIS. Boston: S.G. Robinson for Wellesley College, 1896.

Bates and Godfrey still appear in bibliographies, but the age of the volume works against its current usefulness.

Battenhouse, Roy [W.]. "Recent Studies in Elizabethan and Jacobean Drama." STUDIES IN ENGLISH LITERATURE, 12 (1972), 391-428.

Title annotates.

Bergeron, David M. TWENTIETH-CENTURY CRITICISM OF ENGLISH MASQUES, PAGEANTS, AND ENTERTAINMENTS: 1558-1642. SUPPLEMENT ON THE FOLK-PLAY AND RELATED FORMS BY HARRY B. CALDWELL. Checklists in the Humanities and Education. San Antonio, Tex.: Trinity University Press, 1972.

The series is described as directed towards "selection and limitation." There is no annotation.

Bergquist, G. William, ed. THREE CENTURIES OF ENGLISH AND AMERICAN

PLAYS, A CHECKLIST. ENGLAND: 1500-1800; UNITED STATES: 1714-1830. New York and London: Hafner Publishing Co., 1963.

The CHECKLIST provides an index and location guide to Wells, Henry W., ed., THREE CENTURIES OF DRAMA (see Section 2 C: Serial and Multi-Volume Editions) and is "a valuable reference tool for every student of the drama and for reference librarians." Bergquist notes that "[o]f the 836 titles in Walter W. Greg--BIBLIOGRAPHY OF THE ENGLISH PRINTED DRAMA TO THE RESTORATION, 772 plays are included" (p. v). Both the CHECKLIST and Wells's microprint edition are highly useful.

Brockett, Oscar G., Samuel L. Becker, and Donald C. Bryant. A BIBLIOGRAPHICAL GUIDE TO RESEARCH IN SPEECH AND DRAMATIC ART. Chicago: Scott, Foresman, & Co., 1963.

Provides a limited number of basic titles, mostly bibliographical tools, which are clearly described.

Brown, Arthur. "Studies in Elizabethan and Jacobean Drama Since 1900." SHAKESPEARE SURVEY, 14 (1961), 1-14.

Title annotates.

BULLETIN OF BIBLIOGRAPHY AND DRAMATIC INDEX, THE. Vols. 6-21 (1906-53).

Volume 6, number 1, page [3], announces that THE BULLETIN OF BIBLIOGRAPHY will begin to publish "a quarterly Dramatic Index covering all the important periodicals in England and America," providing "in one alphabet an index to the theatre and its plays and players." Volume 21, number 2, carries a notice that the dramatic index has been dropped and that the name of the periodical will henceforth be BULLETIN OF BIBLIOGRAPHY. Among magazines indexed are COSMOPOLITAN, LADIES' HOME JOURNAL, WOMAN'S HOME COMPANION, along with some others more likely to yield material relevant to the Medieval-Renaissance period.

Caldwell, Harry B., and David L. Middleton. ENGLISH TRAGEDY, 1370-1600: FIFTY YEARS OF CRITICISM. Checklists in the Humanities and Education. San Antonio: Texas University Press, 1971.

Both dramatic and nondramatic works are included. Very restricted list; no annotation.

Cheshire, David. THEATRE: HISTORY, CRITICISM, AND REFERENCE. The Readers Guide Series. Hamden, Conn.: Archon Books; London: Clive Bingley, 1967.

The "Introduction" indicates that the focus is specifically on "material on the way plays have been or could be staged in theatres" (p. 7, italics his). The bibliography is classified and annotated.

In paragraph form but with an "Author, Title and Subject Index."

Chicorel, Marietta, general ed. CHICOREL INDEX SERIES.

The Chicorel Index Series runs to several volumes, not all relevant to this bibliography and none restricted to the time period to 1660. Useful information may be found in these volumes:

CHICOREL THEATER INDEX TO PLAYS IN ANTHOLOGIES, PERIODICALS, DISCS, AND TAPES. 3 vols. New York: Chicorel Library Publishing Corp., 1970-72.

The volumes index plays of all periods and countries; for English, see especially Volume 3.

Volume 3A, CHICOREL BIBLIOGRAPHY TO THE PERFORMING ARTS, 1972, is described as a "buying guide."

Volumes 7 and 7A, CHICOREL INDEX TO THE SPOKEN ARTS ON DISCS, TAPES, AND CASSETTES, 1973, give prices and include all spoken arts, from Will Rogers to Will Shakespeare.

Clarence, Reginald [pseud.]. See Eldredge, H.J.

Coleman, Arthur, and Gary R. Tyler. DRAMA CRITICISM; Volume 1, A CHECKLIST OF INTERPRETATIONS SINCE 1940 OF ENGLISH AND AMERICAN PLAYS. Denver: Alan Swallow, Publisher, 1966.

The "Introduction" indicates the limit and extent of coverage: Coleman and Tyler index 1,050 periodicals, academic and other, for the years 1940-64, omitting monographs "which are, in effect, 'histories,' or broad 'surveys'" (p. [7]). They index books, but not those to be found in "a library card catalog under a particular dramatist's name and which deal only with that dramatist and his works." Reprints of materials originally printed before 1940 and dissertations are in general omitted. Included, with these exceptions, however, is "all drama criticism--notable and obscure."

Coleman, Edward D. THE BIBLE IN ENGLISH DRAMA. AN ANNOTATED LIST OF PLAYS INCLUDING TRANSLATIONS FROM OTHER LANGUAGES FROM THE BEGINNINGS TO 1931, WITH A SURVEY OF RECENT MAJOR PLAYS (1968) BY ISAIAH SHEFFER. New York: New York Public Library and KTAV Publishing House, 1968.

Described on the verso of the title page as "originally published in the BULLETIN OF THE NEW YORK PUBLIC LIBRARY, Oct.-Dec. 1930 and Jan.-March 1931," the volume provides a list of plays and some secondary material, with full, clear annotations and various indexes.

______. THE JEW IN ENGLISH DRAMA: AN ANNOTATED BIBLIOGRAPHY, with a preface by Joshua Bloch, printed with Edgar Rosenberg, THE JEW IN WESTERN DRAMA: AN ESSAY AND CHECK LIST (1968). New York: New York Public Library and KTAV Publishing House, 1968, 1970.

THE JEW IN ENGLISH DRAMA appeared in the BULLETIN OF THE NEW YORK PUBLIC LIBRARY, November 1938-November 1940, and in book form with revisions in 1943. The 1968, 1970 reprints have an "Addenda to THE JEW IN ENGLISH DRAMA (1968)" by Flola L. Shepard. The material surveyed is not confined to the Medieval-Renaissance period. Useful annotations.

Connor, John M., and Billie M. Connor. OTTEMILLER'S INDEX TO PLAYS IN COLLECTIONS: AN AUTHOR AND TITLE INDEX TO PLAYS APPEARING IN COLLECTIONS PUBLISHED BETWEEN 1900 AND MID-1970. 5th ed., rev. and enl. Metuchen, N.J.: Scarecrow Press, 1971.

In addition to the "Author and Title Index" promised by the title of the volume, there is an extensive "List of Collections Analyzed and Key to Symbols," pages 177-371, making the INDEX fully usable.

Davis, Caroline Hill. "Pageants in Great Britain and the United States. A List of References." BULLETIN OF THE NEW YORK PUBLIC LIBRARY, 20 (1916), 753-91.

Much that is irrelevant to the period of this bibliography but also some basic and some obscure materials listed.

DRAMATIC INDEX, THE.

See ANNUAL MAGAZINE SUBJECT-INDEX, above.

Eldredge, H.J. [Reginald Clarence]. "THE STAGE" CYCLOPEDIA. A BIBLIOGRAPHY OF PLAYS: AN ALPHABETICAL LIST OF PLAYS AND OTHER STAGE PIECES OF WHICH ANY RECORD CAN BE FOUND SINCE THE COMMENCEMENT OF THE ENGLISH STAGE, TOGETHER WITH DESCRIPTIONS, AUTHORS' NAMES, DATES AND PLACES OF PRODUCTION, AND OTHER USEFUL INFORMATION, COMPRISING IN ALL NEARLY 50,000 PLAYS, AND EXTENDING OVER A PERIOD OF UPWARDS OF 500 YEARS. London: "The Stage," 1909.

Title annotates. Entries are very brief.

Gamble, William Burt. DEVELOPMENT OF SCENIC ART AND STAGE MACHINERY: A LIST OF REFERENCES IN THE NEW YORK PUBLIC LIBRARY. Rev. with additions. New York: The New York Public Library, 1928.

Organized by period and topic.

Greg, W[alter] W[ilson]. A BIBLIOGRAPHY OF THE ENGLISH PRINTED DRAMA.

See the main entry in Section 9: Playlists, Early Records of Publication, Etc.

GUIDE TO THE PERFORMING ARTS. Vol. 1--. New York: Scarecrow Press, 1960--.

The GUIDE is published annually and is designed as a "listing from periodicals over the world . . . to aid editors, producers and scholars, including students in college and secondary school" (Vol. 1, p. [iii]). By its scope and the fact of the preponderance of contemporary performances, the GUIDE will yield more references to Lawrence Welk than to John Webster, but it gives information about recent performances, etc., of Medieval and Renaissance drama. Volume 1 indexes publications for the year 1957.

Hazlitt, W[illiam] Carew. A MANUAL FOR THE COLLECTOR AND AMATEUR OF OLD ENGLISH PLAYS, EDITED FROM THE MATERIAL FORMED BY KIRKMAN, LANGBAINE, DOWNES, OLDYS, AND HALLIWELL-PHILLIPPS, WITH EXTENSIVE ADDITIONS AND CORRECTIONS. London: Pickering & Chatto, 1892.

An alphabetical list of plays with brief notes on each, followed by a list of "The Collected Works of Dramatic Authors," "Collections of Old English Plays," and "Collections of Miracle Plays." Indexed.

Heninger, S.K., Jr. "French Scholarship on Elizabethan Drama: A Survey." ETUDES ANGLAISES, 13 (1960), [283]-92.

Useful survey; identifies French works of particular importance to a given topic.

Henshaw, Millett. "A Survey of Studies in Medieval Drama, 1933-1950." PROGRESS OF MEDIEVAL AND RENAISSANCE STUDIES IN THE UNITED STATES AND CANADA. Bulletin No. 21 (August 1951), 7-35.

Henshaw evaluates the various items judiciously.

Houle, Peter J. THE ENGLISH MORALITY AND RELATED DRAMA: A BIBLIOGRAPHICAL SURVEY. Hamden, Conn.: Shoe String Press, Archon, 1972.

Section 1 lists all the plays with "pertinent facts of publication," selected editions, summaries of the plays, and criticisms of individual plays. Section 2 is made up of six appendices: "Coming of Death," "Debate of the Body and Soul," "Debate of the Heavenly Graces or The Parliament in Heaven," "The Devil in the Moralities," "The Psychomachia (Prudentius)," and "Staging of Morality Plays." Section 3 is "a listing of critical materials . . . dealing with the moralities in general" (pp. xi-xiii). Of great use.

Huffman, Clifford Chalmers. "Tudor and Stuart Drama: A Bibliography, 1966-1971." EDUCATIONAL THEATRE JOURNAL, 24 (1972), 169-78.

A continuation of Ribner's TUDOR AND STUART DRAMA (see Ribner, Irving).

Hunter, Frederick J. DRAMA BIBLIOGRAPHY: A SHORT-TITLE GUIDE TO EXTENDED READING IN DRAMATIC ART FOR THE ENGLISH-SPEAKING AUDIENCE AND STUDENTS IN THEATRE. Boston: G.K. Hall & Co., 1971.

Good guide to general reference works. Brief entries under particular periods. Designed to provide "information concerning reference works, play titles, theatre history, the lives of artists and performers, the techniques of theatre, the art of dance and the criticism of dramatic art as a whole" (p. v).

Keyishian, Harry. MEDIEVAL AND RENAISSANCE PLAYS (EXCLUDING SHAKESPEARE) ON RECORD, FILM, AND TELEVISION TAPE: A CATALOGUE IN PROGRESS. Madison, N.J.: Department of English, Fairleigh Dickinson University, 1972.

I have not seen this catalog.

Litto, Fredric M. AMERICAN DISSERTATIONS ON THE DRAMA AND THE THEATRE: A BIBLIOGRAPHY. Kent, Ohio: Kent State University Press, 1969.

Indexed by Author, Key-Word, and Subject. The availability of dissertations in microform makes the bibliography valuable.

Loewenberg, Alfred. THE THEATRE OF THE BRITISH ISLES EXCLUDING LONDON. A BIBLIOGRAPHY. London: Printed for the Society for Theatre Research, 1950.

Although the bibliography is marked "Distributed Only to Members of the Society," it can be found in libraries. The "General Section" is followed by an alphabetical arrangement by place; some brief annotations.

Logan, Terence P., and Denzell S. Smith, general eds. THE PREDECESSORS OF SHAKESPEARE: A SURVEY AND BIBLIOGRAPHY OF RECENT STUDIES IN ENGLISH RENAISSANCE DRAMA. Lincoln: University of Nebraska Press, 1973.

The "Preface" states: "This volume is part of a larger project, Recent Studies in English Renaissance Drama, which in additional volumes will survey scholarship and criticism exclusive of Shakespeare." The present volume deals with Marlowe, Greene, Kyd, Nashe, Lyly, Peele, Lodge, various anonymous plays, and, in a section entitled "Other Dramatists," with a miscellaneous group. The sections have been prepared by various hands. Each provides a discussion of materials, grouped under such headings as "Biographical," "General Studies of Plays," etc.; then gives an unannotated list of additional materials under the heading "See Also."

Lowe, Robert W. A BIBLIOGRAPHICAL ACCOUNT OF ENGLISH THEATRICAL LITERATURE FROM THE EARLIEST TIMES TO THE PRESENT DAY. London: John C. Nimmo, 1888.

Not only a bibliography but, as the "Preface" states (p. [vii]), "much that in a Bibliography, would be looked for in vain." This last includes a good deal of theatre gossip. For a revision of Lowe, see Arnott, James Fullarton, and John William Robinson.

MATERIALS FOR THE STUDY OF THE ENGLISH DRAMA (EXCLUDING SHAKESPEARE): A SELECTED LIST OF BOOKS IN THE NEWBERRY LIBRARY. Chicago: The Newberry Library, 1912.

Not concentrated in any period and somewhat limited in utility by age, but a good checklist of basic books in its time. No annotation.

Mikhail, E.H. COMEDY AND TRAGEDY: A BIBLIOGRAPHY OF CRITICAL STUDIES. Troy, N.Y.: Whitson Publishing Co., 1972.

Designed as "a comprehensive 'general' bibliography" (p. iii), the volume aims at completeness through 1970, with some later publications also included. No annotation.

New York Public Library. CATALOG OF THE THEATRE AND DRAMA COLLECTIONS. 21 vols. Boston: G.K. Hall & Co., 1967.

I have not seen this catalog.

Nicoll, Allardyce. "Studies in the Elizabethan Stage Since 1900." SHAKESPEARE SURVEY, 1 (1948), 1-16.

Useful review of publications on the stage, actors, audiences, and the like.

Ottemiller, John H.

See Connor, John M., and Billie M. Connor.

Palmer, Helen H., and Anne Jane Dyson. EUROPEAN DRAMA CRITICISM. Hamden, Conn.: Shoe String Press, 1967; SUPPLEMENT I, 1970.

The "Introduction" provides a clear discussion of the extent of coverage: plays and playwrights are selected; articles are listed only if they are "directly concerned with the play as a whole, or with a large or important part of it." The editors also point out that the "quality of the articles was not considered." There are multiple listings of a given item concerned with several plays. The SUPPLEMENT provides various lists of materials indexed. Books as well as articles are considered, of course.

Pennel, Charles A., general ed. ELIZABETHAN BIBLIOGRAPHIES SUPPLEMENTS. Vol. 1--. London: Nether Press, 1967--.

These are supplements to the Tannenbaum ELIZABETHAN BIBLIOGRAPHIES (see Tannenbaum, Samuel A[aron], and Dorothy R. Tannenbaum). Pennel, in the "Editor's Note," says the SUPPLEMENTS are designed to bring Tannenbaum "up to date" and will in some instances include authors not in Tannenbaum. Being "intended for use at the advanced rather than the elementary level," they aim at including "all relevant material, with the following exceptions: (1) brief mentions; (2) anthology texts; (3) M.A. theses; (4) Ph.D. dissertations other than American and English." See relevant individual supplements under the particular authors surveyed: Beaumont and Fletcher, Chapman, Daniel, Dekker, Ford, Gascoigne, Greene, J. Heywood, T. Heywood, Jonson, Kyd, Lodge, Lyly, Marlowe, Marston, Massinger, Middleton, Nashe, Peele, Shirley, Tourneur, Webster.

RESEARCH OPPORTUNITIES IN RENAISSANCE DRAMA.

This periodical began as mimeographed reports, with the title "Opportunities for Research in Renaissance Drama (Exclusive of Shakespeare), The Report of Conference 12 of the Seventieth Meeting of the Modern Language Association (Chicago, 1955)." Numbers 1-3, 1955-57, and Numbers 4-6, 1958-64, have been made available in a reprint edition (New York: AMS Press, 1967). In Volume 7 (1964), the "Editor's Preface" (p. [3]), states: "The earliest numbers furnished Conference minutes, texts of papers delivered at the meetings, and listings of works in progress. . . . [T]he publication has grown in size and scope, and has come to include, besides other features, essays not directly prepared for the Conference. With this installment, RENAISSANCE DRAMA becomes an independent annual publication." In 1968, a New Series was initiated, with an "Editorial Note" (p. v), announcing: "Past numbers have been collections of miscellaneous essays; the new policy is to build the volume around a specified subject, but also to allow for a few papers on unrelated topics." These topics are, giving volume numbers in the New Series, 1: ESSAYS PRINCIPALLY ON MASQUES AND ENTERTAINMENTS, with a review article, "Masque Criticism"; 2: ESSAYS PRINCIPALLY ON DRAMATIC THEORY AND FORM; 3: ESSAYS PRINCIPALLY ON DRAMA IN ITS INTELLECTUAL CONTEXT; 4: ESSAYS PRINCIPALLY ON THE PLAYHOUSE AND STAGING, with an essay by T.J. King, "The Stage in the Time of Shakespeare: A Survey of Major Scholarship"; 5: ESSAYS PRINCIPALLY ON COMEDY; 6: ESSAYS ON DRAMATIC ANTECEDENTS. Volumes 1-5 of the New Series were edited by Samuel Schoenbaum, Volume 6 by Alan C. Dessen. Publication continues under the name RENAISSANCE DRAMA.

The title notwithstanding, RENAISSANCE DRAMA, beginning with Volume 10 (1967) includes a "Medieval Supplement."

Ribner, Irving. TUDOR AND STUART DRAMA. Goldentree Bibliographies. New York: Appleton-Century-Crofts, 1966.

Subdivided into various major topics; well indexed. See Huffman, Clifford Chalmers, for a supplement to 1971.

Santaniello, A.E. THEATRE BOOKS IN PRINT. New York: Drama Book

Shop, 1963.

The list is annotated. It is generally limited to materials in English and covers "the literature of the theatre, drama, the technical arts of the theatre," but excludes "plays and collections of plays" (p. vii).

SHAKESPEARE ASSOCIATION BULLETIN, THE. Published by the Shakespeare Association of America. Vols. 1-24, 1924-49.

The BULLETIN includes an annual bibliography, "Shakespeare and His Contemporaries (A Classified Bibliography)," selective but rather full, quite usable for its period.

Stoddard, Francis H. REFERENCES FOR STUDENTS OF MIRACLE PLAYS AND MYSTERIES. Library Bulletin, No. 8. Berkeley: University of California, 1887.

Not confined to English plays and old, but useful for its period.

Stratman, Carl J. AMERICAN THEATRICAL PERIODICALS, 1789-1967: A BIBLIOGRAPHICAL GUIDE. Durham, N.C.: Duke University Press, 1970.

Broadly inclusive of periods, aspects of theatre, etc.

_____. BIBLIOGRAPHY OF ENGLISH PRINTED TRAGEDY, 1565-1900. Carbondale and Edwardsville: Southern Illinois University Press; London and Amsterdam: Feffer & Simons, 1966.

In the "Introduction" Stratman states that "the present bibliography gives the names of all English tragedies which I have been able to locate, and whose first editions were printed between 1565 and 1900" and that it "notes the various editions of each" (p. [vii]).

_____. BIBLIOGRAPHY OF MEDIEVAL DRAMA. Berkeley and Los Angeles: University of California Press, 1954. 2nd ed., rev. and enl. 2 vols. New York: Ungar, 1972.

Includes both English and European drama and both secondary and primary materials. Collections are analyzed as to contents, and editions of single plays and of small groups of plays are listed. The arrangement of the second edition differs from that of the first.

_____. BRITAIN'S THEATRICAL PERIODICALS, 1720-1967: A BIBLIOGRAPHY. 2nd ed. New York: New York Public Library, 1972.

The first edition has the title A BIBLIOGRAPHY OF BRITISH DRAMATIC PERIODICALS, 1720-1960. Compare Stratman's AMERICAN THEATRICAL PERIODICALS, above.

_____. DRAMATIC PLAY LISTS, 1591-1963. New York: New York Public

Library, 1966. See also the BULLETIN OF THE NEW YORK PUBLIC LIBRARY, 70 (1966), 71-85, 169-88.

Limited strictly to play lists; omits such kinds of lists as manuscript lists, certain booksellers' and auction catalogs, and the like, but the more useful because it is brief and selective.

_____. "The History and Theory of Tragedy: Unpublished Dissertations, 1889-1957." INDEX: BULLETIN OF BIBLIOGRAPHY AND MAGAZINE NOTES, 22 (September 1956-December 1959), 161-64, 190-92, 214-16.

These three parts of Stratman's list are relevant to the period of this bibliography. The two remaining parts are out of period.

Tannenbaum, Samuel A[aron], and Dorothy R. Tannenbaum. ELIZABETHAN BIBLIOGRAPHIES. 1937-50; reprint ed. Port Washington, N.Y.: Kennikat Press, 1967.

The "Prefatory Note" states that these bibliographies are "not intended for the professed bibliographer or the collector of rarities but for the student engaged in research." While Tannenbaum points out the impossibility of absolute completeness, he aims at identifying "what has been written on any subject relating to the Elizabethans" as well as editions and matters related to editions, such as "what music has been written for their plays and lyrics, and so forth." Among the dramatists in the various volumes are: Volume 1: Beaumont and Fletcher, Chapman; Volume II: Daniel, Dekker, Drayton, Ford, Gascoigne; Volume III: Greene, J. Heywood, T. Heywood; Volume IV: Jonson, Kyd, Lodge; Volume V: Lyly, Middleton, Marlowe, Marston; Volume VI: Massinger, Mundy, Nashe, Peele, Randolph; Volumes VII and VIII: Shakespeare; Volume IX: Shakespeare, Shirley; Volume X: Tourneur, Webster. Every bibliography has its limitations. Tannenbaum, in seeking to be as all-inclusive as possible, will tell some users more than they wish to know, though the inclusiveness will be the great virtue of these bibliographies for others. Tannenbaum provides no annotations beyond an occasional comment, and the entries are compressed. See Pennel, Charles A., for supplements to Tannenbaum.

Vowles, Richard B. DRAMATIC THEORY: A BIBLIOGRAPHY. New York: New York Public Library, 1956.

Self-described as "selective." Vowles says he has "endeavored to comprehend all significant items, book or periodical, since 1930, and all other classical treatments of the subject. Coverage attempts to be thorough for America and England, substantial for Germany, France, and Spain" (p. 8). No annotation, but items are grouped under various headings: "Theory in General," "Aristotle's POETICS," "Form," "Content," "Genre," "Mode," "Language and Poetry in the Theatre," "Audience and Illusion," and "Drama Criticism."

2. EDITIONS

How to arrange one's materials is the bibliographer's never-ending quandary. Even if authors could be persuaded to write in tidy time periods or types--as they cannot--editors would undoubtedly contrive to publish mixed assortments. Some order other than one alphabetical list seems needed here, however, and I have endeavored to make it sensible. Medieval texts are entered under several major types, followed by a section of editions of miscellaneous Medieval plays. Then comes a section of various kinds of editions: assortments of Medieval plays together with later works, collections of Tudor plays, and some post-Tudor material. Included are a few editions of Shakespeare apocrypha. For the Tudor-Stuart periods, see also Part 2, where editions of the collected works of major playwrights, and occasionally editions of single plays, are listed under individual playwrights. In general, I have not listed anthologies devoted to the Elizabethan or Stuart periods, since the plays represented in these anthologies will usually not be difficult to find within the works of major authors. I have, however, provided a short section of collected editions which are not collections of the works of a single author and are not of the textbook type. Some of these are more historically than immediately important, but important nonetheless. In general, space has not allowed the listing of editions of single plays or small sets of plays. I have entered a few which seem to me to offer important or at least unusual possibilities. I have also listed a few series providing plays in editions of single titles or small sets and have tried to characterize them. An occasional bibliography is mentioned here; for others, see Section 1: Bibliographies. Annotation may be limited to a group note for some of these entries. If the explanations of Medieval drama seem too obvious, the user may pass them by. Certain series--Bang, De Vocht, Shakespeare Society--include volumes of scholarship as well as texts.

A. EDITIONS OF PLAYS: MEDIEVAL DRAMA

Medieval drama does not lend itself to easy classification. Lacking any other system, one can arrange most plays by author or by date of composition or performance. Medieval plays are mostly anonymous and are not susceptible to exact dating. All other systems of classification run into contradictions, overlaps, and inconsistencies. It is not even possible to draw an absolute line between Medieval and Renaissance, however one defines those labels. Since some system must be chosen, let us resort to the most usual one, of dividing the principal surviving body of Medieval drama into liturgical, Corpus Christi (or mystery), miracle, and morality plays. Folkplays, in addition to being unusually problematical in text, present the additional difficulties of being rather rare in printed versions and rather brief. They are likely to be printed in collections of other plays. I have, therefore, included the few collections of folkplays per se which I have noted in Section 2 A v: Miscellaneous Editions and Collections of Editions of Medieval Plays. Folkplays in mixed collections with later materials will be found in Section 2 A v and also in Section 2 B: Miscellaneous Medieval and Tudor Plays. Folkplay texts are also often included in discussions of the type; see Section 7 B: Studies of Medieval Drama--Folklore and the Folkplay.

Let us assume that the Middle Ages end about the year 1500.

i. Liturgical Plays

Liturgical plays obviously means plays somehow related to the liturgy of the Church and will include plays in Latin rather than in English. Because the Roman Catholic liturgy in the Middle Ages transcended national boundaries, there is no useful way to separate plays of English and non-English origin.

For a fine example of a Latin play edited for presentation on the modern stage, see Greenberg, Noah, ed., under Section 2 A v: Miscellaneous Editions and Collections of Editions of Medieval Plays.

The great collection of liturgical texts is:

Young, Karl. THE DRAMA OF THE MEDIEVAL CHURCH. 2 vols. Oxford: Clarendon Press, 1933; reprint ed. 1951.

> Young prints the texts and comments on them extensively. The commentary is so thorough that the reader lacking facility in the Latin of the plays may use the volumes profitably. Young's conclusions--even his basic arrangement of material--have not been universally accepted, but his collection is an indispensable tool.

ii. Corpus Christi Plays and the Cornish Cycle

The group of plays sometimes called "cycles," sometimes "mysteries," and sometimes--less frequently now--"miracles" or "pageants," is clearly defined with respect to its major body of texts, the four more or less complete cycles, or sets of plays which run a full course, or cycle, from the creation of the world to doomsday. These cycles of plays draw directly and almost exclusively from the Bible for episodes. Within a cycle, the first group of plays deals with the creation, the fall of Lucifer, the fall of Adam and Eve, and their expulsion from the Garden of Eden. Then there are plays about certain other Old Testament materials, a group centered in the Nativity, one centered in the Crucifixion and Resurrection, with a few matters between Nativity and Crucifixion, a few post-Resurrection plays, and a Doomsday play. Sometimes there is rather extended treatment of the Virgin Mary. The extant cycles are called CHESTER; HEGGE (for the longtime owners of the manuscript), LUDUS COVENTRIAE (because of the no-longer-held assumption that it originated in Coventry), or N-TOWN (because N-Town appears in a set of "banns" or announcements of performances); TOWNELEY (again for owners of the manuscript) or WAKEFIELD (because of the likelihood, not fully provable, of their having been acted originally at Wakefield); and YORK. These plays have been given various generic names: mysteries, miracles, pageants, cycles; but the old name Corpus Christi has recently come into widespread use and is more descriptive, not only of the day when the cycles were often performed, but also of their thematic focus in Christ, than are the other names used.

There are also extant some fragments of other English cycles and a few plays of a similar Biblical nature which show no evidence of having ever belonged to cycles, and a Cornish cycle.

See Stratman, Carl J., BIBLIOGRAPHY OF MEDIEVAL DRAMA, Section 1 C: Bibliographies of Drama, for comprehensive lists of manuscripts and of editions of full cycles, selections, and single plays. Shown here are selected editions of full cycles or substantial parts thereof and occasional notices of editions of small segments when these are of particular interest. Also shown are some editions of plays without a surviving cycle context.

The materials are arranged as follows: There is a section for each of the four more or less complete cycles, then a group of miscellaneous English Corpus Christi plays; and then the Cornish cycle. Within the group of editions for each of the four cycles, the arrangement is: complete editions in Middle English, followed by complete editions in Modern English, and then by part-editions in Middle and Modern English arranged chronologically. In the miscellaneous group, the cycle fragments come first, then the noncycle plays.

CHESTER

THE CHESTER PLAYS. RE-EDITED FROM THE MSS. Part 1, ed. Hermann Deimling; Part 2, ed. G.W. Matthews. Early English Text Society, Extra Series, Nos. 62, 115. 1892, 1916; reprint ed. London, New York, Toronto: Oxford University Press for the Early English Text Society, 1959.

> In Middle English. Part 2 carries a "Prefatory Note": "This final section of the Chester plays has long been printed off. It is now [1916] issued, without the usual apparatus, in response to requests which have been made that it should be at the service of scholars." While a modern edition of this, and the other cycles, is needed, the Early English Text Society has done careful work.

THE CHESTER MIRACLE PLAYS. DONE INTO MODERN ENGLISH AND ARRANGED FOR ACTING. Ed. I. King and O. Bolton King, with an introduction by Sir Barry V. Jackson. London: S.P.C.K.; New York: Macmillan, 1930.

About half the cycle, with "Hints on Production" and "The Songs," including music for all but one of these.

"THE TRIAL & FLAGELLATION."

See the main entry under Salter, F[rederick] M[illet] and W[alter] W[ilson] Greg, eds., in Section 7 C: Studies of Medieval Drama--Corpus Christi and Miracle Plays.

THE CHESTER MYSTERY PLAYS. SIXTEEN PAGEANT PLAYS FROM THE CHESTER CRAFT CYCLE. ADAPTED INTO MODERN ENGLISH. Ed. Maurice Hussey. Melbourne, London, Toronto: Heinemann, 1957.

There is an appendix, "Hints on Production."

LUDUS COVENTRIAE

LUDUS COVENTRIAE OR THE PLAIE CALLED CORPUS CHRISTI, COTTON MS, VESPASIAN D. VIII. Ed. K.S. Block. Early English Text Society, Extra Series, No. 120. London: Oxford University Press for the Early English Text Society, 1922.

In Middle English. Somewhat old but with extensive apparatus.

THE CORPUS CHRISTI PLAY OF THE ENGLISH MIDDLE AGES. Ed. R.T. Davies. Totowa, N.J.: Rowman & Littlefield; Frome: Butler & Tanner; London: Faber and Faber, 1972.

The text is modernized and is divided into two parts. Part 1 contains most of the LUDUS COVENTRIAE cycle, the editor explaining that he has "omitted only the episodes of the Baptism and Temptation of Christ, the episodes of Mary's Assumption, and those episodes involving Mary which are not found in the other cycles." Part 2 contains the Abraham and Isaac episode in the various texts of "all the known cycles" (p. 15). In addition to the introduction and texts, Davies provides a bibliography, a "Comparison of the Cycles: Episodes before the Passion," and notes.

TOWNELEY

THE TOWNELEY PLAYS. RE-EDITED FROM THE UNIQUE MS. Ed. George England, with introduction and notes by Alfred W. Pollard. Early English Text Society, Extra Series, No. 71. London: Oxford University Press for the Early English Text Society, 1897; reprint eds. 1907, 1925, 1952.

The Middle English text, with extensive apparatus. A new edition would be helpful, of course.

THE WAKEFIELD MYSTERY PLAYS. Ed. Martial Rose. London: Evans Brothers, 1961; New York: W.W. Norton & Co., 1969.

Intended as "a complete acting version" (p. 6), the edition represents the work of an editor who has had a hand in the production of some of the plays and whose long introduction deals not only with such problems as provenience and authorship but with production. The text is in Modern English, which, together with the paperback price, makes the material readily accessible, though for scholarly purposes the Middle English is essential.

THE WAKEFIELD PAGEANTS IN THE TOWNELEY CYCLE. Ed. A.C. Cawley. Old and Middle English Texts. Manchester: Manchester University Press, 1958.

The six pageants concerned with Abel, Noah, the shepherds (both the FIRST and SECOND SHEPHERDS' PLAYS), Herod, and the COLIPHIZACIO are here "newly transcribed from photographs of the manuscript" (p. vii). Consult the "Note on the Edited Text" (p. xxxix), for indications of such departures from the manuscript--in punctuation, etc.--as the editor has made. Cawley provides extensive introduction, notes, appendices, glossary, bibliography.

YORK

YORK PLAYS: THE PLAYS PERFORMED BY THE CRAFTS OR MYSTERIES OF YORK ON THE DAY OF CORPUS CHRISTI IN THE 14TH, 15TH, AND 16TH CENTURIES; NOW FIRST PRINTED FROM THE UNIQUE MANUSCRIPT IN THE LIBRARY OF LORD ASHBURNHAM, WITH INTRODUCTION AND GLOSSARY. Ed. Lucy Toulmin Smith. Oxford: Clarendon Press, 1885.

Middle English text, with extensive apparatus, but of course, again, in need of replacement.

THE YORK CYCLE OF MYSTERY PLAYS. A COMPLETE VERSION. Ed. J.S. Purvis. New York: Macmillan; London: S.P.C.K., 1957; reprint ed. 1971.

See next item.

THE YORK CYCLE OF MYSTERY PLAYS: A SHORTER VERSION OF THE ANCIENT CYCLE, WITH A NOTE ON THE PRODUCTION STAGED AT THE YORK FESTIVAL OF 1951 BY E. MARTIN BROWNE. Ed. J.S. Purvis. London: S.P.C.K., 1951.

York has had spectacular success with the revival of its cycle, in which Purvis had a large hand. The two texts he has prepared are in modern English.

MISCELLANEOUS CORPUS CHRISTI OR MYSTERY PLAYS, INCLUDING THE "TRUE" COVENTRY

TWO COVENTRY CORPUS CHRISTI PLAYS: 1. THE SHEARMEN AND TAYLORS' PAGEANT, RE-EDITED FROM THE EDITION OF THOMAS SHARP, 1825; AND 2. THE WEAVERS' PAGEANT, RE-EDITED FROM THE MANUSCRIPT OF ROBERT CROO, 1534; WITH A PLAN OF COVENTRY, AND APPENDICES CONTAINING THE CHIEF RECORDS OF THE COVENTRY PLAYS. Ed. Hardin Craig. Early English Text Society, Extra Series, No. 87. 1902; 2nd ed. London: Oxford University Press for the Early English Text Society, 1957; reprint ed. 1967.

Of the cycle of plays known to have been performed at Coventry, these two texts remain. The plays called LUDUS COVENTRIAE have their name from the error in taking them to be the Coventry plays.

A DISSERTATION ON THE PAGEANTS . . . ANCIENTLY PERFORMED AT COVENTRY.

See Sharp, Thomas, in Section 7 C: Studies of Medieval Drama--Corpus Christi Plays and Miracle Plays.

THE NON-CYCLE MYSTERY PLAYS, TOGETHER WITH "THE CROXTON PLAY OF THE SACRAMENT" AND "THE PRIDE OF LIFE." Ed. Osborn Waterhouse. Early English Text Society, Extra Series, No. 104. London: Published for the Early English Text Society by Kegan Paul, Trench, Trubner & Co., and Oxford University Press, 1909.

See next item.

NON-CYCLE PLAYS AND FRAGMENTS. EDITED ON THE BASIS OF THE EDITION BY OSBORN WATERHOUSE. WITH AN APPENDIX ON THE SHREWSBURY MUSIC BY F. LL. HARRISON. Ed. Norman Davis. Early English Text Society Supplementary Texts, No. 1. London: Oxford University Press for the Early English Text Society, 1970.

The Waterhouse edition carries on the title page the notice that it is "Re-Edited from the Manuscripts." The texts are identified as three from THE SHREWSBURY FRAGMENTS (OFFICIUM PASTORUM, OFFICIUM RESURRECTIONIS, and OFFICIUM PEREGRINORUM), the Norwich CREATION OF EVE AND THE FALL, the Newcastle NOAH'S SHIP, the Dublin and Brome plays of ABRAHAM'S SACRIFICE, the Croxton PLAY OF THE SACRAMENT, and THE PRIDE OF LIFE. Davis sometimes retains the titles Waterhouse uses and sometimes does not, and he adds some titles. THE SHREWSBURY FRAGMENTS are given the same designations in both editions. In Davis, the Norwich play is given as THE NORWICH GROCERS' PLAY and the Newcastle as simply THE NEWCASTLE PLAY. Davis identifies the two ABRAHAM plays as Northampton and Brome, gives the same title as Waterhouse for THE PRIDE OF LIFE, and adds in his TABLE of texts these: DUX MORAUD; THE CAMBRIDGE PROLOGUE; THE

RICKINGHALL (BURY ST. EDMUNDS) FRAGMENT; THE DURHAM PROLOGUE; THE ASHMOLE FRAGMENT; and THE REYNES EXTRACTS. Both editions provide the usual Early English Text Society apparatus, and are, of course, in Middle English. See Davis for a current bibliography.

THE CORNISH CYCLE

THE CORNISH ORDINALIA: A MEDIEVAL DRAMATIC TRILOGY: I. BEGINNING OF THE WORLD, II. CHRIST'S PASSION, III. RESURRECTION OF OUR LORD. Trans. Markham Harris. Washington, D.C.: Catholic University of America Press, 1969.

In addition to the four-plus Middle English Corpus Christi cycles, there exists another in Cornish, rather different in form from the English plays. The Harris edition provides a new translation, with introduction, notes, and bibliography.

iii. Miracle Plays

If miracle and mystery designate truly distinct types of the drama, the miracle is a saint's life, Biblical or not. (See Section 7 C: Corpus Christi Plays and Miracle Plays, introductory note, on the problem of naming these types of Medieval plays.) The saint's life play is not very plentiful in English. Two examples appear in the "Digby Plays."

THE DIGBY PLAYS, WITH AN INCOMPLETE "MORALITY" OF "WISDOM, WHO IS CHRIST" (PART ONE OF THE MACRO MORALITIES). Re-issued from the Plates of the Text Edited by F.J. Furnivall for the New Shakspere Society in 1882. Early English Text Society, Extra Series, No. 70. 1896; reprint ed. London: For the Early English Text Society by Oxford University Press, 1930.

The four plays in the Digby MS. have no demonstrable relation except for their joint presence in a manuscript collection. They are the two miracles, the CONVERSION OF ST. PAUL and MARY MAGDALENE, with the MASSACRE OF THE INNOCENTS and WISDOM, a morality.

iv. Moralities

The two major titles among English moralities are the single play EVERYMAN and the collection, THE MACRO PLAYS. EVERYMAN has been edited repeatedly, as a single play and in collections. A text often recommended is:

EVERYMAN, REPRINTED . . . FROM THE EDITION BY JOHN SKOT PRESERVED AT BRITWELL COURT. ED. W.W. GREG. In W. Bang, general ed. MATERIALIEN ZUR KUNDE DES ALTEREN ENGLISCHEN DRAMAS, 4. 1904; reprint ed. Vaduz: Kraus Reprint, 1963.

"EVERYMAN," WITH OTHER INTERLUDES, INCLUDING EIGHT MIRACLE PLAYS. Everyman's Library. London: J.M. Dent; New York: E.P. Dutton, 1909; frequently reprinted.

> Since the Everyman's Library series takes its name and motto from the play, the edition deserves notice.

Editions of the Macro Plays, arranged chronologically, include:

THE MACRO PLAYS: 1. MANKIND (AB. 1475). 2. WISDOM (AB. 1460). 3. THE CASTLE OF PERSEVERANCE (AB. 1425). Ed. F.J. Furnivall and Alfred W. Pollard. Early English Text Society, Extra Series, No. 91. London: Published by Kegan Paul, Trench, Trubner & Co., for the Early English Text Society, 1904.

THE MACRO PLAYS: THE CASTLE OF PERSEVERANCE, WISDOM, MANKIND. Ed. Mark Eccles. Early English Text Society, Original Series, No. 262. London, New York, and Toronto: Oxford University Press, for the Early English Text Society, 1969.

THE MACRO PLAYS: THE CASTLE OF PERSEVERANCE; WISDOM; MANKIND. A FACSIMILE EDITION WITH FACING TRANSCRIPTIONS. Ed. David Bevington. The Folger Facsimiles, Manuscript Series, Vol. 1. New York: Johnson Reprint Corp.; Washington, D.C.: The Folger Shakespeare Library, 1972.

> This facsimile has full scholarly apparatus, including a short bibliography.

v. Miscellaneous Editions and Collections of Editions of Medieval Plays, Including Collections of Folkplays

Browne, E. Martin, ed. RELIGIOUS DRAMA 2: MYSTERY AND MORALITY PLAYS. Cleveland and New York: World, 1958; various reprintings.

> The mystery plays in the paperback collection are from various cycles; the morality is EVERYMAN. The texts are modernized. Browne provides an introduction and a concluding essay as well as a bibliography, this last being made up chiefly of "the most useful editions to work from."

Cawley, A.C., ed. EVERYMAN AND MEDIEVAL MIRACLE PLAYS. 2nd ed. New York: E.P. Dutton & Co., 1959.

> Another paperback with modernized texts, the plays representing the extant English Corpus Christi cycles and the Cornish cycle.

Greenberg, Noah, ed. THE PLAY OF DANIEL: A THIRTEENTH-CENTURY

MUSICAL DRAMA, EDITED FOR MODERN PERFORMANCE . . . , BASED ON THE TRANSCRIPTION FROM BRITISH MUSEUM EGERTON 2615 BY REV. REMBERT WEAKLAND, NARRATION BY W.H. AUDEN. New York: Oxford University Press, 1959.

The edition includes a preface by E. Martin Browne, the music (edited), the Latin text with a key to pronunciation, a translation, notes on staging and costumes, and illustrations. It is intended for use in the effort to stage the play, for guidance in viewing a production, or for aid in listening to the phonograph recording of the New York Pro Musica production. The Pro Musica has done much to make Medieval music-drama an auditory and visual experience for the twentieth century. Its recent disbandment can be only partly compensated by the phonograph records.

Helm, Alex, ed. EIGHT MUMMERS' PLAYS. London: Ginn & Co., 1971.

See next item.

______. FIVE MUMMING PLAYS FOR SCHOOLS. London: English Folk Dance and Song Society and Folk-lore Society, 1965.

See next item.

Helm, Alex, and E.C. Cawte, eds. SIX MUMMERS' ACTS. Ibnstock, Leicestershire: Guizer Press, 1967.

Helm and Cawte have worked extensively with the surviving remnants of the folkplay, as these editions indicate. (I have not seen these editions.)

Hemingway, Samuel B., ed. ENGLISH NATIVITY PLAYS. Yale Studies in English, Vol. 38. New York: Holt, 1909.

The introduction attempts not only to set out facts but to evaluate the plays as drama.

Hopper, Vincent F., and Gerald B. Lahey, eds. MEDIEVAL MYSTERY PLAYS: ABRAHAM AND ISAAC, NOAH'S FLOOD, THE SECOND SHEPHERDS' PLAY; MORALITY PLAYS: THE CASTLE OF PERSEVERANCE, EVERYMAN; AND INTERLUDES: JOHAN, THE HUSBAND, THE FOUR PP. Woodberry, N.Y.: Barron's Educational Series, 1962.

Modernized texts. The portions of Genesis and Luke relevant to the Biblical plays are supplied. Introduction, brief bibliography.

Malcolmson, Anne, ed. MIRACLE PLAYS. SEVEN MEDIEVAL PLAYS FOR MODERN PLAYERS. Illustrated by Pauline Baynes. Boston: Houghton Mifflin, 1956, 1959.

Five plays from cycles and two St. Nicholas plays adapted for children.

Osgood, Phillips Endecott, ed. OLD-TIME CHURCH DRAMA ADAPTED: MYSTERY PLAYS AND MORALITIES OF EARLIER DAYS FOR SUNDRY CHURCHLY USES TO-DAY. New York and London: Harper & Bros., 1928.

Several Corpus Christi plays, chiefly of the Nativity; EVERYMAN; some plays from the early Greek church; the QUEM QUAERITIS; and others; with some suggestions for staging within the church, etc.

Schenkkan, Robert Frederick, and Kai Jurgenson, eds. FOURTEEN PLAYS FOR THE CHURCH. New Brunswick, N.J.: Rutgers University Press, 1948.

The plays come from Brome, York, Coventry, Wakefield, and various French and German sources; all are given in modern English. Costume sketches, songs with music, and "Notes on Production" are supplied.

Switz, Theodore MacLean, and Robert A. Johnston, eds. GREAT CHRISTIAN PLAYS. A COLLECTION OF CLASSICAL RELIGIOUS PLAYS IN ACTING VERSIONS AND SELECTED CHORAL READINGS SUITABLE FOR A WORSHIP SERVICE. Greenwich, Conn.: Seabury Press, 1956.

The plays are "The BROME Abraham and Isaac," "The YORK Resurrection," "The DIGBY Conversion of St. Paul," "Totentanz, a Morality Play," and "Everyman, a Morality Play." Each play is modernized and has an introduction and music.

Thomas, R. George, ed. TEN MIRACLE PLAYS. York Medieval Texts. Evanston, Ill.: Northwestern University Press; London: E. Arnold, 1966.

Plays from LUDUS COVENTRIAE, TOWNELEY, CHESTER, YORK, and the "true" COVENTRY cycles make up a kind of abridged, mixed cycle, with a brief but sound introduction, notes (mostly glossary), and bibliography. The general editors of the York Medieval Texts, Elizabeth Salter and Derek Pearsall, state that the purpose of the series is "to provide editions of major pieces of Middle English writing in a form which will make them accessible without loss of historical authenticity." Texts have been selected "because of their importance and artistic merit" and edited "to preserve the character of the English while eliminating unnecessary encumbrances." Paperback publication makes the York Medieval Texts further accessible to the scholarly budget. They constitute a significant series.

Tickner, F[rederick] J., ed. EARLIER ENGLISH DRAMA FROM ROBIN HOOD TO EVERYMAN. EDITED AND ARRANGED FOR ACTING. London and Edinburgh: T. Nelson & Sons, 1926.

A miscellaneous collection of plays, in modern English, with brief notes.

B. MISCELLANEOUS MEDIEVAL AND TUDOR PLAYS (WITH SOME POST-TUDOR MATERIAL)

Included here are editions that run from the Middle Ages into the Tudor period; miscellaneous editions of early Tudor plays, mostly anonymous; collections focused in some particular topic; a few editions of single titles of some particular import; and a very few editions of later pieces.

Adams, Joseph Quincy, ed. CHIEF PRE-SHAKESPEAREAN DRAMA: A SELECTION OF PLAYS ILLUSTRATING THE HISTORY OF THE ENGLISH DRAMA FROM ITS ORIGIN DOWN TO SHAKESPEARE. 1924; reprint ed. Cambridge, Mass.: Houghton Mifflin, 1952.

Adams includes various examples of Latin liturgical drama with translations into English and examples of cycle and non-cycle plays, moralities, and folkplays, as well as THE FOUR PP., JOHN JOHN, THE PLAY OF THE WETHER, ROISTER DOISTER, GAMMER GURTON, GORBODUC, SUPPOSES, DAMON AND PITHIAS, CAMPASPE, CAMBISES, THE FAMOUS VICTORIES, and GEORGE A GREENE. The critical apparatus is not extensive, but the collection brings together an important body of plays.

Boas, Frederick S., ed. FIVE PRE-SHAKESPEAREAN COMEDIES. 1934; reprint ed. London, Oxford, New York: Oxford University Press, 1970.

Boas supplies introduction, notes, modernized texts. The plays are Medwall, FULGENS & LUCRECE; J. Heywood, THE FOUR PP; Udall, RALPH ROISTER DOISTER; "Mr. S.," GAMMER GURTON'S NEEDLE; Gascoigne, SUPPOSES. The reprint makes the collection available in paperback.

______. "THE TAMING OF A SHREW," BEING THE ORIGINAL OF SHAKESPEARE'S "TAMING OF THE SHREW." New York: Duffield; London: Chatto & Windus, 1908.

Introduction, notes, various appendices, as well as text.

Bond, R. Warwick, ed. EARLY PLAYS FROM THE ITALIAN. 1911; reprint ed. New York: Benjamin Blom, n.d.

The plays are Gascoigne's SUPPOSES and two anonymous plays, THE BUGGBEARS and MISOGONUS. Bond says of his intention: "I have endeavored . . . something wider than an edition" in order "to show how ancient Greek and Roman comedy finds representation in our own, not only in subject and spirit, but in matters of form and technique" (p. iii). He provides a long introductory essay to the whole and an introduction to each individual play.

Brooke, C[harles] F[rederick] Tucker, ed. THE SHAKESPEARE APOCRYPHA, BEING A COLLECTION OF FOURTEEN PLAYS WHICH HAVE BEEN ASCRIBED

TO SHAKESPEARE. Oxford: Clarendon Press, 1908.

The plays are: ARDEN OF FEVERSHAM, LOCRINE, EDWARD III, MUCEDORUS, SIR JOHN OLDCASTLE, THOMAS LORD CROMWELL, THE LONDON PRODIGAL, THE PURITAN, A YORKSHIRE TRAGEDY, THE MERRY DEVIL OF EDMONTON, FAIR EM, THE TWO NOBLE KINSMEN, THE BIRTH OF MERLIN, and SIR THOMAS MORE. Brooke supplies introduction, notes, bibliography.

Brown, Carleton, ed. THE STONYHURST PAGEANTS. Hesperia Erganzungsreihe: Schriften zur Englischen Philologie, Vol. 7. Gottingen: Vandenhoeck & Ruprecht; Baltimore: Johns Hopkins Press, 1920.

Brown describes the pageants, "here printed for the first time," as having "a distinct interest for the student of literature as a curiously belated survival of an earlier form of drama . . . written after Shakespere's work had already been completed" (p. 7). The author has been identified as "a Roman Catholic [writing] during the reign of James I," but Brown cannot state the occasion of the writing of the pageants or whether they were ever performed (see pp. 7-30).

Creeth, Edmund, ed. TUDOR PLAYS: AN ANTHOLOGY OF EARLY ENGLISH DRAMA. INTRODUCTION, NOTES, AND VARIANTS. Garden City, N.Y.: Doubleday (Anchor); New York: W.W. Norton & Co., 1966.

The plays in this paperback edition are FULGENS AND LUCRES, JOHAN JOHAN, KYNG JOHAN, ROYSTER DOYSTER, GAMMER GURTONS NEDLE, FERREX AND PORREX, OR GORBODUC, and CAMBISES. Creeth points up the rationale of the collection as representing "the chief varieties of Tudor drama from its emergence as a secular art under Henry VII until the first manifestations of English tragedy early in the reign of Elizabeth I" (p. [xi]). The long introduction provides much useful information. The texts are "taken from photographic facsimiles either of original editions or, in the case of KYNG JOHAN, of the unique MS" (p. xliv). Creeth offers an old spelling text to preserve "the distinctive character and subtle associations" of the original. Apparatus includes lists of variants, substantial notes. Creeth seeks to provide scholarly editing in an inexpensive form.

Cunliffe, John W., ed. EARLY ENGLISH CLASSICAL TRAGEDY. Oxford: Clarendon Press, 1912.

Cunliffe edits GORBODUC, JOCASTA, GISMOND OF SALERNE, and THE MISFORTUNES OF ARTHUR.

Elson, John James, ed. THE WITS, OR, SPORT UPON SPORT. Ithaca, N.Y.: Cornell University Press; London: Oxford University Press, 1932.

Elson writes: "The principal purpose of this edition is to provide a complete and accurate text of a rare and little-known dramatic miscellany" (p. vii), a collection of "drolls and playlets" made up of bits from various plays: the first piece in the first part, for example, is "The Bounding Knight" from Shakespeare's I HENRY IV; and various playwrights are then called upon in the compilation. Part I was published by Henry Marsh in 1662 and by Francis Kirkman in 1672; Part 2 by Kirkman, in two editions, 1673, the matter being recommended for recitation or acting (see Elson's "Introduction," p. 1). More a curiosity than a serious dramatic phenomenon, but a curious curiousity.

Evans, Herbert Arthur, ed. ENGLISH MASQUES. London: Blackie, 1897.

Evans provides an "Introduction" and sixteen masques. Jonson, Daniel, Campion, Beaumont, Shirley, and Davenant contribute to the collection.

Everitt, E.B., and R.L. Armstrong, eds. SIX EARLY PLAYS RELATED TO THE SHAKESPEARE CANON. Anglistica, No. 14. Copenhagen: Rosenkild and Bagger, 1965.

The plays are LEIR, THE WEAKEST GOETH TO THE WALL, EDMUND IRONSIDE, THE TROUBLESOME REIGN, EDWARD III, and WOODSTOCK. The texts are modernized. Each play has a brief introduction, and most of them also have both general and textual notes.

Fairholt, Frederick W. LORD MAYORS' PAGEANTS: BEING COLLECTIONS TOWARDS A HISTORY OF THESE ANNUAL CELEBRATIONS, WITH SPECIMENS OF THE DESCRIPTIVE PAMPHLETS PUBLISHED BY THE CITY POETS. Percy Society Publications, Vol. 10. London: Printed for the Percy Society by T. Richards, 1843-44.

Part I, HISTORY OF LORD MAYORS' PAGEANTS, 1843, and Part II, REPRINTS OF LORD MAYORS' PAGEANTS, 1844, are bound in one volume with separate title pages and pagination. Part II includes both pre- and post-Restoration pageants, with extensive notes: Thomas Dekker, TROIA-NOVA TRIUMPHANS, 1612, and LONDON'S TEMPE, 1629; Thomas Heywood, PORTA PIETATIS, OR THE PORT OR HARBOUR OF PIETY, 1638; John Tatham, THE ROYAL OAKE, 1660; Thomas Jordan, LONDON'S RESURRECTION TO JOY AND TRIUMPH, 1671, THE TRIUMPH OF LONDON, 1678, and REPRESENTATIONS IN PARTS (dates of publication and/or performance, the Jordan REPRESENTATIONS IN PARTS constituting an "Appendix" with a note: "Reprinted from 'A Nursery of Novelties in variety of Poetry. Planted for the delightful Leisures of Nobility and Ingenuity.' No date"). See also Section 8: Studies of Tudor and Stuart Drama.

Franklin, Alexander, ed. SEVEN MIRACLE PLAYS. London and New York: Oxford University Press, 1963.

The collection, which I have not seen, is described as containing very modernized versions of Old and New Testament plays.

Furnivall, Frederick J., ed. THE FIRST PART OF THE CONTENTION. THE FIRST QUARTO. 1594 . . . . A FACSIMILE . . . BY CHARLES PRAETORIUS, WITH FOREWORDS EMBODYING THE LATE R. GRANT WHITE'S ARGUMENT ON SHAKSPERE'S RIGHT TO THE WHOLE OF "2 & 3 HENRY VI." London: C. Praetorius, 1889.

The "Forewords" contain an argument on the various hands which have been found in the play--Marlowe's, Greene's, Peele's.

Gassner, John, ed. MEDIEVAL AND TUDOR DRAMA. WITH INTRODUCTIONS AND MODERNIZATIONS. Toronto, New York, London: Bantam Books, 1963, 1968.

Not seen.

Gayley, Charles Mills, ed. REPRESENTATIVE ENGLISH COMEDIES, WITH INTRODUCTORY ESSAYS AND NOTES, AN HISTORICAL VIEW OF OUR EARLIER COMEDY, AND OTHER MONOGRAPHS, BY VARIOUS WRITERS. Vols. 1-3. New York and London: Macmillan, 1903-14.

Old but rather famous.

Greg, W[alter] W[ilson]. TWO ELIZABETHAN STAGE ABRIDGEMENTS: "THE BATTLE OF ALCAZAR" & "ORLANDO FURIOSO." AN ESSAY IN CRITICAL BIBLIOGRAPHY. Oxford: Clarendon Press for The Malone Society, Extra Volume, 1922.

A study of what contemporary texts may reveal or imply about the Renaissance stage.

Happe, Peter, ed. TUDOR INTERLUDES. Harmondsworth: Penguin, 1972.

Happe includes THE PRIDE OF LIFE, MANKIND (extracts), FULGENS & LUCRES (extracts), YOUTH, THE PLAY OF THE WETHER, WIT AND SCIENCE, RESPUBLICA (extracts), APIUS AND VIRGINIA, LIKE WILL TO LIKE, SIR THOMAS MORE (extracts), in slightly modernized texts. He provides introduction, notes, glossary, and a short bibliography.

Hawkins, Thomas, ed. THE ORIGIN OF THE ENGLISH DRAMA, ILLUSTRATED IN ITS VARIOUS SPECIES, VIZ., MYSTERY, MORALITY, TRAGEDY, AND COMEDY, BY SPECIMENS FROM OUR EARLIEST WRITERS. WITH EXPLANATORY NOTES. 3 vols. Oxford: Printed at the Clarendon Press for S. Leacroft, 1773.

The selections run from the Digby CANDLEMAS-DAY, OR THE KILLING OF THE CHILDREN OF ISRAEL, which Hawkins ascribes to "Iham Parfre in 1512," EVERYMAN, HYCKE-SCORNER, etc., to WILY BEGUILED.

Heilman, Robert B., ed. AN ANTHOLOGY OF ENGLISH DRAMA BEFORE

SHAKESPEARE. New York and Toronto: Rinehart, 1952, with various reprints.

Heilman includes four examples from the Corpus Christi cycles, EVERYMAN, GAMMER GURTON, FRIAR BACON AND FRIAR BUNGAY, THE SPANISH TRAGEDY, and DR. FAUSTUS, in modern spelling, with introduction, light notes, and a "Bibliographical Note."

Lamb, Charles, ed. SPECIMENS OF ENGLISH DRAMATIC POETS, WHO LIVED ABOUT THE TIME OF SHAKSPEARE, WITH NOTES, INCLUDING EXTRACTS FROM THE GARRICK PLAYS. 1808; reprint ed. London: G. Bell & Sons, 1901.

Lamb, in his "Preface," says: "My leading design has been, to illustrate what may be called the moral sense of our ancestors. . . . Another object which I had . . . was, to bring together the most admired scenes in Fletcher and Massinger, in the estimation of the world the only dramatic poets of that age who are entitled to be considered after Shakspeare, and to exhibit them in the same volume with the more impressive scenes of old Marlowe, Heywood, Tourneur, Webster, Ford, and others. To show what we have slighted, while beyond all proportion we have cried up one or two favourite names" (p. iv). The chief value of the volume is perhaps its demonstration of Lamb's taste; but on that subject, Samuel C. Chew, in A LITERARY HISTORY OF ENGLAND (ed. A.C. Baugh, 2nd ed., p. 1182), says this is "one of the finest of all anthologies. Save for an inadequate appreciation of Marlowe's genius Lamb's taste is faultless."

Loomis, Roger Sherman, and Henry W. Wells, eds. REPRESENTATIVE MEDIEVAL AND TUDOR PLAYS, TRANSLATED AND MODERNIZED. New York: Sheed & Ward, 1942.

A very miscellaneous collection: three Saint Nicholas plays, De la Vigne's THE MIRACLE OF THE BLIND MAN AND THE CRIPPLE, the Wakefield ANNUNCIATION and SECOND SHEPHERDS' PLAY, the Hegge REDEMPTION, EVERYMAN, JOHN, TYB, AND SIR JOHN, and THE PARDONER AND THE FRIAR. Introduction, bibliography.

Manly, John Matthews, ed. SPECIMENS OF THE PRE-SHAKSPEREAN DRAMA. 2 vols. 1897; reprint ed. New York: Dover Publications, 1967.

The Dover paperback makes Manly's old but famous collection again available. Volume I contains some liturgical materials; a series of plays from the various cycles, making up an abridged cycle; the Digby THE CONVERSION OF ST. PAUL; THE PLAY OF THE SACRAMENT; several folkplays; several moralities: MANKIND, MUNDUS ET INFANS, HYCKE-SCORNER, WIT AND SCIENCE, and NICE WANTON; THE FOURE PP; KYNGE JOHAN. Volume 2 contains ROISTER DOISTER, GAMMER GURTON, CAMBISES, GORBODUC, CAMPASPE, JAMES IV, DAVID AND BETHSABE, THE

SPANISH TRAGEDIE. Manly's notes are brief but reflect his learning.

Pollard, Alfred W., ed. ENGLISH MIRACLE PLAYS, MORALITIES, AND INTERLUDES: SPECIMENS OF THE PRE-ELIZABETHAN DRAMA. 8th ed., rev. Oxford: Clarendon; London: Humphrey Milford, 1927.

Pollard provides five plays from York, Chester, Towneley, and LUDUS COVENTRIAE; also MARY MAGDALENE, THE CASTELL OF PERSEVERANCE, EVERYMAN, THE FOUR ELEMENTS, MAGNYFYCENCE, THE PARDONER AND THE FRERE, THERSYTES, and KING JOHN, with rather extensive notes and an appendix.

Sabol, Andrew J., ed. SONGS AND DANCES FOR THE STUART MASQUE.

See Section 8: Studies of Tudor and Stuart Drama.

Spencer, T.J.B., S[tanley] W. Wells, et al., eds. A BOOK OF MASQUES IN HONOUR OF ALLARDYCE NICOLL. London: Cambridge University Press, 1967.

The "General Introduction" is by Gerald Eades Bentley. There are forty-eight plates and fourteen masques: Samuel Daniel, THE VISION OF THE TWELVE GODDESSES; Ben Jonson, OBERON, THE FAIRY PRINCE and LOVE FREED FROM IGNORANCE AND FOLLY; Thomas Campion, THE LORDS' MASQUE; Francis Beaumont, THE MASQUE OF THE INNER TEMPLE AND GRAY'S INN; THE MASQUE OF FLOWERS (anonymous); William Browne, THE MASQUE OF THE INNER TEMPLE; Ben Jonson, LOVERS MADE MEN and PLEASURE RECONCILED TO VIRTUE; Thomas Middleton, THE INNER TEMPLE MASQUE, OR MASQUE OF HEROES; James Shirley, THE TRIUMPH OF PEACE; Thomas Nabbes, THE SPRING'S GLORY; Inigo Jones and William Davenant, SALMACIDA SPOLIA; and James Shirley, CUPID AND DEATH. The masques are edited by various hands, and the whole ends with an essay by Inga-Stina Ewbank, "'These pretty devices': A Study of Masques in Plays."

[Steevens, George, and John Nichols, eds.] SIX OLD PLAYS ON WHICH SHAKSPEARE FOUNDED HIS "MEASURE FOR MEASURE," "COMEDY OF ERRORS," "TAMING THE SHREW," "KING JOHN," "K. HENRY IV" and "K. HENRY V," "KING LEAR." 2 vols. London: S. Leacroft, 1779.

The plays are: George Whetstone, Gent., THE . . . HISTORYE OF PROMOS AND CASSANDRA; W.W., MENAECMI, A . . . COMOEDIE TAKEN OUT OF THE MOST EXCELLENT WITTIE POET PLAUTUS; THE TAMING OF A SHREW; THE FIRST AND SECOND PART OF THE TROUBLESOME RAIGNE OF JOHN KING OF ENGLAND; THE FAMOUS VICTORIES OF HENRY THE FIFTH, CONTAINING THE HONOURABLE BATTELL OF AGIN-COURT; THE TRUE CHRONICLE HISTORY OF KING LEIR AND HIS THREE DAUGHTERS, GONORILL, RAGAN, AND CORDELLA. Texts only, no apparatus.

Thorndike, Ashley H., ed. THE MINOR ELIZABETHAN DRAMA. Everyman's Library. 2 vols. London: Dent; New York: E.P. Dutton & Co., 1910, with various reprintings.

Volume 1, PRE-SHAKESPEAREAN TRAGEDIES, includes GORBODUC, ARDEN OF FEVERSHAM, DAVID AND BETHSABE, and THE SPANISH TRAGEDY; Volume 2, PRE-SHAKESPEAREAN COMEDIES: RALPH ROISTER DOISTER, ENDIMION, OLD WIVES' TALE, FRIAR BACON AND FRIAR BUNGAY, and JAMES IV. A small but well-chosen collection. Little apparatus.

C. SERIAL AND MULTI-VOLUME EDITIONS

Bang, W., ed. MATERIALIEN ZUR KUNDE DES ALTEREN ENGLISCHEN DRAMAS. 39 vols. 1902-13; reprint ed. Vaduz: Kraus Reprint, 1963.

Bang's work was continued by Henry de Vocht with a slightly modified title:

Vocht, Henry de, ed. MATERIALS FOR THE STUDY OF THE OLD ENGLISH DRAMA, BEING THE COMPLETING AND CONTINUATION OF THE "MATERIALIEN ZUR KUNDE DES ALTEREN ENGLISCHEN DRAMAS" FOUNDED BY PROFESSOR W. BANG. New Series, 21 vols. 1927-50; reprint ed. Vaduz: Kraus Reprint, 1963.

The Bang-De Vocht series contains both texts of plays and critical materials, including concordances. In spite of Bang's German title, the materials are more often in English than in another language. In the course of time, some of the editions have been superseded, but by no means all of them.

Bergquist, G. William, ed. THREE CENTURIES OF ENGLISH AND AMERICAN PLAYS. A CHECKLIST.

See Wells, Henry W., ed., below, and Bergquist, G. William, ed., in Section 1 C: Bibliographies of Drama.

Bullen, A.H., ed. A COLLECTION OF OLD ENGLISH PLAYS. 4 vols. London: Privately Printed by Wyman & Sons, 1882-85.

These four volumes contain: Volume I: THE TRAGEDY OF NERO, THE MAYDE'S METAMORPHOSIS, THE MARTYR'D SOULDIER, and THE NOBLE SOULDIER; Volume II: DICK OF DEVONSHIRE, THE LADY MOTHER, THE TRAGEDY OF SIR JOHN VAN OLDEN BARNAVELT, and CAPTAIN UNDERWIT; Volume III: SIR GYLES GOOSECAPPE, THE WISDOME OF DR. DODYPOLL, THE DISTRACTED EMPEROR, and THE TRYALL OF CHEVALRY; Volume IV: TWO TRAGEDIES IN ONE, THE CAPTIVES, OR, THE LOST RECOVERED, THE COSTLIE WHORE, and EVERIE WOMAN IN HER HUMOR. This edition was followed by another edition by Bullen, see below.

______. OLD ENGLISH PLAYS. New Series. 3 vols. London: Privately Printed by Wyman & Sons, 1887-90.

The New Series contains: Volumes I and II: THE WORKS OF THOMAS NABBES; Volume III, THE WORKS OF ROBERT DAVENPORT.

In 1964, Benjamin Blom reprinted Bullen's editions, using the title A COLLECTION OF OLD ENGLISH PLAYS and printing four volumes. Of these, Volume I corresponds to Volume I in the original Bullen series and Volume II to Bullen's original Volume III; in the Blom reprint, Volume III contains THE WORKS OF THOMAS NABBES and Volume IV, THE WORKS OF ROBERT DAVENPORT, both from Bullen's New Series.

[Dilke, C.W., ed.]. OLD ENGLISH PLAYS: BEING A SELECTION FROM THE EARLY DRAMATIC WRITERS. 6 vols. in 3. London: Whittingham and Rowland for John Martin, 1814-15.

The writers selected are: Volume I: Marlowe and Lyly; Volume II: Lyly and Marston; Volume III: Dekker and Chapman; Volume IV: Chapman, Middleton and William Rowley, and Middleton; Volume V: Middleton and Rowley, and Webster; Volume VI: Webster and William Rowley, and Thomas Heywood. Dilke's collection is famous, although it provides little beyond texts. Its notes are represented, perhaps not quite fairly, by the annotation for the line "Come, Mephostophilis, let us dispute again," from DR. FAUSTUS: "The remainder of this scene, an ostentatious display of school-learning, with which the authors before Shakspeare abound, may be passed over without loss to the reader" (Vol. 1, p. 33).

Dodsley, Robert, ed. A SELECT COLLECTION OF OLD PLAYS. 12 vols. London: Printed for Dodsley, 1744.

When Dodsley printed his first edition, he could hardly have foreseen what he had begun. The second edition, with the added editorial hand of Isaac Reed, appeared in twelve volumes, 1780. In 1825-27, again in twelve volumes, there came "A New Edition: with Additional Notes and Corrections, by the Late Isaac Reed, Octavius Gilchrist, and the Editor [John Payne Collier]."

Then, in THE SHAKESPEARE SOCIETY'S PAPERS, a sufficiently complicated printing venture in itself, appeared:

> Amyot, Thomas; J. Payne Collier; W. Durrant Cooper; A. Dyce; Barron Field; J.O. Halliwell [-Phillipps]; and Thomas Wright, eds. A SUPPLEMENT TO DODSLEY'S OLD PLAYS. 4 vols. London: Printed for the Shakespeare Society, 1853.

There is also:

> Hazlitt, W. Carew, ed. A SELECT COLLECTION OF OLD ENGLISH PLAYS . . . ORIGINALLY PUBLISHED

BY ROBERT DODSLEY IN THE YEAR 1744. 4TH ED. NOW FIRST CHRONOLOGICALLY ARRANGED, REVISED, AND ENLARGED WITH THE NOTES OF ALL THE COMMENTATORS AND NEW NOTES. 15 vols. 1874-76; reprint ed. New York: Benjamin Blom, 1964.

Farmer, John S., ed. EARLY ENGLISH DRAMATISTS. 13 vols. 1906; reprint ed. Guildford, England: Charles W. Traylen, 1966.

Originally printed for the Early English Drama Society, Farmer's thirteen volumes include several series of anonymous plays and works by John Heywood, Ulpian Fulwell, Nicholas Udall, Norton and Sackville, Richard Edwards, Henry Medwall, John Redford, Bale, Wever, and Ingelend. See entries under individual authors in Part 2 for separate entries for some of these. The scholarly apparatus provided by Farmer is rather slight.

_____. TUDOR FACSIMILE TEXTS: OLD ENGLISH PLAYS, PRINTED & MS. RARITIES. EXACT COLLOTYPE REPRODUCTIONS IN FOLIO AND QUARTO, UNDER THE GENERAL EDITORSHIP AND SUPERVISION OF JOHN S. FARMER ASSISTED BY CRAFTSMEN OF REPUTE AND STANDING. London: Issued for Subscribers by John S. Farmer, 1907-14.

Volume 129 is A HAND LIST TO THE TUDOR FACSIMILE TEXTS . . . AUGUST 1914, CANCELLING PREVIOUS ANNOUNCEMENTS.

FOUNTAINWELL DRAMA SERIES.

The FOUNTAINWELL DRAMA texts, under the general editorship of T.A. Dunn, Andrew Gurr, John Horden, A. Norman Jeffares, R.L.C. Lorimer, and Brian W.M. Scobie, have been issued by Oliver & Boyd of Edinburgh and by the University of California Press. Mr. Geoffrey Ashton of the University of California Press informs me by letter, July 5, 1972, that Oliver & Boyd expects to continue issuing volumes in the series but that the University of California does not. The announcement of available texts supplied by Mr. Ashton describes the series as designed to provide, for each play, "a text based on fresh critical study of the original sources, together with an introduction, textual notes, commentary, and glossary. The original spelling and punctuation are normalized but not modernized." Texts are issued in both cloth and paper bindings. Among those already in print are THE MAID'S TRAGEDY, TWELFTH NIGHT, FATAL DOWRY, WOMEN BEWARE WOMEN, THE WHITE DEVIL, A CHASTE MAID IN CHEAPSIDE, THE SPANISH TRAGEDY, THE ALCHEMIST, VOLPONE, A TRICK TO CATCH THE OLD ONE, THE KNIGHT OF THE BURNING PESTLE, THE DUTCH COURTESAN, and THE SHOEMAKERS' HOLIDAY. (A list of titles for a continuing series cannot be complete, obviously.)

MALONE SOCIETY.

The Malone Society has issued two major series: THE MALONE

SOCIETY COLLECTIONS and THE MALONE SOCIETY REPRINTS. These were begun under the editorship of W.W. Greg and have been edited by various hands. In the COLLECTIONS, various materials are issued separately, then "collected" when a suitable body of material has appeared. Volume I, Part 1, appeared in 1907; Volume VII was collected in 1965. The COLLECTIONS include both reprints of plays and various scholarly articles. THE MALONE SOCIETY REPRINTS (1907--) are facsimile reprints with little apparatus. See Eleanora A. Baer, TITLES IN SERIES, 2nd ed. (New York and London: Scarecrow Press, 1964; Supplements, 1967, 1971), for a list of the titles in the REPRINTS.

MERMAID SERIES: THE BEST PLAYS OF THE OLD DRAMATISTS.

The original Mermaids are collections of selected plays by one or more authors in small volumes. Each volume has one or more editors and the contents are described as "Literal Reproductions of the Old Text." These were printed in London by T. Fisher Unwin, and in New York by Charles Scribner's Sons. Editions in THE MERMAIDS are not necessarily of Renaissance plays, and the texts are intended as convenient readers' texts rather than as scholars' tools. See also next item for a recent series reviving the old name.

NEW MERMAID DRAMABOOKS.

The NEW MERMAID DRAMABOOKS is a current series being edited by Philip Brockbank and Brian Morris and published by Hill and Wang, New York. Titles currently in print in the series, as shown in the PUBLISHERS' TRADE LIST ANNUAL 1973, include: BUSSY D'AMBOIS, THE BROKEN HEART, THE DUCHESS OF MALFI, DOCTOR FAUSTUS, THE ALCHEMIST, THE JEW OF MALTA, THE REVENGER'S TRAGEDY, A GAME AT CHESS, EVERYMAN IN HIS HUMOUR, THE WHITE DEVIL, EDWARD THE SECOND, THE MALCONTENT, 'TIS PITY SHE'S A WHORE, SEJANUS HIS FALL, VOLPONE, WOMEN BEWARE WOMEN, LOVE FOR LOVE, THE SPANISH TRAGEDY, and TAMBURLAINE THE GREAT. Brian Morris, the editor of Ford's THE BROKEN HEART, describes the editorial practice employed in preparing that volume as including modernization of spelling, capitalization, and punctuation. The NEW MERMAID series is also publishing volumes of critical essays on the various dramatists.

REGENTS RENAISSANCE DRAMA SERIES.

The REGENTS RENAISSANCE DRAMA SERIES, under the general editorship of Cyrus Hoy and G.E. Bentley and published by the University of Nebraska Press, Lincoln, has been issuing volumes, usually of single plays, since 1963. A statement, signed by Hoy and printed in each volume, indicates that the purpose of the series is "to provide soundly edited texts, in modern spelling, of the more significant plays of the Elizabethan, Jacobean, and Caroline theater. Each text . . . is based on a fresh collation of all sixteenth- and seventeenth-century editions. The textual notes . . . record all substantive departures from the edition used as the copy-text." Each edition has textual and explanatory notes. Titles available in the series, as of the winter of 1972, include: FRIAR BACON AND FRIAR BUNGAY; A KING AND NO KING; BARTHOLOMEW FAIR; THE JEW OF MALTA; THE CITY MADAM; BUSSY D'AMBOIS; THE MALCONTENT; ANTONIO AND MELLIDA; ANTONIO'S REVENGE; THE FAWN; THE DUTCH COURTESAN; A MAD WORLD, MY MASTERS; THE TRAITOR; PERKIN WARBECK; THE CHANGELING; 'TIS PITY SHE'S A WHORE; EPICOENE; THE WIDOW'S TEARS; THE REVENGER'S TRAGEDY; THE ANTIPODES; MICHAELMAS TERM; THE FIRST PART OF HIERONIMO and THE SPANISH TRAGEDY; TAMBURLAINE, Parts I and II; THE KNIGHT OF THE BURNING PESTLE; THE MAID'S TRAGEDY; THE LONGER THOU LIVEST and ENOUGH IS AS GOOD AS A FEAST; THE FAIR MAID OF THE WEST, Parts I and II; THE BROKEN HEART; A JOVIAL CREW; ALL FOOLS; THE WOUNDS OF CIVIL WAR; GALLATHEA and MIDAS; THE WHITE DEVIL; THE TWO NOBLE KINSMEN; GORBODUC, OR, FERREX AND PORREX; EVERY MAN IN HIS HUMOR; THE DEVIL'S LAW-CASE; and THE GENTLEMAN USHER. There is also a REGENTS CRITICS SERIES.

REVELS PLAYS

The REVELS PLAYS, edited by Clifford Leech and F.D. Hoeniger, began to appear (from Methuen, London, and Harvard University Press, Cambridge, Massachusetts) in 1958. The "General Editor's Preface," prepared in 1969 by Leech, reads in part: "The introduction to each volume includes a discussion of the provenance of the text, the play's stage-history and reputation, its significance as a contribution to dramatic literature, and its place within the work of its author." Leech points out that editorial policy stresses a balance of consistency and flexibility. Spelling and punctuation are modernized. The series began with better-known plays, aims at moving into lesser-known works. The titles are now listed in the Harper and Row catalog, under the Barnes & Noble imprint. The titles shown as available in the PUBLISHERS' TRADE LIST ANNUAL 1974, augmented with a few additional titles apparently now out of print, include: THE ALCHEMIST; THE ATHEIST'S TRAGEDY; BARTHOLOMEW FAIR; BUSSY D'AMBOIS; THE CHANGELING; CHASTE MAID IN CHEAPSIDE; CHRONICLE HISTORY OF PERKIN WARBECK; DIDO, QUEEN OF CARTHAGE and THE MASSACRE AT PARIS; DOCTOR FAUSTUS; THE DUCHESS OF MALFI; PHILASTER; OR, LOVE LIES A-BLEEDING; THE REVENGER'S TRAGEDY; THE SCOTTISH HISTORY OF JAMES THE FOURTH; THE SPANISH TRAGEDY; THE TRAGEDY OF MASTER ARDEN OF FAVERSHAM; THE WHITE DEVIL; A WOMAN KILLED WITH KINDNESS; and THE WIDOW'S TEARS.

SHAKESPEARE SOCIETY'S PAPERS, THE.

These papers present a complicated maze, perhaps too complex to make an analysis of their contents worthwhile here. A number of volumes are entered separately in other parts of this bibliography, particularly under Section 10: Contemporary and Other Early Records, Allusions, Criticism, Etc. Both editions of plays and various other kinds of materials are included. Various pieces were printed separately, then collected into volumes, which have a general title page with the imprint: London: Printed for the Shakespeare Society, 1853, and a number of additional title pages, usually with dates earlier than 1853. The hand of John Payne Collier in the editing raises the usual doubts about the reliability of the materials, but many of the editors are above suspicion. A day spent browsing through the various volumes will entertain and probably instruct.

Vocht, Henry de, ed.

See the entry included under Bang, W., ed.

Wells, Henry W., ed. THREE CENTURIES OF DRAMA. New York: Readex Microprint, 1953.

This thirty-two-box microcard edition of the plays in the Larpent Collection makes better than 5,000 plays available, often from valuable early editions, though not all from the period to 1660. G. William Bergquist, ed., THREE CENTURIES OF ENGLISH AND AMERICAN PLAYS, A CHECKLIST. ENGLAND: 1500-1800, UNITED STATES, 1714-1830 (New York: Hafner, 1963), lists the plays reproduced and identifies the original edition from which each is taken. Microprinting allows for the exact reproduction of a text but not for editorial guidance into its mysteries.

3. AVAILABILITY AND PRICES

Indicated here are some guides to prices, old and current, of rare or otherwise valuable books and also to prices of current, generally available books. The guides concerned with "collectors' items" will supply information about demand and bibliographical descriptions of old and rare books, information often needed by the scholar as well as the buyer.

A. OLD BOOKS

AMERICAN BOOK-PRICES CURRENT . . . A RECORD OF LITERARY PROPERTIES SOLD AT AUCTION IN ENGLAND, THE UNITED STATES, AND IN CANADA. New York and London: Columbia University Press, 1894--.

Published annually, this RECORD provides information about prices of rare or otherwise valuable books, with a brief description of the book--author, title, date, edition, number of volumes, size, binding, condition, and the like.

BOOK-PRICES CURRENT: A RECORD OF THE PRICES AT WHICH BOOKS HAVE BEEN SOLD AT AUCTION. London: H.F. & G. WITHERBY, 1886/87--. (Imprint varies over the years.)

To be used the same way as (and in conjunction with) AMERICAN BOOK PRICES CURRENT for information on auction book prices and the like.

Livingston, Luther S., ed. AUCTION PRICES OF BOOKS. A REPRESENTATIVE RECORD ARRANGED IN ALPHABETICAL ORDER FROM THE COMMENCEMENT OF THE ENGLISH "BOOK-PRICES CURRENT" IN 1886 AND THE "AMERICAN BOOK-PRICES CURRENT" IN 1894 TO 1904, AND INCLUDING SOME THOUSANDS OF IMPORTANT QUOTATIONS OF EARLIER DATE. 4 vols. New York: Dodd, Mead & Co., 1905.

Title annotates.

McGrath, Daniel F. BOOKMAN'S PRICE INDEX: A[N ANNUAL] GUIDE TO THE VALUES OF RARE AND OTHER OUT-OF-PRINT BOOKS [AND SETS OF

PERIODICALS]. Detroit, Mich.: Gale Research Co., 1964--.

Volume 7 of this continuing series appeared in 1973. Prices are derived from sales catalogs of what are described as "leading dealers," whose addresses are among the useful materials included.

Ricci, Seymour de, comp. THE BOOK COLLECTOR'S GUIDE: A PRACTICAL HANDBOOK OF BRITISH AND AMERICAN BIBLIOGRAPHY. Philadelphia and New York: Rosenbach, 1921.

De Ricci describes the GUIDE as containing "in the alphabetical order of the authors, the two or three thousand British and American books which fashion has decided are the most desirable for the up-to-date collector" (pp. [vii]-viii). Although the GUIDE itself is no longer up-to-date, it remains valuable for its careful bibliographical descriptions of the books.

Shapiro, S.R., ed. U.S. CUMULATIVE BOOK AUCTION RECORDS. 3 vols. New York, 1946-51.

No publisher's name is given. The RECORDS are designed to report "American book auction prices" for "all books, pamphlets, manuscripts, periodicals, autographs and other property selling in American auction rooms for $3.00 or more." The three volumes represent cumulations for 1940-45, 1945-50, and 1950-51. The RECORDS have apparently ceased publication.

B. CURRENT PRICES OF READILY AVAILABLE BOOKS

"Ready availability" is subject to unexpected change, especially in the current world of shortages, but information about prices, publishers, hardback and paperback editions, publishers' addresses, and the like, are obtainable from certain standard lists, as well, of course, as from the catalogs of individual publishers. These include:

BOOKS IN PRINT. New York and London: R.R. Bowker, A Xerox Education Company.

The 1973 edition is the 26th Annual Edition. BOOKS IN PRINT gives current prices and supplies addresses of publishers. It includes paperback editions, but there is also:

PAPERBOUND BOOKS IN PRINT. New York and London: R.R. Bowker, A Xerox Education Company.

This volume also appears annually.

Note: One advantage enjoyed by the twentieth-century scholar is the fact that many standard and classic titles in the drama have been reprinted. The user of this bibliography may want to consult the reprint catalogs issued by such companies as AMS, H.P. Kraus, Walter Johnson, Russell & Russell, and others. These may be found in university, college, and research library acquisitions departments and sometimes in reference departments as well.

4. FESTCHRIFTEN AND OTHER COLLECTIONS OF ESSAYS, INCLUDING SOME SERIALS

Short essays are often valuable and may rather easily be lost sight of. As my "Foreword" states, periodical materials are in general omitted from this bibliography for reasons of space. Similarly only a portion of the nonperiodical collections of essays can be shown, in general those which contain a fairly large number of essays on Medieval and Renaissance drama. Shown are collections of essays by one author and collections by various hands, one-volume collections and multivolume collections such as papers of annual meetings and other serials. Some of these collections are on a variety of subjects; some are centered on a single topic and might be shown under a particular section. Some collections, in fact, have been so placed; see further the various divisions of the bibliography, especially for collections focused on a single dramatist, none of these last being included here.

The collections are entered under the name of the author if there is a single author, or of the editor or compiler. If these are not shown, the collection is given under the name of the honoree or under the first word of the title.

Allen, Don Cameron, ed. STUDIES IN HONOR OF T.W. BALDWIN. Urbana: University of Illinois Press, 1958.

> Essays relevant to the drama to 1660 include: Hardin Craig, "Criticism of Elizabethan Dramatic Texts"; Fredson Bowers, "Old-Spelling Editions of Dramatic Texts"; Robert Adger Law, "KING LEIR and KING LEAR: An Examination of the Two Plays"; Marvin T. Herrick, "Susanna and the Elders in Sixteenth-Century Drama"; Una Ellis-Fermor, "Marlowe and Greene: A Note on Their Relations as Dramatic Artists"; Baldwin Maxwell, "Conjectures on THE LONDON PRODIGAL"; and some essays on Shakespeare.

Bennett, Josephine W., Oscar Cargill, and Vernon Hall, Jr., eds. STUDIES IN THE ENGLISH RENAISSANCE DRAMA IN MEMORY OF KARL JULIUS HOLZKNECKT. New York: New York University Press, 1959.

> The essays are: Albert C. Baugh, "A Medieval Survival in Elizabethan Punctuation"; Matthew Black, "Enter Citizens"; Fredson Bowers, "The Death of Hamlet: A Study in Plot and Character"; Har-

din Craig, "Revised Elizabethan Quartos: An Attempt to Form a Class"; Giles E. Dawson, "Robert Walker's Editions of Shakespeare"; Rhodes Dunlap, "James I, Bacon, Middleton, and the Making of THE PEACE-MAKER"; Mark Eccles, "Anthony Munday"; Vernon Hall, Jr., "JULIUS CAESAR: A Play Without Political Bias"; Alfred Harbage, "The Mystery of PERKIN WARBECK"; Richard C. Harrier, "Troilus Divided"; S.F. Johnson, "The Tragic Hero in Early Elizabethan Drama"; Donald J. McGinn, "A Quip from Tom Nashe"; Waldo F. McNeir, "Heywood's Sources for the Main Plot of A WOMAN KILLED WITH KINDNESS"; L.J. Mills, "The Acting in University Comedy of Early Seventeenth-Century England"; T.M. Pearce, "Evidence for Dating Marlowe's TRAGEDY OF DIDO"; George F. Reynolds, "MUCEDORUS, Most Popular Elizabethan Play?"; Irving Ribner, "Then I Denie You Starres: A Reading of ROMEO AND JULIET"; Samuel Schoenbaum, "A CHASTE MAID IN CHEAPSIDE and Middleton's City Comedy"; Frederick W. Sternfeld, "Song in Jonson's Comedy: A Gloss on VOLPONE"; Dick Taylor, Jr., "Clarendon and Ben Jonson as Witnesses for the Earl of Pembroke's Character"; Elkin Calhoun Wilson, "Falstaff--Clown and Man."

Bentley, Gerald Eades, ed. THE SEVENTEENTH-CENTURY STAGE: A COLLECTION OF CRITICAL ESSAYS. Chicago: University of Chicago Press, 1968.

Bentley has collected previously published materials, dating from 1609 to 1967, and grouped them around three topics: Part 1. "Contemporary Discussions," containing Thomas Dekker, "The Gull's Hornbook"; Thomas Heywood, "An Apology for Actors"; Ben Jonson, "Induction to BARTHOLOMEW FAIR"; and the anonymous "Praeludium for Thomas Goffe's THE CARELESS SHEPHERDESS"; Part II. "Actors and Acting," containing John Russell Brown, "On the Acting of Shakespeare's Plays"; Muriel C. Bradbrook, "The Status Seekers: Society and the Common Player in the Reign of Elizabeth I"; Michael Jamieson, "Shakespeare's Celibate Stage"; Marvin Rosenberg, "Elizabethan Actors: Men or Marionettes?"; William A. Ringler, Jr., "The Number of Actors in Shakespeare's Early Plays"; Part III. "Theaters and Production," containing F.P. Wilson, "Ralph Crane, Scrivener to the King's Players"; Louis B. Wright, "Stage Duelling in the Elizabethan Theater"; Charles J. Sisson, "Introduction to BELIEVE AS YOU LIST"; Richard Hosley, "The Discovery-Space in Shakespeare's Globe"; William A. Armstrong, "The Audience of the Elizabethan Private Theaters"; and J.W. Saunders, "Staging at the Globe, 1599-1613." The collection includes a short bibliography.

Bluestone, Max, and Norman Rabkin, eds. SHAKESPEARE'S CONTEMPORARIES: MODERN STUDIES IN ENGLISH RENAISSANCE DRAMA. 2nd ed. Englewood Cliffs, N.J.: Prentice-Hall, 1970.

Bluestone and Rabkin reprint essays or sections of books by various hands on Preston, Lyly, Peele, Greene, Kyd, Marlowe, Dekker,

Thomas Heywood, Jonson, Marston, Webster, Chapman, Tourneur, Beaumont, Fletcher, Middleton, William Rowley, Massinger, Ford, Shirley, and on GAMMER GURTON'S NEEDLE and ARDEN OF FEVERSHAM.

Brown, John Russell, and Bernard Harris, general eds. STRATFORD-UPON-AVON STUDIES. Nos. 1-10; Nos. 11 and following, ed. Malcolm Bradbury and David Palmer.

These studies have been in progress since 1960, published by Edward Arnold in London and St. Martin's Press, New York. The subject is not necessarily drama. See the following numbers:

1. JACOBEAN THEATRE, 1960, containing: Maynard Mack, "The Jacobean Shakespeare: Some Observations on the Construction of the Tragedies"; William A. Armstrong, "Ben Jonson and Jacobean Stagecraft"; Arthur Brown, "Citizen Comedy and Domestic Drama"; G.K. Hunter, "English Folly and Italian Vice: The Moral Landscape of John Marston"; Geoffrey Hill, "The World's Proportion: Jonson's Dramatic Poetry in SEJANUS and CATILINE"; David William, "THE TEMPEST on the Stage"; Philip Edwards, "The Danger Not the Death: The Art of John Fletcher"; R.B. Parker, "Middleton's Experiments with Comedy and Judgement"; J.R. Mulryne, "THE WHITE DEVIL and THE DUCHESS OF MALFI"; and Peter Ure, "Chapman's Tragedies."

9. ELIZABETHAN THEATRE, 1966, 1967, containing: D.J. Palmer, "Elizabethan Tragic Heroes"; T.W. Craik, "The Tudor Interlude and Later Elizabethan Drama"; J.A. Barish, "THE SPANISH TRAGEDY, or The Pleasures and Perils of Rhetoric"; N. Brooke, "Marlowe the Dramatist"; P. Russell, "Romantic Narrative Plays: 1570-1590"; R. Hosley, "The Formal Influence of Plautus and Terence"; J. Powell, "John Lyly and the Language of Play"; M. Jones, "The Court and the Dramatists"; J.C. Meagher, "Hackwriting and the Huntingdon Plays"; E.B. Partridge, "Ben Jonson: The Makings of the Dramatist (1596-1602)."

16. MEDIEVAL DRAMA, 1973. See the main entry under Bradbury, Malcolm, and David Palmer, eds., in Section 7 A: Studies of Medieval Drama--Broad Approaches, for contents.

See also numbers 3, 8, and 14, on Shakespeare, with some essays touching other aspects of the drama than Shakespeare only.

Campbell, Lily B. COLLECTED PAPERS OF LILY B. CAMPBELL, FIRST PUBLISHED IN VARIOUS LEARNED JOURNALS, 1907-1952, with an Introduction by Louis B. Wright. New York: Russell & Russell, 1968.

Essays bearing on the drama include "Theories of Revenge in Renaissance England," "The Lost Play of AESOP'S CROW," "The Use of Historical Patterns in the Reign of Elizabeth," "Richard Tarlton and the Earthquake of 1580," "DOCTOR FAUSTUS: A Case of Conscience."

Coffman, George Raleigh. STUDIES IN PHILOLOGY, Vol. 48, No. 3 (July 1951), with the special title: STUDIES IN MEDIAEVAL CULTURE, DEDICATED TO GEORGE RALEIGH COFFMAN.

Essays on drama include: Timothy Fry, "The Unity of LUDUS COVENTRIAE"; Waldo F. McNeir, "The Corpus Christi Passion Plays as Dramatic Art"; E.S. Miller, "Antiphons in Bale's Cycle of Christ"; and Jesse Byers Reese, "Alliterative Verse in the York Cycle."

Colquitt, Betsy Feagan, ed. STUDIES IN MEDIEVAL, RENAISSANCE, [AND] AMERICAN LITERATURE: A FESTSCHRIFT [Honoring Troy C. Crenshaw, Lorraine Sherley, and Ruth Speer Angell]. Fort Worth: Texas Christian University Press, 1971.

Essays on Medieval and Renaissance drama include: William G. Stryker, "An Easter Play in Finland," which adds a very brief Latin liturgical play to those collected by Karl Young; Jim W. Corder, "EVERYMAN: The Way to Life"; John P. Cutts, "'By Shallow Riuers': A Study of Marlowe's DIDO QUEEN OF CARTHAGE"; James T. Bratcher, "Peele's OLD WIVES' TALE and Tale-Type 425A"; Karl E. Snyder, "'These Are But Toyes,'" concerning Thomas Heywood's LOVE'S MISTRESS.

Craig, Hardin. RENAISSANCE STUDIES IN HONOR OF HARDIN CRAIG. Stanford, Calif.: Stanford University Press; London: Oxford University Press, 1942.

Among the essays directly on drama and dramatists are: Mendal G. Frampton, "The York Play of CHRIST LED UP TO CALVARY (Play XXXIV)"; George R. Coffman, "The Miracle Play: Notes and Queries"; Paul H. Kocher, "Backgrounds for Marlowe's Atheist Lecture"; Henry David Gray, "THE TAMING OF A SHREW"; Baldwin Maxwell, "THE TWO ANGREY WOMEN OF ABINGTON and WILY BEGUILED"; George F. Reynolds, "Aims of a Popular Elizabethan Dramatist"; T.M. Parrott, "Comedy in the Court Masque: A Study of Ben Jonson's Contribution"; G.F. Sensabaugh, "John Ford and Elizabethan Tragedy"; together with various essays on Shakespeare and some others touching drama or dramatists.

______, ed. ESSAYS IN DRAMATIC LITERATURE: THE PARROTT PRESENTATION VOLUME BY PUPILS OF PROFESSOR THOMAS MARC PARROTT OF PRINCETON UNIVERSITY, PUBLISHED IN HIS HONOR. 1935; reprint ed. New York: Russell & Russell, 1967.

Not all the twenty-one essays in the volume concern the drama to

1660. Those with some greater or lesser relevance to the period include: Hardin Craig, "Ethics in the Jacobean Drama: The Case of Chapman"; De W.C. Croissant, "Early Sentimental Comedy" (sentimental comedy is assigned Renaissance beginnings); C.W. Kennedy, "Political Theory in the Plays of George Chapman"; Hubertis Cummings, "For Shakespeare's Hamlet"; Lacy Lockert, "The Greatest of Elizabethan Melodramas" (i.e., THE REVENGER'S TRAGEDY); W.B.D. Henderson, "Shakespeare's TROILUS AND CRESSIDA, Yet Deeper in Its Tradition"; T.W. Baldwin, "A Note Upon William Shakespeare's Use of Pliny"; G.R. Stewart, Jr., "The Drama in a Frontier Theater" (the frontier is the nineteenth-century American West, but Renaissance plays cut a modest figure on its stage); T.B. Hunt, "The Scenes as Shakespeare Saw Them"; H.B. Walley, "Shakespeare's Portrayal of Shylock"; R.H. Ball, "Sir Giles Mompesson and Sir Giles Overreach"; D.A. Stauffer, "A Deep and Sad Passion"; P.W. Timberlake, "Milton and Euripides"; G.M. Kahrl, "The Influence of Shakespeare on Smollett"; Edward Hubler, "The Verse Lining of the First Quarto of KING LEAR"; Rudolph Kirk, "Jane Bell: Printer at the East End of Christ-Church"; and J.E. Baker, "The Philosophy of Hamlet."

Davis, Richard Beale, and John Leon Lievsay, eds. STUDIES IN HONOR OF JOHN C. HODGES AND ALWIN THALER. Tennessee Studies in Literature, Special Number. Knoxville: University of Tennessee Press, 1961.

Among the essays are Roscoe E. Parker, "Some Records of the 'Somyr Play'"; Bain Tate Stewart, "Characterization through Dreams in the Drama of Shakespeare's Day"; Carolyn Blair, "On the Question of Unity in Peele's DAVID AND BETHSABE"; and Thomas Wheeler, "Magic and Morality in COMUS."

Dunn, E. Catherine, Tatiana Fotitch, and Bernard M. Peebles, eds. THE MEDIEVAL DRAMA AND ITS CLAUDELIAN REVIVAL.

See the full entry, with analysis of contents, in Section 7 A: Medieval Drama--Broad Approaches.

Eliot, T[homas] S[tearns]. ELIZABETHAN ESSAYS. 1934; reprint ed. New York: Haskell House, 1964.

The essays are "Four Elizabethan Dramatists" (Webster, Tourneur, Middleton, and Chapman), "Christopher Marlowe," "Shakespeare and the Stoicism of Seneca," "Hamlet," "Ben Jonson," "Thomas Middleton," "Thomas Heywood," "Cyril Tourneur," "John Ford," "Philip Massinger," and "John Marston."

_____. ESSAYS ON ELIZABETHAN DRAMA. New York: Harcourt, Brace & World, 1932, 1956.

The essays overlap with the collection above to a substantial degree. They are "Seneca in Elizabethan Translation," "Christopher Marlowe,"

"Ben Jonson," "Thomas Middleton," "Thomas Heywood," "Cyril Tourneur," "John Ford," "Philip Massinger," and "John Marston."

_____. THE SACRED WOOD: ESSAYS ON POETRY AND CRITICISM. London: Methuen & Co., 1920; various reprintings.

The collection includes theoretical essays on the drama: "The Possibility of a Poetic Drama" and "'Rhetoric' and Poetic Drama" as well as essays on individual playwrights: "Notes on the Blank Verse of Christopher Marlowe," "Ben Jonson," "Philip Massinger," together with essays out of the area of this bibliography. Perhaps there is now a generation of students who need to be reminded of the major role Eliot played in calling attention to seventeenth-century literature which had fallen into neglect.

_____. SELECTED ESSAYS, 1917-1932. New York: Harcourt, Brace, & World, 1932; new ed. 1950.

Part II contains four essays on drama, including "Seneca in Elizabethan Translation." Part III includes "Four Elizabethan Dramatists (Webster, Tourneur, Middleton, Chapman)," "Christopher Marlowe," "Shakespeare and the Stoicism of Seneca," "Hamlet and His Problems," "Ben Jonson," "Thomas Middleton," "Thomas Heywood," "Cyril Tourneur," "John Ford," and "Philip Massinger."

Ellis-Fermor, Una [M.], comp. ESSAYS AND STUDIES BY MEMBERS OF THE ENGLISH ASSOCIATION. Vol. 29 for 1943. Oxford: Clarendon Press, 1944.

Essays on drama include: Gladys D. Willcock, "Shakespeare and Rhetoric"; F.S. Boas, "Charles Lamb and the Elizabethan Dramatists"; Evelyn M. Simpson, "Jonson and Dickens: A Study in the Comic Genius of London"; and Katharine A. Esdaile, "Ben Jonson and the Devil Tavern."

FOUR STUDIES IN ELIZABETHAN DRAMA. The Emporia State Research Studies, Kansas State Teachers College, Emporia, Kans., Vol. 10, No. 4 (June 1962).

The essays are: Roma Ball, "The Choirboy Actors of St. Paul's Cathedral"; Jim C. Pogue, "THE TWO GENTLEMEN OF VERONA and Henry Wotton's A COURTLIE CONTROUERSIE OF CUPIDS CAUTELS"; John L. Somer, "Ralph Crane and 'an old play called Winter's Tale'"; and Eugene J. Kettner, "LOVE'S LABOUR'S LOST and the Harvey-Nashe-Greene Quarrel."

Galloway, David, ed. THE ELIZABETHAN THEATRE: PAPERS GIVEN AT THE INTERNATIONAL CONFERENCE ON ELIZABETHAN THEATRE HELD AT THE UNIVERSITY OF WATERLOO, ONTARIO, IN JULY 1968. Toronto: Macmillan of Canada in collaboration with the University of Waterloo, 1969; [Hamden, Conn.]: Archon Books, 1970.

Galloway, in the "Introduction," asserts: "For many years now it has been clear that we shall have to re-examine certain traditional preconceptions about Elizabethan theatres in general. . . . [T]he familiar black and white timbered 'olde worlde' theatre of Cranford Adams crumbles in the mind" (pp. ix-x). The essays are: T.J.B. Spencer, "Shakespeare: The Elizabethan Theatre-Poet"; Glynne Wickham, "The Privy Council Order of 1597 for the Destruction of All London's Theatres"; Herbert Berry, "The Playhouse in the Boar's Head Inn, Whitechapel"; Richard Hosley, "A Reconstruction of the Second Blackfriars"; D.F. Rowan, "The Cockpit-in-Court"; Clifford Leech, "The Function of Locality in the Plays of Shakespeare and His Contemporaries"; and Terence Hawkes, "Postscript: Theatre Against Shakespeare?"

_____. THE ELIZABETHAN THEATRE II: PAPERS GIVEN AT THE SECOND INTERNATIONAL CONFERENCE ON ELIZABETHAN THEATRE HELD AT THE UNIVERSITY OF WATERLOO, ONTARIO, IN JULY 1969. Toronto: Macmillan of Canada in collaboration with the University of Waterloo; Hamden, Conn.: Archon Books, 1970.

The essays are: S. Schoenbaum, "Shakespeare and Jonson: Fact and Myth"; Trevor Lennam, "The Children of Paul's, 1551-1582"; R.A. Foakes, "Tragedy of the Children's Theatre after 1600: A Challenge to the Adult Stage"; D.F. Rowan, "A Neglected Jones/ Webb Theatre Project, Part II: A Theatrical Missing Link"; J.A. Lavin, "The Elizabethan Theatre and the Inductive Method"; Lise-Lone Marker, "Nature and Decorum in the Theory of Elizabethan Acting"; Bernard Beckerman, "A Shakespearean Experiment: the Dramaturgy of MEASURE FOR MEASURE"; and Peter Davison, "Marry, Sweet Wag."

_____. THE ELIZABETHAN THEATRE III. PAPERS GIVEN AT THE THIRD INTERNATIONAL CONFERENCE ON ELIZABETHAN THEATRE HELD AT THE UNIVERSITY OF WATERLOO, ONTARIO, IN JULY 1970. Hamden, Conn.: Archon Books, 1973.

The papers are: T.J. King, "Shakespearian Staging, 1599-1642"; Clifford Leech, "Three Times HO and a Brace of Widows: Some Plays for the Private Theatre"; Herbert Berry, "The Boar's Head Again"; J.A. Lavin, "Shakespeare and the Second Blackfriars"; Glynne Wickham, "Romance and Emblem: A Study in the Dramatic Structure of THE WINTER'S TALE"; W.R. Gair, "The Politics of Scholarship: A Dramatic Comment on the Autocracy of Charles I"; George R. Kernodle, "The Mannerist Stage of Comic Detachment"; John Lawlor, "Continuity and Innovation in Shakespeare."

Gaw, Allison, ed. STUDIES IN ENGLISH DRAMA, FIRST SERIES. Publications of the University of Pennsylvania, Series in Philology and Literature, Vol. 14. Introduction by Felix E. Schelling. Philadelphia: University of Pennsylvania; New York: D. Appleton and Co., 1917.

Made up principally of essays "originally designed to serve as the matter introductory to a critical edition" of certain plays (p. v), the collection includes: Allison Gaw, "Tuke's ADVENTURE OF FIVE HOURS in Relation to the 'Spanish Plot' and to John Dryden" (1663); Ross Jewell, "Heywood's FAIR MAID OF THE WEST"; John Linton Carver, "THE VALIANT SCOT, by 'J.W.'"; Charles Clayton Gumm, "Sir Ralph Freeman's IMPERIALE"; Clarence Stratton, "The Cenci Story in Literature and in Fact" (treats no Renaissance play); Martha Gause McCaulley, "Function and Content of the Prologue, Chorus, and Other Non-Organic Elements in English Drama, from the Beginnings to 1642."

Greg, W[alter] W[ilson]. COLLECTED PAPERS. Ed. J.C. Maxwell. Oxford: Clarendon Press, 1966.

This large collection includes these essays on drama to 1660: "Webster's WHITE DEVIL: An Essay in Formal Criticism," "Theatrical Repertories of 1662," "The Bakings of Betsy," "Massinger's Autograph Corrections in THE DUKE OF MILAN," "More Massinger Corrections," "THE SPANISH TRAGEDY--a Leading Case," "THE ESCAPES OF JUPITER," "The Riddle of Jonson's Chronology," "A Question of Plus or Minus," "Three Manuscript Notes by Sir George Buc," "Entrance in the Stationers' Register: Some Statistics," "The Damnation of Faustus," "Was There a 1612 Quarto of EPICENE?" Some others of the essays deal with Shakespeare or with special problems related to the drama.

Hart, Alfred. SHAKESPEARE AND THE HOMILIES; AND OTHER PIECES OF RESEARCH INTO THE ELIZABETHAN DRAMA. 1934; reprint ed. New York: Octagon Books, 1970.

The second part of the collection, entitled "Play Abridgement," contains these essays relevant to the drama to 1660: "The Length of Elizabethan and Jacobean Plays," "The Time Allotted for the Representation of Elizabethan and Jacobean Plays," "Acting Versions of Elizabethan and Jacobean Plays." Also see "The Vocabulary of EDWARD III" and "Shakespeare and the Vocabulary of THE TWO NOBLE KINSMEN," with other essays on Shakespeare.

Hosley, Richard, ed. ESSAYS ON SHAKESPEARE AND ELIZABETHAN DRAMA IN HONOR OF HARDIN CRAIG. Columbia: University of Missouri Press, 1962.

In addition to essays on Shakespeare, this collection contains: Richard Southern, "The Contribution of the Interludes to Elizabethan Staging"; Marvin T. Herrick, "Trissino's ART OF POETRY"; S.F. Johnson, "THE SPANISH TRAGEDY, or Babylon Revisited"; Alfred Harbage, "Intrigue in Elizabethan Tragedy"; Kenneth Muir, "Robert Greene as Dramatist"; Don Cameron Allen, "Marlowe's DIDO and the Tradition"; Clifford Leech, "Marlowe's Humor" (on HERO AND LEANDER, but priceless); Muriel C. Bradbrook, "Marlowe's DOCTOR FAUSTUS and the Eldritch Tradition"; Irving Ribner, "Marlowe's 'Tragicke Glasse'"; Paul H. Kocher, "Francis Bacon on the Drama";

Allardyce Nicoll, "THE REVENGER'S TRAGEDY and the Virtue of Anonymity"; John Leon Lievsay, "Italian Favole boscarecce and Jacobean Stage Pastoralism"; Arthur Brown, "Thomas Heywood's Dramatic Art"; Philip Edwards, "Massinger the Censor"; G.E. Bentley, "Lenten Performances in the Jacobean and Caroline Theaters"; and George F. Reynolds, "The Return of the Open Stage." The volume contains illustrations.

Jacquot, Jean, ed. LES FETES DE LA RENAISSANCE. I. JOURNEES INTERNATIONALES D'ETUDES, ABBAYE DE ROYAUMONT, 8-13 JUILLET 1955. Collection le Choeur des Muses. Paris: Editions du Centre National de la Recherche Scientifique, 1956.

The volume contains: Denis Stevens, "Pieces de Theatre et 'Pageants' a l'Epoque des Tudor"; Glynne Wickham, "Contribution de Ben Jonson et de Dekker aux Fetes du Couronnement de Jacques Ier"; John P. Cutts, "Le Role de la Musique dans les Masques de Ben Jonson et Notamment dans OBERON (1610-1611)"; D.J. Gordon, "Le 'Masque Memorable' de Chapman," with other essays less directly in the area of the bibliography. Volume II, FETES ET CEREMONIES AU TEMPS DE CHARLES QUINT, contains very little material relevant to England.

Jacquot, Jean, ed., with the collaboration of Elie Konigson and Marcel Oddon. DRAMATURGIE ET SOCIETE: RAPPORTS ENTRE L'OEUVRE THEATRALE, SON INTERPRETATION, ET SON PUBLIC AUX XVIe ET XVIIe SIECLES. 2 vols. Paris: Editions du Centre National de la Recherche Scientifique, 1968.

Volume I is primarily concerned with European drama but discusses connections with the English stage at some points. Volume II, pages 525-888, contains a section, "Angleterre," with these fifteen essays: L.G. Salingar, Gerald Harrison, and Bruce Cochrane, "Les Comediens et leur Public en Angleterre de 1520 a 1640"; Antoine Demadre, "Un Temoin: Thomas Nashe"; Jean Fuzier, "Carriere et Popularite de la TRAGEDIE ESPAGNOLE en Angleterre"; Claude Dudrap, "La TRAGEDIE ESPAGNOLE face a la Critique Elisabethaine et Jacobeenne"; Henri Plard, "Adaptations de la TRAGEDIE ESPAGNOLE dans les Pays-Bas et en Allemagne (1595-1640)"; W.R. Gair, "La Compagnie des Enfants de St. Paul, Londres (1599-1606)"; Louis Lecoco, "Le Theatre de Blackfriars de 1596 a 1606"; Andre Bry, "Middleton et le Public des 'City Comedies'"; Jean Jacquot, "Le Repertoire des Compagnies d'Enfants a Londres (1600-1610): Essai d'Interpretation Socio-Dramatique"; T.J.B. Spencer, "Le Masque a la Cour d'Angleterre a la Veille de la Guerre Civile"; Douglas Sedge, "La Question de la Monarchie au Theatre sous le Regne de Charles Ier: La Cour, le Dramaturge, et le Censeur"; Peter Davison, "La Dramaturgie en Angleterre a la Veille de la Guerre Civile: John Ford et la Comedie"; Robert Weimann, "La Declin de la Scene 'Indivisible' Elisabethaine: Beaumont, Fletcher, et Heywood"; E. Schoenbaum, "Peut-on Parler d'une 'Decadence' du Theatre au temps des Premiers Stuart?"; Pierre Danchin,

"Le Public des Theatres Londoniens a l'Epoque de la Restauration d'apres les Prologues et les Epilogues."

_____. LE LIEU THEATRAL A LA RENAISSANCE. COLLOQUES INTERNATIONAUX DU CENTRE NATIONAL DE LA RECHERCHE SCIENTIFIQUE. ROYAUMONT, 22-27 MARS 1963. Paris: Editions du Centre National de la Recherche Scientifique, 1964.

Among the many items in this collection are: Sydney Anglo, "La Salle de Banquet et le Theatre Construits a Greenwich pour les Fetes Franco-Anglaises de 1527"; Richard Southern, "Les Interludes au Temps des Tudor"; Richard Hosley, "Reconstitution du Theatre du Swan"; Glynne Wickham, "Embleme et Image: Quelques Remarques sur la Maniere de Figurer et de Representer le Lieu sur la Scene Anglaise aux XVIe Siecle." A few other items have relevance to English drama to 1660, especially James G. McManaway, "L'Heritage de la Renaissance dans la Mise en Scene en Angleterre (1642-1700)."

Kaufmann, R.J., ed. ELIZABETHAN DRAMA: MODERN ESSAYS IN CRITICISM. New York: Oxford University Press, 1961.

Reprints of articles and sections of books concerned with "the drama of the English contemporaries of Shakespeare" assembled so as to "constitute a virtually unified interpretation" and also to illustrate various approaches to criticism. (See the "Preface" for the plan of the collection.)

Ker, W.P., A.S. Napier, and W.W. Skeat, eds. AN ENGLISH MISCELLANY PRESENTED TO DR. FURNIVALL IN HONOUR OF HIS SEVENTY-FIFTH BIRTHDAY. 1901; reprint ed. New York and London: Benjamin Blom, 1969.

Contains, among other materials: Pierce Butler, "A Note on the Origin of the Liturgical Drama"; W.A. Craigie, "The Gospel of Nicodemus and the York Mystery Plays"; Ewald Flugel, "Nicholas Udall's Dialogues and Interludes"; J.J. Jusserand, "A Note on Pageants and 'Scaffolds Hye'"; Arthur F. Leach, "Some English Plays and Players (1220-1548)"; and M.W. MacCallum, "The Authorship of the Early HAMLET."

Kittredge, George Lyman. ANNIVERSARY PAPERS BY COLLEAGUES AND PUPILS OF GEORGE LYMAN KITTREDGE, PRESENTED ON THE COMPLETION OF HIS TWENTY-FIFTH YEAR OF TEACHING IN HARVARD UNIVERSITY, JUNE, MCMXIII. 1913; reprint ed. New York: Russell & Russell, 1967.

Contains, among others, Carleton Brown, "Caiphas as a Palm-Sunday Prophet"; Ashley H. Thorndike, "From Outdoors to Indoors on the Elizabethan Stage"; Edward Kennard Rand, "Mediaeval Lives of Judas Iscariot" (not on drama per se, but on a character who figures largely there); James Holly Hanford, "The Debate Element in the Elizabethan Drama."

Lawrence, W[illiam] J. PRE-RESTORATION STAGE STUDIES.

See the main entry in Section 11: The Theatre and Stagecraft.

_____. SPEEDING UP SHAKESPEARE: STUDIES OF THE BYGONE THEATRE AND DRAMA. 1937; reprint ed. New York and London: Benjamin Blom, 1968.

Includes: "On the Underrated Genius of Dick Tarleton," "The Dedication of Early English Plays," "A Quaint Old Playhouse Trick," "The Elizabethan Plotter," "Dekker's Theatrical Allusiveness and What It Reveals," "Stage Dummies," "The Origin of Bulls," "New Facts from Sir Henry Herbert's Office Book," "Playwriting for Love," "The Folly of the Gravedigger's Waistcoats," and other essays on Shakespeare.

_____. THOSE NUT-CRACKING ELIZABETHANS: STUDIES OF THE EARLY THEATRE AND DRAMA. London: Argonaut Press, 1935.

The "Preface" calls this a "sheaf of Elizabethan studies." The essays, previously published in various journals and revised or rewritten for the book, deal with a number of topics: "Those Nut-Cracking Elizabethans," "The Elizabethan Private Playhouses," "Bearers for the Dead," "Bells in Elizabethan Drama," "The Evolution of the Tragic Carpet," "Bygone Stage Furniture and its Removers," "Bacon on Masques and Triumphs," "The Wedding of Poetry and Song," "The Secret of the 'Bad Quartos,'" "Double Titles in Elizabethan Drama," and "Massinger's Punctuation and What It Reveals," together with some essays directly on Shakespeare.

Leech, Clifford. THE DRAMATIST'S EXPERIENCE. WITH OTHER ESSAYS IN LITERARY THEORY. New York: Barnes & Noble, 1970.

Not all eleven of the essays bear immediately on the drama to 1660: "'The Servants Will Do That For Us,'" "A School of Criticism," "Comedy in the Grand Style," "When Writing Becomes Absurd," "The Shaping of Time," "Art and the Concept of Will," "*Catharsis* in English Renaissance Drama," "Elizabethan and Jacobean," "Congreve and the Century's End," "On Seeing a Play," and "The Dramatist's Experience."

_____. SHAKESPEARE'S TRAGEDIES AND OTHER STUDIES IN SEVENTEENTH CENTURY DRAMA. London: Chatto & Windus, 1950.

Includes, with various essays on Shakespeare, these: "The Implications of Tragedy," "The Tragic Picture," "The Tragic Style," "The Tragic Effect," "The Caroline Audience," "Love as a Dramatic Theme," "Catholic and Protestant Drama."

Long, John H., ed. MUSIC IN ENGLISH RENAISSANCE DRAMA.

See the main entry in Section 8: Studies of Tudor and Stuart Drama, for an analysis of contents.

McManaway, James G., Giles E. Dawson, and Edwin E. Willoughby, eds. JOSEPH QUINCY ADAMS MEMORIAL STUDIES. Washington, D.C.: The Folger Shakespeare Library, 1948.

Together with a number of essays on Shakespeare, these on the drama to 1660: George C. Taylor, "Did Shakespeare, Actor, Improvise in EVERY MAN IN HIS HUMOR?"; John Elson, "Studies in the King John Plays"; Robert Adger Law, "Belleforest, Shakespeare, and Kyd"; Willard Farnham, "The Mediaeval Comic Spirit in the English Renaissance"; Theodore Spencer, "The Elizabethan Malcontent"; T.M. Parrott, "Two Late Dramatic Versions of the Slandered Bride Theme" (on MUCH ADO ABOUT NOTHING and THE PARTIAL LAW); Gerald J. Eberle, "Dekker's Part in THE FAMILIE OF LOVE"; C.J. Sisson, "A Topical Reference in THE ALCHEMIST"; Baldwin Maxwell, "Middleton's THE PHOENIX"; Gerald E. Bentley, "Randolph's PRAELUDIUM and the Salisbury Court Theatre"; William Van Lennep, "Thomas Killigrew Prepares His Plays for Production," with other essays at least touching on drama or dramatists.

Manly, John Matthews. THE MANLY ANNIVERSARY STUDIES IN LANGUAGE AND LITERATURE. Chicago, Ill.: University of Chicago Press, 1923.

Among much else, these essays on drama: Walter K. Smart, "The CASTLE OF PERSEVERANCE: Place, Date and a Source"; George F. Reynolds, "Another Principle of Elizabethan Staging"; Baldwin Maxwell, "Fletcher and HENRY THE EIGHTH"; Evelyn May Albright, "A Stage Cartoon of the Mayor of London in 1613"; Thornton S. Graves, "Jonson in the Jest Books"; Edgar A. Hall, "COMUS, OLD WIVES' TALE, and Drury's ALVREDUS"; and Karl Young, "Concerning the Origin of the Miracle Play."

Prouty, Charles T., ed. STUDIES IN HONOR OF A.H.R. FAIRCHILD. University of Missouri Studies, Vol. 21, No. 1. Columbia: University of Missouri, 1946.

Essays on various subjects, including several on Shakespeare, and these: Hardin Craig, "The Origin of the Passion Play: Matters of Theory as Well as Fact"; Harry R. Hoppe, "JOHN OF BORDEAUX: A Bad Quarto That Never Reached Print"; and R.C. Bald, "Charles Lamb and the Elizabethans."

_____. STUDIES IN THE ELIZABETHAN THEATRE. Hamden, Conn.: Shoe String Press, 1961.

Contains: Morton Paterson, "The Stagecraft of the Revels Office During the Reign of Elizabeth"; James Stinson, "Reconstruction of Elizabethan Public Playhouses," with an "Appendix: Commonly Reproduced Maps and Views of London," providing a bibliography indicating where these may be seen, and a section of plates; Robert K. Sarlos, "Development and Operation of the First Blackfriars Theatre." Bibliography.

Rabkin, Norman, ed. REINTERPRETATIONS OF ELIZABETHAN DRAMA: SELECTED PAPERS FROM THE ENGLISH INSTITUTE. New York and London: Columbia University Press, 1969.

Together with several essays on Shakespeare, these two: Jonas A. Barish, "The New Theater and the Old: Reversions and Rejuvenations," and Max Bluestone, "Libido Speculandi: Doctrine and Dramaturgy in Contemporary Interpretations of Marlowe's DOCTOR FAUSTUS."

RENAISSANCE DRAMA

See Section 1 C: Bibliographies of Drama, under the title RESEARCH OPPORTUNITIES IN RENAISSANCE DRAMA, for a brief description of the various metamorphoses of this periodical.

Ricks, Christopher, ed. ENGLISH DRAMA TO 1710. History of Literature in the English Language, Vol. 3. London: Barrie & Jenkins in association with Sphere Books, 1971.

The "Introduction" states that the essays, which were commissioned for the collection, "are intended to give a modern reader a sense of the many contexts within which literature--in this case drama --exists" (p. 9). There are nine sections: Glynne Wickham, "Stage and Drama till 1660"; Brian Morris, "Elizabethan and Jacobean Drama"; Gamini Salagado, "Christopher Marlowe"; a section by various hands entitled "Shakespeare"; Ian Donaldson, "Ben Jonson"; Christopher Ricks, "The Tragedies of Webster, Tourneur and Middleton: Symbols, Imagery, and Conventions"; Stephen Orgel, "The Masque"; Glynne Wickham, "The Restoration Theatre"; and John Barnard, "Drama from the Restoration till 1710." Bibliography.

Shafer, Robert, ed. SEVENTEENTH CENTURY STUDIES BY MEMBERS OF THE GRADUATE SCHOOL, UNIVERSITY OF CINCINNATI. Princeton, N.J.: Princeton University Press for the University of Cincinnati; London: Oxford University Press, First Series, 1933; Second Series, 1937.

Series I includes Benjamin Townley Spencer, "Philip Massinger" and Mary Edith Cochnower, "John Ford"; Series II, Kathleen Ressler, "Jeremy Collier's Essays."

Sisson, Charles J., ed. THOMAS LODGE AND OTHER ELIZABETHANS. Cambridge, Mass.: Harvard University Press, 1933.

There are five biographical studies here: Charles J. Sisson, "Thomas Lodge and His Family"; Mark Eccles, "Barnabe Barnes" (possibly the "Rival Poet"); Deborah Jones, "Lodowick Bryskett and his Family" and "John Lyly at St. Bartholomew's, or Much Ado about Washing"; and Mark Eccles, "Sir George Buc, Master of the Revels." Not all the subjects are drama, obviously.

Sticca, Sandro, ed. THE MEDIEVAL DRAMA.

See the main entry under Section 7 A: Studies of Medieval Drama--Broad Approaches.

Tillotson, Geoffrey. ESSAYS IN CRITICISM AND RESEARCH. Cambridge: University Press, 1942.

The essays include "The Prose of Lyly's Comedies," "OTHELLO and THE ALCHEMIST at Oxford in 1610," and "Two Productions of Elizabethan Plays."

Ward, Adolphus William. COLLECTED PAPERS: HISTORICAL, LITERARY, TRAVEL AND MISCELLANEOUS. 5 vols. Cambridge: University Press, 1921.

Volume III contains "Introduction to THE SPIDER AND THE FLIE" (not on a play, of course, but on a playwright's poem), "Ben Jonson's Prose," "Introduction to A WOMAN KILLED WITH KINDNESS," "James Shirley," "THE FEMALE REBELLION," "The Parnassus Plays"; Volume IV contains "Creizenach's ENGLISH DRAMA (IV, 1)" (a review), and "EVERY-MAN at the Charterhouse" (on William Poel's production of the morality play, called "an unequivocal success").

Wendell, Barrett. THE TEMPER OF THE SEVENTEENTH CENTURY IN ENGLISH LITERATURE. Clark Lectures Given at Trinity College, Cambridge, in the Year 1902-1903. New York: Charles Scribner's Sons, 1904.

This famous volume contains a general lecture on "Elizabethan Literature" and two on drama, "The Disintegration of the Drama" and "The Decline of the Drama."

[West, E.J., ed.]. ELIZABETHAN STUDIES AND OTHER ESSAYS IN HONOR OF GEORGE F. REYNOLDS. University of Colorado Studies, Series B. Studies in the Humanities, Vol. 2, No. 4. Boulder, Colo., 1945.

This large collection of essays contains, on drama or dramatists: Homer A. Watt, "The Staging of GAMMER GURTONS NEEDLE"; George Coffin Taylor, "Marlowe's 'Now'"; Richard L. Hillier, "The Imagery of Color, Light, and Darkness in the Poetry of Christopher Marlowe"; Hallett Smith, "Tamburlaine and the Renaissance"; Hardin Craig, "The Shrew and A Shrew"; T.M. Parrott, "The Taming of a Shrew"; Tucker Brooke, "The Royal Fletcher and the Loyal Heywood"; Baldwin Maxwell, "A Note on the Date of Middleton's THE FAMILY OF LOVE, with a Query on the Porters Hall Theatre," together with some material on Shakespeare and on drama after 1660 and much that is not directly on the drama.

Williams, Arnold, ed. A TRIBUTE TO GEORGE COFFIN TAYLOR: STUDIES AND ESSAYS, CHIEFLY ELIZABETHAN, BY HIS STUDENTS AND FRIENDS. Chapel Hill: University of North Carolina Press, 1952.

Contains, on drama to 1660: Beach Langston, "Marlowe's FAUSTUS and the Ars Moriendi Tradition"; George F. Sensabaugh, "Platonic Love in Shirley's THE LADY OF PLEASURE"; W.J. Olive, "SEJANUS and HAMLET"; and Joseph T. McCullen, Jr., "The Function of Songs Aroused by Madness in Elizabethan Drama." Other essays, notably Hardin Craig's "A Cutpurse of the Empire," bear upon the drama.

5. GENERAL LITERARY HISTORIES

Represented here are a few of the many histories of English or Medieval and Tudor-Stuart literature. Most of them are of current value; a few are shown for their historical importance.

Baugh, Albert C., ed. A LITERARY HISTORY OF ENGLAND. New York: Appleton-Century-Crofts, 1948; rev. ed. 1967.

> Baugh himself prepared the section on "The Middle English Period"; Tucker Brooke, and for the revised edition, Matthias A. Shaaber, "The Renaissance." There is material on the Medieval drama and extensive material on the Renaissance drama, with full bibliographical footnotes (the revision carries additional bibliography in notes at the back of the volume). Far more critical discussion than one ordinarily encounters in a one-volume literary history.

Brink, Bernhard ten. THE HISTORY OF ENGLISH LITERATURE.

> Brink's GESCHICHTE DER ENGLISCHEN LITTERATUR, 2 volumes (Berlin: R. Oppenhain, 1877-93), has been frequently printed in English translation, beginning with an edition in 3 volumes printed by G. Bell & Sons (London, 1883-96). In this edition, Volume II includes "Earliest Drama"; Volume III is FROM THE FOURTEENTH CENTURY TO THE DEATH OF SURREY.

CAMBRIDGE HISTORY OF ENGLISH LITERATURE, THE.

> See Ward, A[dolphus] W[illiam], and A[lfred] R[ainey] Waller, general eds.

Chambers, E[dmund] K[erchever]. ENGLISH LITERATURE AT THE CLOSE OF THE MIDDLE AGES. Oxford History of English Literature. Vol. 2, Part 2. Oxford: Clarendon Press, 1945; reprint ed., with corrections, 1947; various additional reprintings.

> Chambers has written extensively on the drama, which he here treats in the context of late Medieval literature generally. One of the features of the Oxford History series is the extensive annotated bibliography in each volume. (This is the volume which

opens with Chambers's famous judgment: "Medieval drama, in England as elsewhere, owes nothing to the tragedy and comedy of insolent Greece and haughty Rome.")

Daiches, David. A CRITICAL HISTORY OF ENGLISH LITERATURE. 2 vols. New York: Ronald Press, 1960.

A readable general history, the "Critical" of the title being a key work to the approach. Volume I covers the Middle Ages and Renaissance.

Day, Martin S. HISTORY OF ENGLISH LITERATURE TO 1660: A COLLEGE COURSE GUIDE. Garden City, N.Y.: Doubleday & Co., 1963. (Vol. I of the 3-vol. set.)

A general survey, largely factual and rather summary. Useful as an outline though not for depth analysis.

D'Israeli, Isaac. AMENITIES OF LITERATURE, CONSISTING OF SKETCHES AND CHARACTERS OF ENGLISH LITERATURE. 2nd ed., 2 vols. New York: J. & H.G. Langley, 1841.

The "Preface" indicates the tone: D'Israeli wished, he says, "not to furnish any arid narrative . . . but following the steps of the human mind through the wide track of time, to trace from their beginnings the rise, the progress, and the decline of public opinions, and to illustrate, as the objects presented themselves, the great incidents in our national annals" (p. [iii]). Volume I deals briefly with "Primitive Dramas"; Volume II treats drama more extensively. D'Israeli, as a representative of his era and of his own point of view, can make interesting reading, though he needs to be measured against more modern scholarship.

Dunn, Esther Cloudman. THE LITERATURE OF SHAKESPEARE'S ENGLAND. New York: Cooper Square Publishers, 1969. (Copyright, 1936.)

The "Foreword" states: "This is not a history. . . . It has few dates and makes no claim to inclusiveness" (p. v). The author wishes to show "the gradual evolution of old ideas into new, the changing values of life in this century of prelude to modern English literature." Included are "Reading Lists" designed "as a practical guide for the general reader" (p. 311). About half the volume is concerned with drama.

Ford, Boris, ed. THE AGE OF SHAKESPEARE. The Pelican Guide to English Literature, Vol. 2. Harmondsworth, England, and Baltimore, Md.: Penguin Books, 1955; rev. and reprinted 1956; various additional reprintings.

Essays, many of them on drama, by various hands. Easily available at small cost in paperback. Conveniently arranged bibliography.

Garnett, Richard, and Edmund Gosse. ENGLISH LITERATURE: AN ILLUSTRATED RECORD. 4 vols. New York: Macmillan, 1923.

Volumes 1 and 2 and part of 3 deal with the period to 1660. The history is oldish and general but is widely known; profusely illustrated in black and white.

Halkett, Samuel, and John Laing. DICTIONARY OF ANONYMOUS AND PSEUDONYMOUS ENGLISH LITERATURE. New and enl. ed. by James Kennedy and others. 8 vols. Edinburgh and London: Oliver and Boyd, 1926-56. Vol. 9, ADDENDA, by Dennis E. Rhodes and Anna E.C. Simoni, 1962.

Title annotates.

Jusserand, J[ean] [Adrien] [Antoine] J[ules]. A LITERARY HISTORY OF THE ENGLISH PEOPLE. 2 vols. in 3 parts. London: Unwin [1895]; New York and London: G.P. Putnam's, The Knickerbocker Press, 1895-1909.

A general literary history, now rather old, but well regarded over the years. (Translated from the French.)

Legouis, Emile, and Louis Cazamian. A HISTORY OF ENGLISH LITERATURE. 2 vols. Vol. I: THE MIDDLE AGES & THE RENASCENCE (650-1660), by Legouis. Trans. Helen Douglas Irvine. New York: Macmillan, 1926-27.

About a quarter of the volume concerns drama. Also published in a revised edition, two volumes in one, by Macmillan (New York, 1929), and in various other editions.

Moody, William Vaughn, and Robert Morss Lovett. 8th ed. by Fred B. Millett. A HISTORY OF ENGLISH LITERATURE. New York: Charles Scribner's Sons, 1964.

The first edition of Moody and Lovett appeared in 1922. Together with general literary history, it provides useful bibliographies.

Morley, Henry, and W. Hall Griffin. ENGLISH WRITERS: AN ATTEMPT TOWARDS A HISTORY OF ENGLISH LITERATURE. 11 vols. London, Paris, New York, Melbourne: Cassel & Co., 1887-95.

At Morley's death, Volume 11 was finished by Griffin. Volumes 10 and 11 bring the history down to "Shakespeare and His Time: Under Elizabeth" and "Under James I."

Morris, Helen. ELIZABETHAN LITERATURE. The Home University Library of Modern Knowledge, No. 233. London, New York, Toronto: Oxford University Press, 1958.

A brief introduction to the period for the general reader; a very selective annotated bibliography, pages 220-28.

Moulton, Charles Wells, ed. THE LIBRARY OF LITERARY CRITICISM OF

ENGLISH AND AMERICAN AUTHORS. 8 vols. 1901-5; reprint ed. New York: Peter Smith, 1935.

See Volumes 1 and 2. Moulton arranges the critical discussion under each author in chronological order. Volume 1 covers authors from 680 to 1638; Volume 2, 1639-1729. See Tucker, Martin, ed., for an extension of Moulton's work.

Muir, Kenneth. INTRODUCTION TO ELIZABETHAN LITERATURE. New York: Random House, 1967.

The book is brief, designed, as the title says, as an introduction. It provides lists of "Suggested Reading" at the ends of chapters and a "Selective Bibliography" at the end.

OXFORD HISTORY OF ENGLISH LITERATURE.

See Wilson, F[rank] P[ercy], and Bonamy Dobree, general eds.

Pinto, V. de Sola. THE ENGLISH RENAISSANCE, 1510-1688, WITH A CHAPTER ON LITERATURE AND MUSIC BY BRUCE PATTISON. 3rd ed. London: Cresset Press, 1966.

The book is Volume 2 of INTRODUCTIONS TO ENGLISH LITERATURE, general ed. Bonamy Dobree. The first edition appeared in 1938. A major part of the book is the "Student's Guide to Reading," a classified, annotated bibliography of primary and secondary materials.

Sampson, George. THE CONCISE CAMBRIDGE HISTORY OF ENGLISH LITERATURE. Cambridge: University Press; New York: Macmillan, 1941; various reprints; 3rd ed., Revised Throughout . . . by R.C. Churchill. Cambridge: University Press, 1970.

Very concise.

Schelling, Felix E. ENGLISH LITERATURE DURING THE LIFETIME OF SHAKESPEARE. Rev. ed. New York: Henry Holt, 1927.

The "Preface" describes the book as an attempt to narrate "as far as possible at first hand, the fascinating story of Elizabethan literature," not chronologically but "by the recognition of a succession of literary movements, developments, and varieties in poetry, drama, and prose" (p. v). Drama figures largely in the discussion.

Taine, Hippolyte A. HISTORY OF ENGLISH LITERATURE. Trans. H. Van Laun. 1871; reprint ed., from the 1883 ed., New York: Frederick Ungar Publishing Co., 1965.

The tenth edition, revised, appeared in five volumes (Paris: Hachette, 1899), with the title HISTOIRE DE LA LITTERATURE ANGLAISE. There are several editions of the Van Laun translation, varying in imprint and in the number of volumes. Taine devotes a large section of his history to the theatre, and the fame of the work makes it worth noticing even though it is now old and is rather general in its approach.

Tucker, Martin, ed. THE CRITICAL TEMPER: A SURVEY OF MODERN CRITICISM ON ENGLISH AND AMERICAN LITERATURE FROM THE BEGINNINGS TO THE TWENTIETH CENTURY. Volume 1: FROM OLD ENGLISH TO SHAKESPEARE. New York: Frederick Ungar Publishing Co., 1969.

Designed along the lines of Moulton's LIBRARY OF LITERARY CRITICISM, THE CRITICAL TEMPER is "an attempt to present a panoramic view of the best twentieth-century criticism on English and American literature from the period of Old English to the beginning of modern times" (Vol. 1, p. xv). The volume contains little on Medieval drama but much on Renaissance. The editor for the section "Elizabethan and Jacobean Literature" is Irving Ribner.

Ward, A[dolphus] W[illiam], and A[lfred] R[ainey] Waller, general eds. THE CAMBRIDGE HISTORY OF ENGLISH LITERATURE. 15 vols. Cambridge: University Press, 1907-27. Reissued without bibliographies, 1932; reissued, 1949-53.

To say the CHEL is famous is hardly necessary. Volumes 5 and 6 are THE DRAMA TO 1642, beginning with "The Origins of English Drama." The list of contributors to these volumes yields an impressive roll of scholars: A.W. Ward, Harold H. Child, W. Creizenach, John W. Cunliffe, F.S. Boas, G.P. Baker, G. Gregory Smith, George Saintsbury, F.W. Moorman, Ernest Walder, J.G. Robertson, Ronald Bayne, Ashley H. Thorndike, W. Macneile Dixon, Arthur Symons, G.C. Macaulay, Emil Koeppel, C.E. Vaughan, W.A. Neilson, J.M. Manly, and J. Dover Wilson.

Warton, Thomas. THE HISTORY OF ENGLISH POETRY FROM THE ELEVENTH TO THE SEVENTEENTH CENTURY. London: Ward, Lock, and Co., n.d.

The title page of the Ward, Lock edition says: "A full Reprint--Text and Notes of the Edition, London, 1778 & 1781." Warton's comments have now achieved such age as to lend them the respect and charm of antiquity. They make a more substantial claim, however; Rene Wellek, in THE RISE OF ENGLISH LITERARY HISTORY (see below), says: "Warton's three large volumes were the first history of English literature 'in form,' and determined the whole future development of English literary history" (p. vi). See also next item.

_____. HISTORY OF ENGLISH POETRY FROM THE TWELFTH TO THE CLOSE OF THE SIXTEENTH CENTURY. Ed. W. Carew Hazlitt. 4 vols. 1871; reprint ed. New York: Haskell House, 1970.

Wellek, Rene. THE RISE OF ENGLISH LITERARY HISTORY. Chapel Hill:

University of North Carolina, 1941.

Wellek traces "the origins and growth of English literary history from its beginnings during the Renaissance to Thomas Warton's HISTORY OF ENGLISH POETRY (1774-1781)" (p. v). The bibliography contains a section of primary bibliography which "attempts to list all publications up to 1774, which can be called English literary scholarship or history" (p. 237).

Whipple, Edwin P. THE LITERATURE OF THE AGE OF ELIZABETH. Boston: Fields, Osgood, & Co., 1869.

Originally delivered as Lowell Institute lectures in 1859 and printed in THE ATLANTIC MONTHLY in 1867-68, about half the lectures deal with drama: Marlowe, Shakespeare, Jonson, Heywood, Middleton, Marston, Dekker, Webster, Chapman, Beaumont, Fletcher, Massinger, and Ford figure to greater or lesser degrees. The discussions are rather general.

Wilson, F[rank] P[ercy], and Bonamy Dobree, general eds. OXFORD HISTORY OF ENGLISH LITERATURE. Oxford: Clarendon Press, 1945--.

Each volume of the OXFORD HISTORY has its own author. For those on drama, see the main entries under Chambers, E[dmund] K[erchever], in this section, and under Wilson, F[rank] P[ercy] in Section 7: Studies of Tudor and Stuart Drama.

6. GENERAL STUDIES OF THE DRAMA

Included here are general studies of the drama, studies of particular topics broadly viewed (dramatic theory, stock types, and the like), and a few general lists and dictionaries, in one alphabetical list. See, immediately following, Sections 7 and 8: Studies of Medieval Drama and Studies of Tudor and Stuart Drama.

Bartley, J.O. TEAGUE, SHENKIN AND SAWNEY: BEING AN HISTORICAL STUDY OF THE EARLIEST IRISH, WELSH, AND SCOTTISH CHARACTERS IN ENGLISH PLAYS. Cork: Cork University Press, 1954.

Organized for quick location of the information sought. Bibliography.

Bates, Alfred, ed.-in-chief; James P. Boyd and John P. Lamberton, associate eds. THE DRAMA: ITS HISTORY, LITERATURE AND INFLUENCE ON CIVILIZATION. 20 vols. 1903; reprint ed. New York: AMS Press, 1970.

Volume IV, RELIGIOUS DRAMA, contains a good deal on the drama of Medieval England. Volumes XIII and XIV stress Shakespeare and his predecessors, contemporaries, and successors through the Restoration.

Boas, Frederick S. SHAKSPERE AND HIS PREDECESSORS. London: J. Murray, 1896. Various reprintings.

A general survey, from the Middle Ages down, with a heavy emphasis on Shakespeare.

Bowman, Walter Parker, and Robert Hamilton Ball. THEATRE LANGUAGE: A DICTIONARY OF TERMS IN ENGLISH OF THE DRAMA AND STAGE FROM MEDIEVAL TO MODERN TIMES. New York: Theatre Arts Books, 1961.

Clear, straightforward definitions; little exploration of the latent complexities of words or terms.

Bradbrook, M[uriel] C[lara]. ENGLISH DRAMATIC FORM: A HISTORY OF

ITS DEVELOPMENT. New York: Barnes & Noble; London: Chatto & Windus, 1965.

Part I, "A Psychological Theory of Drama," discusses the "Theatre of the Icon," or drama drawn from pageantry in which icons "represent the ideals or fears of a community" and lead "to plays of heroic monolithic design" and to the tragedy (pp. 13-14), and the "Theatre of the Dream" based in the "medieval ritual of the dream" and leading to comedy. Part II, "The Evolution of Poetic Drama," considers chiefly Marlowe and Shakespeare. Part III, "Contemporary Theatre of Imagination," is concerned with the modern stage.

Bridges-Adams, W. THE IRRESISTIBLE THEATRE. Vol. I: FROM THE CONQUEST TO THE COMMONWEALTH. London: Secker & Warburg; Cleveland: World Publishing Co., 1957.

The "Foreword" (p. vii) indicates firmly that the book, a general introduction dealing with all aspects of the drama, is intended for "the general reader," not the scholar or specialist. Bibliography.

Chetwood, W[illiam] R[ufus]. A GENERAL HISTORY OF THE STAGE, FROM ITS ORIGIN IN GREECE DOWN TO THE PRESENT TIME. WITH THE MEMOIRS OF MOST OF THE PRINCIPAL PERFORMERS THAT HAVE APPEARED ON THE ENGLISH AND IRISH STAGE FOR THESE LAST FIFTY YEARS. WITH NOTES, ANCIENT, MODERN, FOREIGN, DOMESTIC, SERIOUS, COMIC, MORAL, MERRY, HISTORICAL, AND GEOGRAPHICAL, CONTAINING MANY THEATRICAL ANECDOTES; ALSO SEVERAL PIECES OF POETRY, NEVER BEFORE PUBLISHED. COLLECTED AND DIGESTED BY W.R. CHETWOOD, TWENTY YEARS PROMPTER TO HIS MAJESTY'S COMPANY OF COMEDIANS AT THE THEATRE-ROYAL IN DRURY-LANE, LONDON. London: W. Owen, 1749.

Title annotates.

Clark, William Smith. THE EARLY IRISH STAGE: THE BEGINNINGS TO 1720. Oxford: Clarendon Press, 1955.

The period to 1660 is treated only briefly in this general history. Appendices include "Plays Acted at the Dublin Theatres, 1637-1720" and "Actors and Actresses at the Dublin Theatres, 1637-1720." Bibliography.

Collier, J[ohn] Payne. THE HISTORY OF ENGLISH DRAMATIC POETRY TO THE TIME OF SHAKESPEARE: AND ANNALS OF THE STAGE TO THE RESTORATION. 3 vols. London: John Murray, 1831.

In three parts, "Annals of the Stage" (1182-1656), "The History of Dramatic Poetry" (beginning with "Miracle Plays"), and "An Account of the Old Theatres of London." Collier should be used with care and checked against other sources, in this and all his publications.

A COMPENDIOUS HISTORY OF THE ENGLISH STAGE, FROM THE EARLIEST

PERIOD TO THE PRESENT TIME, CONTAINING A CANDID ANALYSIS OF ALL DRAMATIC WRITINGS, A LIBERAL AND IMPARTIAL CRITICISM ON THE MERITS OF THEATRICAL PERFORMERS, AND A SKETCH OF THE LIVES OF SUCH AS HAVE BEEN EMINENT IN THEIR PROFESSION, BY WALDRON, DIBDIN, ETC. London: J.S. Jordon, 1800.

This COMPENDIOUS HISTORY begins in 1170, reaches 1574 by page 4 and the Restoration by page 31, and treats its whole subject in 174 pages. In addition, it is likely to be found only in rare book rooms. It is, nevertheless, worth a look.

Creizenach, Wilhelm. THE ENGLISH DRAMA IN THE AGE OF SHAKESPEARE. Trans. Cecile Hugon and ed. Alfred Schuster and R.B. McKerrow. 1916; reprint ed. New York: Haskell House, 1964; Russell & Russell, 1967.

See especially Volume IV, Books I-VIII. This is a translation of the following:

______. GESCHICHTE DES NEUEREN DRAMAS. 5 vols. 1893-1916; reprint ed., from Vols. 1-3 of the rev. ed. of 1911-23, New York: Benjamin Blom, 1965.

Cushman, L[ysander] W[illiam]. THE DEVIL AND THE VICE IN THE ENGLISH DRAMATIC LITERATURE BEFORE SHAKESPEARE. Studien zur Englischen Philologie, Vol. VI. 1900; reprint ed. London: Frank Cass, 1970.

Cushman argues that "[t]he devil, Vice, clown, fool and villian are parallel figures of quite independent origin and function" (p. [vii]). The discussion is organized for easy discovery of the specific information sought.

Derrick, Samuel [T. Wilkes]. A GENERAL VIEW OF THE STAGE BY MR. WILKES. London: J. Coote and W. Whetstone, 1759.

The discussion is divided into four parts. The first, without an overall title, discusses the stage and various types of drama--comedy, tragedy, farce, opera, etc. Part II is headed "Of the Art of Acting"; Part III, "A Short Historical Account of the Stage, Ancient and Modern to the Restoration"; Part IV, "A Critical Examination of the Merits and Demerits of the principal Performers in England and Ireland." "Wilkes" is likely to be found only in rare book rooms, but like most books of its antiquity, it will usually reward the reader. See the Library of Congress, THE NATIONAL UNION CATALOG; the British Museum, GENERAL CATALOGUE OF PRINTED BOOKS TO 1955; and NOTES AND QUERIES, 11th series, Volume 5, page 366, concerning the possibility that Wilkes is the true author.

Dibdin, [Charles].

See COMPENDIOUS HISTORY.

_____. A COMPLETE HISTORY OF THE ENGLISH STAGE. INTRODUCED BY A COMPARATIVE AND COMPREHENSIVE REVIEW OF THE ASIATIC, THE GRECIAN, THE ROMAN, THE SPANISH, THE ITALIAN, THE PORTUGESE, THE GERMAN, THE FRENCH, AND OTHER THEATRES, AND INVOLVING BIOGRAPHICAL TRACTS AND ANECDOTES, INSTRUCTIVE AND AMUSING, CONCERNING A PRODIGIOUS NUMBER OF AUTHORS, COMPOSERS, PAINTERS, ACTORS, SINGERS, AND PATRONS OF DRAMATIC PRODUCTIONS IN ALL COUNTRIES. THE WHOLE WRITTEN, WITH THE ASSISTANCE OF INTERESTING DOCUMENTS, COLLECTED IN THE COURSE OF FIVE AND THIRTY YEARS, BY MR. DIBDIN. 5 vols. London: Printed for the author, [1800].

In the "Preface" Dibdin says, "The prodigious mass of materials perpetually at variance with one another, that I have had the slavery to wade through precluded all possibility of a particular elucidation; for they were a complete chaos of jarring atoms." Volumes 2, 3, and 4 contain most of the material relevant to the Middle Ages and Renaissance. In addition to all else, the author himself emerges from his pages in a text so written that the world should not willingly let it die. The book is likely to be found only in rare book collections.

Dibdin, James C. THE ANNALS OF THE EDINBURGH STAGE WITH AN ACCOUNT OF THE RISE AND PROGRESS OF DRAMATIC WRITING IN SCOTLAND. Edinburgh: Richard Cameron, 1888.

The author writes: "As far as possible I have availed myself of every scrap of information bearing on my subject; and . . . I have endeavored to extract and set down in as concise a form as possible every important date and circumstance of the Edinburgh Stage" (p. [v]). The arrangement is chronological. The "First Period, Extending to 1691" is brief: two chapters, "Origin and Popular Development of the Drama in Scotland" and "The Drama in Scotland under Court Patronage," pages [3]-29.

Downer, Alan S. THE BRITISH DRAMA: A HANDBOOK AND BRIEF CHRONICLE. New York: Appleton-Century-Crofts, 1950.

The book "is intended as a guide and companion to those undertaking for the first time a study of the drama." The facts "have been selected and arranged to focus attention on the development of the drama as a form of communication and artistic expression" (p. v). The "List of Suggested Readings" includes "English Drama by Period" and "Individual Authors" and provides both primary and secondary materials.

Downes, John. ROSCIUS ANGLICANUS (1708). The Augustan Reprint Society, Publication No. 134, William Andrews Clark Memorial Library. Introduction by John Loftis. Los Angeles: University of California, 1969.

Facsimile reproduction. The original title page runs, in part: "ROSCIUS ANGLICANUS, OR AN HISTORICAL REVIEW OF THE STAGE: AFTER IT HAD BEEN SUPPRES'D BY MEANS OF THE

LATE UNHAPPY CIVIL WAR, BEGUN IN 1641. . . . London: Printed and sold by H. Playford, at his House in Arundel-street, near the Water-side, 1708." Downes describes himself as having long been "Book-keeper and Prompter" at the Lincoln's Inn Fields theatre and therefore not likely to be "very Erronius in his Relation" (sig. A2, recto). The book is largely concerned with the Restoration stage, but it reveals something of the Restoration treatment of Renaissance drama. The "Index of Performers and Plays" supplied in the modern edition enables the user to locate the materials he seeks.

Duggan, G.C. THE STAGE IRISHMAN: A HISTORY OF THE IRISH PLAY AND STAGE CHARACTERS FROM THE EARLIEST TIMES. Dublin & Cork: Talbot Press, 1937.

The study contains two parts, on English-language plays on Irish topics and on Irish characters in British plays.

Ellis-Fermor, Una [M.]. THE FRONTIERS OF DRAMA. With an Introduction by Allardyce Nicoll and a Bibliography by Harold Brooks. 2nd ed. London: Methuen & Co., 1964.

The "Author's Preface" describes the book as "an attempt to investigate some of the means by which an art form" is sometimes able to "transcend its normal and seemingly inevitable limitations. It is therefore the picture of a conflict, now between form and some stubborn content . . . , now between the dramatic process and the limitations of a medium that is nevertheless essential" (p. xi). Ellis-Fermor considers in particular some plays by Shakespeare and Milton's SAMSON AGONISTES. In addition, she discusses "The Functions of Imagery," "The Revelation of Unspoken Thought," and "The Equilibrium of Tragedy." The author's authority as a scholar is enormous. Bibliography.

Fergusson, Francis. THE IDEA OF A THEATRE: A STUDY OF TEN PLAYS. THE ART OF DRAMA IN CHANGING PERSPECTIVE. Princeton, N.J.: Princeton University Press, 1949; reprint ed., paperback, Garden City, N.Y.: Doubleday & Co., 1955.

Of the ten plays in the title, only HAMLET belongs to English drama before 1660. Fergusson's study, however, has been so influential in the criticism of the quarter century and more since its publication that it requires attention.

Frye, Northrup. ANATOMY OF CRITICISM: FOUR ESSAYS. Princeton, N.J.: Princeton University Press, 1957; reprint ed., paperback, New York: Atheneum Publishers, 1970.

The four essays are "Historical Criticism: Theory of Modes," "Ethical Criticism: Theory of Symbols," "Archetypal Criticism: Theory of Myths," "Rhetorical Criticism: Theory of Genres." Frye draws frequently on drama for examples. He has made himself so much the exponent of a critical school and has aroused so much interest, enthusiastic and hostile, that one must consider what he says. The index will locate specific references to authors cited, but the book really needs to be read through.

Fuller, Edmund. A PAGEANT OF THE THEATRE. Rev. ed. New York: Thomas Y. Crowell, 1965.

Pageant is a key to the focus of the book, "a display, an exhibit, of aspects of the history and variety" of the theatre designed "for general readers, for those who enjoy the theatre but have not thought about studying it formally" (p. ix). Bibliography.

Gayley, Charles Mills. PLAYS OF OUR FOREFATHERS AND SOME OF THE TRADITIONS UPON WHICH THEY WERE FOUNDED. New York: Duffield, 1907.

Important in the history of twentieth-century dramatic criticism, though now rather old.

[Genest, Rev. John]. SOME ACCOUNT OF THE ENGLISH STAGE FROM THE RESTORATION IN 1660 TO 1830. 10 vols. Bath: H.E. Carrington, 1832.

Genest supplies a straightforward enumeration of facts heavily interwoven with opinions, of which he says in Volume I, page 29: [E]very body has a right to think for himself and to say what he thinks." Of the ten volumes in the ACCOUNT, only Volume I, pages [1]-29, "A Short Account of the Stage Previously to 1660" is immediately relevant to the period of this bibliography, but Genest should be remembered. See Genest also for revivals of early plays.

Gilliland, Thomas. THE DRAMATIC MIRROR: CONTAINING THE HISTORY OF THE STAGE, FROM THE EARLIEST PERIOD TO THE PRESENT TIME; INCLUDING A BIOGRAPHICAL AND CRITICAL ACCOUNT OF ALL THE DRAMATIC WRITERS, FROM 1660; AND ALSO THE MOST DISTINGUISHED PERFORMERS, FROM THE DAYS OF SHAKESPEARE TO 1807; AND A HISTORY OF THE COUNTRY THEATRES, IN ENGLAND, IRELAND, AND SCOTLAND. EMBELLISHED WITH SEVENTEEN ELEGANT ENGRAVINGS. 2 vols. London: C. Chapple, 1808.

Gilliland covers the period to 1660 in Volume I, in a section entitled, "History of the Stage, from Julius Caesar to the Death of James the First, including the Lives of the early English Actors," ending on page 76.

Hartnoll, Phyllis, ed. THE CONCISE OXFORD COMPANION TO THE THEATRE. London, Oxford, New York: Oxford University Press, 1972.

Brief entries with "A Guide to Further Reading" compiled by Simon Trussler.

_____. THE OXFORD COMPANION TO THE THEATRE. 3rd ed. London, New York, Toronto: Oxford University Press, 1967.

Brief entries, with a "Select List of Theatre Books" compiled by D.M. Moore.

Herrick, Marvin T. THE POETICS OF ARISTOTLE IN ENGLAND. Cornell Studies in English, Vol. 17. New Haven, Conn.: Yale University Press, published for Cornell University; London: Oxford University Press, 1970.

Brief review of a basic topic.

Hoffman, Frederick A. POETRY: ITS ORIGIN, NATURE, AND HISTORY. BEING A GENERAL SKETCH OF POETIC AND DRAMATIC LITERATURE. COMPREHENDING CRITICAL, HISTORICAL AND BIOGRAPHICAL NOTICES, WITH SPECIMENS, OF THE MOST DISTINGUISHED WRITERS FROM THE EARLIEST PERIOD TO THE MIDDLE OF THE PRESENT CENTURY; TO WHICH IS ADDED (SEPARATELY BOUND) A COMPENDIUM OF THE WORKS OF THE POETS OF ALL TIMES AND COUNTRIES, WITH EXPLANATORY NOTES, SYNOPTICAL TABLES, A CHRONOLOGICAL DIGEST AND A COPIOUS INDEX. London: Thurgate & Sons, 1884.

Hoffman explains further: "I feel that I am contributing to literature both a treasure and curiosity. . . . [M]y object has been, not merely to give a collection of elegant extracts, but to show, by a series of notes, the growth and development of poetry up to the middle of this century" (p. [iii]).

Hoy, Cyrus. THE HYACINTH ROOM: AN INVESTIGATION INTO THE NATURE OF COMEDY, TRAGEDY, & TRAGICOMEDY. New York: Alfred A. Knopf, 1964.

Hoy deals with the concepts of comedy, tragedy, and tragicomedy and with their resemblances and differences, drawing upon a wealth of examples, sometimes Renaissance, but not limited in time or place.

Hudson, H[enry] N[orman]. SHAKESPEARE: HIS LIFE, ART AND CHARACTERS. WITH AN HISTORICAL SKETCH OF THE ORIGIN AND GROWTH OF THE DRAMA IN ENGLAND. 4th ed., rev. 2 vols. Boston: Ginn and Co., 1872.

Hudson treats the "Origin and Growth of the Drama in England" in pages 53-95. Much has been learned since Hudson's day, and his treatment is very brief, but it is not without a certain slightly antique charm for the wary reader.

Hunningher, Benjamin. THE ORIGIN OF THE THEATRE. 1955; reprint ed. New York: Hill & Wang, 1961.

Hunningher see Christian drama as having "its genesis in pagan drama" (p. 117).

Jackson, John. THE HISTORY OF THE SCOTTISH STAGE, FROM ITS FIRST ESTABLISHMENT TO THE PRESENT TIME; WITH A DISTINCT NARRATIVE OF SOME RECENT THEATRICAL TRANSACTIONS, THE WHOLE NECESSARILY INTERSPERSED WITH MEMOIRS OF HIS OWN LIFE, BY JOHN JACKSON, TEN YEARS MANAGER OF THE THEATER ROYAL OF EDINBURGH. Edinburgh: Printed for Peter Hill and G.G.J. and J. Robinson, London, [1793].

The "Dedication" is dated 1793. This old and rare book has been reproduced by the Lost Cause Press (Louisville, Ky.) on microcards (eleven cards for the ten volumes).

Jusserand, J[ean] Adrien [Antoine] [Jules]. LE THEATRE EN ANGLETERRE DEPUIS LA CONQUETE JUSQU'AUX PREDECESSEURS IMMEDIATS DE SHAKESPEARE. 2nd ed. Paris: Ernest Leroux, 1881.

Famous old general history of the early theatre.

Klein, David. MILESTONES TO SHAKESPEARE: A STUDY OF THE DRAMATIC FORMS AND PAGEANTRY THAT WERE THE PRELUDE TO SHAKESPEARE. New York: Twayne Publishers, 1970.

A brief survey, from the early Biblical plays through (and including) Shakespeare. One-page "List of Books," page 121.

Landa, M[yer] J[ack]. THE JEW IN DRAMA. London: King, 1926; New York: William Morrow & Co., 1927.

Landa sees the stage Jew as "either grossly libeled or ruthlessly travestied." About one-third of his study concerns the drama to 1660. "Index of Plays."

Langbaine, Gerard. ACCOUNT OF THE ENGLISH DRAMATICK POETS. OR, SOME OBSERVATIONS AND REMARKS ON THE LIVES AND WRITINGS, OF ALL THOSE THAT HAVE PUBLISH'D EITHER COMEDIES, TRAGEDIES, TRAGI-COMEDIES, PASTORALS, MASQUES, INTERLUDES, FARCES, OR OPERA'S IN THE ENGLISH TONGUE. Oxford: George West and Henry Clements, 1691.

The arrangement is alphabetical by author, with an index of plays. Langbaine, one of the very early writers on "The English Dramatick Poets," is still much referred to.

_____. MOMUS TRIUMPHANS: OR, THE PLAGIARIES OF THE ENGLISH STAGE. [London: Nicholas Cox, 1688]; reprint ed. The Augustan Reprint Society, Publication No. 150, William Andrews Clark Memorial Library. Introduction by David Stuart Rodes. Los Angeles: University of California, 1971.

Rodes's "Introduction" points up the continuing importance of MOMUS TRIUMPHANS as an early, comprehensive, and bibliographically competent study and as a foundation for Langbaine's longer ACCOUNT OF THE ENGLISH DRAMATICK POETS (p. 1). The reprint makes this highly interesting work readily available to the modern scholar. The full title is MOMUS TRIUMPHANS: OR, THE PLAGI-

ARIES OF THE ENGLISH STAGE; EXPOSED IN A CATALOGUE OF ALL THE COMEDIES, TRAGI-COMEDIES, MASQUES, TRAGEDIES, OPERA'S, PASTORALS, INTERLUDES, &C BOTH ANCIENT AND MODERN, THAT WERE EVER YET PRINTED IN ENGLISH. THE NAMES OF THEIR KNOWN AND SUPPOSED AUTHORS. THEIR SEVERAL VOLUMES AND EDITIONS: WITH AN ACCOUNT OF THE VARIOUS ORIGINALS, AS WELL ENGLISH, FRENCH, AND ITALIAN, AS GREEK AND LATINE; FROM WHENCE MOST OF THEM HAVE STOLE THEIR PLOTS.

[Langbaine, Gerard, and Charles Gildon]. THE LIVES AND CHARACTERS OF THE ENGLISH DRAMATICK POETS. ALSO AN EXACT ACCOUNT OF ALL THE PLAYS THAT WERE EVER YET PRINTED IN THE ENGLISH TONGUE; THEIR DOUBLE TITLES, THE PLACES WHERE ACTED, AND DATES WHEN PRINTED, AND THE PERSONS TO WHOM DEDICATED; WITH REMARKS AND OBSERVATIONS ON MOST OF THE SAID PLAYS. FIRST BEGUN BY MR. LANGBAINE, IMPROV'D AND CONTINUED DOWN TO THIS TIME, BY A CAREFUL HAND. London: William Turner, 1699.

The title leaves us only the need to comment on the importance of Langbaine and Gildon to the development of the history and biography of English drama and dramatists, and to point out that all this information is compressed into about 200 pages, indexed.

Lawson, Robb. STORY OF THE SCOTS STAGE. 1917; reprint ed. New York: E.P. Dutton & Co., n.d.

A general and now somewhat old study.

Malone, Edmond, ed. THE PLAYS AND POEMS OF WILLIAM SHAKSPEARE, IN TEN VOLUMES, COLLATED VERBATIM WITH THE MOST AUTHENTICK COPIES, AND REVISED: WITH THE CORRECTIONS AND ILLUSTRATIONS OF VARIOUS COMMENTATORS; TO WHICH ARE ADDED, AN ESSAY ON THE CHRONOLOGICAL ORDER OF HIS PLAYS; AN ESSAY RELATIVE TO SHAKSPEARE AND JONSON; A DISSERTATION ON THE THREE PARTS OF KING HENRY VI; AN HISTORICAL ACCOUNT OF THE ENGLISH STAGE; AND NOTES. London: J. Rivington and Sons, 1790.

See Volume I, pages [387]-414, for the essay, "Shakspeare, Ford, and Jonson." See Volume I, part 2, pages [1]-284, for the essay, "An Historical Account of the Rise and Progress of the English Stage, And of The Economy and Usages of Our Ancient Theatres," which begins: "The drama before the time of Shakspeare was so little cultivated, or so ill understood, that to many it may appear unnecessary to carry out theatrical researches higher than that period. Dryden has truly observed, that he 'found not, but created first the stage;' of which no one can doubt, who considers, that of all the plays issued from the press antecedent to the year 1592, when there is reason to believe he commenced a dramatick writer, the titles are scarcely known, except to antiquaries; nor is there one of them that will bear a second perusal. Yet these, contemptible and few as they are, we may suppose to have been the most popular productions of the time, and the best that have been exhibited before the appearance of Shakspeare." On page 284, suitably enough, Malone ends: "Here therefore I conclude this imperfect account of the origin and progress of the English Stage." The rise and progress of studies in the early drama since Malone's day have radically altered our view of those early plays, but to understand the history of the history of drama, one must go back to such early points of view. It should be remembered that Malone worked without benefit of modern research and modern critical methods and did much to establish the study of drama.

In the 1821 edition of Malone, "Mr. Malone's Historical Account of the Rise and Progress of the English Stage" appears in Volume III, with two additional essays: "Farther Account of The Rise and Progress of the English Stage" by George Chalmers, and "Chester Mysteries" by James Heywood Markland.

Nicoll, Allardyce. BRITISH DRAMA. 5th ed., rev. New York: Barnes & Noble, 1963.

A general survey, "from earliest times to the present," with a bibliography "designed to serve both as a guide to essential reference works and to suggest further reading (p. [5]). Chapters 1-3 are relevant to the period to 1660.

______. THE ENGLISH STAGE. London: Benn, 1928.

Among the great diversity of books published in Benn's Sixpenny Library (titles range from NUTRITION AND DIETETICS to ENGLISH WATER COULOUR PAINTERS), there is Nicoll's eighty-page review of THE ENGLISH STAGE, from QUEM QUAERITIS to "The Modern Period"; yet for all its breadth in time and its narrow compass in print, the volume has a good deal to say, said with Nicoll's authority.

______. AN INTRODUCTION TO DRAMATIC THEORY. London: Harrap, 1923; New York: Brentano's, n.d.

A discussion of comedy, tragedy, and tragicomedy in such aspects as "Fable," "Characterization," "Conflict," "Universality," "Spirit," "Style," "Hero," and "Types." An appendix contains two short annotated bibliographies: "Brief Bibliography of Dramatic Theory" and "Brief Bibliography of Select Dramatic Works."

______. THE THEATRE AND DRAMATIC THEORY. London: Harrap; New York: Barnes & Noble, 1962.

Although the book is specifically directed to the question of the success of the modern theatre in "giving to the general public what subconsciously it seeks for in the theatre," Nicoll points out that a proper answer will necessarily involve a consideration "of some general trends in earlier dramatic theory" and "of the prevailing forms assumed by the drama in preceding epochs" (p. [5]). Chapters on "The Theatre," "The Drama," "The Dramatic Kinds," "Tragedy," "Comedy," and "Dramatic Dialogue."

_____. THE THEORY OF DRAMA. New York: Thomas Y. Crowell, [1931].

The "Preface" describes the book as "in some respects a revised edition of AN INTRODUCTION TO DRAMATIC THEORY," which has, however, been "entirely rewritten" and increased "by over half its length" (p. 5). The major divisions of the discussion are "The Theory of Drama," "Tragedy," "Comedy," and "Tragicomedy," with "Suggestions for Reading" in theory and in the drama itself.

Peacock, Ronald. THE ART OF DRAMA. London: Routledge & Kegan Paul, 1957.

The book undertakes to establish "the nature of drama . . . through a study of images and imagery" as "related to both form and expression" (p. 1), thus "illuminating the nature of dramatic art and its affinities with poetry and other art forms" (p. 241). Bibliography.

Ricks, Christopher, ed. ENGLISH DRAMA TO 1710.

See main entry in Section 4: Festschriften and Other Collections of Essays.

Rossister, Arthur Percival. ENGLISH DRAMA FROM EARLY TIMES TO THE ELIZABETHANS: ITS BACKGROUND, ORIGINS AND DEVELOPMENT. 1950; reprint ed., paperback, New York: Barnes & Noble, 1967.

An historical account coupled with critical opinions.

Roston, Murray. BIBLICAL DRAMA IN ENGLAND FROM THE MIDDLE AGES TO THE PRESENT DAY. Evanston: Northwestern University Press, 1968.

Rigorously selecting plays which he judges to be of literary significance, Roston devotes about a third of the book to Medieval and Renaissance Biblical drama. He emphasizes the theme of the "spiritual struggle of men committed to an ideal yet torn from it by their human weaknesses and strength" (p. 3). He is also concerned with the development of comedy through the Biblical drama and with the influence of the form of Medieval drama on Renaissance drama. "Select List of Plays."

Schelling, Felix E. ENGLISH DRAMA. London: J.M. Dent & Sons; New York: E.P. Dutton & Co., 1914.

A general account, "in scale and with a due regard to proportion" ("Preface") to 1779, with a brief outline of later drama.

Sharpe, Robert Boies. IRONY IN THE DRAMA: AN ESSAY ON IMPERSONATION, SHOCK, AND CATHARSIS. Chapel Hill: University of North Carolina Press, 1959.

Sharpe draws on material from the classical to the modern; authors in the period to 1660 can be located through the index.

SOURCE MATERIALS IN THE FIELD OF THE THEATRE. University Microfilms, Film, 22 reels.

For the guide to these materials, see Angotti, Vincent L., ed., in Section 1 C: Bibliographies of Drama.

Spek, Cornelius van der. THE CHURCH AND THE CHURCHMAN IN ENGLISH DRAMATIC LITERATURE BEFORE 1642. Amsterdam: H.J. Paris, 1930.

The study runs from "Mysteries and Miracles" through "Shakespeare and the Roman Catholic Church," with a chapter devoted to John Heywood. The author is concerned (see the "Introduction," p. 1) with "how far the social and political position of the English clergy" can be discerned in the plays and also with the attitude of "dramatists toward the clergy and the church" and with drama as a tool and a weapon in religious matters.

Stuart, Donald Clive. THE DEVELOPMENT OF DRAMATIC ART. New York and London: D. Appleton and Co., 1928.

A general review.

Symonds, John Addington. SHAKSPERE'S PREDECESSORS IN THE ENGLISH DRAMA. 1884; reprint ed. New York: Cooper Square Publishers, 1967.

General in scope, rather old, but of sufficient renown to warrant mention.

Taylor, John Russell. THE PENGUIN DICTIONARY OF THE THEATRE. Baltimore, Md.: Penguin Books, 1966.

Brief discussion of various words or phrases related to the drama.

Taylor, Joseph Richard. THE STORY OF THE DRAMA. Vol. I: BEGINNINGS TO THE COMMONWEALTH. Boston: Expression Co., 1930.

The "Preface," Volume I, page ix, states that the aim of the volumes is "to provide at a moderate cost authentic material sufficient to furnish an adequate working equipment for every student and teacher of drama." Authentic is not to be construed as meaning the reproduction of early documents, though BEGINNINGS does mean early beginnings, Greek, Roman, Eastern.

Thorndike, Ashley H. ENGLISH COMEDY. New York: Macmillan, 1929.

Thorndike's attempt to define and analyze what he calls a "heterogeneous" and not "readily classified" genre, comedy ("Preface," p. v), deals with the period to 1660 in part I, through page 266.

Tomlins, F[rederick] G[uest]. A BRIEF VIEW OF THE ENGLISH DRAMA, FROM THE EARLIEST PERIOD TO THE PRESENT TIME: WITH SUGGESTIONS FOR ELEVATING THE PRESENT CONDITION OF THE ART, AND OF ITS PROFESSORS. London: C. Mitchell, 1840.

Interesting as a period piece; largely reprinted from THE SUNDAY TIMES. (See the "Preface," p. [v].)

Waldron, [Francis Godolphin].

See A COMPENDIOUS HISTORY.

Ward, Adolphus William. A HISTORY OF ENGLISH DRAMATIC LITERATURE TO THE DEATH OF QUEEN ANNE. Rev. ed. 3 vols. London and New York: Macmillan, 1899.

Old and therefore somewhat dated, but a full, systematic general survey.

White, Richard Grant. MEMOIRS OF THE LIFE OF WILLIAM SHAKESPEARE, WITH AN ESSAY TOWARD THE EXPRESSION OF HIS GENIUS, AND AN ACCOUNT OF THE RISE AND PROGRESS OF THE ENGLISH DRAMA. Boston: Little, Brown, 1865.

The "Account of the Rise and Progress," pages [315]-425, takes no very favorable view of the early drama. Concerning the plays of which Henslowe supplies records, for instance, White says: "Happily, nearly all of these have perished, and of those which have survived, the best claim the attention of posterity only because Shakespeare lived when they were written" (p. 425).

Whiting, B.J. PROVERBS IN THE EARLIER ENGLISH DRAMA WITH ILLUSTRATIONS FROM CONTEMPORARY FRENCH PLAYS. Harvard Studies in Comparative Literature, Vol. 14. Cambridge, Mass.: Harvard University Press; London: Oxford University Press, 1938.

The "Preface" outlines the scope of the study: "[T]he proverbs and other proverbial materials . . . are studied in relation to their context. The documents considered are the Biblical plays, moralities, early comedies, and early tragedies" (p. [ix]). These make it "possible to trace an unbroken line of usage within a definite literary type from earlier than 1400 to later than 1600." The proverbs are classified, indexed, and so on, for ready reference. Whiting is a scholar of particular authority on the subject of proverbs.

Wickham, Glynne. SHAKESPEARE'S DRAMATIC HERITAGE: COLLECTED STUD-

IES IN MEDIAEVAL, TUDOR, AND SHAKESPEAREAN DRAMA. New York: Barnes & Noble, 1969.

The four studies, "The Mediaeval Heritage of Shakespearean Drama," "Reformation and Renaissance," "Stages and Stage Directions," and "Studies in Shakespeare," are directed towards the exploration of what Shakespeare owed to "his own society" and of what "that society" owed to "the mediaeval past" (p. xvi).

Wilkes, T. [pseud.]. See Derrick, Samuel.

Winslow, Ola Elizabeth. LOW COMEDY AS A STRUCTURAL ELEMENT IN ENGLISH DRAMA FROM THE BEGINNINGS TO 1642. Chicago: Private ed., distributed by the University of Chicago Libraries, 1926.

This doctoral dissertation argues that low comedy, if it is to succeed, must necessarily be episodic and that its interruptions must constitute, "in Freytag's term . . . 'advantageous addition.'" Winslow finds Elizabethan playwrights more likely to disregard than obey these principles, "but the few supreme examples of their application leave no doubt that low comedy, may, in the hands of genius, serve drama effectively" (p. 170).

Wynne, Arnold. THE GROWTH OF ENGLISH DRAMA. Oxford: Clarendon Press, 1914.

"The "Preface" calls attention to the fact that the book supplies "details of the plots and characters, and specimens of the verse" and to the fact--more pertinent in 1914 than now--that plays neglected in earlier studies are discussed, plays previously mentioned only briefly are so treated as to "cease to be mere names appended to an argument" (p. [5]). Readers not wishing such basic information may look elsewhere.

7. STUDIES OF MEDIEVAL DRAMA

A. BROAD APPROACHES

(See Subdivisions B, C, and D for studies of particular types: Folklore and the Folkplay, Corpus Christi Plays and Miracle Plays, and Morality Plays.)

Anderson, M[ary] D[esiree]. DRAMA AND IMAGERY IN ENGLISH MEDIEVAL CHURCHES. Cambridge: At the University Press, 1963.

In a valuable and well-documented study, using a considerable number of black and white illustrations, Anderson argues that religious drama and religious art are both didactic and that they teach the same lessons. She adduces evidence that art and drama not only show parallels but demonstrate "direct interaction" (p. 2).

Bates, Katharine Lee. THE ENGLISH RELIGIOUS DRAMA. New York and London: Macmillan, 1902.

As the "Prefatory Note" indicates, the book is made up of lectures originally delivered in 1893, and it should be read with an awareness of developments which have occurred in the intervening eighty years and more. Its early recognition of the dramatic significance of the Corpus Christi plays gives it a lasting place in the history of dramatic criticism, however--a recognition expressed in words which may seem an exaggeration to those who have not read Medieval drama sympathetically--for example: "Londoners had looked already on a more heart-moving tragedy than HAMLET" (p. 200).

Bradbury, Malcolm, and David Palmer, eds.; Neville Denny, associate ed. MEDIEVAL DRAMA. Stratford-Upon-Avon Studies, No. 16. London: Edward Arnold, 1973.

Earlier volumes in this series were edited by John Russell Brown and Bernard Harris. The essays in this number are: Richard Axton, "Popular Modes in the Earliest Plays"; Paula Neuss, "Active and Idle Language: Dramatic Images in 'Mankind'"; David L. Jeffrey, "English Saints' Plays"; David Bevington, "Popular and Courtly Traditions on the Early Tudor Stage"; Arnold Williams, "The Comic in the Cycles"; Neville Denny, "Arena Staging and Dramatic Quality in the Cornish Passion Play"; Kevin Roddy, "Epic Qualities in the Cycle Plays"; T.W. Craik, "Violence in the English Miracle Plays"; Martial Rose, "The Staging of the Hegge Plays"; and John R. Elliott, Jr., "Medieval Rounds and Wooden O's: The Medieval Heritage of the Elizabethan Theatre."

Brooks, Neil C. THE SEPULCHRE OF CHRIST IN ART AND LITURGY, WITH SPECIAL REFERENCE TO THE LITURGIC DRAMA. University of Illinois Studies in Language and Literature, Vol. 7, No. 2, 1921; reprint ed. New York: Johnson Reprint Corp., 1970.

Brooks's study is directed towards assembling and offering an interpretation of "the essential facts about the sepulchre as known from art, architecture, and archives, and from liturgic rubrics" and to using these materials "to enlarge our knowledge of the mise en scene of the liturgical Easter plays" (p. 8). See especially Chapter 8, "Easter Sepulchres in England." There are an appendix, "Texts of the DEPOSITIO, ELEVATIO, and VISITATIO," and extensive illustrations.

Cargill, Oscar. DRAMA AND LITURGY. Columbia University Studies in English and Comparative Literature. New York: Columbia University Press, 1930.

Cargill proposes to refute the theory of liturgical origins for the drama. He sums up his own argument: "[T]here appears to be evidence to support the view" that the authors were "professional entertainers . . . hired by the monks to entertain, to instruct, and to draw to the shrines the populace" but "that there is any generic connection between the drama and the liturgy has been most strenuously denied" (p. 140; italics his). That Cargill's argument has not met universal acceptance is indicated by the number of recent studies on the relation of drama to liturgy.

Chambers, E[dmund] K[erchever]. THE MEDIAEVAL STAGE. 2 vols. Oxford: Clarendon Press, 1903. Several reprintings.

Volume I discusses "Minstrelsy" and "Folk Drama"; Volume II, "Religious Drama" and "The Interlude." See Volume I, pages [xiii]-xlii, for a "List of Authorities" and Volume II for various appendices, A-X. Medieval drama and particularly the folkplay have received a great deal of recent attention which challenges some of Chambers's assumptions and conclusions.

Craig, Hardin. ENGLISH RELIGIOUS DRAMA OF THE MIDDLE AGES. Oxford: Clarendon Press, 1955; reprint ed. 1960.

Drawn from a long lifetime of study, Craig's book provides an abundance of fact and critical deduction about Medieval drama in general and about the Corpus Christi plays in particular. Not all of

Craig's speculations have met universal acceptance, of course, but they are worth due consideration. Bibliography.

Dunn, E. Catherine, Tatiana Fotitch, and Bernard M. Peebles, eds. THE MEDIEVAL DRAMA AND ITS CLAUDELIAN REVIVAL. PAPERS PRESENTED AT THE THIRD SYMPOSIUM IN COMPARATIVE LITERATURE HELD AT THE CATHOLIC UNIVERSITY OF AMERICA, APRIL 3 AND 4, 1968. With a Foreword by Helmut A. Hatzfeld. Washington, D.C.: Catholic University of America Press, 1970.

The essays are: E. Catherine Dunn, "The Origin of the Middle English Saints' Plays"; Bert Nagel, "The Dramas of Hrotsvit von Gandersheim"; O. B. Hardison, Jr., "Gregorian Easter Vespers and Early Liturgical Drama"; Richard B. Donovan, "Two Celebrated Centers of Medieval Liturgical Drama"; Alexander Mavrocordato, "[Paul Claudel's] 'The Tidings Brought to Mary' and Medieval Drama."

Frank, Grace. THE MEDIEVAL FRENCH DRAMA. Oxford: Clarendon Press, 1954.

Confined to the discussion of French plays, and with respect to "the liturgical plays . . . almost entirely to those produced in France" (p. [vii]). Among the "Transitional Plays" which are the subject of Chapter 8, however, the Anglo-Norman LE MYSTERE D'ADAM is considered at some length, pages 76-84, and very sympathetically. Bibliography.

Hardison, O[sborne] B., Jr. CHRISTIAN RITE AND CHRISTIAN DRAMA IN THE MIDDLE AGES: ESSAYS IN THE ORIGIN AND EARLY HISTORY OF MODERN DRAMA. Baltimore, Md.: Johns Hopkins Press, 1965; paperback ed., 1969.

Hardison makes a careful re-examination of theories of dramatic form and of the relation of drama to Christian rite, arguing that the Church's "ritual *was* the drama of the early Middle Ages" (p. viii). Hardison takes a very different view from that of Karl Young or Hardin Craig, as he himself explains in some detail. Appendix II provides a "Chronological Index of Early Liturgical Plays."

Jones, Charles W. THE SAINT NICHOLAS LITURGY AND ITS LITERARY RELATIONSHIPS (NINTH TO TWELFTH CENTURIES) WITH AN ESSAY ON THE MUSIC BY GILBERT REANEY. University of California Publications, English Studies, 27. Berkeley and Los Angeles: University of California Press, 1963.

See especially Chapter 8, "The Miracle Plays." (Miracle plays, strictly defined as plays of saints' lives, are not of major importance in England, of course.)

Kinghorn, A.M. MEDIEVAL DRAMA. Literature in Perspective. London: Evans Brothers, 1968.

One of a series of guides designed for the layman, Kinghorn's volume surveys the types of Medieval plays and includes chapters on "The Nature of Drama," "Realism in the Miracle Plays," and "The Classical Tradition in England" among others. The bibliography includes a section of "Illustrated works on medieval religious art."

Kretzmann, Paul Edward. THE LITURGICAL ELEMENT IN THE EARLIEST FORMS OF THE MEDIEVAL DRAMA, WITH SPECIAL REFERENCE TO THE ENGLISH AND GERMAN PLAYS. University of Minnesota Studies in Language and Literature, No. 4. Minneapolis: University of Minnesota, 1916.

Kretzmann provides a substantial collection of liturgical elements to be found in the plays as evidence of the weight of liturgical influence. He also offers as a "probable reason" for this influence "a brief chapter on the psychology of the medieval dramaturgical method, cycle construction, and the interrelation of cycle plays" (p. [162]).

Mill, Anna Jean. MEDIAEVAL PLAYS IN SCOTLAND. St. Andrews University Publications, No. 24. Edinburgh and London: Blackwood, 1927.

Mill provides a general survey. She points out the difficulty of absolute conclusions on the basis of such documents as have survived. The appendices reproduce generously from those documents.

Moore, E. Hamilton. ENGLISH MIRACLE PLAYS AND MORALITIES. London: Sherratt & Hughes, 1907.

The "Foreword" declares the intention of the book to be "rather popular than scholastic" in answering such basic questions as "What is a Morality? What are these Mystery Plays? Are they English or foreign? Who wrote them? Who acted them, and how? What are they all about?" (pp. [v]-vi).

Owst, G[erald] R. LITERATURE AND PULPIT IN MEDIEVAL ENGLAND: A NEGLECTED CHAPTER IN THE HISTORY OF ENGLISH LETTERS & OF THE ENGLISH PEOPLE. 1933; reprint ed. New York: Barnes & Noble, 1961.

Specific reference to the drama makes up only a part of the whole, but the background material supplied by Owst is valuable in the extreme. See especially Chapter 8, "Sermon and Drama."

Selz, William A., ed. MEDIEVAL DRAMA: A COLLECTION OF FESTIVAL PAPERS. Vermillion: Dakota Press, University of South Dakota, 1968.

This collection of papers from the University of South Dakota "Festival of Medieval Drama," March 1967, constitutes Volume III of the University's FESTIVAL PAPERS. It contains: Wayne R. Rood, "Mystery and Drama"; J.W. Robinson, "Ad Majorem Dei Gloriam"; Leon E. Lewis, "The Complexion of Medieval English Drama"; E. Catherine Dunn, "The Origin of the Saints' Plays: The Question Reopened"; Merle Fifield, "'The Castle of Perseverance': A Moral Trilogy"; George R. Adams, "Comedy and Theology in the 'Second Shepherds' Play'"; Robert W. Ackerman, "Sir Frederic Madden and the Study of Medieval Literature"; David C. Fowler, "Poetry and the Liberal Arts: The Oxford Background of 'Piers the Plowman'"; and George K. Anderson, "Chaucer: A Suggested Portrait." The volume is not, obviously, entirely on drama in spite of its title.

Sticca, Sandro, ed. THE MEDIEVAL DRAMA. PAPERS OF THE THIRD ANNUAL CONFERENCE OF THE CENTER FOR MEDIEVAL AND EARLY RENAISSANCE STUDIES. STATE UNIVERSITY OF NEW YORK AT BINGHAMTON, 3-4 MAY, 1969. Albany: State University of New York Press, 1972.

The collection contains: Omer Jodogne, "Le Theatre Francais du Moyen Age: Recherches sur l'Aspect Dramatique des Textes"; Wolfgang Michael, "Tradition and Originality in the Medieval Drama in Germany"; Sandro Sticca, "The Literary Genesis of the Latin Passion Play and the PLANCTUS MARIAE: A New Christocentric and Marian Theology"; V.A. Kolve, "EVERYMAN and the Parable of the Talents"; Glynne Wickham, "The Staging of Saint Plays in England"; William L. Smoldon, "The Origins of the QUEM QUAERITIS Trope and the Easter Sepulchre Music-Dramas, as Demonstrated by their Musical Settings." The Binghamton conference has gained considerable fame as a center for productive discussions.

Tunison, Joseph S. DRAMATIC TRADITIONS OF THE DARK AGES. Chicago: University of Chicago Press; London: Unwin, 1907.

Not designed as a "history of the drama in the Dark Ages" but as a study of "the process of the transfer of theatrical aptitudes from the East to the West, and from ancient to modern times" (p. vii), Tunison's work discusses both the hostility of "church and stage" and (in Chapter 2) "Traditions of Dramatic Impulses in Religion."

Vriend, J[ohannes]. THE BLESSED VIRGIN MARY IN THE MEDIEVAL DRAMA OF ENGLAND, WITH ADDITIONAL STUDIES IN MIDDLE ENGLISH LITERATURE. Purmerend, Holland: J. Muusses, 1928.

Vriend studies the role of Mary in detail, in Old Testament as well as New Testament plays, and builds up a background of Medieval attitudes towards Mary, arguing that "[l]ike the rest of Christendom during the middle ages medieval England had a special devotion to the Blessed Virgin Mary" (p. 1).

Williams, Arnold. THE DRAMA OF MEDIEVAL ENGLAND. East Lansing: Michigan State University Press, 1961.

In this history of "the liturgical drama of Western Europe and of the vernacular drama of England from the late tenth century to about 1500 . . . addressed to the general reader" (p. vi), Williams urges recognition of the fact that these Medieval plays constitute "a vital dramatic literature which, even in the fragmentary state it has come down to us, can stand on its own excellence" (p. 174). Bibliography.

Young, Karl. THE DRAMA OF THE MEDIEVAL CHURCH. 2 vols. Oxford: Clarendon Press, 1933; corrected reprint eds. 1951, 1962, 1967.

The "Preface," Volume I, page [vii], states: "The essential purpose of the present treatise is to assemble, in their authentic forms, the dramatic compositions which were employed by the medieval Church in Western Europe as a part of public worship, and which are commonly regarded as the origins of modern drama." Young provides texts and extensive commentary upon them. Later scholars have not entirely agreed with Young's conclusions but all have been indebted to him for the massive job of editing and annotating. Illustrations. Bibliography. (Also listed in Section 2 A i: Editions of Plays: Medieval Drama--Liturgical Plays.

B. FOLKLORE AND THE FOLKPLAY

Alford, Violet. SWORD DANCE AND DRAMA. London: Merlin Press, 1962.

The sword dance in the whole of Europe is the subject of this book, but one chapter, pages [31]-76, is on "The Sword Dance in Great Britain," and the discussion of the basic characteristics of the sword dance is generally applicable. See especially the "Summary" provided in the last chapter. Illustrations. Bibliography.

Baskervill, Charles Read. THE ELIZABETHAN JIG AND RELATED SONG DRAMA. 1929; reprint ed., paperback, New York: Dover Publications, 1965.

In two parts, "The History of the Jig" and "Texts," the book is done with great care and casts interesting light on one of the side developments of the drama, though Baskervill points out that "much of this material lacks literary significance" (p. v).

Beatty, Arthur. "The St. George, or Mummers', Plays: A Study in the Protology of the Drama." TRANSACTIONS OF THE WISCONSIN ACADEMY OF SCIENCES, ARTS, AND LETTERS, 15 (1906), 273-324.

Beatty sees the St. George play as part of a widespread folk tradition, influenced late in its history by Christianity but going back probably to "the earliest agricultural magic rites." He thinks further that the St. George plays illustrate what Aristotle meant by mimesis (p. 323).

Brand, John. OBSERVATIONS ON THE POPULAR ANTIQUITIES OF GREAT BRITAIN: CHIEFLY ILLUSTRATING THE ORIGIN OF OUR VULGAR AND PROVINCIAL CUSTOMS, CEREMONIES, AND SUPERSTITIONS, ARRANGED, RE-

VISED, AND GREATLY ENLARGED BY SIR HENRY ELLIS. A NEW EDITION, WITH FURTHER ADDITIONS BY J.Q. HALLIWELL. 3 vols. London: Bohn, 1848-49.

Along with material on various holidays and Holy Days and on games like hot cockles and see-saw, there are sections on customs related to drama: "Morris-Dancers," "Corpus Christi Day, and Plays," and the like. There is an index in Volume 3. See also Hazlitt, W[il-liam] Carew.

Brody, Alan. THE ENGLISH MUMMERS AND THEIR PLAYS: TRACES OF ANCIENT MYSTERY. Philadelphia: University of Pennsylvania Press, 1969, 1970; London: Routledge and Kegal Paul, n.d.

Brody says: "My thesis is based . . . on the idea that drama, as explained action requiring some separation between performer and audience, can emerge from ritual at any stage of religious consciousness" (p. viii). Drawing on the Cambridge anthropologists (p. ix), Brody argues that for all their many variants, the mummers' plays have a common basic core: "They are all seasonal and they all contain a death and resurrection" (p. 3). The appendices include examples of plays, and there are a number of illustrations, chiefly photographs of contemporary mummers. The bibliography, pages 177-85, is especially useful on folklore.

Cawte, E.C., Alex Helm, and N. Peacock. ENGLISH RITUAL DRAMA: A GEOGRAPHICAL INDEX. London: Published for The Folk-Lore Society, 1967.

The attempt here made to deal systematically with an unsystematic body of material provides a useful perspective, with maps and tables of distribution and appendices of "Old Plays Impossible to Classify" and "Examples of Texts."

Chambers, E[dmund] K[erchever]. THE ENGLISH FOLK PLAY. Oxford: Clarendon Press, 1933.

The study has two main sections, "The Mummers' Play and its Congeners" and "The Problem of Origin." Folklore studies have rather shifted point of view since Chambers wrote, and his judgments should be measured against new developments.

Ditchfield, P[eter] H[ampson]. OLD ENGLISH CUSTOMS EXTANT AT THE PRESENT TIME: AN ACCOUNT OF LOCAL OBSERVANCES, FESTIVAL CUSTOMS, AND ANCIENT CEREMONIES YET SURVIVING IN GREAT BRITAIN. 1896; reprint ed. Detroit: Singing Tree Press, 1968.

The "Preface" points out as the distinctive quality of this collection of folklore that it deals with what, at least at the time of its first publication, were "actual folk-customs yet extant, which may be witnessed to-day by the folk-lorist and lover of rural manners" (p. v). Some of the customs--"Mumming," for example--relate to drama, though most, of course, do not.

Gable, J. Harris. BIBLIOGRAPHY OF ROBIN HOOD.

See main entry in Section 1 B: General Literary Bibliographies.

Gailey, Alan. IRISH FOLK DRAMA. Cork: Mercier Press, 1969.

Gailey discusses Mummers, Christmas Rhymers, "The Sources of the Texts," "The Origins of the Action," "Seasonal Festivals," "Weddings and Wakes," and "The Life-Cycle Drama in Ireland." He provides some texts of plays.

Hazlitt, W[illiam] Carew. FAITH AND FOLKLORE: A DICTIONARY OF NATIONAL BELIEFS, SUPERSTITIONS, AND POPULAR CUSTOMS, PAST AND CURRENT, WITH THEIR CLASSICAL AND FOREIGN ANALOGUES, DESCRIBED AND ILLUSTRATED. FORMING A NEW EDITION OF "THE POPULAR ANTIQUITIES OF GREAT BRITAIN" BY BRAND AND ELLIS, LARGELY EXTENDED, CORRECTED, BROUGHT DOWN TO THE PRESENT TIME, AND NOW FIRST ALPHABETICALLY ARRANGED. 2 vols. London: Reeves and Turner, 1905.

See Brand, John.

Helm, Alex. THE CHAPBOOK MUMMERS' PLAY: A STUDY OF THE PRINTED VERSIONS OF THE NORTH-WEST OF ENGLAND. Ibstock, Leicestershire: Guizer Press, 1969.

Helm attempts to determine what role the chapbook texts have played in the shaping and survival of the mummers' play and concludes (p. [32]): "The normal effect of tampering with tradition is to cause it to decline if not vanish completely: the chapbooks had the opposite effect, producing a blend of tradition and re-writing which was apparently acceptable." The chapbooks date from 1771 forward, so that the study concerns the survival of a Medieval form into the modern world. "Check List of Known Play Chapbooks," pages [34]-39.

______. CHESHIRE FOLK DRAMA. Ibstock, Leicestershire: Guizer Press, 1968.

Helm provides an account of a recently surviving folkplay and some assessment of its ramifications and implications. Such records of folk drama, for all the hazards they offer the scholar who attempts to generalize from them, are important to our hope of arriving at some knowledge of the origins of drama. Helm observes: "In Cheshire, as elsewhere, the surviving actions are only fragments: one could perhaps guess at the form the whole ceremony took, but it would only be a guess, impossible to prove" (p. 55). "References," pages 57-58.

Hone, William. ANCIENT MYSTERIES DESCRIBED, ESPECIALLY THE ENGLISH MIRACLE PLAYS, FOUNDED ON APOCRYPHAL NEW TESTAMENT STORY, EXTANT AMONG THE UNPUBLISHED MANUSCRIPTS IN THE BRITISH MUSEUM; INCLUDING NOTICES OF ECCLESIASTICAL SHOWS, THE FESTIVALS OF FOOLS

AND ASSES--THE ENGLISH BOY-BISHOP--THE DESCENT INTO HELL--THE LORD MAYOR'S SHOW--THE GUILDHALL GIANTS--CHRISTMAS CAROLS, &C. 1823; reprint ed. Trowbridge and London: Redwood Press Limited for Ward Lock Reprints, 1970.

Full of pictures, odd facts, and much "&c," Hone's book is entirely charming and casts occasional light on the drama.

Miles, Clement A. CHRISTMAS IN RITUAL AND TRADITION, CHRISTIAN AND PAGAN. London and Leipsic: Unwin, 1912, 1913.

Miles offers chapters on "Christmas Drama" and "Masking, The Mummers' Play, The Feast of Fools, and the Boy Bishop."

Sharp, Cecil J. THE SWORD DANCES OF NORTHERN ENGLAND TOGETHER WITH THE HORN DANCE OF ABBOTS BROMLEY. London: Novello and Co., [1912].

See next item.

_____. THE SWORD-DANCES OF NORTHERN ENGLAND. Part II. London: Novello and Co., [1913].

Of the three volumes of Sharp's study, I have seen only these two, which provide photographs, diagrams.

Smith, Horatio. FESTIVALS, GAMES AND AMUSEMENTS: ANCIENT AND MODERN. London: Henry Colburn and Richard Bentley, 1831.

Smith says, page [v], that his book is less new than compressed and popularized material. Much of it relates to dramatic activity.

Strutt, Joseph. THE SPORTS AND PASTIMES OF THE PEOPLE OF ENGLAND FROM THE EARLIEST PERIOD, INCLUDING THE RURAL AND DOMESTIC RECREATIONS, MAY GAMES, MUMMERIES, SHOWS, PAGEANTS, PROCESSIONS, AND POMPOUS SPECTACLES, ILLUSTRATED BY REPRODUCTIONS FROM ANCIENT PAINTINGS IN WHICH ARE REPRESENTED MOST OF THE POPULAR DIVERSIONS, BY JOSEPH STRUTT, 1801. A NEW EDITION, MUCH ENLARGED AND CORRECTED BY J. CHARLES COX, WITH A PREFACE TO THE 1969 EDITION BY NORRIS MCWHIRTER AND ROSS MCWHIRTER. New York: Augustus M. Kelley, 1970.

The "Preface" of 1969 (p. [iii]) dates the Cox revisions as 1903. A note (p. xv) advises that asterisks mark "all the newly written paragraphs throughout." This accessible edition can, therefore, be used without undue confusion of original and added matters. See the index for references to dramatic materials.

Tiddy, R[eginald] J.E. THE MUMMERS' PLAY. 1923; reprint ed. Chicheley: Paul P.B. Minit, 1972.

The book contains two parts, a discussion of "The Mummers' Play," including "Popular Taste, as reflected in Miracle and Morality Plays" and "Popular Taste in Elizabethan and Later Drama," and in the second part, texts. Tiddy died before his book reached print. He has been warmly remembered by those who knew him as a folklorist in genuine contact and sympathy with the tradition he sought to record. See the "Editor's Note," page [140], on the texts.

C. CORPUS CHRISTI PLAYS AND MIRACLE PLAYS

The "Three M's" of Medieval drama are Mystery, Miracle, and Morality. But while the greatest part of Medieval drama falls under these three labels, what the Middle Ages and the modern scholar mean in using them is not altogether clear. The morality play is rather easily described: it presents an allegorical fable, generally about a representative of the human species facing death and the eternal consequences of his life. In a strict definition, miracle plays are the plays of saints' lives. More broadly, the designation may be applied to the saints' lives plays and also to all the plays which fall under the label mystery plays. Mystery itself is an eighteenth-century designation, first used by Robert Dodsley; it lacks Medieval authority and also lacks clear definition. Among the characteristics of the play sometimes called a mystery are these: its episodes are Biblical (with some exceptions--the Mak and Gil episode in the Towneley SECOND SHEPHERDS' PLAY, for example). It is often but not always part of a cycle or set of plays running from the creation to doomsday, and so the sequence may be called a cycle. It may have been performed from a pageant or wagon--hence the name pageants for the plays themselves. The name guild plays reflects the enactment of the cycle by guilds of workmen. It was probably performed at the time of a Church feast, Whitsuntide or Corpus Christi, for example. While modern scholars have not universally agreed on the separation of miracle plays into a narrowly defined group, to call the plays of saints' lives miracle plays makes a useful distinction. For the Biblical plays which are not by this definition miracle plays, the term Corpus Christi plays has great currency now, it is of Medieval origin, and it identifies the focus of these plays on Corpus Christi, the body of Christ. In Section 2 A, ii and iii, I have separated editions of Corpus Christi and miracle plays because the separation can be easily and usefully made. To separate scholarly books into three categories, those which discuss miracle plays only, Corpus Christi plays only, and both, would be cumbersome and uninstructive. They are, therefore, given here in one list. Subdivision iv treats morality plays.

Beuscher, Elisabeth. DIE GEGANSEINLAGEN IN DEN ENGLISCHEN MYSTERIEN. Munster: Helios-Verlag, 1930.

Beuscher provides useful charts showing occurrences of songs in the mystery plays.

Carey, Millicent. THE WAKEFIELD GROUP IN THE TOWNELEY CYCLE. A STUDY TO DETERMINE THE CONVENTIONAL AND ORIGINAL ELEMENTS IN FOUR PLAYS COMMONLY ATTRIBUTED TO THE WAKEFIELD AUTHOR. Hesperia Ergänzungsreihe: Schriften zur Englischen Philologie, Vol. 11. Gottingen: Vandenhoeck & Ruprecht; Baltimore, Md.: Johns Hopkins Press, 1930.

The study is "an attempt . . . to estimate accurately the contribution of the Wakefield Author to the development of the drama" (p. [v]).

Clarke, Sidney W. THE MIRACLE PLAY IN ENGLAND: AN ACCOUNT OF THE EARLY RELIGIOUS DRAMA. 1897; reprint ed. New York: Haskell House, 1964.

A consideration of "what these Miracle Plays really were in matter and in representation" and of "the manner in which the people at large entered into the spirit of the performances" (p. [v]). A rather slight book (77 pages plus appendices) and rather old, but important in the history of the criticism of Medieval drama.

Coffman, George Raleigh. A NEW THEORY CONCERNING THE ORIGIN OF THE MIRACLE PLAY. Menasha, Wis.: Collegiate Press, George Banta Publishing Co., 1914.

The "Preface" states Coffman's thesis: "[C]ircumstances and conditions of the eleventh century explain the origin of the Miracle Play, not only as to its type, but also as to its form and spirit" (p. [v]). Among Coffman's conclusions is the theory that "[t]he Miracle Play originated in musical services as an unecclesiastical feature of St. Nicholas' feast day celebration" (p. [79]).

Cornelius, Brother Luke. THE ROLE OF THE VIRGIN MARY IN THE COVENTRY, YORK, CHESTER, AND TOWNELEY CYCLES. Washington, D.C.: Catholic University of America, 1933.

Directed towards showing the Virgin's role to be "thoroughly Christocentric" and then at exploring (1) the effect of the use of apocryphal material on this focus, and (2) the distinctiveness of the handling of the Virgin Mary in each of the cycles (p. 1).

Davidson, Charles. STUDIES IN THE ENGLISH MYSTERY PLAYS. New Haven, Conn.: Printed by the Authority of Yale University, 1892.

Davidson's dissertation argues for the origin of the Corpus Christi plays in a "spirit of devotion" and in "the liturgy and its sources" (p. 171) and for the plays as "the most important source of literary history for their time, and the determining factor in many dialectical questions" (p. 173).

Deasy, C. Philip. ST. JOSEPH IN THE ENGLISH MYSTERY PLAYS. Washington, D.C.: Catholic University of America, 1937.

The study endeavors "to establish the definite nature and status of the Saint's dramatic role, and to determine thereby, at least partially, the popular medieval conception of Christ's foster-father" (p. v).

Foster, Frances A. A STUDY OF THE MIDDLE-ENGLISH POEM KNOWN AS THE "NORTHERN PASSION" AND ITS RELATION TO THE CYCLE PLAYS. London and Bungay: R. Clay, 1914.

Foster provides an extensive treatment of the poem itself, culminating in a chapter on "The NORTHERN PASSION and the Drama," with particular reference to the York, Towneley, and Hegge cycles.

Gardiner, Harold C. MYSTERIES' END: AN INVESTIGATION OF THE LAST DAYS OF THE MEDIEVAL RELIGIOUS STAGE. Yale Studies in English, Vol. 103. New Haven, Conn.: Yale University Press; London: Oxford University Press, 1946.

This important study, based on extensive research in many libraries and archives, reaches two basic conclusions: "that the popular religious stage of the Middle Ages owed its discontinuance to measures of repression" and that it remained "tremendously popular" to the end for the reason that "it was still a religious drama" (p. [113]). Bibliography.

Garth, Helen Meredith. "Saint Mary Magdalene in Mediaeval Literature." THE JOHNS HOPKINS UNIVERSITY STUDIES IN HISTORICAL AND POLITICAL SCIENCE, Series 67, No. 3 (1949), 339–452.

The essay considers various forms of literature and literature in languages other than English but draws extensively from Medieval English drama to provide "an exposition" of Medieval views of "the identity of Mary Magdalene" and of "the events of her life" as well as "her personality and character" and of the way Medieval writers "used their subject for the endless symbolism in which they delighted." The study provides "one method of illustration and approach to the mind and spirit of the Middle Ages" (p. 107). (The essay has both separate and continuous pagination with the remainder of the volume; it has a separate title page with the date 1950.)

Greg, W[alter] W[ilson]. "Bibliographical and Textual Problems of the English Miracle Cycles." LIBRARY, 3rd Series, 5 (1914), 1-30, 168-205, 280-319, 365-99.

Greg's study also appeared as a separate publication from A. Moring (London, 1914). Time has not much diminished either the problems or Greg's authority on the subject of bibliography.

Hildburgh, W[alter] L[eo]. ENGLISH ALABASTER CARVINGS AS RECORDS OF THE MEDIEVAL RELIGIOUS DRAMA. Oxford: Society of Antiquaries of London, 1949. (Reprinted from ARCHAEOLOGIA, 93 (1949), [51]-101 plus plates.)

Hildburgh points out that little English art relevant to the drama except these carvings has survived but that the carvings are "a source of information concerning the medieval English stage whose value has never adequately been realized" (p. 52). Extensive plates.

Janicka, Irena. THE COMIC ELEMENTS IN THE ENGLISH MYSTERY PLAYS AGAINST THE CULTURAL BACKGROUND (PARTICULARLY ART). Poznanskie Towarzystwo Przyjaciol Nauk, Wydzial Filologiczno-Filozoficzny Prace Komisji Filologicznej Tom. 16, Zeszyt 6. Poznan: Praca Wydana z Zasilku Polskiej Akademii Nauk, 1962.

The two aims of the book are "to analyse the comic element in the English mystery cycles and to try to find links between the comic in the mysteries and that in other fields of contemporary culture" (p. [3]). Bibliography. Forty-two black and white plates.

Kolve, V.A. THE PLAY CALLED CORPUS CHRISTI. Stanford, Calif.: Stanford University Press, 1966.

Kolve's distinguished study attempts to establish the Medieval frame of reference within which the plays were viewed. Kolve relates the plays to the typological reading of the Scripture and regards the play as game, not ritual. Bibliography.

Longsworth, Robert. THE CORNISH ORDINALIA: RELIGION AND DRAMATURGY. Cambridge, Mass.: Harvard University Press, 1967.

Longsworth deliberately limits his study to one aspect of the complex problem of the ORDINALIA, "the religious ideas that it contains," wishing "in effect, to set aside the question of its dramatic appeal in order to consider the moral, theological, and doctrinal ideas with which it deals and by which it developed in the church" (p. 20). Not only does this limit enable Longsworth to work in depth with one problem; he sees the intent of the ORDINALIA as didactic, "shaped" by "pedagogical genius" (p. 124). Bibliography.

Lucken, Brother Linus Urban. ANTICHRIST AND PROPHETS OF ANTICHRIST IN THE CHESTER CYCLE. Washington, D.C.: Catholic University of America, 1940.

This dissertation is directed towards the study of "the popular conception of the End of the World as embodied in non-exegetical literature" (p. [vii]), more specifically of the Antichrist materials in the Chester plays.

Lyle, Marie C. THE ORIGINAL IDENTITY OF THE YORK AND TOWNELEY CYCLES. Research Publications of the University of Minnesota, Vol. 8, No. 3, Studies in Language and Literature, No. 6. Minneapolis: University of Minnesota, 1919.

Lyle argues that the York and Towneley cycles are related, not through the process of one cycle's borrowing certain plays from the other, but through having been, at some time before the hands of "redactors, revisers, and mere tinkerers" wrought "changes and modifications" on "the work of older and simpler originals" (p. [iii]), identical.

Meyers, Walter E. A FIGURE GIVEN: TYPOLOGY IN THE WAKEFIELD PLAYS. A Modern Humanities Research Association Monograph: Duquesne Studies, Philological Series, No. 14. Pittsburgh, Pa.: Duquesne University Press; Louvain: Editions E. Nauwelaerts, [1969].

Meyers sees the cycle, for all the variety of its matter and the many hands involved in its composition, as essentially unified by the typological method and by the projection of its time which it makes.

Phillips, William J. CAROLS, THEIR ORIGIN, MUSIC, AND CONNECTION WITH MYSTERY-PLAYS. With A Foreword by Sir Frederick Bridge. London: G. Routledge & Sons; New York: E.P. Dutton & Co., 1921.

The book is charmingly written but probably oversimplifies all the great questions.

Pierson, Merle. "The Relation of the Corpus Christi Procession to the Corpus Christi Play in England." TRANSACTIONS OF THE WISCONSIN ACADEMY OF SCIENCES, ARTS AND LETTERS, 18 (1915), [110]-65.

Pierson argues cogently that close examination of relevant documents casts doubt on the theory that the plays developed out of the processions.

Prosser, Eleanor. DRAMA AND RELIGION IN THE ENGLISH MYSTERY PLAYS: A RE-EVALUATION. Stanford Studies in Language and Literature, No. 23. Stanford, Calif.: Stanford University Press, 1961.

Arguing that Medieval drama has failed to achieve critical recognition as drama because critics have approached it wrongly, this study proposes to try to "look at the drama as drama, through the eyes of the medieval audience," a perspective requiring an understanding of "the religion that gave birth to the drama of the Middle Ages" (p. 15). The study concentrates on "only those plays in which the penetential doctrine is crucial" (p. 17).

Salter, F[rederick] M[illet]. MEDIAEVAL DRAMA IN CHESTER. The Alexander Lectures, 1953-54. 1955; reprint ed. New York: Russell & Russell, 1968.

The old city of Chester has remarkably full Medieval records, which Salter has mined thoroughly for information about the Corpus Christi plays. While much must be estimated in the way of costs of productions and so on, the text makes clear what is recorded fact, what is estimate.

Salter, F[rederick] M[illet], and W[alter] W[ilson] Greg, eds. "THE TRIAL & FLAGELLATION" WITH OTHER STUDIES IN THE CHESTER CYCLE. Malone

Society Studies. London: Oxford University Press, 1935.

A study stemming from a then-newly-discovered manuscript of "The Coopers' Play, Play XVI" in the Chester "Enrolment Book of 1597-1776," copied there by George Bellin "On 'the 22th day of August 1599'" (p. 3).

Sharp, Thomas. A DISSERTATION ON THE PAGEANTS OR DRAMATIC MYSTERIES ANCIENTLY PERFORMED AT COVENTRY, BY THE TRADING COMPANIES OF THAT CITY; CHIEFLY WITH REFERENCE TO THE VEHICLE, CHARACTERS, AND DRESSES OF THE ACTORS. COMPILED, IN A GREAT DEGREE, FROM SOURCES HITHERTO UNEXPLORED. TO WHICH ARE ADDED, "THE PAGEANT OF THE SHEARMEN & TAYLORS' COMPANY." AND OTHER MUNICIPAL ENTERTAINMENTS OF A PUBLIC NATURE. Coventry: Merridew and Son, 1825.

Sharp is remarkably optimistic in asserting that "the history of the English Stage has been investigated with a perseverance and minuteness . . . which scarcely leaves an expectation of any additional facts or illustrations remaining to be discovered." He is entirely correct, for his day, however, in his lament that the "Religious Dramas or Mysteries, the unquestionable groundwork of the Stage, have been treated in a very superficial and unsatisfactory manner" (p. [1]). His handsome folio volume provided an auspicious step on the way to a better grasp of the importance of that drama, only now coming fully into its own again. Ten plates.

Spencer, M[atthew] Lyle. CORPUS CHRISTI PAGEANTS IN ENGLAND. New York: Baker & Taylor, 1911.

Spencer says (p. 2): "One field not yet adequately understood is that which includes the decorations, the management, and the general stage business of the Corpus Christi pageants." His discussion centers on these problems, which remain problems today, of course.

Swenson, Esther L. AN INQUIRY INTO THE COMPOSITION AND STRUCTURE OF "LUDUS COVENTRIAE." WITH A NOTE ON THE HOME OF "LUDUS COVENTRIAE" BY HARDIN CRAIG. University of Minnesota Studies in Language and Literature, No. 1. Minneapolis: Bulletin of the University of Minnesota, 1914.

In an early modern exploration of a cycle more than usually vexed with problems, Swenson is concerned not only with "Composition," "Structure," and "Home," but with speculations about staging.

Williams, Arnold. THE CHARACTERIZATION OF PILATE IN THE TOWNELEY PLAYS. East Lansing: Michigan State College Press, 1950.

Proposing to examine characterization from "four points of view: literary heritage, dramatic structure, social satire, and textual problems" (p. [v]), Williams uses the study to point up the "understanding of the dramatic principle of unity" and the "vast progress towards true tragedy" in the composite Passion group of the Towneley cycle (p. 76). Bibliography.

Woolf, Rosemary. THE ENGLISH MYSTERY PLAYS. Berkeley and Los Angeles: University of California Press, 1972.

Drawing upon the renewed interest and the critical perceptions of very recent years, Woolf offers a penetrating analysis of the dramatic values of the mystery plays, beginning with an assessment of their relation to the Latin liturgical play and ending with an analysis of their "decline," on the stage and in the eyes of Renaissance and later scholars who failed to recognize their learning and literary value. Brief but very useful "Select Bibliography" of English and continental plays and of secondary sources, pages 425-28; extensive notes; two appendices.

D. MORALITY PLAYS

Bevington, David M. FROM "MANKIND" TO MARLOWE: GROWTH OF STRUCTURE IN THE POPULAR DRAMA OF TUDOR ENGLAND. Cambridge, Mass.: Harvard University Press, 1962.

Bevington argues that the moralities have form and that the form is not static but can be seen to evolve. Much of his concern is with the manner of performance, by a troupe of fixed size, and with the effect of the manner of performance on the playwright's work. The argument culminates in an analysis of DR. FAUSTUS as the result of a "diversity of aim between realistic expression of factual occurrence and the traditional rendition of a moral pattern" (p. 262). One of the strengths of the book is its careful documentation at every point. Bibliography.

Coogan, Sister Mary Philippa. AN INTERPRETATION OF THE MORAL PLAY "MANKIND." Washington, D.C.: Catholic University of America Press, 1947.

The study urges the need to read MANKIND as a play in itself, not simply as part of the morality continuum. The interpretation here offered relates the play to Shrovetide and provides a reading of the allegory.

Fifield, Merle. THE CASTLE IN THE CIRCLE. Ball State Monograph No. 6. Muncie, Ind.: Ball State University, 1967.

Referring to Southern's THE MEDIEVAL THEATRE IN THE ROUND (see below) for a full discussion of the CASTLE OF PERSEVERANCE, Fifield argues for the stage "theoretically suggested by the CASTLE OF PERSEVERANCE MS sketch" (p. 17) as the type used in other moralities. The stage here hypothesized from the evidence of "text and action" (p. 48) is of the "Castle in the Circle" type which gives the study its title. Fifield discusses in detail PRIDE OF LIFE,

WISDOM WHO IS CHRIST, MANKIND, and EVERYMAN.

MacKenzie, W[illiam] Roy. THE ENGLISH MORALITIES FROM THE POINT OF VIEW OF ALLEGORY. Harvard Studies in English, Vol. 2. 1914; reprint ed. New York: Gordian Press, 1966; New York and London: Johnson Reprint Corp., 1968.

MacKenzie's study, rather old but full of information, argues for the dramatic worth of the moralities when viewed rightly.

Molloy, John Joseph. A THEOLOGICAL INTERPRETATION OF THE MORAL PLAY, "WISDOM, WHO IS CHRIST." Washington, D.C.: Catholic University of America, 1952.

Molloy argues against the opinions of a number of earlier scholars to assert that the play has a "unified theological theme" and that it was not written "for those in the religious state" (p. 184). He suggests that it may be "an early Inns of Court play" and that it may be "a forerunner of plays like FULGENCE AND LUCRECE and NATURE" (pp. 191-92). Appendices: "A Working Outline of WISDOM" and "For Whom Was WISDOM Written?" Bibliography.

Smart, Walter Kay. SOME ENGLISH AND LATIN SOURCES AND PARALLELS FOR THE MORALITY OF "WISDOM." Menasha, Wis.: George Banta, 1912.

This University of Chicago dissertation demonstrates, in parallel columns, the relation of the play to nine sources.

Southern, Richard. THE MEDIEVAL THEATRE IN THE ROUND: A STUDY OF THE STAGING OF "THE CASTLE OF PERSEVERANCE" AND RELATED MATTERS. London: Faber and Faber, 1957.

Southern's "Foreword" describes the purpose of this and the others of his books which make up an informal series as to provide an examination of "the purpose and history of scenery in its widest sense on the British stage" (p. xiii). Five plates, twenty-two figures. An appendix, "On the Use of the 'Place' and the Platea in Medieval Theatre Generally," pages [217]-36, and also bibliographical references in an appendix.

Thompson, Elbert N.S. "The English Moral Plays." TRANSACTIONS OF THE CONNECTICUT ACADEMY OF ARTS AND SCIENCES, 14 (1908-10), 291-414.

Among various theories about the rise and progress of the morality, Thompson subscribes to the view that the drama began as an "Alliance of the Pulpit and the Stage" (the title of Chapter 1) but became increasingly "engrossed in mirth" and "neglectful of godliness," while the Church found "other and more naturally effective means of teaching morality and religion" (pp. 402-3).

8. STUDIES OF TUDOR AND STUART DRAMA

The possibilities for subdividing the material here presented are so numerous and so overlapping that one alphabetical list has finally seemed more useful than a series of partly satisfactory subdivisions.

Adams, Henry Hitch. ENGLISH DOMESTIC OR, HOMILETIC TRAGEDY, 1575 TO 1642, BEING AN ACCOUNT OF THE DEVELOPMENT OF THE TRAGEDY OF THE COMMON MAN, SHOWING ITS GREAT DEPENDENCE ON RELIGIOUS MORALITY, ILLUSTRATED WITH STRIKING EXAMPLES OF THE INTERPOSITION OF PROVIDENCE FOR THE AMENDMENT OF MEN'S MANNERS. 1943; reprint ed. New York: Benjamin Blom, 1965.

> Recognizing the need for "an interpretation which would establish the place of the genre in dramatic history and . . . relate the plays to the intellectual movement of their own times" (p. vii), Adams characterizes domestic tragedy as having as its hero the common man, as its purpose the homiletic, and as its atmosphere the realistic. Bibliography, including a list of domestic tragedies. Appendix: "Lost Domestic Tragedies."

Albright, Evelyn May. DRAMATIC PUBLICATION IN ENGLAND, 1580-1640: A STUDY OF CONDITIONS AFFECTING CONTENT AND FORM OF DRAMA. Modern Language Association of America, Monograph Series, No. 2. New York: D.C. Heath and Co.; London: Oxford University Press, 1927.

> Albright recalls, page 1, the "theory that the publication of plays in the period 1580-1640 was for the most part surreptitious or unauthorized if it took place while the plays were still in demand for the stage." She argues, however, that in fact "each text must be fairly judged on its own evidence" (p. 5).

Anglo, Sydney. SPECTACLE, PAGEANTRY, AND EARLY TUDOR POLICY. Oxford-Warburg Studies. Oxford: Clarendon Press, 1969.

> The focus of the book is on "Early Tudor spectacle and pageantry" as "a small but significant part of the multiform historical materials through which the making of the Tudor Idea can be traced" (p. 2). Various forms of spectacle and pageant, for example, tournaments,

which "became an incipient drama" (p. 98), figure in the discussion.

Baker, Howard. INDUCTION TO TRAGEDY: A STUDY IN A DEVELOPMENT OF FORM IN "GORBODUC," "THE SPANISH TRAGEDY," AND "TITUS ANDRONICUS." 1939; reprint ed. New York: Russell & Russell, 1965.

Baker views Renaissance English tragedy as largely a development from Medieval English roots. He sees the notoriously Senecan SPANISH TRAGEDY, for example, as derived from English traditions in "technical and moral" ways (p. 2).

Baldwin, T.W. SHAKSPERE'S FIVE-ACT STRUCTURE: SHAKSPERE'S EARLY PLAYS ON THE BACKGROUND OF RENAISSANCE THEORIES OF FIVE-ACT STRUCTURE FROM 1470. Urbana: University of Illinois Press, 1947.

Baldwin explores Classical and Renaissance dramatic theory and practice, with extensive treatment of the early Renaissance English stage, as background to Shakespeare.

Barber, C[harles] L[aurence]. THE IDEA OF HONOUR IN THE ENGLISH DRAMA, 1591-1700. Gothenburg Studies in English, No. 6. Goteburg: Elanders Boktryckeri Antiebolag, 1957. Distributor: Almqvist & Wiksell (Stockholm).

Barber has studied the "use of the noun honour . . . in 235 plays," examining its use in two modes, tragedy and comedy, and in the comedy as designed for two audiences, that of the public and that of the private theatres, in two time periods, 1591-1640 and 1661-1700. He suggests that changes in the connotation of the noun honour reflect both social and linguistic changes (pp. 330-33). Much of the material is presented through charts. Appendix A is a "Chronological list of plays used as materials." Bibliography.

Bastiaenen, Johannes Adam. THE MORAL TONE OF JACOBEAN AND CAROLINE DRAMA. 1930; reprint ed. New York: Haskell House, 1966.

Bastiaenen concludes that a number of Jacobean and Caroline dramatists "may be safely considered as the precursors of the immoral dramatic period which followed in the train of the Restoration." He asserts, however, that "claims to honourable mention" of a few--Bastiaenen names Heywood, Massinger, Shirley, Habington, and Nabbes--"will not be opposed by any who have proper notions of morality" (p. 196).

Bentley, Gerald Eades. THE JACOBEAN AND CAROLINE STAGE. 7 vols. 1941-56; reprint ed. Oxford: Clarendon Press, 1949-68.

Bentley sets the general dates of 1616-42 for his work, adding a few items outside those limits, and designing the whole as a sequel to Chambers, THE ELIZABETHAN STAGE (see Chambers, E[dmund] K[erchever]). The work is an indispensable source of information within the limits set by Bentley's intention, to provide, not criticism or evaluation, but facts: titles, dates, authors, and the like. The volumes have individual titles: Volumes 1 and 2: DRAMATIC COMPANIES AND PLAYERS; Volumes 3-5: PLAYS AND PLAYWRIGHTS; Volume 6, THEATRES; Volume 7: APPENDICES TO VOLUME VI, GENERAL INDEX.

Bergeron, David M. ENGLISH CIVIC PAGEANTRY, 1558-1642. Columbia: University of South Carolina Press; London: Edward Arnold, 1971.

Bergeron calls his work an "historical reconstruction and analysis" designed for "both the specialist and the person approaching the subject of civic pageantry for the first time" (p. ix). The study has three divisions: "Progresses and Royal Entries," "The Lord Mayors' Shows," and "Pageants: Body and Soul." Illustrations. Bibliography.

Berlin, Normand. THE BASE STRING: THE UNDERWORLD IN ELIZABETHAN DRAMA. Rutherford, N.J.: Fairleigh Dickinson University, 1968.

The author concedes that a study of the plays from the standpoint of the underworld provides "only the beginning of a critical evaluation" but he regards it as "an important beginning" (p. 230). Berlin discusses chiefly Dekker, Jonson, and Shakespeare.

Bernard, Jules Eugene, Jr. THE PROSODY OF THE TUDOR INTERLUDE. New Haven, Conn.: Yale University Press; London: Oxford University Press, 1939.

A technical study of seventy-two interludes, with various useful appendices.

Bevington, David M. FROM "MANKIND" TO MARLOWE.

See main entry in Section 7 D: Studies of Medieval Drama--Morality Plays.

______. TUDOR DRAMA AND POLITICS: A CRITICAL APPROACH TO TOPICAL MEANING. Cambridge, Mass.: Harvard University Press, 1968.

Bevington discusses the anonymous morality plays and the work of Medwall, Skelton, John Heywood, Rastell, and others, to urge that drama is "generic", not personal, and that "[b]ecause dramatists looked beyond immediacies to principles, they sought the perspectives of historical pattern" (p. 301).

Blackburn, Ruth H. BIBLICAL DRAMA UNDER THE TUDORS. The Hague, Paris: Mouton Publishers, 1971.

Blackburn finds the Biblical drama to share with other Tudor drama "rugged native roots, capacity for assimilating foreign elements without being enslaved by them, deep concern with morality in the individual and society, awareness of theatrical values, and remarkable variety" (p. 193). She suggests as a probable chief cause for the demise of Biblical drama "the continuing spread of Puritanism, the deepening austerity of the Puritans" (p. 194). Bibliography.

Boas, Frederick S. AN INTRODUCTION TO STUART DRAMA. London: Oxford University Press, 1946.

A brief introduction to the chief dramatists, taken one by one, set into a general framework. Boas speaks of the book as "complet[ing] a trilogy, which began with an INTRODUCTION TO THE READING OF SHAKESPEARE in 1927, and was followed by an INTRODUCTION TO TUDOR DRAMA in 1933" (p. v). Dramatists given extended treatment are Chapman, Jonson, Marston, Dekker, T. Heywood, Webster, Tourneur, Middleton, W. Rowley, Beaumont, Fletcher, Massinger, Field, Ford, Shirley, and Brome, with concluding chapters on "Masques and University Plays" and "The Drolls--Sir William Davenant."

_____. AN INTRODUCTION TO TUDOR DRAMA. Oxford: Clarendon Press, 1933; reprint ed., with corrections, 1950.

A general introductory study in which, Boas says, he has "endeavoured to set forth briefly the broad results of recent research and criticism." He also points out that the "term 'Tudor' has been strictly interpreted" (p. [v]). Topics and authors discussed include Udall, the Inns of Court, Oxford, Cambridge, Lyly, Kyd, Marlowe, the University Wits, and others.

_____. UNIVERSITY DRAMA IN THE TUDOR AGE. Oxford: Clarendon Press, 1914.

Designed to treat the subject "on a comprehensive scale," the study deals with sources, productions, relations to the professional stage, University attitudes towards drama, and the like (pp. [iii]-v).

Boughner, Daniel C. THE BRAGGART IN RENAISSANCE COMEDY: A STUDY IN COMPARATIVE DRAMA FROM ARISTOPHANES TO SHAKESPEARE. Minneapolis: University of Minnesota Press, 1954.

The study runs from Aristophanes and Terence into the Renaissance, with a consideration of Italian, Spanish, and French, as well as English plays. Bibliography.

Bourgy, Victor. LE BOUFFON SUR LA SCENE ANGLAISE AU XVIe SIECLE (C. 1495-1594). Paris: O[ffice] C[entral] d[e] L[ibrairie], 1969.

Bourgy discusses the various types, the repertory, and the dramatic values of the bouffon. Bibliography.

Bowden, William R. THE ENGLISH DRAMATIC LYRIC, 1603-42: A STUDY IN STUART DRAMATIC TECHNIQUE. Yale Studies in English, Vol. 118. New Haven, Conn.: Yale University Press; London: Oxford University Press, 1951.

Bowden sees the song as used variously: to induce or express emotion, to provide characterization, and so on. He also suggests that whether songs occur may have been determined by factors other than dramatic theme or structure: by the interest of the playwright or the abilities of the players, for example. An appendix lists plays with songs. Bibliography.

B[ower], G[eorge] S[pencer]. A STUDY OF THE PROLOGUE AND EPILOGUE IN ENGLISH LITERATURE FROM SHAKESPEARE TO DRYDEN. London: Kegan Paul, Trench, & Co., 1884.

Bower's concern is with the vast amount of assorted information, particularly on "stage-usages," to be derived from the Prologues and Epilogues. He provides a pleasant--and relevant--side-journey for the student of drama.

Bowers, Fredson. ELIZABETHAN REVENGE TRAGEDY, 1587-1642. 1940; reprint ed. Gloucester, Mass.: Peter Smith, 1959.

A standard treatment of the subject.

Boyer, Clarence Valentine. THE VILLAIN AS HERO IN ELIZABETHAN TRAGEDY. 1914; reprint ed. New York: Russell & Russell, 1964.

Much of the discussion is centered in Marlowe, under whose influence, together with that of Seneca and Machiavelli and the general mood of the period, Boyer urges, the Aristotelean "good" man as hero is replaced by the hero-villain.

Bradbrook, M[uriel] C[lara]. THE GROWTH AND STRUCTURE OF ELIZABETHAN COMEDY. London: Chatto & Windus, 1955; Berkeley and Los Angeles: University of California Press, 1956.

The "Introduction" points out the relative dearth of critical attention to comedy. The discussion is an attempt to classify and analyze the diverse types of Elizabethan comedy. "Chronological Table of Plays," pages 207-10.

_____. THEMES AND CONVENTIONS OF ELIZABETHAN TRAGEDY. Cambridge: At the University Press, 1935; reprint ed., paperback, 1960, 1964, 1966, 1969.

The object of the book is "to discover how an Elizabethan would approach a tragedy by Chapman, Tourneur, or Middleton" (p. 1). Part I deals with such topics as "Conventions of Presentation and Acting," "Conventions of Action," "Elizabethan Habits of Reading, Writing and Listening," and "Conventions of Speech." Part II treats Marlowe, Tourneur, Webster, Middleton, and "The Decadence."

Brereton, John LeGay.

Brereton has published several small volumes of notes and essays: ELIZABETHAN DRAMATISTS. NOTES (Sydney: Sydney University Library, 1906), which I have not seen; ELIZABETHAN DRAMA. NOTES AND STUDIES (Sydney: Brooks, 1909); WRITINGS ON ELIZABETHAN DRAMA, collected by R.G. Howarth (Carlton, Victoria: Melbourne University Press, 1948). These are collections of various small pieces on individual dramatists, the theatre, and similar topics.

Briggs, K[atharine] M. THE ANATOMY OF PUCK: AN EXAMINATION OF FAIRY BELIEFS AMONG SHAKESPEARE'S CONTEMPORARIES AND SUCCESSORS. London: Routledge and Kegan Paul, 1959.

By no means a whimsical or quaint piece, but a seriously conceived study, based on the premise that "[f]undamental beliefs often betray themselves more by superstitions than by creeds" (p. 4). Much of the discussion is immediately related to drama. Bibliography.

Brodwin, Leonora Leet. ELIZABETHAN LOVE TRAGEDY, 1587-1625. New York: New York University Press, 1971; London: University of London Press, 1972.

A complex analysis, involving theme and dramatic pattern, with stimulating evaluations. Three major sections: "Tragedies of Courtly Love," "False Romantic Love," and "Tragedies of Worldly Love." There is a "Chart of Elizabethan Love Tragedies" (p. 359).

Brooke, C[harles] F[rederick] Tucker. THE TUDOR DRAMA: A HISTORY OF ENGLISH NATIONAL DRAMA TO THE RETIREMENT OF SHAKESPEARE. 1911; reprint ed. London and Hamden, Conn.: Archon Books, 1964.

Chapters on Medieval drama, the interlude, classical influences, comedy, history, realism, and the like. Even in such a broad survey and after more than half a century, Brooke's learning and insight make him worth reading.

Brown, John Russell, and Bernard Harris, eds. STRATFORD-UPON-AVON STUDIES. Nos. 1-10. Nos. 11 and following, general eds., Malcolm Bradbury and David Palmer. London: Edward Arnold; New York: St. Martin's Press, 1960--.

Each number in this series is directed to a particular topic, not always on the drama. See Section 4: Festschriften and Other Collections of Essays for an analysis of the contents of Number 1, JACOBEAN THEATRE, and Number 9, ELIZABETHAN THEATRE; see Section 7 A: Studies of Medieval Drama--Broad Approaches for an analysis of Number 16, MEDIEVAL DRAMA. Numbers 3, 8, and 14 in general deal with Shakespeare.

Buland, Mable. THE PRESENTATION OF TIME IN THE ELIZABETHAN DRAMA.

Yale Studies in English, Vol. 44. New York: H. Holt and Co., 1912.

Concerned with "[t]he double-time scheme . . . whereby two impressions are given simultaneously--one of swiftness and one of slowness" (p. 4), and with the relation of "the intricacies of time-schemes" to "constructive skill" (p. 184). Extensive appendices, pages [187]-347, provide time-scheme charts for plays of various periods.

Busby, Olive Mary. STUDIES IN THE DEVELOPMENT OF THE FOOL IN THE ELIZABETHAN DRAMA. London and New York: Oxford University Press, 1923.

This rather brief study, prepared as an MA thesis for the University of London, traces the development of the fool "from a crudely sketched personage" through his development as "a character possessing true dramatic value" and a "decay . . . not so much in quality as a decrease in quantity" (p. [85]).

Campbell, Lily B. DIVINE POETRY AND DRAMA IN SIXTEENTH CENTURY ENGLAND. Cambridge: At the University Press; Berkeley and Los Angeles: University of California Press, 1959.

Part 1 concerns poetry; Part 2, drama. The aim is to tell "a very small part" of the "story of the use of the Bible to combat the influence of the new paganism and the new secularism which accompanied the rediscovery of ancient works of literature and art" (p. vii). The assertion that the part told is small is auctorial modesty; Campbell in fact reveals a great deal about drama for a variety of audiences.

Campbell, Oscar James. COMICALL SATYRE AND SHAKESPEARE'S "TROILUS AND CRESSIDA." 1938; reprint ed. San Marino, Calif.: C.F. Braun & Co., 1970.

Exploring the thesis that certain works--EVERY MAN OUT OF HIS HUMOUR, CYNTHIAS REVELS, POETASTER, JACK DRUM'S ENTERTAINMENT, WHAT YOU WILL, and TROILUS AND CRESSIDA--were written as "plays that would serve as effective substitutes" for satires destroyed and banned "by an edict of the bishops issued on June 1, 1599" (p. vii), Campbell provides a broad view of classical and Renaissance theories of satire and an interesting interpretation of the plays mentioned.

Cardozo, Jacob Lopes. THE CONTEMPORARY JEW IN THE ELIZABETHAN DRAMA. 1925; reprint ed. New York: Burt Franklin, n.d.

The reprint is one of the Burt Franklin series, Research and Source Works Series, No. 175. Cardozo argues that Elizabethan and early Stuart playwrights had little direct contact with Jews and that the Jews in their plays are not realistic but stylized portraits, that the word "Jew" is used and readily understood in these plays as a metaphorical, not a literal, expression.

Carpenter, Frederic Ives. METAPHOR AND SIMILE IN THE MINOR ELIZABETHAN DRAMA. Chicago: University of Chicago Press, 1895.

Carpenter argues that the minor Elizabethan drama, deficient in many ways, nevertheless represents "the most vital and the most popular form of literature existing in its day" and "presents an imaginative transcript of life . . . reflected in the metaphor and simile employed in the drama" (pp. 212-13). The technique of analyzing metaphor has, of course, altered a good deal since Carpenter published this doctoral dissertation in 1895.

Cawley, Robert Ralston. UNPATHED WATERS: STUDIES IN THE INFLUENCE OF THE VOYAGERS ON ELIZABETHAN LITERATURE. Princeton, N.J.: Princeton University Press; London: Oxford University Press, 1940.

See next entry.

______. THE VOYAGERS AND ELIZABETHAN DRAMA. 1938; reprint ed. New York: Kraus Reprint Corp., 1966.

These are companion volumes. THE VOYAGERS collects large quantities of information on voyaging and its impact on literature, especially the drama; UNPATHED WATERS draws "conclusions and inferences" (p. [vii], UNPATHED WATERS). Bibliography.

Chambers, E[dmund] K[erchever]. THE ELIZABETHAN STAGE. 4 vols. Oxford: Clarendon Press, 1923; reprint ed. 1945, with corrections, 1951, 1961, 1965, 1967.

Books 1 and 2 deal with the Elizabethan Court and "the settlement of the players in London," Books 3 and 4 with "the fortunes of the individual playing companies and the individual theatres," and Book 5 "with the surviving plays . . . as documents helping to throw light upon the history of the institution which produced them" (Vol. 1, pp. [vii]-viii). While later scholarship has suggested some revisions, for instance in hypothesized dates, Chambers provides a body of fact which must be consulted constantly. Chambers expresses regret at not having included the period from the death of Shakespeare to the closing of the theatres, a gap which Bentley, in THE JACOBEAN AND CAROLINE STAGE (see Bentley, Gerald Eades), has now filled. To say that Chambers provides bibliography is to offer an understatement. See White, Beatrice, comp., for AN INDEX providing useful aid in finding one's way in Chambers.

Chapman, J[ohn] K., ed. A COMPLETE HISTORY OF THEATRICAL ENTERTAINMENTS, DRAMAS, MASQUES, AND TRIUMPHS, AT THE ENGLISH COURT, FROM THE TIME OF KING HENRY THE EIGHTH TO THE PRESENT DAY, INCLUDING THE SERIES OF PLAYS PERFORMED BEFORE HER MAJESTY AT WINDSOR CASTLE, CHRISTMAS, 1848-9. CONTAINING MANY CURIOUS PARTICULARS OF OUR EARLY DRAMATIC LITERATURE AND ART. EMBELLISHED WITH BEAUTIFUL ENGRAVINGS ON STEEL, BY FINDEN, FROM

DESIGNS BY GRIEVE, TELBIN, AND ABSOLON. London: John Mitchell, [1849?].

The "Curious Particulars" are compressed into fewer than a hundred pages.

Charlton, H.B. THE SENECAN TRADITION IN RENAISSANCE TRAGEDY. 1921; reprint ed. Manchester: Manchester University Press, 1946.

The study treats the Senecan tradition in Italy, France, and England.

Clarkson, Paul S., and Clyde T. Warren. THE LAW OF PROPERTY IN SHAKESPEARE AND THE ELIZABETHAN DRAMA. Baltimore, Md.: Johns Hopkins Press, 1942.

The authors are lawyers who have read a vast array of Elizabethan dramatists and have proceeded to "group and discuss all legal allusions by all the playwrights surveyed according to legal subject matters" (p. xxiv). Pleasantly written. Fully indexed.

Clemen, Wolfgang [H.]. ENGLISH TRAGEDY BEFORE SHAKESPEARE: THE DEVELOPMENT OF DRAMATIC SPEECH. Trans. T.S. Dorsch. London: Methuen & Co., 1961.

Clemen's work was originally published in 1955, in German, with the title DIE TRAGODIE VOR SHAKESPEARE: IHRE ENTWICKLUNG IN SPEIGEL DER DRAMATISCHEN REDE. Clemen studies the development of the "set speech," that is, "any continuous spoken passage that stands out noticeably from the general run of the dialogue by reason of its length and structure, its theme, or its significance" (p. 12), as a means of studying the development of dramatic skill.

Colby, Elbridge. ENGLISH CATHOLIC POETS: CHAUCER TO DRYDEN. 1936; reprint ed. Freeport, N.Y.: Books for Libraries, 1967.

Colby proposes "to record the noteworthy Catholic elements found in a reading of those early authors whose writings are universally accepted as part of the canon of classic English letters" (p. xv). John Heywood, Marlowe, Lodge, Jonson, Shakespeare, Shirley, Massinger, and D'Avenant are among his subjects.

Cope, Jackson I. THE THEATER AND THE DREAM: FROM METAPHOR TO FORM IN RENAISSANCE DRAMA. Baltimore and London: Johns Hopkins Press, 1973.

Cope draws upon Renaissance and modern sources to formulate a complex analysis of dramatic form, with extended discussion of Chapman and Jonson among others. He says: "Ultimately . . . this book offers itself as a critical history of dramatic form in the Renaissance" (p. 13).

Cowling, George Herbert. MUSIC ON THE SHAKESPEARIAN STAGE. 1913; reprint ed. New York: Russell & Russell, 1964.

Cowling attempts to assemble "the musical stage-directions" and "to force them to show their own conclusions" about "what kinds of music were used during a play, and when and how the music was performed." The work "concludes by attempting to estimate critically the artistic worth of music to the stage" (p. [1]). Cowling does not automatically assume that the music has dramatic relevance--see, for example, Chapter 6. Ten plates. Bibliography in three divisions, "Books concerning Music and the Stage," "Books concerning Elizabethan Music," and "Reprints of Elizabethan Music."

Craik, T.W. THE TUDOR INTERLUDE: STAGE, COSTUME, AND ACTING. Leicester: At the University Press, 1958.

The "Foreword" is by M.C. Bradbrook. The study, focused on performance, has chapters on "The Setting," "The Performers," "Dress," "Changes of Costume," and "Action." Bibliography.

Cunliffe, John W. THE INFLUENCE OF SENECA ON ELIZABETHAN TRAGEDY. 1893; reprint ed. New York: G.E. Stechert, 1907.

To support the conclusion that "[t]he influence of Seneca was paramount in English tragedy till far into the eighteenth century" (p. 124), Cunliffe examines the work of Kyd, Marlowe, Peele, Greene, Shakespeare, Jonson, Chapman, Marston, Chettle, Dekker, Webster, Tourneur, Ford, Beaumont and Fletcher, Massinger, Shirley, and others; he also discusses a number of anonymous plays.

Cunningham, John E. ELIZABETHAN AND EARLY STUART DRAMA. Literature in Perspective. London: Evans Brothers, 1965.

The series "Literature in Perspective" is published with the expectation "that each book will be easily understood [and] that it will adequately describe its subject without pretentiousness" (see the general note prefixed to the volume). Cunningham provides a brief discussion of Marlowe, Kyd, Jonson, Beaumont and Fletcher, and Webster, with a "General Introduction" and a final chapter, "The Last Phase," touching on several additional authors. Bibliography.

Curry, John V. DECEPTION IN ELIZABETHAN COMEDY. Chicago: Loyola University Press, 1955.

Curry sees deception as having various "structural and functional uses" (p. 167). He considers the natures of the deceiver and the gull and also the question of "audience appeal."

Cutts, John P. LA MUSIQUE DE SCENE DE LA TROUPE DE SHAKESPEARE.

THE KING'S MEN SOUS LE REGNE DE JACQUE Ier. Collection le Choeur des Muses. Paris: Editions du Centre National de la Recherche Scientifique, 1959.

The music itself is here printed, with careful descriptions of the songs, providing a very useful edition of the songs of this particular group.

Davis, Joe Lee. THE SONS OF BEN: JONSONIAN COMEDY IN CAROLINE ENGLAND. Detroit: Wayne State University Press, 1967.

Davis identifies the Sons of Ben as "a somewhat heterogeneous group . . . Richard Brome, William Cartwright, William Cavendish, William Davenant, Henry Glapthorne, Peter Hausted, Thomas Killigrew, Shackerley Marmion, Jasper Mayne, Thomas Nabbes, and Thomas Randolph." His study of "their thirty-two comedies . . . is addressed to the general reader and non-specialized student." It is designed to be "humanistic rather than antiquarian" and to supply "an adequate historical background" (p. 8). Bibliography.

Donaldson, Ian. THE WORLD UPSIDE-DOWN: COMEDY FROM JONSON TO FIELDING. Oxford: Clarendon Press, 1970.

Donaldson studies the "topos of mundus inversus," arguing that a study of comedy in the light of the mundus inversus figure provides "one way of tracing the continuity of a variety of comic traditions, problems, and techniques from the time of Ben Jonson to that of Henry Fielding" (pp. 21-23). Not all the evidence is drawn from drama, but Jonson's EPICOENE and BARTHOLOMEW FAIR and Brome's THE ANTIPODES are studied at some length.

Doran, Madeleine. ENDEAVORS OF ART: A STUDY OF FORM IN ELIZABETHAN DRAMA. Madison: University of Wisconsin Press, 1954; reprint ed. 1963.

The "Preface" calls the book "an essay in historical criticism . . . based on the premise that to know and understand the frame of artistic reference within which the practising dramatists of the Elizabethan and Jacobean periods worked is to understand better their artistic achievement" (p. v). Various appendices, including "'Tragedy' and 'Comedy' in Tudor and Early Stuart Dictionaries." This is a study of considerable renown.

ELIZABETHAN STUDIES.

See SALZBURG STUDIES IN ENGLISH LITERATURE.

Ellis-Fermor, U[na] M. THE JACOBEAN DRAMA: AN INTERPRETATION. 4th ed., rev. London: Methuen & Co., 1958.

Ellis-Fermor's long-famous study deals particularly with Chapman,

Marston, Jonson, Dekker, Middleton, Tourneur, Webster, Greville, Beaumont and Fletcher, and Ford. There are "Biographical Notes" and "Book Lists."

Ellison, Lee Monroe. THE EARLY ROMANTIC DRAMA AT THE ENGLISH COURT. Menaska, Wis.: Collegiate Press, George Banta, 1917.

Ellison's published dissertation is a study of "the survival of mediaeval literary conventions in the sixteenth century court drama" (p. vi).

Erskine, John. THE ELIZABETHAN LYRIC. New York: Columbia University Press, 1903.

Chapter 8, pages 244-74, considers "The Lyric in the Drama," touching on the Mystery plays, RALPH ROISTER DOISTER, LUSTY JUVENTUS, GORBODUC, GAMMER GURTON'S NEEDLE, and plays by Lyly, Peele, Nashe, Kyd, Dekker, Shakespeare, Jonson, Beaumont and Fletcher.

Fairholt, Frederick W. LORD MAYORS' PAGEANTS: BEING COLLECTIONS TOWARDS A HISTORY OF THESE ANNUAL CELEBRATIONS, WITH SPECIMENS OF THE DESCRIPTIVE PAMPHLETS PUBLISHED BY THE CITY POETS. Percy Society Publications, Vol. 10. London: Printed for the Percy Society by T. Richards, 1843-44.

Part I, HISTORY OF LORD MAYORS' PAGEANTS (1843), and Part II, REPRINTS OF LORD MAYORS' PAGEANTS (1844), are bound in one volume with separate title pages and pagination. The Lord Mayors' Pageants represent a curious by-way in the history of drama, and Fairholt's material is worth looking into even if one does not wish to dwell long with these ephemera.

Farnham, Willard. THE MEDIEVAL HERITAGE OF ELIZABETHAN TRAGEDY. 1936; reprint ed. Oxford: Basil Blackwell, 1956, 1963.

Much has been done in the field of Medieval drama since Farnham first said of the mystery plays that they represent "a commemorative folk drama" composed "with little more than the unstudied simplicity and the casual art of the folk ballad" (p. 174). His study of "a consistently developing tragic spirit as it found more than one specialized form of artistic and critical approach to the mystery of man's suffering on earth" (p. xi) offers insights of continuing value, however.

Feldman, Sylvia D. THE MORALITY-PATTERNED COMEDY OF THE RENAISSANCE. De Proprietatibus Litterarum edenda curat C.H. Van Schooneveld, Series Practica, No. 12. The Hague and Paris: Mouton Publishers, 1970.

Feldman quotes Charles Mills Gayley (ed.), "An Historical View of the Beginnings of English Comedy," REPRESENTATIVE ENGLISH COMEDIES (see Section 2 B: Editions--Miscellaneous Medieval and Tudor Plays), for the thesis that the morality play, with its concern with "'the vicissitudes of the conflict and the certainty of peace'" led the way to comedy (Feldman, pp. 8-9). She draws upon a large number of plays in making her case. Bibliography.

Fenton, Doris. THE EXTRA-DRAMATIC MOMENT IN ELIZABETHAN PLAYS BEFORE 1616. Philadelphia: University of Pennsylvania, 1930.

The "extra-dramatic moment" of the title is that moment "in which . . . consciousness of the audience is openly expressed" through "a stepping out of the world of make-believe into that of reality" (p. 8). Especially in view of the return in modern drama to a complex view of real and make-believe, the study provides an interesting basis for critical speculation. Fenton provides a "List of Plays, Written, Acted, or Printed Between 1558 and 1616, Which Contain Passages Directly Recognizing the Audience."

Feuillerat, Albert. LE BUREAU DES MENUS-PLAISIRS (OFFICE OF THE REVELS) ET LA MISE EN SCENE A LA COUR D'ELIZABETH. THESE PRESENTE A LA FACULTE DES LETTRES DE L'UNIVERSITE DE RENNES. Louvain: A. Uystpruyst, 1910.

Feuillerat outlines the history of the Revels office and argues its influence on the "mise en scene au XVIe siecle."

Fleay, Frederick Gard. A BIOGRAPHICAL CHRONICLE OF THE ENGLISH DRAMA, 1559-1642. 2 vols. 1891; reprint ed. New York: Burt Franklin, 1969.

Fleay provides an "Introduction" and an "Excursus on the 'Mirror for Magistrates'" before he begins the "Biographies of the Playwrights: 1557-1642." The biographies are followed by discussions of anonymous plays and masks, "University Plays," "Translations," "Addenda," "Index," a "Table of Authors who Wrote for more than One Company," and finally an "Afterword." See also the annotation for the next entry.

______. A CHRONICLE HISTORY OF THE LONDON STAGE, 1559-1642. 1890; reprint ed. New York: C.E. Stechert & Co., 1909.

The book is divided into time periods: 1559-86, 1587-93, and so on. Within each there are sections headed "Introduction," "Court Performances," "Companies," "Theatres," "Authors," "General Stage History"; and in some divisions there are "Intercalatory" sections and an "Appendix." Fleay offers a monumental collection of material, organized so that it can be recovered and providing a foundation for much that has come after him. He must be read with a little caution, however, since information which has come to light since he worked alters some of his conclusions. Indeed, E.K. Chambers, who in his "List of Authorities" (see THE ELIZABETHAN STAGE, Vol. I, pp. [xv]-xli) takes no very charitable view of some of his predecessors, says of these two and other volumes by Fleay: "Some new ground was broken by F.G. Fleay, who gave real stimulus to investigation by the series of hasty generalizations and unstable hypotheses contained in [various works]" (p. [xv]).

Foxon, D[avid] F. THOMAS J. WISE AND THE PRE-RESTORATION DRAMA: A STUDY IN THEFT AND SOPHISTICATION. Supplement to the Bibliographical Society's Publications No. 19. London: Bibliographical Society, 1959.

A careful account of a curious literary theft, in which Wise stole from one copy of certain valuable books leaves lacking in other copies and used these leaves to make up presumably "perfect" copies from the defective volumes. That Wise had a fancy for stealing from copies of plays gives him relevance to the study of the drama.

Freehafer, John. "John Warburton's Lost Plays." STUDIES IN BIBLIOGRAPHY: PAPERS OF THE BIBLIOGRAPHICAL SOCIETY OF THE UNIVERSITY OF VIRGINIA, 23 (1970), 154-64.

Warburton's famous story of having owned copies of plays which were inadvertently destroyed by his cook has generally been discredited. (See Greg, W[alter] W[ilson], "The Bakings of Betsy," reprinted in his COLLECTED PAPERS, entered here under Section 4: Festschriften and Other Collections of Essays.) Freehafer believes that his own "new examination of Warburton's list, memorandum, sale catalogue, and surviving manuscripts suggests that Warburton's list and memorandum record plays that he owned or information that he believed to be correct" and that "a study of his statements and collection . . . could add considerably to existing knowledge of the finest period of English drama" (p.164). The article serves as a reminder that we ought not to leap too readily to the conclusion that a subject is closed to further investigation.

Frey, Albert R. SOBRIQUETS AND NICKNAMES. Boston and New York: Houghton, Mifflin; Cambridge: Riverside Press, 1887.

From Frey's alphabetical lists we can learn the identity of the Merry Devil of Edmonton and hundreds more and also discover not only such sobriquets for Jonson as "Father Ben," "Old Ben," "Rare Ben," but for Elizabeth I, "Astraea," "Belphoebe," and "The Untamed Heifer."

Frost, David L. THE SCHOOL OF SHAKESPEARE: THE INFLUENCE OF SHAKESPEARE ON ENGLISH DRAMA, 1600-42. Cambridge and London: Cambridge University Press, 1968.

The question of the direction of influence between Shakespeare on the one hand and certain contemporaries (Beaumont and Fletcher in particular) on the other, has been variously argued. Frost holds "that both Marston and Beaumont and Fletcher took advantage of

[Shakespeare's] success rather than inspired any new departure" (p. 246) but that "Webster and Ford seem both to reject the Shakespearean type of tragedy" (p. 247). Bibliography.

Gagen, Jean Elisabeth. THE NEW WOMAN: HER EMERGENCE IN ENGLISH DRAMA, 1600-1730. New York: Twayne Publishers, 1954.

The study treats drama before 1660 briefly. Bibliography.

Gerrard, Ernest A. ELIZABETHAN DRAMA AND DRAMATISTS, 1583-1603. Oxford: At the University Press, 1928.

In Part 1, Gerrard argues that Shakespeare did not belong to "Lord Strange's men from 1592 to 1594" or to the Lord Chamberlain's in 1594-97 and therefore that "none of the Strange nor Chamberlain plays written from 1592 to 1597 were written by Shakespeare." In the "various Chamberlain plays . . . printed after 1597" as Shakespeare's, Gerrard argues that Shakespeare's part took the form of "corrections and additions" (p. [376]). Part 2 is then concerned with finding authors for these plays.

Gibbons, Brian. JACOBEAN CITY COMEDY: A STUDY OF SATIRIC PLAYS OF JONSON, MARSTON, AND MIDDLETON. Cambridge, Mass.: Harvard University Press, 1968.

Defining his subject as "satiric" plays with "urban settings" deriving in form from "the medieval Morality" and from "the Tudor Interlude" and dating between 1597 and 1616 (pp. 24-25), Gibbon sees these plays as rooted in world views in conflict, asserting that they take their "essential dynamic" from "the conflict between order and authority on the one hand, and intelligently aggressive insubordination on the other" (p. 202). Bibliography.

Gildersleeve, Virginia C. GOVERNMENT REGULATION OF THE ELIZABETHAN DRAMA. Columbia University Studies in English, Series 2, Vol. 4, No. 1. 1908; reprint ed. New York: Burt Franklin, 1961.

This reprint is Number 23 in the Burt Franklin Research and Source Works Series. Its presentation of the material is made in six major divisions: "National Regulation," "The Master of the Revels," "The Nature of the Censorship," "Local Regulations in London, 1543-1592," "Local Regulations in London, 1592-1642," "The Puritan Victory." The aim, to collect "the government regulations of the drama under the Tudors and the early Stuarts . . . in complete and orderly form" (p. 1), is well realized.

Gotch, J[ohn] Alfred. INIGO JONES. London: Methuen & Co., 1928.

Gotch provides an extensive treatment of the masque, with thirty-four illustrations. He endeavors to be objective in such matters as the Jones-Jonson quarrel.

Green, A. Wigfall. THE INNS OF COURT AND EARLY ENGLISH DRAMA. New Haven, Conn.: Yale University Press; London: Oxford University Press, 1931.

Green studies an aspect of the development of drama not always sufficiently taken into account.

Greenfield, Thelma N. THE INDUCTION IN ELIZABETHAN DRAMA. Eugene: University of Oregon Books, 1969.

Greenfield studies the forms which inductions take, their frequency of occurrence, their use, especially in establishing the relation of actor to audience, and what they reveal of the dramatist's "attitudes toward his art" (p. 150). Appendix 2 provides "A List of Plays with Inductions."

Greg, Walter W[ilson]. PASTORAL POETRY & PASTORAL DRAMA: A LITERARY INQUIRY, WITH SPECIAL REFERENCE TO THE PRE-RESTORATION STAGE IN ENGLAND. 1906; reprint ed. New York: Russell & Russell, 1959.

Greg discusses the origin, rise, and decline of the pastoral drama and analyzes three plays which he considers masterpieces: THE FAITHFUL SHEPHERDESS (Fletcher), AMYNTAS (Randolph), and THE SAD SHEPHERD (Jonson). Bibliography.

Harbage, Alfred. CAVALIER DRAMA: AN HISTORICAL AND CRITICAL SUPPLEMENT TO THE STUDY OF THE ELIZABETHAN AND RESTORATION STAGE. New York: Modern Language Association of America; London: Oxford University Press, 1936.

Directing his study particularly "to illustrating the continuity of an English literary tradition," Harbage points out that what was in 1936 "modern" scholarship has shown "that the interruption effected by Puritan rule was less complete than used generally to be supposed" (p. 1) and finally speculates that even if the theatres had not been closed, the development of English drama would have been substantially the same, because he sees a "natural progression from the dramatic types familiar before 1642 toward the two most conspicuous types of the Restoration--Drydenesque heroic tragedy and Etheregean social comedy" (p. 255). Harbage provides, pages 259-85, "A List, Chronologically Arranged of All Plays of the Caroline, Commonwealth, and Early Restoration Periods." See also the next two entries, concerned largely with Shakespeare but also useful for the Elizabethan theatre generally, especially on theatre management and audiences.

_____. SHAKESPEARE AND THE RIVAL TRADITIONS. New York: Macmillan, 1952.

_____. SHAKESPEARE'S AUDIENCE. New York: Columbia University Press, 1941.

Harrison, G[eorge] B[agshawe]. ELIZABETHAN PLAYS AND PLAYERS. London: G. Routledge and Sons, 1940; Ann Arbor: University of Michigan Press, 1956.

The study is designed "to show something of the world in which Elizabethan players and dramatists worked," the complex world of "Burbage, the Chamberlain's Men, the Globe Theatre, the Stage War, the melancholy of the generation, and the whole turmoil of life" (p. [vii]).

_____. SHAKESPEARE'S FELLOWS. BEING A BRIEF CHRONICLE OF THE SHAKESPEAREAN AGE. London: John Lane, The Bodley Head Ltd., 1923.

The book is "intended as a brief introduction to the study of the personal side of Elizabethan drama," assembling in "one place much that is widely scattered" ("Preface"). There are chapters on "Stage and University," "Greene and Marlowe," "The Chamberlain's and the Admiral's," "Poetomachia," and "The New Generation." Harrison insists that the book represents collection rather than discovery, but the author is a very knowledgeable collector.

_____. THE STORY OF ELIZABETHAN DRAMA. Cambridge: At the University Press, 1924.

The book, "written for those who have not hitherto become acquainted with the Elizabethan dramatists" ("Preface"), discusses in particular Kyd, Marlowe, Greene, Shakespeare, and Jonson.

Hawkins, Harriett. LIKENESSES OF TRUTH IN ELIZABETHAN AND RESTORATION DRAMA. Oxford: Clarendon Press, 1972.

A "survey of dramatic perspectives in a number of Elizabethan and Jacobean plays, and in three Restoration comedies," the study argues that the truths of these plays "are not just imaginative visions of reality, but that they are truths about human experience . . . explored and exhibited in different ways by different kinds of artists" (p. [ix]).

Hazlitt, William. LECTURES ON THE ENGLISH POETS, AND THE ENGLISH COMIC WRITERS. Ed. William Carew Hazlitt. London: George Bell and Sons, 1884.

The section THE ENGLISH COMIC WRITERS contains "On Wit and Humour" and "On Shakspeare and Ben Jonson."

_____. LECTURES ON THE LITERATURE OF THE AGE OF ELIZABETH, AND CHARACTERS OF SHAKESPEAR'S PLAYS. London: George Bell and Sons, 1878.

A series of eight lectures, most of them on drama.

Herndl, George C. THE HIGH DESIGN: ENGLISH RENAISSANCE TRAGEDY AND THE NATURAL LAW. Lexington: University Press of Kentucky, 1970.

Herndl attempts to account for the development and disappearance of the school of great Renaissance tragedy through the thesis that a "certain, originally medieval, conception of the natural law was vital in Elizabethan tragedy." Under the influence of Calvin, Bacon, and Descartes, "the old conviction of the natural law" disappeared, taking the great age of tragedy with it (p. 10).

Herrick, Marvin T. COMIC THEORY IN THE SIXTEENTH CENTURY. Illinois Studies in Language and Literature, Vol. 34, Nos. 1-2. 1950; reprint ed., paperback, Urbana: University of Illinois Press, 1964.

Herrick argues that for the sixteenth century "Donatus and the Terentian commentators of the fifteenth and sixteenth centuries, with aid from Horace, Cicero, Quintillian, and other rhetoricians, provided a satisfactory theory of comedy" (p. 224) which was "an intellectual theory emphasizing a strict decorum" and "the philosophical lessons in human conduct to be gained from literary comedy" (p. 226). Bibliography.

_____. ITALIAN COMEDY IN THE RENAISSANCE. Urbana: University of Illinois Press, 1960.

The study is designed to provide both students and novice teachers with "the proper background for a better understanding of the dramaturgy of Shakespeare, Jonson, Chapman, Marston, Middleton, and other English writers of Comedy" (p. [v]). Bibliography.

_____. TRAGICOMEDY: ITS ORIGIN AND DEVELOPMENT IN ITALY, FRANCE, AND ENGLAND. Illinois Studies in Language and Literature, Vol. 39. 1955; reprint ed. Urbana: University of Illinois, 1962.

Herrick offers a broad survey, from "The Classical Background" to "The Aftermath of Tragicomedy." Bibliography.

Hogg, James, ed.

See SALZBURG STUDIES IN ENGLISH LITERATURE.

Hogrefe, Pearl. THE SIR THOMAS MORE CIRCLE: A PROGRAM OF IDEAS AND THEIR IMPACT ON SECULAR DRAMA. Urbana: University of Illinois Press, 1959.

Part 1 treats "the main ideas which More and his friends wished to use for the reform of society," under such topics as "Nature and the Law of Nature," "The Bases of True Nobility," "Religious Reform," "Law and Government," "Education in General," and "Education of Women: Love and Marriage" (see pp. 6-7 for an outline of Part 1). Part 2 treats the same topics in the context of the drama. Among the dramatists considered are Henry Medwall, John

Rastell, and, as a printer of plays, his son, William Rastell, John Heywood, and John Redford, with other playwrights sometimes drawn into the discussion.

Hotson, Leslie. COMMONWEALTH AND RESTORATION STAGE. Cambridge, Mass.: Harvard University Press, 1928.

Valuable for material, much of it of Hotson's finding, on the Commonwealth stage, when officially there was no stage.

Hussey, Maurice. THE WORLD OF SHAKESPEARE AND HIS CONTEMPORARIES: A VISUAL APPROACH. London: Heinemann, 1971.

The book is designed "as an unusual and attractive step towards the understanding of some of the best-known plays of Shakespeare, Marlowe, and Jonson" and others through illustrations chosen to reveal "some of the common assumptions of educated people in Tudor and Stuart England" (p. vii). The stress is on the visual. The comment may be not much more than a caption identifying the picture; for example, there is a picture of Chaucer on page 114, with the remark: "Jonson highly revered Chaucer." Bibliography.

Irving, David. THE LIVES OF THE SCOTISH POETS, WITH PRELIMINARY DISSERTATIONS ON THE LITERARY HISTORY OF SCOTLAND AND THE EARLY SCOTISH DRAMA. 2nd ed. 2 vols. London: B. Crosby & Co.; Longman, Hurst, Rees, & Orme, 1810.

Title annotates.

JACOBEAN DRAMA STUDIES.

See SALZBURG STUDIES IN ENGLISH LITERATURE.

Jewkes, Wilfred T. ACT-DIVISION IN ELIZABETHAN AND JACOBEAN PLAYS, 1583-1616. Hamden, Conn.: Shoe String Press, 1958.

By examining "the bibliographical and textual history of two hundred and thirty-six printed plays which survive from the period 1583-1616" ("Preface"), Jewkes concludes that it was the practice of "university men" to divide their plays into acts, whereas the early public theatre practice was not to make divisions, a practice which gave way to act division later in the period under discussion (pp. 102-3). See pages 337-53 for a "Table of the Textual Origin and Act Division of All Plays Acted between 1583 and 1616."

Jones, Eldred. OTHELLO'S COUNTRYMEN: THE AFRICAN IN ENGLISH RENAISSANCE DRAMA. London: Oxford University Press for Fourah Bay College, the University of Sierra Leone, 1965.

Jones provides an examination of "the background of knowledge available to playwrights through works published during the sixteenth and early seventeenth centuries, and the use they made of such knowledge in their plays," with two useful appendices: a "Chart of Plays, Masques and Pageants involving African Characters" and a two-part bibliography, "Early Printed Books on Geography, History, and Travel" and "Select List of General Works and Editions of Plays and Masques."

Kastner, L.E., and H.B. Charlton, eds. THE POETICAL WORKS OF SIR WILLIAM ALEXANDER, EARL OF STIRLING. Vol. 1. Scottish Text Society, New Series, Vol. 11. Edinburgh and London: Printed for the Society by William Blackwood and Sons, 1921.

Kastner and Charlton supply an "Introductory Essay on the Growth of the Senecan Tradition in Renaissance Tragedy," which is almost 200 pages long and which provides a discussion of "the Senecan Tradition" in Italy, France, and England.

Kerr, Mina. INFLUENCE OF BEN JONSON ON ENGLISH COMEDY, 1598-1642. New York: University of Pennsylvania, D. Appleton, Agents, 1912.

Kerr argues that the pervasive influence of Jonson's theory and practice came, for his "immediate contemporaries," chiefly through "his theory of humors and his ideal of constructive excellence" (p. 120).

Kingsley, Charles. WORKS, Vol. 16: PLAYS AND PURITANS AND OTHER HISTORICAL ESSAYS. London: Macmillan, 1880.

In a longish essay, Kingsley treats sympathetically the Puritan antipathy for plays.

Kirsch, Arthur C. JACOBEAN DRAMATIC PERSPECTIVES. Charlottesville: University Press of Virginia, 1972.

Kirsch sees "the harmonies of plays written on Shakespearian principles and those written on Fletcherian principles" as "different both in kind and dimension" (p. 127). He explores the relation of dramatic development to world view, not only discussing Shakespeare and Fletcher but also giving extended consideration to Jonson, Marston, Ford, Beaumont, Middleton, and Webster.

Knights, L.C. DRAMA & SOCIETY IN THE AGE OF JONSON. 1937; reprint ed. New York: Barnes & Noble, 1968.

Knights provides "a study of economic conditions and the drama, in conjunction, in order to throw light on . . . the relation between economic activities and general culture" (p. ix). He discusses Shakespeare, Jonson, Dekker, Thomas Heywood, Massinger, and Middleton in particular, together with a number of others treated less extensively.

Kokeritz, Helge. SHAKESPEARE'S PRONUNCIATION. New Haven, Conn.: Yale University Press, 1953.

As the "Preface," page vi, points out, the rules for Shakespeare's pronunciation here promulgated can be carried over to the works of his contemporaries. There is a phonograph record, made by Kokeritz, entitled SHAKESPEARE'S PRONUNCIATION: A SELECTION OF PASSAGES FROM SHAKESPEARE AS SPOKEN IN THE POET'S TIME, Yale University Press (TV 19232), which illustrates the pronunciation advocated in the printed text.

Koskenniemi, Inna. STUDIES IN THE VOCABULARY OF THE ENGLISH DRAMA 1550-1600, EXCLUDING SHAKESPEARE AND BEN JONSON. Annales Universitatis Turkuensis, sarja B., osa 84. Turku. Turun Yliopisto, 1962.

A study of "certain types of words and phrases" from the standpoints of "word formation and phraseology" and of "style and dramatic characterization" (p. [9]).

[Lamb, Charles]. THE ART OF THE STAGE AS SET OUT IN LAMB'S DRAMATIC ESSAYS, WITH A COMMENTARY BY PERCY FITZGERALD. London: Remington & Co., 1885.

Lamb comments briefly on a number of Shakespeare's contemporaries; Fitzgerald comments further, often to refute Lamb's position.

Lanier, Sidney. THE CENTENNIAL EDITION OF THE WORKS. Ed. Kemp Malone. Vol. 3: SHAKSPERE AND HIS FORERUNNERS. Baltimore, Md.: Johns Hopkins Press, 1945.

Lanier supplies a good deal on Shakespeare, includes some dramatists among the forerunners, and indulges in some poetic license.

Lea, Kathleen M. ITALIAN POPULAR COMEDY: A STUDY IN THE COMMEDIA DELL'ARTE, 1560-1620, WITH SPECIAL REFERENCE TO THE ENGLISH STAGE. 2 vols. 1934; reprint ed. New York: Russell & Russell, 1962.

See especially Volume 2, THE CONTACTS AND COMPARISONS WITH ELIZABETHAN DRAMA.

Lever, J[ulius] W[alter]. THE TRAGEDY OF STATE. London: Methuen & Co., 1971.

The book, made up of lectures delivered at Simon Fraser University in 1970, is concerned with the contemporary relevance of certain Renaissance plays and with the producer's ways of dealing with them. The discussion centers on ANTONIO'S REVENGE, THE REVENGER'S TRAGEDY, the "Bussy" plays, SEJANUS, CAESAR AND POMPEY, THE WHITE DEVIL, and THE DUCHESS OF MALFI.

Levin, Richard. THE MULTIPLE PLOT IN ENGLISH RENAISSANCE DRAMA. Chicago and London: University of Chicago, 1971.

Levin classifies a great number of multiple-plot plays as to type and analyzes their artistic effectiveness. Bibliography.

Lindabury, Richard Vliet. A STUDY OF PATRIOTISM IN THE ELIZABETHAN DRAMA. Princeton, N.J.: Princeton University Press; London: Oxford University Press, 1931.

Lindabury challenges the assumption that Elizabethan drama "profited" by its "stamp of Elizabethan patriotism" (p. vii).

Long, John H., ed. MUSIC IN ENGLISH RENAISSANCE DRAMA. Lexington: University of Kentucky Press, 1968.

The essays are: Nan Cooke Carpenter, "Music in the English Mystery Plays"; Ernest Brennecke, "The Entertainment at Elvetham, 1591"; Ian Spink, "Campion's Entertainment at Brougham Castle, 1617"; R.W. Ingram, "Patterns of Music and Action in Fletcherian Drama"; MacDonald Emslie, "Milton on Lawes: The Trinity MS Revision"; Willa McClung Evans, "Cartwright's Debt to Lawes"; Vincent Duckles, "The Music for the Lyrics in Early Seventeenth-Century English Drama: A Bibliography of Primary Sources." Special attention might be directed to the last article, a useful bibliography.

Lucas, F[rank] L. SENECA AND ELIZABETHAN TRAGEDY. Cambridge: At the University Press, 1922.

Lucas believes that Seneca taught the Elizabethans "the Classic sense of form and structure, of Unity," as well as "the tragic splendour of Human Will in the face of eyeless Destiny," and other Greek and Roman attitudes (pp. 132-33).

McDonald, Charles Osborne. THE RHETORIC OF TRAGEDY: FORM IN STUART DRAMA. Amherst: University of Massachusetts Press, 1966.

Probing "the influences of the modes of rhetorical instruction used in fifth century B.C. Greece, First Century A.D. Rome, and Sixteenth and Seventeenth Century A.D. England upon the form of tragic drama," McDonald argues that dramatists were schooled by rhetoric to regard an issue "as a proposition having mutually contradictory answers" capable of expression through "a variety of characters from heroes to villains" (p. v). Rhetorical Index.

McGinn, Donald Joseph. SHAKESPEARE'S INFLUENCE ON THE DRAMA OF HIS AGE STUDIED IN "HAMLET." New Brunswick, N.J.: Rutgers University Press, 1938.

Part 1 studies the influence of HAMLET on other plays of the period. Part 2 contains "Allusions to HAMLET from 1600 to 1642."

Mackenzie, Agnes Mure. THE PLAYGOER'S HANDBOOK TO THE ENGLISH

RENAISSANCE DRAMA. New York: Macmillan, n.d.

Mackenzie proposes to treat the Elizabethan plays as plays rather than as literature, writing for "those like myself, plain men and women without claim to scholarship and with a considerable objection to highbrows and such vermin of the arts" (p. 10).

Manifold, John S. THE MUSIC IN ENGLISH DRAMA, FROM SHAKESPEARE TO PURCELL. London: Rockliff, 1956.

Manifold provides a book "about the musical resources and the theatrical convention . . . and the way the two things interact" (p. vii). Bibliography.

Margeson, J.M.R. THE ORIGINS OF ENGLISH TRAGEDY. Oxford: Clarendon Press, 1967.

Margeson undertakes "an inquiry into the origins of tragedy on the medieval and Elizabethan stages and into the different kinds of tragedy which that theatre produced" (p. [vii]). Bibliography.

Matthews, Honor. THE PRIMAL CURSE: THE MYTH OF CAIN AND ABEL IN THE THEATRE. London: Chatto & Windus; New York: Schocken Books, 1967.

Part 1, "The Myth of Cain and Abel in the Theatre of an Ordered Society," studies some Medieval and Renaissance treatments, including A SPANISH TRAGEDY and works by Webster and Chapman among others. Part 2 deals with "The Myth of the Warring Brothers in the Contemporary Theatre."

Mehl, Dieter. THE ELIZABETHAN DUMB SHOW: THE HISTORY OF A DRAMATIC CONVENTION. London: Methuen & Co., 1965; Cambridge, Mass.: Harvard University Press, 1966.

Mehl's study was published in German in 1964, with the title DIE PANTOMIME IM DRAMA DER SHAKESPEAREZEIT. Mehl sees the dumb show as part of the total history of Elizabethan drama, casting light on "the particular style of the individual author" and on "the general tendencies of dramatic writing during this period" (p. 169). Appendix I provides a "List of Plays Containing Dumb Shows" and Appendix II, "Further Texts of Dumb Shows."

Meyer, Edward. MACHIAVELLI AND THE ELIZABETHAN DRAMA. Literarhistorische Forschungen, Vol. 1. Weimar: Emil Felber, 1897.

Noting "395 references to Machiavelli in Elizabethan literature," Meyer proposes that the dramatists drew not so much on Machiavelli as on Gentillet, "Discours sur les Moyens de bien gouverner et maintenir en bonne paix un Royaume ou autre Principaute . . . Contre Nicolas Machiavel, Florentin, 1576" (p. x).

Mills, Laurens J. ONE SOUL IN BODIES TWAIN: FRIENDSHIP IN TUDOR

LITERATURE AND STUART DRAMA. Bloomington, Ind.: Principia Press, 1937.

Mills sees the friendship theme as more classical than Medieval as it emerges into Renaissance literature, "combined with medieval motifs of various sorts, and metamorphosed into a romantic theme. Especially fruitful was the conflict that ensued when love and friendship interests clashed" (p. iii). The argument, meticulously documented, is in general developed chronologically, with a final chapter, "From Socrates to Shirley."

Myers, A.M. REPRESENTATION AND MISREPRESENTATION OF THE PURITAN IN ELIZABETHAN DRAMA. Philadelphia: University of Pennsylvania, 1931.

The title denotes exactly the content of this dissertation.

Nares, Robert. A GLOSSARY; OR, COLLECTION OF WORDS, PHRASES, NAMES, AND ALLUSIONS TO CUSTOMS, PROVERBS, &C WHICH HAVE BEEN THOUGHT TO REQUIRE ILLUSTRATION, IN THE WORKS OF ENGLISH AUTHORS, PARTICULARLY SHAKESPEARE, AND HIS CONTEMPORARIES. LONDON: ROBERT TRIPHOOK, MESSRS. RIVINGTON AND CO., W. AND C. TAIT, AND GEORGE MULLEN, 1822. A NEW EDITION WITH CONSIDERABLE ADDITIONS BOTH OF WORDS AND EXAMPLES BY JAMES O. HALLIWELL AND THOMAS WRIGHT. 2 vols. London: Gibbings and Co., 1901.

Title annotates.

Nicoll, Allardyce. STUART MASQUES AND THE RENAISSANCE STAGE. WITH ONE HUNDRED AND NINETY-SEVEN ILLUSTRATIONS. 1938; reprint ed. New York: Benjamin Blom, 1968.

For no drama perhaps is the understanding of staging more important than for the masque. Nicoll studies the techniques of staging used by Inigo Jones and his contemporaries to determine "so far as such a determination is possible--the precise methods employed in the production of these royal entertainments" (p. 9). Appendix: "List of Masques (1603-41)."

Olson, Elder. TRAGEDY AND THE THEORY OF DRAMA. Detroit: Wayne State University Press, 1966.

In this "inquiry into dramatic principles" (p. 1), the discussion focuses particularly on KING LEAR, but plays by such dramatists as Jonson, Marlowe, Middleton, Tourneur, Webster, the writings of the critic Rymer, and such anonymous works as ARDEN OF FEVERSHAM, EVERYMAN, and THE YORKSHIRE TRAGEDY provide material for the construction of the argument.

Oras, Ants. PAUSE PATTERNS IN ELIZABETHAN AND JACOBEAN DRAMA: AN EXPERIMENT IN PROSODY. University of Florida Monographs, Humanities Series, No. 3. Gainesville: University of Florida Press, 1960.

Much of the material is, quite suitably, presented in graphs and tables. The bibliography is "A Note on Sources."

Orgel, Stephen, and Roy Strong. INIGO JONES: THE THEATRE OF THE STUART COURT. INCLUDING THE COMPLETE DESIGNS FOR PRODUCTIONS AT COURT FOR THE MOST PART IN THE COLLECTION OF THE DUKE OF DEVONSHIRE, TOGETHER WITH THEIR TEXTS AND HISTORICAL DOCUMENTATION. 2 vols. London: Sotheby Parke Bernet; Berkeley: University of California Press, 1973.

Title annotates.

Ornstein, Robert. THE MORAL VISION OF JACOBEAN TRAGEDY. Madison: University of Wisconsin Press, 1960; reprint ed. 1965.

Ornstein argues that for all "their imperfect and ambiguous ethical sympathies, the Jacobeans cherished those virtues which literature has immemorially enshrined" but gave them such diverse definitions "that we cannot generalize about the 'moral vision' of Jacobean tragedy" (p. 46). He explores those evolving values, "those qualities of the human mind which reduce tragic anguish to the beauty and order of art" (p. 276), considering in particular Chapman, Jonson, Tourneur, Webster, Marston, Beaumont and Fletcher, Middleton, Ford, and Shakespeare.

Orr, David. ITALIAN RENAISSANCE DRAMA IN ENGLAND BEFORE 1625: THE INFLUENCE OF "ERUDITA" TRAGEDY, COMEDY, AND PASTORAL ON ELIZABETHAN AND JACOBEAN DRAMA. University of North Carolina Studies in Comparative Literature, No. 49. Chapel Hill: University of North Carolina Press, 1970.

Orr examines "some of the primary and all the significant secondary material relating to the influence exercised by the formal drama of Italy on that of England before 1625" (p. viii). He concludes that it "had very little influence on English drama as a whole" (p. 109). Appendices: "Plots of Italian plays" and "Some scholarly arguments." Bibliography.

Parr, Johnstone. TAMBURLAINE'S MALADY AND OTHER ESSAYS ON ASTROLOGY IN ELIZABETHAN DRAMA. University: University of Alabama Press, 1953.

Essays on Marlowe, Lyly, Greene, Shakespeare, Chapman, Webster, and Jonson. The "Bibliography: Sources of the Renaissance Englishman's Knowledge of Astrology: A Bibliographical Survey and a Bibliography, 1473-1625," offers annotation as well as titles.

Parrott, Thomas Marc, and Robert Hamilton Ball. A SHORT VIEW OF ELIZABETHAN DRAMA. Rev. ed. New York: Charles Scribner's Sons, 1958.

A general history (first published in 1943) running from "The Medieval Background: Cycles, Morals, and Interludes" to "The Curtain

Falls: Massinger, Shirley, Davenant, Court Masques, Summary." Bibliography.

Partridge, A[stley] C. ORTHOGRAPHY IN SHAKESPEARE AND ELIZABETHAN DRAMA: A STUDY OF COLLOQUIAL CONTRACTIONS, ELISION, PROSODY AND PUNCTUATION. London: E. Arnold; Lincoln: University of Nebraska Press, 1964.

The study is oriented towards developing a "knowledge of the textual history of the plays" (p. [1]).

Peers, Edgar Allison. ELIZABETHAN DRAMA AND ITS MAD FOLK. Cambridge: W. Heffer, 1914.

Title annotates.

Penniman, Josiah H. THE WAR OF THE THEATRES. Publications of the University of Pennsylvania, Series in Philology, Literature and Archaeology, Vol. 4, No. 3. Boston: Ginn & Co.; Halle a. S.: Max Niemeyer, 1897.

Table I shows the plays involved in the quarrel as Penniman analyzes it. Table II equates characters in the plays to real-life counterparts. The dramatists considered by Penniman as warring are Jonson, Marston, Dekker, Chettle, Haughton, Shakespeare, and Kyd, although (p. [152]) Penniman says that whether the plays he discusses "were the only plays concerned in the quarrel is by no means certain."

Pickel, Margaret Barnard. CHARLES I AS PATRON OF POETRY AND DRAMA. London: Frederick Muller, 1936.

There are chapters on "Court Drama" and "Court Masques."

Pineas, Rainer. TUDOR AND EARLY STUART ANTI-CATHOLIC DRAMA. Bibliotheca Humanistica & Reformatorica, Vol. 5. Nieuwkoop: B. de Graaf, 1972.

Pineas offers a reconsideration of "Tudor and Stuart religious polemical drama," which has often "been dismissed as regrettable and lacking in literary interest," in order to show "the not inconsiderable debt Tudor and Stuart drama generally owes to contemporary polemics" (p. 5). This short study touches on a great number of authors and of types of drama, to argue finally that the continuity of a native tradition gives rise to the genius of Shakespeare.

Prior, Moody E. THE LANGUAGE OF TRAGEDY. New York: Columbia University Press, 1947.

In the attempt "to discover the relationship between the language of plays written in verse and the dramatic nature of the form" (p. vii), Prior draws heavily on the Elizabethans.

Reed, A[rthur] W. EARLY TUDOR DRAMA: MEDWALL, THE RASTELLS, HEYWOOD, AND THE MORE CIRCLE. 1926; reprint ed. New York: Octagon Books, 1969.

Reed provides a substantial factual background. Harris, in SKELTON'S "MAGNYFYCENCE" (see in Part 2, Section 29: John Skelton), calls Reed's the "definitive study of this group" (p. v).

Reed, Robert Rentoul, Jr. BEDLAM ON THE JACOBEAN STAGE. Cambridge, Mass.: Harvard University Press, 1952.

A study of "Bethlehem Hospital and Its Background," "Theories of Mental Pathology and Conduct," "The Pathological Studies of Melancholy," as well as of various aspects of theatrical use of Bedlamites. Especially useful for its study of John Ford. Useful bibliography in two parts, "Historical Sources" and "Dramatic Works."

_____. THE OCCULT ON THE TUDOR AND STUART STAGE. Boston: Christopher Publishing House, 1965.

The "Preface" points to the comprehensive scope of the treatment of the occult and to a particular concern with mechanics, "with the importance of supernatural agents as a function of plot and theme" (p. 7). The bibliography includes a section on "Dramatic Works That Emphasize the Supernatural."

Reyher, Paul. LES MASQUES ANGLAIS: ETUDE SUR LES BALLETS ET LA VIE DE COUR EN ANGLETERRE (1512-1640). Paris and London: Librairie Hachette et Cie, 1909.

Reyher reprints various documents. His appendices include a "Note sur la Musique des Ballets" and a "Liste des principales pieces ou se trouvent inseres des Masques." There is a "Bibliographie des Ballets de 1603 a 1640."

Ribner, Irving. THE ENGLISH HISTORY PLAY IN THE AGE OF SHAKESPEARE. Rev. ed. New York: Barnes & Noble, 1965.

The objectives declared in the "Preface to the First Edition" (1957): the presentation of a full body of "factual information," the demonstration that each play fulfills the given specifications for a history play, and the demonstration "that the plays together form a continuous dramatic tradition . . . from the Middle Ages to the closing of the theatres in 1642" (p. x), are well realized. Ribner provides three useful appendices: "A Note on Tudor Political Doctrine," "A Chronological List of Extant English History Plays, 1519-1653," and "The Principal Sources of the English History Play." Bibliography.

_____. JACOBEAN TRAGEDY: THE QUEST FOR MORAL ORDER. New

York: Barnes & Noble; London: Methuen & Co., 1962.

Ribner explores the role in great tragedy of "the artist's moral concern," his struggle with "the fact of evil in the world" and his vision of the relation of human suffering to human joy" (p. xi). Ribner studies in particular the work of Chapman, Thomas Heywood, Tourneur, Webster, Middleton, and Ford, urging that "the tragedies they wrote are all conditioned by this quest for moral order, and when they are examined in these terms they reveal new dimensions" (p. xi).

Ristine, Frank Humphrey. ENGLISH TRAGICOMEDY: ITS ORIGIN AND HISTORY. Columbia University Studies in English. New York: Columbia University Press, 1910; reprint ed. 1963.

Ristine traces tragicomedy from "Origin" to "Decline." He seeks to define the type and to account for its rise and fall within "an attempt to present a comprehensive survey" (p. v). Appendix: "A List of English Tragicomedies." Bibliography.

Rollins, Hyder. "A Contribution to the History of the English Commonwealth Drama." STUDIES IN PHILOLOGY, 18 (1921), 267-333. Supplemented by: "The Commonwealth Drama: Miscellaneous Notes," STUDIES IN PHILOLOGY, 20 (1923), 52-69.

Rollins assembles evidence of theatrical activity during the period when the theatres were "closed."

Sabol, Andrew J., ed. SONGS AND DANCES FOR THE STUART MASQUE. AN EDITION OF SIXTY-THREE ITEMS OF MUSIC FOR THE ENGLISH COURT MASQUE FROM 1604 TO 1641. Providence, R.I.: Brown University Press, 1959.

An edition of songs with musical scores.

SALZBURG STUDIES IN ENGLISH LITERATURE.

The STUDIES are under the direction of Professor Erwin A. Storzl and Dr. James Hogg. Studies in this group are in four fields, two of them relevant to this bibliography. One is published with the series title ELIZABETHAN STUDIES. The announced list of publications--which I understand to include both works published and those expected to be available soon--indicates these on drama:

3. Russell E. Leavenworth, DANIEL'S "CLEOPATRA."

4. Arthur F. Kinney, MARKETS OF BAWDRIE: THE DRAMATIC CRITICISM OF STEPHEN GOSSON.

6. Steven C. Young, THE INDUCTION IN TUDOR AND STUART DRAMA.

7. David H. Zucker, STAGE AND IMAGE IN THE PLAYS OF MARLOWE.

8. Frederick D. Horn, A CRITICAL EDITION OF "EDWARD III."

10. Martha H. Fleischer, THE ICONOGRAPHY OF THE ENGLISH HISTORY PLAY.

12. Norbert Platz, JONSON'S "ARS POETICA": AN INTERPRETATION OF "POETASTER" IN ITS HISTORICAL CONTEXT. Published with Philip Dust's "GORBODUC," and Hans-Joachim Hermes's FRANK'S SINGING IN "THE FAIR MAID OF THE EXCHANGE."

16. TWO UNIVERSITY LATIN PLAYS: PHILIP PARSONS' "ATALANTA" AND THOMAS ATKINSON'S "HOMO," with texts by William E. Mahaney and Walter K. Sherwin; translated by Walter K. Sherwin, Jay Freyman, and Eve Parrish; introduction and notes by William E. Mahaney.

18. Frances E. Bolen, IRONY AND SELF-KNOWLEDGE IN THE CREATION OF TRAGEDY.

Note: This list is taken from Number 20 (Camoin) in the JACOBEAN DRAMA STUDIES. The list for the Jacobean series, together with the statement about it, comes from Number 22 (Williams). There are some differences in the lists; compare Number 12, above, with Number 10, below; notice also Number 13, below. The series JACOBEAN DRAMA STUDIES is self-described as "founded in 1972 for the publication of doctoral theses and other learned studies . . . which, though they have failed in the present economic situation to find a commercial publisher, yet deserve to be made available to a wider public." The various volumes are edited by James Hogg and carry the imprint: Salzburg: Dr. James Hogg, Institut fur Englische Sprache und Literatur, Univ. Salzburg, or some slight variant thereon. The Williams volume carries a list of titles in print or expected to "be published by the end of 1973":

1. Sanford Sternlicht, JOHN WEBSTER'S IMAGERY AND THE WEBSTER CANON. Published with Derek de Silva's JONSON: WIT AND THE MORAL SENSE IN "VOLPONE" AND THE MAJOR COMEDIES.

2. Richard A. Bodtke, TRAGEDY AND THE JACOBEAN TEMPER: THE MAJOR PLAYS OF JOHN WEBSTER.

3. Suzanne K. Blow, A STUDY OF RHETORIC IN THE PLAYS OF THOMAS DEKKER.

4. Robert F. Whitman, BEYOND MELANCHOLY: JOHN WEBSTER AND THE TRAGEDY OF DESPAIR.

5. Thomas M. Grant, THE COMEDIES OF GEORGE CHAPMAN: A STUDY IN DEVELOPMENT.

6. Bertha Hensman, THE SHARES OF FLETCHER, FIELD

AND MASSINGER IN TWELVE PLAYS OF THE BEAUMONT AND FLETCHER CANON.

7. Alice Shalvi, THE RELATIONSHIP OF RENAISSANCE CONCEPTS OF HONOUR TO SHAKESPEARE'S PROBLEM PLAYS.

8. Peter Bement, ACTION AND CONTEMPLATION IN THE TRAGEDIES OF GEORGE CHAPMAN.

9. William E. Mahaney, DECEPTION IN THE JOHN WEBSTER PLAYS: AN ANALYTICAL STUDY.

10. ______, A BIBLIOGRAPHY OF JOHN WEBSTER. Published with Norbert Platz's JONSON'S "ARS POETICA": AN INTERPRETATION OF "POETASTER" IN ITS HISTORICAL CONTEXT.

11. Muriel West, THE DEVIL AND JOHN WEBSTER.

12. Robert Griffin, JOHN WEBSTER: POLITICS AND TRAGEDY.

13. Agnes Dinn, NATURE AND ART THEMES IN THE MIDDLE COMEDIES OF BEN JONSON. (In the Camoin volume, Number 13 is given as Jay Louis Funston, A CRITICAL EDITION OF "LOVE'S HOSPITAL" BY GEORGE WILDE.)

14. Francis D. Evenhuis, MASSINGER'S IMAGERY.

15. Melvin Seiden, JOHN WEBSTER.

16. Derek Crawley, GEORGE CHAPMAN'S PLAYS.

17. Winifred Kittredge Eaton, CONTRASTS IN THE REPRESENTATION OF DEATH BY SOPHOCLES, WEBSTER AND STRINDBERG.

18. William G. Dwyer, A STUDY OF JOHN WEBSTER'S USE OF RENAISSANCE NATURAL AND MORAL PHILOSOPHY.

19. John F. McElroy, PARODY AND BURLESQUE IN THE TRAGICOMEDIES OF THOMAS MIDDLETON.

20. Francois A. Camoin, THE REVENGE CONVENTION IN TOURNEUR, WEBSTER AND MIDDLETON.

21. Tucker Orbison, THE TRAGIC VISION OF JOHN FORD.

22. Mary C. Williams, SOURCES OF UNITY IN BEN JONSON'S COMEDY.

23. Charlotte N. Clay, ANXIETY IN ENGLISH TRAGEDY.

24. Annette Drew-Bear, RHETORIC IN BEN JONSON'S MIDDLE PLAYS.

25. and 26. James Hogg, WEBSTER "REFORMED": A STUDY OF POST-RESTORATION VERSIONS OF JOHN WEBSTER'S PLAYS (publication expected in 1975).

27. William D. Wolf, THE REFORM OF THE FALLEN WORLD: THE "VIRTUOUS PRINCE" IN JONSONIAN TRAGEDY AND COMEDY.

The user of these lists should bear in mind the possibility of delays and changes in publication plans. I have not examined all the in-print volumes. Both the Elizabethan and Jacobean series are prepared in offset printing.

Schelling, Felix E. ELIZABETHAN DRAMA, 1558-1642: A HISTORY OF THE DRAMA IN ENGLAND FROM THE ACCESSION OF QUEEN ELIZABETH TO THE CLOSING OF THE THEATRES, TO WHICH IS PREFIXED A RESUME OF THE EARLIER DRAMA FROM ITS BEGINNINGS. 2 vols. Boston and New York: Houghton, Mifflin & Co., 1908.

The study is based largely on "the original texts of the plays themselves" (Vol. 1, p. xi). Volume 2 contains a "Bibliographical Essay" and "A List of Plays and Like Productions."

______. ELIZABETHAN PLAYWRIGHTS: A SHORT HISTORY OF THE ENGLISH DRAMA FROM MEDIAEVAL TIMES TO THE CLOSING OF THE THEATERS IN 1642. New York and London: Harper & Brothers, 1925; reprint ed. 1965.

A general chronological survey, with bibliography and "A Chronological List of Principal Dates."

______. THE ENGLISH CHRONICLE PLAY: A STUDY IN THE POPULAR HISTORICAL LITERATURE ENVIRONING SHAKESPEARE. New York and London: Macmillan, 1902.

The "Preface" describes the book as "an attempt . . . to tell the history of one of the many and various strands which, twisted and interwoven, form the brilliant and heterogeneous Elizabethan Drama" (p. v). Schelling provides a "Table of Extant Plays" and a "List of Plays on English Historical Subjects."

______. FOREIGN INFLUENCES IN ELIZABETHAN PLAYS. New York and London: Harper & Brothers, 1923.

A consideration of classical, Italian, French, and Spanish influences.

Schrickx, W. SHAKESPEARE'S EARLY CONTEMPORARIES.

See main entry in Part 2, Section 24: Thomas Nashe.

Seccombe, Thomas, and J.W. Allen. THE AGE OF SHAKESPEARE (1579-1631). Introduction by [John] [Wesley] Hales. Vol. 2: THE DRAMA. 1903; reprint ed. Freeport, N.Y.: Books for Libraries, 1971; 2nd ed. 1904.

A general survey.

Sharpe, Robert Boies. THE REAL WAR OF THE THEATRES: SHAKESPEARE'S FELLOWS IN RIVALRY WITH THE ADMIRAL'S MEN, 1594-1603. REPERTORIES, DEVICES, AND TYPES. Boston: D.C. Heath and Co.; London: Oxford University Press; Published by the Modern Language Association of America, 1935.

Sharpe presents "a chronological survey of the theatrical events of Queen Elizabeth's last decade . . . tak[ing] up systematically season by season those complex interrelationships among happenings in the nation and on the stage" relative to "the rivalry between Shakespeare's fellows and the other chief London company, the Admiral's men" (p. v).

Silvette, Herbert. THE DOCTOR ON THE STAGE: MEDICINE AND MEDICAL MEN IN SEVENTEENTH-CENTURY ENGLAND. Ed. Francelia Butler. Knoxville: University of Tennessee Press, 1967.

Silvette collects and explains a world of medical allusions in drama. Readably put together, the curious lore offers a fascinating sidelight. The bibliography lists "Editions Consulted."

Simpson, Percy. STUDIES IN ELIZABETHAN DRAMA. 1955; reprint ed. Folcroft, Pa.: Folcroft Press, 1969.

The articles in this collection were for the most part published earlier as separate studies. In addition to a number on Shakespeare, they include: "Marlowe's TRAGICAL HISTORY OF DOCTOR FAUSTUS," "The Art of Ben Jonson," "King Charles the First as a Dramatic Critic," "The Theme of Revenge in Elizabethan Tragedy," and "The Official Control of Tudor and Stuart Printing."

Simpson, Percy, and C.F. Bell. DESIGNS BY INIGO JONES FOR MASQUES & PLAYS AT COURT. A DESCRIPTIVE CATALOGUE OF DRAWINGS FOR SCENERY AND COSTUMES MAINLY IN THE COLLECTION OF HIS GRACE THE DUKE OF DEVONSHIRE, K.G. Oxford: Printed for the Walpole and Malone Societies at the University Press, 1924.

The introduction discusses the masque, largely with respect to production. The drawings are annotated.

Sisson, Charles J. THE ELIZABETHAN DRAMATISTS EXCEPT SHAKESPEARE. London: Benn, 1928.

Sisson states that he has tried "to link up the Elizabethan drama with the stage and with social history, and to place it in relation with what preceded and what followed it, so far as space permits" (p. 3). The space is limited to eighty pages, but Sisson knows his subject well enough to make those eighty profitable.

_____. LE GOUT PUBLIC ET LA THEATRE ELISABETHAIN JUSQU'A LA MORT DE SHAKESPEARE. Dijon: Darantiere, 1922.

Sisson argues that Elizabethans wrote for audiences whose tastes are important to our understanding of the plays. He attempts to heighten our awareness of that taste.

_____. LOST PLAYS OF SHAKESPEARE'S AGE. Cambridge: At the University Press, 1936.

Sisson asserts that he wishes "to tell stories of life and people" as much "as to add to our knowledge of the Elizabethan stage and drama or to record texts rescued from their burial in legal evidences and now submitted to the unforeseen test of literary criticism" (p. [Ix]). He provides insight into the ways of scholarship as well as into obscure facets of drama. He also provides two useful appendices: "Summary of Original Sources" and "Notes Upon the Times."

Small, Roscoe Addison. THE STAGE-QUARREL BETWEEN BEN JONSON AND THE SO-CALLED POETASTERS. Forschungen zur Englischen Sprache und Litteratur, Vol. 1. Breslau: M. & H. Marcus, 1899.

Having examined the available data, Small states briefly what he believes can be known or concluded: "[T]hat only Jonson, Marston, Dekker, Shakspere, and Monday had any share in the quarrel. At all events, careful research fails to show evidence that any other man took part in it" (p. 199). Small provides a "Chronological Table of Literary Works and Identifications."

Smith, G[eorge] C[harles] Moore. THE ACADEMIC DRAMA AT CAMBRIDGE FROM COLLEGE RECORDS. Malone Society Collections, Vol. II, Part ii, pp. [150]-230. London: Printed for the Malone Society at the Oxford University Press, 1923.

The material is described as "such references to the dramatic activities of their members as are to be found in the records of the various Cambridge colleges" (p. [150]).

_____. COLLEGE PLAYS PERFORMED IN THE UNIVERSITY OF CAMBRIDGE. Cambridge: At the University Press, 1923.

In addition to discussing the plays, Smith provides a "Chronological Table of Performance of College Plays" and "Actor-Lists."

Smith, Robert Metcalf. FROISSART AND THE ENGLISH CHRONICLE PLAY. Columbia University Studies in English and Comparative Literature. 1915; reprint ed. New York: Benjamin Blom, 1965.

Smith deals with various plays about Edward III, Richard II, and Jack Straw, and also with Daniel's CIVIL WARS.

Smith, Winifred. THE COMMEDIA DELL'ARTE. Reprint ed. of the 1912 edition, with additions, New York: Benjamin Blom, 1964.

A visually attractive presentation of very visual material, with illustrations "assembled by David Allen and Benjamin Blom" at the end of the volume. The book provides a discussion of "The commedia dell'arte in Elizabethan and Jacobean England," pages 170-99. Appendix: "Relations between English and Italian drama in the 16th, 17th centuries."

Sorelius, Gunnar. "THE GIANT RACE BEFORE THE FLOOD": PRE-RESTORATION DRAMA ON THE STAGE AND IN THE CRITICISM OF THE RESTORATION. Acta Universitatis Upsaliensis, Studia Anglistica Upsaliensia, No. 4. Uppsala: Amqvist & Wiksells, 1966.

Although the main title is whimsical, the subtitle annotates. Bibliography.

Spencer, Theodore. DEATH AND ELIZABETHAN TRAGEDY: A STUDY OF CONVENTION AND OPINION IN THE ELIZABETHAN DRAMA. 1936; reprint ed. New York: Pageant Books, 1960.

Taking the position that the "problems death implies are the central problems of life, and hence they are the central subject matter of art," Spencer's study focuses on the precise problem of an attempt "to define the attitudes toward death in a short period of time and to show how they affected dramatic poetry" (p. [vii]).

Spens, Janet. ELIZABETHAN DRAMA. London: Methuen & Co., 1922.

The book begins with a chapter entitled "Bibliography," offering recommendations about basic and useful material; the advice is good though now dated. The text proper is a readable running commentary on Elizabethan drama.

Stagg, Louis C. INDEX TO THE FIGURATIVE LANGUAGE OF [VARIOUS DRAMATISTS]. 7 parts. Charlottesville: Bibliographical Society of the University of Virginia, 1967-70.

Stagg has prepared indexes to the figurative language of the tragedies of seven dramatists: Jonson, Tourneur, Chapman, Marston, Thomas Heywood, Middleton, and Webster, providing catalogs of figurative speech which can be used for various explorations of the dramatist and his linguistic relations to his peers. See individual listings under each dramatist, in Part 2, for date of publication and full title.

Steele, Mary Susan. PLAYS AND MASQUES AT COURT DURING THE REIGNS OF ELIZABETH, JAMES, AND CHARLES. Cornell Studies in English, Vol. 10. 1926; reprint ed. New York: Russell & Russell, 1968.

An annotated chronology, highly useful and clearly arranged.

Stopes, Mrs. C[harlotte] C[armichael]. WILLIAM HUNNIS AND THE REVELS OF THE CHAPEL ROYAL: A STUDY OF HIS PERIOD AND THE INFLUENCES WHICH AFFECTED SHAKESPEARE. MATERIALIEN ZUR KUNDE DES ALTEREN ENGLISCHEN DRAMAS. Ed. W. Bang, Vol. 29. 1910; reprint ed. Vaduz: Kraus Reprint, 1963.

Mrs. Stopes concedes: "No contemporary monument or record of the Life or death of Master William Hunnis has been preserved, and his existence would have passed into oblivion along with his plays, had it not so strenuously interwoven itself, with the literary, political, and religious developments of the sixteenth century" (p. 278). The study explores a somewhat minor matter, but one which may cast light on the period.

Stroup, Thomas B. MICROCOSMOS: THE SHAPE OF THE ELIZABETHAN PLAY. Lexington: University of Kentucky Press, 1965.

Stroup explores the theory that there is "a relationship between the idea that 'The world's a stage,/And all the men and women merely players'" and "The Shape of the Elizabethan Play." Indeed, he asserts: "I am convinced the basic structure of the Elizabethan play of whatever kind lies in this ancient observation" (p. vii).

Sugden, Edward H. A TOPOGRAPHICAL DICTIONARY TO THE WORKS OF SHAKESPEARE AND HIS FELLOW DRAMATISTS. Publications of the University of Manchester, No. 168. Manchester: At the University Press; London and New York: Longmans, Green & Co., 1925.

Sugden provides an alphabetical list of places, such as "Appian Way" and "Bedlam," and of such other items as "Ishmael, Children of," and "Lyon's Inn," with explanations, of course, and maps.

Sullivan, Mary. COURT MASQUES OF JAMES I: THEIR INFLUENCE ON SHAKESPEARE AND THE PUBLIC THEATRES. New York and London: Putnam's, The Knickerbocker Press, 1913.

The study was Sullivan's University of Nebraska doctoral dissertation. Age has not removed it from view.

Swinburne, Algernon Charles. THE COMPLETE WORKS. Ed. Edmund Gosse and Thomas James Wise. Vols. 11 and 12, comprising THE PROSE WORKS (Vols. 1 and 2). London: William Heinemann; New York: Gabriel Wells, 1926.

Volume I has an essay on Shakespeare and one on "The Age of Shakespeare." Volume II includes several relevant essays, including "Contemporaries of Shakespeare." Swinburne casts a wide net in these studies.

Symons, Arthur. STUDIES IN THE ELIZABETHAN DRAMA. 1919; reprint ed. New York: AMS Press, 1972.

Together with various essays on Shakespeare, the volume contains

"Philip Massinger," "John Day," and "Middleton and Rowley." "The Question of HENRY VIII" argues for Fletcher's hand in the play.

Talbert, Ernest William. ELIZABETHAN DRAMA AND SHAKESPEARE'S EARLY PLAYS: AN ESSAY IN HISTORICAL CRITICISM. Chapel Hill: University of North Carolina Press, 1963.

Talbert describes his study as "based essentially upon a single consideration. Before these dramas could be read . . . , they were seen and heard in performance; and thus their authors must have been concerned with the likely effect of their art upon an Elizabethan audience" (p. [3]). The discussion emphasizes Shakespeare.

_____. THE PROBLEM OF ORDER: ELIZABETHAN POLITICAL COMMONPLACES AND AN EXAMPLE OF SHAKESPEARE'S ART. Chapel Hill: University of North Carolina, 1962.

See especially Part 1, "Current Thought About the Body Politic."

Thaler, Alwin. SHAKESPEARE TO SHERIDAN: A BOOK ABOUT THE THEATRE OF YESTERDAY AND TO-DAY. Cambridge, Mass.: Harvard University Press; London: Oxford University Press, 1922.

A broad survey designed to demonstrate the continuity of the English dramatic tradition. Various appendices, including "Rates of Admission in the Elizabethan Theatre" and "On the Size of the Elizabethan Playhouses."

Thompson, Elbert N.S. THE CONTROVERSY BETWEEN THE PURITANS AND THE STAGE. Yale Studies in English, Vol. 20. New York: H. Holt and Co., 1903.

The discussion is in two basic parts, "The Puritan Attack on the Stage" and "The Dramatists' Reply to the Puritans." The author inclines to the conclusion that "the English Puritan did not attack unfairly the vices of the theater" (p. 261). See the section, "Legislation on the Stage, 1576-1603."

Thorp, Willard. THE TRIUMPH OF REALISM IN ELIZABETHAN DRAMA, 1558-1612. Princeton Studies in English, No. 3. Princeton, N.J.: Princeton University Press; London: Oxford University Press, 1928.

Thorp studies didacticism as it was directed towards "guiding the audience to a correct understanding of the events pictured before it" and then "the decline of didacticism in theme and plot and the consequent triumph of realism" (pp. viii-ix).

Tomlinson, T[homas] B[rian]. A STUDY OF ELIZABETHAN AND JACOBEAN TRAGEDY. Cambridge: At the University Press; Victoria: Melbourne University Press, 1964.

Tomlinson discusses a great number of playwrights but focuses on

Shakespeare, Middleton, and Tourneur as playwrights whose work provides a base for discussing the "general issues which affect English tragedy": the confrontation of good and evil, of order and disorder. He also proposes to examine the role of society in the "defeat [of] the drama" (pp. vii-viii, 3).

Wagner, Max. ENGLISH DRAMATIC BLANK-VERSE BEFORE MARLOWE. 2 parts. Osterode: Druck von F. Albrecht vorm. J.G. Rautenberg, 1881-82.

An analysis of meter and metrical variants in a number of plays. Perhaps a bit pedestrian.

Waith, Eugene M. THE HERCULEAN HERO IN MARLOWE, CHAPMAN, SHAKESPEARE AND DRYDEN. New York: Columbia University Press; London: Chatto & Windus, 1962.

Waith proposes that the seven plays which are his principal subject--TAMBURLAINE, BUSSY D'AMBOIS, ANTONY AND CLEOPATRA, CORIOLANUS, THE CONQUEST OF GRANADA, AURENG-ZEBE, and ALL FOR LOVE--have been misunderstood and often undervalued through failure to understand their particular kind of hero, "a warrior of great stature who is guilty of striking departures from the morality of the society in which he lives" (p. [11]).

_____. IDEAS OF GREATNESS: HEROIC DRAMA IN ENGLAND. London: Routledge & Kegan Paul, 1971.

Waith comments that <u>heroic drama</u> usually connotes a particular type of play belonging to the 1660s. He argues, however, for a strong line of continuity in the concept of the heroic from the Renaissance, and even from the Middle Ages, to the Restoration stage. Bibliography.

Wallace, Malcolm William, ed. "THE BIRTHE OF HERCULES": WITH AN INTRODUCTION ON THE INFLUENCE OF PLAUTUS ON THE DRAMATIC LITERATURE OF ENGLAND IN THE SIXTEENTH CENTURY. Chicago: Scott, Foresman, 1903.

In editing THE BIRTHE OF HERCULES for the first printing from the one surviving manuscript copy, Wallace provides a long introduction (pp. [7]-96) on the growth of classical influence, developed chronologically.

Ward, B[ernard] M[ordaunt]. THE SEVENTEENTH EARL OF OXFORD, 1550-1604. FROM CONTEMPORARY DOCUMENTS. London: John Murray, 1928.

Since Oxford had extensive literary connections and especially since in "1580 the Earl of Warwick's Company of actors transferred to Lord Oxford's service; and John Lyly, who was then his private secretary, was probably appointed manager of the company" (p.

264), the book casts light on the drama. See especially "Interlude: Lord Oxford's Actors, 1580-1602" (pp. 264-82).

Watson, Harold Francis. THE SAILOR IN ENGLISH FICTION AND DRAMA, 1550-1800. New York: Columbia University Press, 1931.

Title annotates.

Watt, Lauchlan MacLean. ATTIC & ELIZABETHAN TRAGEDY. London: J.M. Dent; New York: E.P. Dutton & Co., 1908.

Much of the emphasis is on the Greeks and Shakespeare, but Watt draws general conclusions about tragedy, especially about "The Unities."

Wells, Henry W. ELIZABETHAN AND JACOBEAN PLAYWRIGHTS. 2nd ed., with A CHRONOLOGICAL LIST OF EXTANT PLAYS PRODUCED IN OR ABOUT LONDON, 1581-1642, 1939; reprint ed. Port Washington, N.Y.: Kennikat Press, 1964.

A critical discussion of "major tendencies in the drama from 1576 to 1642" (p. viii), with "Biographical and Bibliographical Notes" as well as the CHRONOLOGICAL LIST mentioned in the title. The LIST has been published separately (see main entry in Section 9: Playlists, Records of Early Publication, Etc.

Wells, Stanley. LITERATURE AND DRAMA WITH SPECIAL REFERENCE TO SHAKESPEARE AND HIS CONTEMPORARIES. Concepts of Literature. London: Routledge & Kegan Paul, 1970.

William Righter, the general editor of "Concepts of Literature," says that the series is designed to describe and evaluate important terms "used in literary discussion," to relate "literature to other intellectual disciplines," and to "account for the methodology of literary study, and . . . define its dimensions" (p. [v]). Wells defines the purpose of his particular study as "to explore something of the area that lies between the two very different experiences of reading plays and seeing them performed." Bibliography.

Welsford, Enid. THE COURT MASQUE: A STUDY IN THE RELATIONSHIP BETWEEN POETRY AND THE REVELS. 1927; reprint ed. New York: Russell & Russell, 1962.

A consideration of the basic but elusive problems of the nature of the artistic or creative impulse and the relationship of one activity--game, religious ritual, play--to another and an examination of these as they manifest themselves in the masque. The masque is here described, interestingly, not only as a sophisticated form (p. [3]), but also as "a peculiarly elaborate example of a rudimentary form of art, of which the first stirrings are seen whenever people express an emotional attitude to life by means of their own bodies" (pp. 356-57).

West, Robert Hunter. THE INVISIBLE WORLD: A STUDY OF PNEUMATOLOGY IN ELIZABETHAN DRAMA. Athens: University of Georgia Press, 1939.

West studies "not only the ghosts but the closely related daemonic figures and . . . the human pursuits, ceremonial magic and witchcraft, that depended upon them" (p. vii).

White, Beatrice, comp. AN INDEX TO "THE ELIZABETHAN STAGE" AND "WILLIAM SHAKESPEARE." 1934; reprint ed. New York: Benjamin Blom, 1964.

The index puts play titles, lost plays, books, names of dramatists, and so on, in one alphabetical list, making E.K. Chambers's massive volumes even more readily usable than their own logical arrangement allows. (See above for Chambers, E.K., THE ELIZABETHAN STAGE.)

Wikland, Erik. ELIZABETHAN PLAYERS IN SWEDEN, 1591-92: FACTS AND PROBLEMS. Trans. Patrick Hort and Carl Erik Holm. Stockholm: Almqvist & Wiksell; Uppsala: Goteborg, 1962.

Wikland provides a detailed, documented account of a relatively small and obscure problem, "the activities of the English players who were at Nykoping in Sweden between 1591-92" (see the "Preface").

Wilson, F[rank] P[ercy]. THE ENGLISH DRAMA, 1498-1585. Ed. with a bibliography by G.K. Hunter. Oxford History of English Literature, Vol. IV, Part 1. New York and London: Oxford University Press; Oxford: Clarendon Press, 1969.

Sound, detailed general history, with chronology, bibliography. Part 2 is to bring the history to the year 1642.

Wimsatt, W[illiam] K[urtz], Jr., ed. ENGLISH STAGE COMEDY. English Institute Essays, 1954. New York: Columbia University Press, 1955.

See especially, for this time period, Wimsatt's "Introduction: The Criticism of Comedy," with bibliographical references in the notes, and "Unifying Symbols in the Comedy of Ben Jonson" by Ray L. Heffner, Jr.

Witherspoon, Alexander Maclaren. THE INFLUENCE OF ROBERT GARNIER ON ELIZABETHAN DRAMA. Yale Studies in English, Vol. 65. New Haven, Conn.: Yale University Press; London: Oxford University Press, 1924.

Witherspoon considers Garnier "the most eminent French tragedian of the sixteenth century" (p. [iii]). His discussion considers particularly "Lady Pembroke and her Circle" and concludes with "A Summary of the Causes of the Failure of Garnier's Influence to Produce any Lasting Results in English Drama," pp. 181-89.

Withington, Robert. ENGLISH PAGEANTRY: AN HISTORICAL OUTLINE. 2 vols. Cambridge, Mass.: Harvard University Press; London: Oxford University Press, 1918-20.

A full outline, from "Folk Mumming" to "Pageantry in the United States," with annotated lists of "Royal Entries" and the like--a useful collection of material on one of the large collateral branches of drama.

Yearsley, [Percival] Macleod. DOCTORS IN ELIZABETHAN DRAMA. London: John Bale, Sons, & Danielsson, 1933.

There are chapters on "Conditions of Medical Education," "Doctors as Characters," "Surgeons and Apothecaries," "Midwives and Nurses," and "Irregular Practitioners." Discussions of individual plays can be located through the index.

9. PLAYLISTS, RECORDS OF EARLY PUBLICATION, ETC.

Included in this section are books that have to do specifically with the question of what plays were written in England before 1660, together with information about their production and publication. Few books are concerned solely with this subject, of course, so that many of the entries here contain other information as well. Conversely, many books entered elsewhere in this bibliography also contain more or less extensive information about the body of English drama to 1660 and its printing. A bibliography cross-referenced for every possibility would be too unwieldy to be of use; the alternative is to leave the user to make some discoveries of his own.

Adams, J[oseph] Q[uincy]. "Hill's List of Early Plays in Manuscript." LIBRARY, 4th Series, 20 (1939), [71]-99.

> Abraham Hill was a seventeenth-century antiquarian given to the collection of books. Adams discusses a list of manuscript plays left by Hill among his many notebooks. The list contains the names of otherwise unknown plays and the like, with many possible significances for the total history of drama. Hill's list and this study of it by Adams are frequently referred to, both Hill and Adams being bookmen of learning and rectitude.

Allibone, S. Austin. A CRITICAL DICTIONARY OF ENGLISH LITERATURE AND BRITISH AND AMERICAN AUTHORS LIVING AND DECEASED FROM THE EARLIEST ACCOUNTS TO THE LATTER HALF OF THE NINETEENTH CENTURY. CONTAINING OVER FORTY-SIX THOUSAND ARTICLES (AUTHORS). WITH FORTY INDEXES OF SUBJECTS. 3 vols. 1858-72; reprint ed. Detroit: Gale Research Co., 1965.

> Allibone recommends his DICTIONARY to a great variety of professions and also to the "individual who follows no particular pursuit" (Vol. I, pp. 5-7). Allibone does not restrict himself to dramatic literature. See Kirk, John Foster, for a SUPPLEMENT.

Arber, Edward, ed. A TRANSCRIPT OF THE REGISTERS OF THE COMPANY OF STATIONERS OF LONDON: 1554-1640 A.D. 5 vols. 1875-94; reprint ed. Gloucester, Mass.: Peter Smith, 1967.

> Arber's "Introduction" explains the nature of the Stationers Com-

pany and of the REGISTERS, which contain entries of titles of books to be printed and provides, in Arber's words, "the most singular and authoritative contemporary List of Books ever preserved in any nation" (p. xvi). The REGISTERS are a mine of information, always cryptic, often with elusive abbreviations or aberrant spelling, but a source for discovering or confirming much about Renaissance literature. See also, Eyre, G.E. Briscoe, ed.

Baker, David Erskine, Isaac Reed, and Stephen Jones. BIOGRAPHIA DRAMATICA; OR, A COMPANION TO THE PLAYHOUSE: CONTAINING HISTORICAL AND CRITICAL MEMOIRS, AND ORIGINAL ANECDOTES, OF BRITISH AND IRISH DRAMATIC WRITERS, FROM THE COMMENCEMENT OF OUR THEATRICAL EXHIBITIONS; AMONG WHOM ARE SOME OF THE MOST CELEBRATED ACTORS: ALSO AN ALPHABETICAL ACCOUNT, AND CHRONOLOGICAL LISTS, OF THEIR WORKS, THE DATES WHEN PRINTED, AND OBSERVATIONS ON THEIR MERITS: TOGETHER WITH AN INTRODUCTORY VIEW OF THE RISE AND PROGRESS OF THE BRITISH STAGE. ORIGINALLY COMPILED, TO THE YEAR 1764, BY DAVID ERSKINE BAKER. CONTINUED THENCE TO 1782, BY ISAAC REED, F.A.S. AND BROUGHT DOWN TO THE END OF NOVEMBER 1811, WITH VERY CONSIDERABLE ADDITIONS AND IMPROVEMENTS THROUGHOUT, BY STEPHEN JONES. 3 vols. London: Printed for Longman, Hurst, Rees, Orme, and Brown, T. Payne, G. and W. Nicol, Nichols and Son, Scatcherd and Letterman, J. Barker, W. Miller, R.H. Evans, J. Harding, J. Faulder, and Gale and Curtis, 1812.

The alphabetical entries are not without editorial comment. For example, under EVERY MAN IN HIS HUMOUR, concerning its long neglect, "until the year 1725," when the BIOGRAPHIA records, "it was again restored to the stage, with alterations, at Lincoln's Inn Field; and, strange to say, the part of Kitely was allotted, to the buffoon Hippisley. . . . In such hands it will be no wonder that it ended in three representations only" (Vol. 2, p. 204).

Barker, James. THE DRAMA RECORDED.

See [Egerton, John].

Barrett, W[ilfred] P[hillips], comp. CHART OF PLAYS, 1584-1623. Published under the Auspices of the Shakespeare Association. Cambridge and London: Cambridge University Press; New York: Maruzen Co., 1934.

Although the chart runs only to thirty-nine pages, it provides, as Barrett's "Introduction" states, a graphic display of the time relationship of various productions and also opens the way to speculation about patterns which are exposed by the chart format (p.[5]).

Beloe, William. ANECDOTES OF LITERATURE AND SCARCE BOOKS. 6 vols. London: Printed for F.C. and J. Rivington by Bye and Law, 1807-12.

As Under Librarian of the British Museum, Beloe says (Vol. 1, pp. viii-ix) he examined printed books and "undertook, from time to time, to give such a description of them and their contents, as might be interesting and useful both to the student and collector." Volumes 3-6 contain little on drama, but Volumes 1 and 2 a great deal. In Volume 1, for example, Beloe describes the "Garrick Collection" and the "Malone Collection"; in Volume 2 there are entries under Chapman, Peele, Dekker, Lodge, and Greene--together with much else, of course. The matter in Beloe's ANECDOTES is so miscellaneous that the student who suspects that there is something of interest to her or him in the volumes will need to make a careful search to uncover what they really hold.

Bentley, Gerald Eades. THE JACOBEAN AND CAROLINE STAGE.

Bentley provides an exceptionally full list of plays, playwrights, companies, actors, theatres, and so on. See the main entry in Section 8: Studies of Tudor and Stuart Drama.

Bowers, Fredson. A SUPPLEMENT TO THE WOODWARD & MCMANAWAY CHECK LIST OF ENGLISH PLAYS, 1641-1700. Charlottesville: Bibliographical Society of the University of Virginia, 1949.

A twenty-two-page supplement. See Woodward, Gertrude L., and James G. McManaway.

Chambers, E[dmund] K[erchever]. THE ELIZABETHAN STAGE.

Chambers offers full lists of plays, playwrights, players, playhouses, and the like. See the main entry in Section 8: Studies of the Tudor and Stuart Drama.

[Egerton, John]. EGERTON'S THEATRICAL REMEMBRANCER, CONTAINING A COMPLETE LIST OF ALL THE DRAMATIC PERFORMANCES IN THE ENGLISH LANGUAGE; THEIR SEVERAL EDITIONS, DATES, AND SIZES, AND THE THEATRES WHERE THEY WERE ORIGINALLY PERFORMED: TOGETHER WITH AN ACCOUNT OF THOSE WHICH HAVE BEEN ACTED AND ARE UNPUBLISHED, AND A CATALOGUE OF SUCH LATIN PLAYS AS HAVE BEEN WRITTEN BY ENGLISH AUTHORS, FROM THE EARLIEST PRODUCTION OF THE ENGLISH DRAMA TO THE END OF THE YEAR MDCCLXXXVII. TO WHICH ARE ADDED NOTITIA DRAMATICA, BEING A CHRONOLOGICAL ACCOUNT OF EVENTS RELATIVE TO THE ENGLISH STAGE. London: Printed for T. and J. Egerton, 1787.

See also:

Barker, James. THE DRAMA RECORDED; OR, BARKER'S LIST OF PLAYS . . . FROM THE EARLIEST PERIOD, TO 1814; TO WHICH ARE ADDED NOTITIA DRAMATICA. . . . Ed. Walley Oulton. London: J. Barker, 1814.

Barker provides a sequel which corrects and supplements Egerton's REMEMBRANCER.

Consult catalogs of the British Museum, the Library of Congress,

(THE NATIONAL UNION CATALOG. PRE-1956 IMPRINTS), and the like, for a fuller history of the publication of these materials.

Eyre, G.E. Briscoe, ed. A TRANSCRIPT OF THE REGISTERS OF THE WORSHIPFUL COMPANY OF STATIONERS: FROM 1640-1708 A.D. Transcribed by H.R. Plomer. 3 vols. 1913-14; reprint ed. Gloucester, Mass.: Peter Smith, 1967.

A companion to A TRANSCRIPT OF THE REGISTERS OF THE COMPANY OF STATIONERS OF LONDON (see Arber, Edward, ed.).

Greg, W[alter] W[ilson]. A BIBLIOGRAPHY OF THE ENGLISH PRINTED DRAMA TO THE RESTORATION. 4 vols. Illustrated Monographs, No. 24, 1-4. London: Printed for the Bibliographical Society at the University Press, Oxford, 1939-59.

Volume I contains materials from the Stationers' Records and Plays to 1616; Volume II, Plays from 1617 to 1689, Latin Plays, and Lost Plays; Volume III, Collections, Appendix, Reference Lists; Volume IV, Introduction, Additions, Corrections, and an Index of Titles. Certain reference tools have been prepared with such care and with such knowledge of what is needed that they may be supplemented and in some points corrected but hardly superseded. This and the following titles prepared by Greg are such tools.

_____. A LIST OF ENGLISH PLAYS WRITTEN BEFORE 1643 AND PRINTED BEFORE 1700. London: Printed for the Bibliographical Society by Blades, East & Blades, 1900.

The title annotates this useful tool. See also the next item.

_____. A LIST OF MASQUES, PAGEANTS, &C. SUPPLEMENTARY TO A LIST OF ENGLISH PLAYS. London: Printed for the Bibliographical Society by Blades, East & Blades, 1902.

In addition to the basic list, Appendix 1, "Advertisement Lists," contains some representative "reprints of the dramatic items from some old stationers' advertisements." Appendix II, "The Early Play Lists," contains a list made up from four catalogs originally published with editions of plays: The Rogers and Ley edition of THE CARELESS SHEPHERDESS, 1656; Archer's THE OLD LAW, 1656; Brook, Kirkman, Johnson, and Marsch's [?] TOM TYLER, 1661; and Kirkman's NICOMEDE, 1671. These lists are frequently referred to and are not easy to secure. Greg's compilation of them is, therefore, most welcome. The volume also contains an essay designed "to supply an introduction to the study of dramatic bibliography, both historical and technical" and "A List of English Plays. Addenda & Corrigenda." (See Greg's "Preface," particularly pages [vii], [xxv], and [xlii] on these matters.)

Greg, W[alter] W[ilson], ed., assisted by C.P. Blagden and I.G. Philip. A COMPANION TO ARBER: BEING A CALENDAR OF DOCUMENTS IN EDWARD ARBER'S "TRANSCRIPT OF THE REGISTERS OF THE COMPANY OF STATIONERS OF LONDON 1554-1640" WITH TEXT AND CALENDAR OF SUPPLEMENTARY DOCUMENTS. Oxford: Clarendon Press, 1967.

The "Preface," signed I.G. Philip, explains the need for A COMPANION TO ARBER: "Arber included in his editions of the registers what he called 'a large mass of illustrative matter.'" This large mass is not chronologically arranged, nor is it indexed. Greg therefore "compiled a chronological calendar of all the documents which Arber had interpolated into his edition" (p. [v]). Greg's material is designed for use in conjunction with Arber's TRANSCRIPT or by itself.

See also Greg's COLLECTED PAPERS under Section 4: Festschriften and Other Collections of Essays especially for a reprinting of "The Bakings of Betsy," concerning John Warburton's claim to having owned some plays inadvertently burned by his cook. See also, under Section 8: Studies of Tudor and Stuart Drama, the essay by John Freehafer which suggests that Warburton's claim may have merit.

Halliwell [-Phillipps], James O. A DICTIONARY OF OLD ENGLISH PLAYS, EXISTING IN PRINT OR IN MANUSCRIPT, FROM THE EARLIEST TIMES TO THE CLOSE OF THE SEVENTEENTH CENTURY; INCLUDING ALSO NOTICES OF LATIN PLAYS WRITTEN BY ENGLISH AUTHORS DURING THE SAME PERIOD. London: John Russell Smith, 1860.

Halliwell-Phillipps lists the plays and comments briefly but often entertainingly about them. He provides supplementary lists of "The Collected Works of Dramatic Authors," "Collections of Old English Plays," and "Collections of Miracle Plays." There is an "Index of Authors."

Harbage, Alfred. ANNALS OF ENGLISH DRAMA, 975-1700: AN ANALYTICAL RECORD OF ALL PLAYS, EXTANT OR LOST, CHRONOLOGICALLY ARRANGED AND INDEXED BY AUTHORS, TITLES, DRAMATIC COMPANIES, &C. Revised by S[amuel] Schoenbaum. Philadelphia: University of Pennsylvania Press, 1940; rev. ed. University of Pennsylvania, and London: Methuen & Co., 1964.

One of several virtues of this list is its comprehensiveness; included are "a list of plays, masks, and other dramatic or quasi-dramatic representations devised in England, or by Englishmen abroad, from . . . the first recorded QUEM QUAERITIS until the year of the death of John Dryden." Latin, French, and English plays, lost plays, unacted plays, translated plays, adapted plays--all are included. All that is required for inclusion in the list is "that the work . . . be of known title or subject matter." "Quasi-dramatic" allows for the inclusion of "descriptions of royal receptions and entertainments" (see p. xi on the scope of the list). The arrangement is chronological, with no annotation. See page xii for an evaluation of the surviving usefulness of the lists provided by Langbaine; Baker, Reed, and Jones; Halliwell [-Phillipps]; and W.C. Hazlitt. See also Schoenbaum, S[amuel] for supplements to these ANNALS.

______. "Elizabethan and Seventeenth-Century Play Manuscripts." PMLA, 50 (1935), 687-99.

Because E.K. Chambers's THE ELIZABETHAN STAGE, Appendix N, lists only "those Plays provedly composed before 1616" and because "the notes concerning manuscripts interspersed in W.C. Hazlitt's MANUAL FOR THE COLLECTOR AND AMATEUR OF OLD ENGLISH PLAYS are incomplete and frequently vague" (p. 687), Harbage has compiled a list of "play manuscripts dating from 1558 to 1700," omitting, however, all Latin plays.

Kirk, John Foster. A SUPPLEMENT TO ALLIBONE'S CRITICAL DICTIONARY OF ENGLISH LITERATURE AND BRITISH AND AMERICAN AUTHORS. CONTAINING OVER THIRTY-SEVEN THOUSAND ARTICLES (AUTHORS), AND ENUMERATING OVER NINETY-THREE THOUSAND TITLES. 1891; reprint ed. Detroit: Gale Research Co., 1965.

See Allibone, S. Austin.

A NEW THEATRICAL DICTIONARY CONTAINING AN ACCOUNT OF ALL THE DRAMATIC PIECES THAT HAVE APPEARED FROM THE COMMENCEMENT OF THEATRICAL EXHIBITIONS TO THE PRESENT TIME TOGETHER WITH THEIR DATES WHEN WRITTEN OR PRINTED, WHERE ACTED, AND OCCASIONAL REMARKS ON THEIR MERITS AND SUCCESS. TO WHICH IS ADDED AN ALPHABETICAL CATALOGUE OF DRAMATIC WRITERS, WITH THE TITLES OF ALL THE PIECES THEY HAVE WRITTEN, ANNEXED TO EACH NAME, AND ALSO A SHORT SKETCH OF THE RISE AND PROGRESS OF THE ENGLISH STAGE. London: Printed for S. Bladon, 1792.

All this is supplied in 400 pages, with an "Addenda" listing one play, presumably the only one overlooked.

Pollard, A[lfred] W., and G.R. Redgrave, with others. A SHORT-TITLE CATALOGUE OF BOOKS PRINTED IN ENGLAND, SCOTLAND, & IRELAND AND OF ENGLISH BOOKS PRINTED ABROAD 1475-1640. London: Bibliographical Society, 1946.

The "STC" must be consulted for an endless variety of details concerning early printed materials.

Schoenbaum, S[amuel]. ANNALS OF ENGLISH DRAMA, 975-1700, A SUPPLEMENT TO THE REVISED EDITION. Evanston, Ill.: Northwestern University, 1966, with A SECOND SUPPLEMENT, 1970.

Complements Harbage, Alfred, ANNALS OF ENGLISH DRAMA.

Sibley, Gertrude Marian. THE LOST PLAYS AND MASQUES, 1500-1642. Cornell Studies in English, Vol. 19. Ithaca, N.Y.: Cornell University Press; London: Oxford University Press, 1933.

The "Preface" indicates the scope of the volume: It includes all the known data about lost plays from 1558 to 1642, treating the masques less completely, since those are dealt with in Steele, Mary Susan, PLAYS AND MASQUES AT COURT, 1558-1642 (see below). The study lists separately "the English plays known to have been acted in Germany, most of which are either lost or hard to identify." The list also gives plays and masques of the period 1550-58 but deals with them less exhaustively than with those of the period 1558-1642.

Stationers Company of London.

See Arber, Edward, ed., and Eyre, G.E. Briscoe, ed.

Steele, Mary Susan. PLAYS AND MASQUES AT COURT, 1558-1642.

See main entry in Section 8: Studies of Tudor Stuart Drama.

Stratman, Carl J. BIBLIOGRAPHY OF MEDIEVAL DRAMA.

Stratman provides a full bibliography from which the canon of Medieval plays can be derived. See main entry in Section 1 C: Bibliographies of Drama.

THE THEATRICAL REMEMBRANCER

See [Egerton, John].

Wells, Henry W. A CHRONOLOGICAL LIST OF EXTANT PLAYS PRODUCED IN OR ABOUT LONDON, 1581-1642, PREPARED . . . AS A SUPPLEMENT TO . . . "ELIZABETHAN AND JACOBEAN PLAYWRIGHTS." New York: Columbia University Press, 1940.

Wells's LIST is printed both separately and in the volume with ELIZABETHAN AND JACOBEAN PLAYWRIGHTS (see Section 8: Studies of Tudor and Stuart Drama).

Whincop, Thomas. SCANDERBEG: OR LOVE AND LIBERTY. A TRAGEDY. WRITTEN BY THE LATE THOMAS WHINCOP, ESQ. TO WHICH ARE ADDED A LIST OF ALL THE DRAMATIC AUTHORS, WITH SOME ACCOUNT OF THEIR LIVES; AND OF ALL THE DRAMATIC PIECES EVER PUBLISHED IN THE ENGLISH LANGUAGE TO THE YEAR 1747. London: W. Reeve, 1747.

"A Compleat List of All the English Dramatic Poets, and of All the Plays Ever Printed in the English Language, to the Present Year M.DCC.LVII," which occupies pages [87]-320, followed by thirty pages of index, is one of the famous early playlists.

Wing, Donald. A SHORT-TITLE CATALOGUE OF BOOKS PRINTED IN ENGLAND, SCOTLAND, IRELAND, WALES AND BRITISH AMERICA AND OF ENGLISH BOOKS PRINTED IN OTHER COUNTRIES, 1641-1700. 3 vols. New York: Printed by Columbia University Press for the Index Society, 1945-51.

A second edition of Volume 1, revised and enlarged, was published in 1972; revised editions of Volumes 2 and 3 are in preparation. See Wing to supplement Pollard and Redgrave for the later seventeenth century. See also Woodward, Gertrude L., and James G. McManaway, immediately below.

Woodward, Gertrude L., and James G. McManaway. A CHECK LIST OF ENGLISH PLAYS, 1641-1700. Chicago: The Newberry Library, 1945.

The Woodward-McManaway list preceded the publication of the Wing SHORT-TITLE CATALOGUE, 1641-1700 which now covers this and additional ground. The CHECK LIST remains, however, a convenient means of securing a list of plays without going through entries for other genres at the same time. See also Bowers, Fredson, for a supplement.

10. CONTEMPORARY AND OTHER EARLY RECORDS, ALLUSIONS, CRITICISM, ETC.

The materials in this section represent an attempt to suggest the attitudes of the Renaissance and the immediately succeeding periods to the stage and dramatic writers. That one will notice, or that one could have space to record if they were found, all the references which might be garnered is too much to hope. I have suggested some important titles, a few collections of materials, and a few guides to Renaissance criticism. See also individual playwrights in Part 2.

Arber, Edward, ed. AN ENGLISH GARNER. Originally published in 8 vols., 1877-90; reprint ed. in 12 vols., New York: Cooper Square Publishers, 1964.

Not all the material bears on the drama. For the sake of completeness, and for possible utility, all may be mentioned: Volume I: Alfred W. Pollard, ed., FIFTEENTH CENTURY PROSE AND VERSE; Volumes II and III: Sidney Lee, ed., ELIZABETHAN SONNETS; Volume IV: A.H. Bullen, ed., SHORTER ELIZABETHAN POEMS; Volume V: A.H. Bullen, ed., SOME LONGER ELIZABETHAN POEMS; Volume VI: A.F. Pollard, ed., TUDOR TRACTS 1532-1588; Volume VII: C.H. Firth, ed., STUART TRACTS 1603-1693; Volume VIII: George A. Aitken, ed., LATER STUART TRACTS; Volume IX: Andrew Lang, ed., SOCIAL ENGLAND ILLUSTRATED: A COLLECTION OF XVIITH CENTURY TRACTS; Volumes X and XI: C. Raymond Beazley, ed., VOYAGES AND TRAVELS MAINLY DURING THE 16TH AND 17TH CENTURIES; Volume XII: J. Churton Collins, ed., CRITICAL ESSAYS AND LITERARY FRAGMENTS.

CALENDAR OF STATE PAPERS.

See Great Britain. Public Record Office.

Collier, Jeremy. A SHORT VIEW OF THE IMMORALITY AND PROFANENESS OF THE ENGLISH STAGE. 1698.

Collier's famous SHORT VIEW is directed primarily at the Restoration stage but is important to the whole argument about stage playing. The tract provoked retort. For an edition which collects Collier's first and second thoughts, see A SHORT VIEW OF THE

PROFANENESS AND IMMORALITY OF THE ENGLISH STAGE, &C. WITH THE SEVERAL DEFENSES OF THE SAME. IN ANSWER TO MR. CONGREVE, DR. DRAKE, &C. (London: G. Strahan, 1730). See also Freeman, Arthur, ed.

Collier, John Payne, ed. THE ALLEYN PAPERS; A COLLECTION OF ORIGINAL DOCUMENTS ILLUSTRATIVE OF THE LIFE AND TIMES OF EDWARD ALLEYN, AND OF THE EARLY ENGLISH STAGE AND DRAMA. 1843; reprint ed. New York: AMS Press, 1970.

George Watson Cole, in "A Survey of the Bibliography of English Literature, 1475-1640" (THE PAPERS OF THE BIBLIOGRAPHICAL SOCIETY OF AMERICA, 23 [1929], 31), says that John Payne Collier "was a rank sensationalist without due regard for veracity. He hesitated at nothing to produce an impression . . . [T]he discoveries of his forgeries have cast doubt upon all his work to such an extent that no statement made by him can be accepted without critical examination." Cole's advice should be heeded, not the less for the fact that Collier edited many valuable pieces and under very respectable auspices. THE ALLEYN PAPERS, for example, originally appeared in the Shakespeare Society's Papers.

Dekker, Thomas. "THE WONDERFUL YEAR"; "THE GULL'S HORN-BOOK"; "PENNY-WISE, POUND-FOOLISH"; "ENGLISH VILLANIES DISCOVERED BY LANTERN AND CANDLELIGHT" AND SELECTED WRITINGS. Ed. E.D. Pendry. Stratford-Upon-Avon Library, No. 4. London: E. Arnold, 1967.

Martin S. Day, in HISTORY OF ENGLISH LITERATURE TO 1660 (see main entry in Section 5: General Literary Histories), says that the sketch, "How a Gallant Should Behave Himself in a Playhouse," in Dekker's GULL'S HORNBOOK, 1609, "offers our only full-length account of conduct in the theater."

Dennis, John. THE CRITICAL WORKS. Ed. Edward Niles Hooker. 2 vols. Baltimore, Md.: Johns Hopkins Press; London: Oxford University Press, 1939-43, with various reprintings.

Volume I contains, together with other matters, "The Impartial Critick: or, some Observations upon a Late Book, Entituled, A Short View of Tragedy by Mr. Rymer" (1693); "The Usefulness of the Stage" (1698); "The Person of Quality's Answer to Mr. Collier's Letter, Being a Disswasive from the Play-House" (1704). Volume II contains, again together with other matters, "The Stage Defended, From Scripture, Reason, Experience, and the Common Sense of Mankind for Two Thousand Years. Occasion'd by Mr. Law's Late Pamphlet Against Stage-Entertainments" (1726).

Dryden, John. ESSAYS. Selected and edited by W.P. Ker. 2 vols. 1900; reprint ed. New York: Russell & Russell, 1961.

Dryden's essays, landmarks of English dramatic criticism, are available in numerous editions. Ker's edition is widely used. A few other editions containing all or part of the drama criticism follow immediately below.

______. LITERARY CRITICISM. Ed. Arthur C. Kirsh. Regents Critics Series. Lincoln: University of Nebraska Press, 1966.

______. OF DRAMATICK POESIE, AN ESSAY. PRECEDED BY A DIALOGUE ON POETIC DRAMA BY T.S. ELIOT. London: Frederick Etchells & Hugh Macdonald, 1928.

The special interest of this edition is Eliot's essay, cast as a dialogue and concerned with the possibility of creating a poetic drama for the modern world.

______. SELECTED CRITICISM. Ed. James Kinsley and George Parfitt. Oxford: Clarendon Press, 1970.

EARLY TREATISES ON THE STAGE; VIZ. NORTHBROOKE'S TREATISE AGAINST DICING, DANCING, PLAYS, AND INTERLUDES; ETC., FROM THE EDITION PRINTED ABOUT 1557. GOSSON'S SCHOOL OF ABUSE . . . AND HEYWOOD'S DEFENCE OF STAGE PLAYS. London: Printed for the Shakespeare Society, 1853.

The fame of these pamphlets requires no annotation.

Feuillerat, Albert, ed. DOCUMENTS RELATING TO THE OFFICE OF THE REVELS IN THE TIME OF QUEEN ELIZABETH AND DOCUMENTS RELATING TO THE OFFICE OF THE REVELS IN THE TIME OF KING EDWARD VI AND QUEEN MARY (THE LOSELY MANUSCRIPTS). MATERIALIEN ZUR KUNDE DES ALTEREN ENGLISCHEN DRAMAS, edited by W. Bang, vols. 21 and 44. 1908, 1914; reprint ed. Vaduz: Kraus Reprint, 1963.

Title annotates.

Freeman, Arthur, ed. THE ENGLISH STAGE: ATTACK AND DEFENSE, 1577-1730: A COLLECTION OF 90 IMPORTANT WORKS REPRINTED IN PHOTO-FACSIMILE IN 50 VOLUMES. New York: Garland Publishing, 1971-74.

The intention of the series is to offer facsimile reprints with modern critical apparatus of all the documents in more than a century and a half of debate, excepting only very slight pieces and those easily obtainable in suitable editions. The ninety titles are: Volume 1: John Northbrooke, A TREATISE WHEREIN DICING, DAUNCING, VAINE PLAYES OR ENTERLUDS . . . ARE REPROVED. Volume 2: Stephen Gosson, THE SHOOLE [SIC] OF ABUSE and [Lodge], REPLY. Volume 3: Gosson, THE EPHEMERIDES OF PHIALO. Volume 4: [Anthony Munday], A SECOND AND THIRD BLAST FOR RETRAIT FROM PLAIES AND THEATERS. Volume 5: A TREA-

TISE OF DAUNCES and John Field, A GODLY EXHORTATION; Volume 6: Gosson, PLAYES CONFUTED IN FIUE ACTIONS. Volumes 7-8: Philip Stubbes, THE ANATOMIE OF ABUSES, Parts 1 and 2. Volume 9: William Rankins, A MIRROUR OF MONSTERS; [Nashe], "Preface" to Greene's MENAPHON; and Henry Chettle, KIND HARTS DREAM. Volume 10: Francis Meres, PALLADIS TAMIA. Volume 11: Rainoldes, Gager, and Gentili, TH'OVERTHROW OF STAGE-PLAYES. Volume 12: Thomas Heywood, AN APOLOGY FOR ACTORS, with the REFUTATION by I.G. Volume 13: William Prynne, HISTRIOMASTIX. Volume 14: [Alexander Leighton], A SHORTE TREATISE AGAINST STAGE-PLAYES and a series of anonymous pieces: THE STAGE-PLAYERS COMPLAINT; DECLARATION . . . ALSO AN ORDINANCE OF BOTH HOUSES, FOR THE SUPPRESSION OF STAGE-PLAYES; THE ACTORS REMONSTRANCE; TWO ORDINANCES; AN ORDINANCE . . . FOR, THE UTTER SUPPRESSION AND ABOLISHING OF ALL STAGE-PLAYES AND INTERLUDES; THE DAGONIZING OF BARTHOLOMEW FAYRE; THE HUMBLE PETITION OF DIVERSE POOR AND DISTRESSED MEN; and THE PLAYERS PETITION. Volume 15: the anonymous MR. WILLIAM PRYNN HIS DEFENCE OF STAGE-PLAYS and [Prynne], VINDICATION OF WILLIAM PRYNNE; also Sir Richard Baker, THEATRUM REDIVIVUM. Volume 16: John Rowe, TRAGI-COMOEDIA. Volume 17: Richard Flecknoe, LOVE'S KINGDOM . . . WITH A SHORT TREATISE OF THE ENGLISH STAGE. Volume 18: Thomas Rymer, THE TRAGEDIES OF THE LAST AGE CONSIDER'D AND EXAMIN'D and his A SHORT VIEW OF TRAGEDY. Volume 19: Gerard Langbaine, MOMUS TRIUMPHANS and his LIVES AND CHARACTERS. Volume 20: Langbaine, AN ACCOUNT OF THE ENGLISH DRAMATICK POETS. Volume 21: John Dennis, THE IMPARTIAL CRITICK and [Charles Gildon], MISCELLANEOUS LETTERS AND ESSAYS. Volume 22: Jeremy Collier, A SHORT VIEW OF THE IMMORALITY, AND PROFANENESS OF THE ENGLISH STAGE. Volume 23: [William Congreve], AMENDMENTS OF MR. COLLIER'S FALSE AND IMPERFECT CITATIONS, &C. FROM THE OLD BATCHELOUR, DOUBLE DEALER, LOVE FOR LOVE, MOURNING BRIDE. Volume 24: ANIMADVERSIONS ON MR. CONGREVE'S LATE ANSWER TO MR. COLLIER, IN DIALOGUE BETWEEN MR. SMITH AND MR. JOHNSON. Volume 25: [Elkanah Settle], A DEFENCE OF DRAMATICK POETRY and his A FARTHER DEFENCE OF DRAMATICK POETRY. Volume 26: John Dennis, THE USEFULNESS OF THE STAGE. Volume 27: THE IMMORALITY OF THE ENGLISH PULPIT and [Charles Hopkins], A LETTER TO A.H. ESQ.: CONCERNING THE STAGE; also the anonymous A LETTER TO MR. CONGREVE ON HIS PRETENDED AMENDMENTS; [Richard Willis], THE OCCASIONAL PAPER; the anonymous SOME REMARKS ON MR. COLLIER'S DEFENCE OF HIS SHORT VIEW OF THE ENGLISH STAGE; and the anonymous A VINDICATION OF THE STAGE. Volume 28: [Sir John Vanbrugh], A SHORT VINDICATION OF THE RELAPSE AND THE PROVOK'D WIFE. Volume 29: [George Ridpath], THE STAGE CONDEMN'D. Volume 30: Jeremy Collier,

A DEFENCE OF THE SHORT VIEW. Volume 31: THE STAGE ACQUITTED, BEING A FULL ANSWER TO MR. COLLIER. Volume 32: [James Drake], THE ANTIENT AND MODERN STAGES SURVEY'D. Volume 33: [John Oldmixon], REFLECTIONS ON THE STAGE, AND MR. COLLYER'S DEFENCE OF THE SHORT VIEW. Volume 34: Jeremy Collier, A SECOND DEFENCE OF THE SHORT VIEW. Volume 35: [Collier], MR. COLLIER'S DISSUASIVE FROM THE PLAY-HOUSE and his A FARTHER VINDICATION OF THE SHORT VIEW; also [John Dennis], THE PERSON OF QUALITY'S ANSWER TO MR. COLLIER'S LETTERS BEING A DISSWASIVE FROM THE PLAY-HOUSE; the anonymous A REPRESENTATION OF THE IMPIETY & IMMORALITY OF THE ENGLISH STAGE; [Collier (?)], SOME THOUGHTS CONCERNING THE STAGE IN A LETTER TO A LADY; and [Charles Gildon], THE STAGE-BEAUX TOSS'D IN A BLANKET. Volume 36: Edward Filmer, A DEFENCE OF PLAYS: OR, THE STAGE VINDICATED. Volume 37: VISITS FROM THE SHADES. Volume 38: [James Wright], HISTORIA HISTRIONICA and [John Downes], ROSCIUS ANGLICANUS. Volume 39: A COMPARISON BETWEEN THE TWO STAGES: IN DIALOGUE. Volume 40: Sir William Anstruther, ESSAYS, MORAL AND DIVINE. Volume 41: [Arthur Bedford], SERIOUS REFLECTIONS; his SECOND ADVERTISEMENT CONCERNING THE PROFANENESS OF THE PLAY-HOUSE; and his A SERMON PREACHED IN THE PARISH-CHURCH OF ST. BUTOLPH'S ALDGATE. Volume 42: Bedford, A SERIOUS REMONSTRANCE IN BEHALF OF THE CHRISTIAN RELIGION. Volume 43: Bedford, THE EVIL AND DANGER OF STAGE-PLAYS. Volume 44: William Ames, STAGE PLAYS ARRAIGNED AND CONDEMNED; Richard Burridge, A SCOURGE FOR THE PLAY-HOUSES; John Feild [sic], AN HUMBLE APPLICATION TO THE QUEEN; A LETTER FROM SEVERAL MEMBERS OF THE SOCIETY FOR REFORMATION OF MANNERS; and William Melmoth, NEW REPRESENTATIONS OF THE CORRUPTION OF THE STAGE. Volume 45: the anonymous THE CONDUCT OF THE STAGE CONSIDER'D and [John James] Heidegger, HEYDEGGER'S LETTER TO THE BISHOP OF LONDON; [P.W.?], A SEASONABLE APOLOGY FOR M. H-G-R. Volume 46: R.C., THE DANGER OF MASQUERADES AND RAREE-SHOWS; the anonymous THE DANCING DEVILS; OR, THE ROARING DRAGON. A DUMB FARCE; and the anonymous A LETTER TO MY LORD ****** ON THE PRESENT DIVERSIONS OF THE TOWN. Volume 47: [James Ralph], THE TOUCH-STONE. Volume 48: [Charles Gildon], REMARKS ON MR. ROWE'S TRAGEDY OF LADY JANE GREY, AND ALL HIS OTHER PLAYS. Volume 49: William Law, THE ABSOLUTE UNLAWFULNESS OF THE STAGE-ENTERTAINMENT FULLY DEMONSTRATED; John Dennis, THE STAGE DEFENDED; Mrs. S- O-, LAW OUTLAW'D; OR, A SHORT REPLY TO MR. LAW'S LONG DECLAMATION AGAINST THE STAGE. Volume 50: the pseudonymous S. Philomusus, MR. LAW'S UNLAWFULNESS OF THE STAGE ENTERTAINMENT EXAMIN'D; the anonymous THE ENTERTAINMENT OF THE STAGE . . . CONSTANTLY TO BE AVOIDED BY ALL SINCERE CHRISTIANS;

and [Allan Ramsay], SOME FEW HINTS, IN DEFENCE OF DRAMATICAL ENTERTAINMENTS.

Furnivall, Frederick J., ed.

See [Laneham, Robert], and also Munro, John James, and E[dmund] K[erchever] Chambers, eds.

Gayton, Edmund. PLEASANT NOTES UPON DON QUIXOT. London: William Hunt, 1654.

Book 4, pages 271-72, contains Gayton's brief but pithy comment on the stage as subject to popular taste, or tastelessness.

Gosson, Stephen.

See EARLY TREATISES ON THE STAGE.

Great Britain. Public Record Office. CALENDAR OF STATE PAPERS. DOMESTIC SERIES.

Northrup Frye is reported to have said that there are two classes of critics, those who can find materials in the Public Record Office and those who cannot find the Public Record Office. For those who wish to launch into the first category, the way is much eased by the publication of the CALENDAR OF STATE PAPERS, DOMESTIC SERIES, among other documents from this office now in print. For the Tudor-Stuart period, one may begin with the CALENDAR OF STATE PAPERS, DOMESTIC SERIES, OF THE REIGNS OF EDWARD VI, MARY, ELIZABETH, 1547-1580, PRESERVED IN THE STATE PAPER DEPARTMENT OF HER MAJESTY'S PUBLIC RECORD OFFICE, Volume I, edited by Robert Lemon (London: Longman, Brown, Green, Longmans, & Roberts, 1856). The Edward-Mary-Elizabeth papers, for the years through 1625, run through Volume 13, Volumes I and II being edited by Lemon and III-XIII by Mary Anne Everett Green. The papers for the years of James I are edited by Green in five volumes, and those for Charles I in twenty-three volumes. The interregnum years occupy thirteen volumes and are also edited by Green. See further the microprint editions available from Microcard Editions in Washington, D.C. Even in print, however, the masses of the material cannot be dealt with lightly.

Greg, W[alter] W[ilson]. DRAMATIC DOCUMENTS FROM THE ELIZABETHAN PLAYHOUSES. STAGE PLOTS: ACTORS' PARTS: PROMPT BOOKS. REPRODUCTIONS & TRANSCRIPTS. Oxford: Clarendon Press, [1931].

Of general interest to the curious; of special interest to the specialist--reproductions in facsimile with transcriptions.

______, ed. HENSLOWE PAPERS: BEING DOCUMENTS SUPPLEMENTARY TO

HENSLOWE'S DIARY. London: A.H. Bullen, 1907.

Included are "Documents relating to the Theatre and Bear Garden," "Papers relating to the Bearbaiting," "Memorandum-Book of Edward Alleyn," "Miscellaneous notes," and "Miscellaneous papers." Among the appendices is one on "Dramatic Plots." (Greg defines dramatic plots as "what may be called the skeleton outlines of the plays they represent, consisting of the entrances and exits of the characters together with such other directions as would require the attention of the prompter or call-boy" [p. 127].)

Greg, W[alter] W[ilson], and E. Boswell, eds. RECORDS OF THE COURT OF THE STATIONERS' COMPANY 1576 TO 1602--FROM REGISTER B. London: Oxford University Press for the Bibliographical Society, 1930.

The "Introduction" recalls that Edward Arber was denied permission to print "a section of Register B" but states that the Bibliograhical Society "has been allowed to make photostatic copies of the Decrees and Ordinances that fill nearly 120 pages of Register B and likewise the whole of Court Book C," making available "the complete records of the Court of the Stationers' Company from July 1576 down to March 1655" (p. v). Greg provides a full introduction as well as facsimiles and transcriptions. Well indexed. See Jackson, William A., ed., for the supplement to Greg and Boswell; see Arber, Edward, ed., in Section 9: Playlists, Records of Early Publication, Etc., for the TRANSCRIPT OF THE REGISTERS.

Harrison, G[eorge] B[agshawe]. THE ELIZABETHAN JOURNALS: BEING A RECORD OF THOSE THINGS MOST TALKED OF DURING THE YEARS 1591-1603, COMPRISING AN ELIZABETHAN JOURNAL 1591-4, A SECOND ELIZABETHAN JOURNAL 1595-8, A LAST ELIZABETHAN JOURNAL 1599-1603. Ann Arbor: University of Michigan Press; London: Lowe and Brydone, 1955.

Harrison's JOURNALS are not "Contemporary Records" in the same way that other materials here listed are. When he published the first of the ELIZABETHAN JOURNALS in 1928, he explained in the "Introduction" his intention to provide "a journal of gossip which should mirror the mind of the English people and give a background to their literature during the years 1591 to 1594" (p. xv). A second JOURNAL appeared in 1931 and a third in 1933; then the 1955 volume combines the three (with certain modifications).

_____. A JACOBEAN JOURNAL: BEING A RECORD OF THOSE THINGS MOST TALKED OF DURING THE YEARS 1603-1609. New York: Macmillan, 1941.

See next item.

_____. A SECOND JACOBEAN JOURNAL: BEING A RECORD OF THOSE

THINGS MOST TALKED OF DURING THE YEARS 1607 TO 1610. Ann Arbor: University of Michigan Press, 1958.

The two JACOBEAN JOURNALS complete a set described by Harrison thirty years after the initial JOURNAL was published as intended to enable us "to see life as the contemporaries of Shakespeare, Donne and Ben Jonson saw it, and to record, day by day, in their own words, or--to use the more grandiloquent and modem phrase--to create the Shakespearean World Picture, not intellectually, impressionistically or symbolically, but as it was" (A SECOND JACOBEAN JOURNAL, p. vii).

Harvey, Gabriel. THE WORKS . . . NOW FOR THE FIRST TIME COLLECTED AND EDITED WITH MEMORIAL-INTRODUCTION, NOTES AND ILLUSTRATIONS, ETC., BY THE REV. ALEXANDER B. GROSART. 3 vols. 50 copies, Printed for Private Circulation Only, 1884-85; reprint ed. New York: AMS Press, 1966.

Harvey published highly partisan reactions to certain of his contemporaries, including dramatists. See especially Volume I, pages [151]-254, "Fovre Letters and Certaine Sonnets," for a vigorous attack on Robert Greene; Volume III, pages [1]-72, for the "Trimming of Thomas Nashe, Gentleman." Selections from Harvey may also be found in other editions in this section of the present Bibliography.

Haslewood, Joseph, ed. ANCIENT CRITICAL ESSAYS UPON ENGLISH POETS AND POESY. 2 vols. London: Robert Triphook, 1811, 1815.

Volume I contains THE ARTE OF ENGLISH POESIE (for other editions, see [Puttenham, George?]). Volume II contains George Gascoigne's CERTAYNE NOTES OF INSTRUCTION CONCERNING THE MAKING OF VERSE OR RYME IN ENGLISH; William Webbe's A DISCOURSE OF ENGLISH POETRIE; King James's A TREATISE OF THE AIRT OF SCOTTIS POESIE; Sir John Harington's AN APOLOGIE OF POETRIE; Francis Meres's A COMPARATIVE DISCOURSE OF OUR ENGLISH POETS; Thomas Campion's OBSERVATIONS IN THE ART OF ENGLISH POESIE; Samuel Daniel's A DEFENCE OF RIME; Edmund Bolton's HYPERCRITICA; OR A RULE OF JUDGMENT FOR WRITING OR READING OUR HISTORY'S; Edmund Spenser's and Gabriel Harvey's THREE PROPER AND WITTIE FAMILIAR LETTERS LATELY PASSED BETVVEENE TWO VNIVERSITIE MEN AND TWO OTHER VERY COMMENDABLE LETTERS OF THE SAME MENS VVRITING.

[Hazlitt, W. Carew]. THE ENGLISH DRAMA AND STAGE UNDER THE TUDOR AND STUART PRINCES, 1543-1664, ILLUSTRATED BY A SERIES OF DOCUMENTS, TREATISES AND POEMS, WITH A PREFACE AND INDEX. London: Printed for the Roxburghe Library by Whittingham and Wilkins, 1869.

The "Preface" declares: "The following pages embrace nearly all the Documents and Treatises directly illustrating the early history of English Dramatic Poetry and of the English Stage, which have not hitherto been made accessible" or which in 1869 needed better editions (p. [v]). There are thirty-two documents--letters, statutes, etc.--and thirteen treatises, including "A sermon Against Miracle-Plays," "A second and third blast of retrait from plaies and Theaters," etc. The declared purpose of the Roxburghe Club, as stated in the "Revised Prospectus" printed in this volume, was to bring "within the reach of everyone who cares for them the best inedited remains of our ancient literature." The endlessly interesting and valuable assortment of materials here printed evidences the worthwhileness of the Club's efforts.

Henslowe, Philip. HENSLOWE AND ALLEYN: BEING THE DIARY OF PHILIP HENSLOWE, FROM 1591 TO 1609, AND THE LIFE OF EDWARD ALLEYN, TO WHICH IS ADDED THE ALLEYN PAPERS. Ed. J. Payne Collier. 2 vols. London: Printed for the Shakespeare Society, 1853.

Henslowe's DIARY is a document of such interest and importance, containing as it does Henslowe's records of his dealings with playwrights, actors, and so on, as manager of the Rose and Fortune theatres, that it has been edited by various hands. On Collier as an editor, see Cole's comment quoted in the entry under Collier, John Payne, ed. Two other editions follow immediately below.

_____. HENSLOWE'S DIARY. Ed. W[alter] W[ilson] Greg. 2 vols. London: A.H. Bullen, 1904, 1908.

Part 1 is TEXT, Part 2, COMMENTARY. The text retains Henslowe's spelling, pagination, abbreviations, and so on, altogether remarkable in themselves. The COMMENTARY has chapters on "Henslowe's Family and Private Affairs," "Henslowe and the Stage," "Plays Mentioned in the Diary," and two "Tables of Reference." The DIARY was a practical record made for Henslowe's own use. Such editorial aid as Greg has supplied is needed to make it meaningful to the general user, and Greg as editor and commentator is thoroughly reliable and well informed.

_____. HENSLOWE'S "DIARY" WITH SUPPLEMENTARY MATERIAL, INTRODUCTION AND NOTES. Ed. R.A. Foakes and R.T. Rickerts. Cambridge: At the University Press, 1961.

In addition to a long "Introduction" (pp. xi-lix), there are appendices: "Manuscripts at Dulwich relating to the DIARY" and "Playhouse inventories now lost." The lost inventories are described by the editors as "inventories of properties, costumes and play-books . . . first printed by Malone in his THE PLAYS AND POEMS OF WILLIAM SHAKESPEARE (1790)." Though the lists are now lost, there "is no reason to doubt that the lists were genuine, and were probably . . . in Henslowe's hand. They were reprinted by Greg, HENSLOWE PAPERS, pp. 113-123" (p. 316). The third appendix is "Actors' Names in Dramatic Plots." This edition, which itself acknowledges generously Greg's work, should be used for the more current researches it brings to bear on the DIARY.

Herbert, Sir Henry. THE DRAMATIC RECORDS OF SIR HENRY HERBERT, MASTER OF THE REVELS, 1623-1673. Ed. Joseph Quincy Adams. 1917; reprint ed. New York: Benjamin Blom, [1964?].

Adams's "Introduction" offers explanations of "The Office of the Revels" and "The Herbert Manuscripts." The materials here edited are "The Office Book, 1622-1642" and "Miscellaneous Documents."

Heywood, Thomas. AN APOLOGY FOR ACTORS (1612), printed with A REFUTATION OF THE APOLOGY FOR ACTORS (1615) BY I.G. Ed. Richard H. Perkinson. New York: Scholars' Facsimiles and Reprints, 1941.

The facsimiles are from the Folger Library copies. The texts are important in the long argument about morality and immorality on the stage. (See also EARLY TREATISES ON THE STAGE.)

Hoskin[s], John. DIRECTIONS FOR SPEECH AND STYLE. Ed. Hoyt H. Hudson. Princeton Studies in English, No. 12. Princeton, N.J.: Princeton University Press; London: Oxford University Press, 1935.

Hoskins's dates are 1566-1638. His book is a rhetoric, supplying "all the figures of Rhetoric and the Art of the best English." Hoskins's remarks are not directed particularly at drama but provide a view of rhetoric contemporary with the great period of Renaissance drama. Hudson's "Introduction" calls attention to Hoskins's influence on Jonson (see p. [ix]).

Inderwick, F.A., ed. A CALENDAR OF THE INNER TEMPLE RECORDS. 3 vols. London: Published by the Masters of the Bench and Sold by Henry Southeran, 1896-1901.

I have seen only Volume I of this set, for 1505-1603. Volume I contains Inderwick's "Introduction" as well as the CALENDAR and various appendices.

Jackson, William A., ed. RECORDS OF THE COURT OF THE STATIONERS' COMPANY, 1602-1640. London: The Bibliographical Society, 1957.

Jackson's work is a continuation of the RECORDS, edited by W[alter] W[ilson] Greg and E. Boswell (see above). It "includes part of the first separate volume of the records of the Court, COURT-BOOK C, as well as the same part of the letter book entitled 'Orders of Parliam.^{t} & Ld Mayor Liber A' and the whole of the 'Book of Entraunce of Fines'" (p. vii). Jackson notes that earlier material in the latter book and the years up to 1654/55 in the Court Book deserve publication. The material is fully indexed.

[Jacob, Giles]. THE POETICAL REGISTER. 2 vols. London: Printed for E. Curll, 1719-20.

Volume I has a full title: THE POETICAL REGISTER: OR, THE LIVES AND CHARACTERS OF THE ENGLISH DRAMATICK POETS. WITH AN ACCOUNT OF THEIR WRITINGS. Volume II has a title page: AN HISTORICAL ACCOUNT OF THE LIVES AND WRITINGS OF OUR MOST CONSIDERABLE ENGLISH POETS, WHETHER EPICK, LYRICK, ELEGIAK, EPIGRAMATISTS, &C. Volume I is directly concerned with dramatists; Volume II has "An Account of the Writings of Our Dramatick Poets, out of the Dramatick way" (pp. 243-86). See also an edition from A. Bettesworth (London, 1723) "Adorned with Curious Sculptures Engraven by the Best Masters."

Jonson, Ben. BEN JONSON'S LITERARY CRITICISM. Ed. James D. Redwine, Jr. Regents Critics Series. Lincoln: University of Nebraska Press, 1970.

The general editor of the series, Paul A. Olson, describes it: "Each volume includes a scholarly introduction which describes how the work collected came to be written, and suggests its uses. All texts are edited in the most conservative fashion consonant with the production of a good reading text." The Jonson material can be found in editions of the complete works, of course, but the collection here is useful because it prints not only obvious pieces such as TIMBER, OR DISCOVERIES and HORACE HIS ART OF POETRY but extracts from other writings arranged under topics: "The Functions of a Poet and a Critic," "Comical Satire," "Comedy," "Tragedy," "Masque," "Contemporary Poets and Playwrights," "Contemporary Actors and Audiences." Brief bibliography.

Kelly, William. NOTICES ILLUSTRATIVE OF THE DRAMA, AND OTHER POPULAR AMUSEMENTS, CHIEFLY IN THE SIXTEENTH AND SEVENTEENTH CENTURIES, INCIDENTALLY ILLUSTRATING SHAKESPEARE AND HIS CONTEMPORARIES; EXTRACTED FROM THE CHAMBERLAINS' ACCOUNTS AND OTHER MANUSCRIPTS OF THE BOROUGH OF LEICESTER. London: John Russell Smith, 1865.

The "Notices" are put together in an essay form.

[Kemp, Will(iam)]. NINE DAIES WONDER: PERFORMED IN A DAUNCE FROM LONDON TO NORWICH. Ed. Alexander Dyce. Camden Society Publications, No. 11. London: Printed for the Society by John Bowyer Nichols and Son, 1840.

Dyce provides an "Introduction" concerned with Kemp's career as a sixteenth-century actor and reproduces the original title page: "Kemps nine daies vvonder. Performed in a daunce from London to Norwich. Containing the pleasure, paines and kinde entertainment of William Kemp betweene London and that Citty in his late Morrice. Wherein is somewhat set downe worth note; to reprooue the slaunders spred of him: many things merry, nothing hurtfull.

Written by himselfe to satisfie his friends. London: Printed by E.A. for Nicholas Ling, and are to be solde at his shop at the west doore of Saint Paules Church 1600." The Dyce edition is available in ultrafiche from National Cash Register (Dayton, Ohio: [1970?]).

Klein, David. THE ELIZABETHAN DRAMATISTS AS CRITICS. 1963; reprint ed. Greenwood Press, 1968.

In this sequel to his LITERARY CRITICISM, 1910 (immediately below) Klein has assembled comments of the dramatists on such topics as "Theory of Poetic Creation," "The Nature of Poetry," "The Dignity of the Poetic Art," and so on, providing transitions between excerpts. He argues that "the doctrines enunciated by the dramatists are superior to those preached by critics, both practically and theoretically" (p. 416).

_____. LITERARY CRITICISM FROM THE ELIZABETHAN DRAMATISTS: REPERTORY AND SYNTHESIS, WITH AN INTRODUCTORY NOTE BY J.E. SPINGARN. New York: Sturgis & Walton, 1910.

Spingarn says that Klein "has collected all the utterances of the Elizabethan dramatists on the subject of their own art" and has "grouped these casual utterances" in such a way as to give "an appearance of unity and completeness . . . that the dramatists themselves should not be held wholly responsible for." So forewarned the reader may make discerning use of Klein's collection.

[Laneham, Robert]. CAPTAIN COX, HIS BALLADS AND BOOKS; OR, ROBERT LANEHAM'S LETTER: WHEARIN PART OF THE ENTERTAINMENT UNTOO THE QUEENS MAJESTY AT KILLINGWORTH CASTL, IN WARWIK SHEER IN THIS SOMMERS PROGRESS, 1575, IS SIGNIFIED; FROM A FREEND OFFICER ATTENDANT IN THE COURT, UNTO HIS FREEND, A CITIZEN AND MERCHAUNT OF LONDON. RE-EDITED, WITH FOREWORDS DESCRIBING ALL THE ACCESSIBLE BOOKS, TALES, AND BALLADS, IN CAPTAIN COX'S LIST AND THE COMPLAYNT OF SCOTLAND, 1548-9 A.D., BY FREDERICK J. FURNIVALL. London: Printed for the Ballad Society by Taylor and Co., 1871.

Title annotates.

Lodge, Thomas. A DEFENCE OF POETRY.

See EARLY TREATISES ON THE STAGE, which includes this piece.

Marcham, Frank, ed. THE KING'S OFFICE OF THE REVELS, 1610-1622, FRAGMENTS OF DOCUMENTS IN THE DEPARTMENT OF MANUSCRIPTS, BRITISH MUSEUM. With a Preface by J.P. Gilson. London: Frank Marcham, 1925.

The documents, reproduced, transcribed, and commented upon, are truly fragments.

Meres, Francis. FRANCIS MERES'S TREATISE "POETRIE": A CRITICAL EDITION. Ed. Don Cameron Allen. University of Illinois Bulletin, Vol. 31, No. 13. University of Illinois Studies in Language and Literature, Vol. 16, Nos. 3-4. Urbana: University of Illinois, 1933.

Meres refers to various dramatists--for example, this somewhat remarkable list: "[T]hese are our best for Tragedie, the Lorde Buckhurst, Doctor Leg of Cambridge, Doctor Edes of Oxforde, maister Edward Ferris, the Authour of the Mirrour for Magistrates, Marlow, Peele, Watson, Kid, Shakespeare, Drayton, Chapman, Decker, and Beniamin Iohnston" (Section XVII, p. 78). Allen's "Introduction" evaluates Meres and establishes him in context. The index enables one to find the allusion sought.

____. PALLADIS TAMIA (1598) WITH AN INTRODUCTION BY DON CAMERON ALLEN. New York: Scholars' Facsimiles & Reprints, 1938.

Allen says of Meres that "almost by chance" he recorded "English artistic activity in an age when the keeping of such records was inconceivable" (pp. v-vi). Allen points out that in "A Comparative Discourse of our English Poets" (a section of Meres's PALLADIS TAMIA), "one finds an appreciative mention of most of the prominent writers of the Tudor age."

Munro, John James, and E[dmund] K[erchever] Chambers, eds. THE SHAKSPERE ALLUSION-BOOK: A COLLECTION OF ALLUSIONS TO SHAKSPERE FROM 1591 to 1700. ORIGINALLY COMPILED BY C.M. INGLEBY, MISS L. TOULMIN SMITH, AND BY DR. F.J. FURNIVALL, WITH THE ASSISTANCE OF THE NEW SHAKSPERE SOCIETY: RE-EDITED, REVISED, AND RE-ARRANGED, WITH AN INTRODUCTION, BY JOHN MUNRO (1909), AND NOW RE-ISSUED WITH A PREFACE BY SIR EDMUND CHAMBERS. 2 vols. London: Oxford University Press, 1932.

The "Preface to the Reprint" points out that it "merely reproduces the text of 1909" with "a brief note as to the fresh material which a complete recast would have had to incorporate" (Vol. 1, p. vii). One can learn something of Shakespeare's contemporaries from their allusions to him. Greene, Chettle, Nashe, Marston, Jonson, Dekker, and many others are represented here.

Nagler, A[lois] M[aria]. SOURCES OF THEATRICAL HISTORY. New York: Theatre Annual, 1952; reprint ed. Dover Publications, 1959, with the title A SOURCE BOOK IN THEATRICAL HISTORY.

Interesting and useful collection of primary materials, in English, with bibliographies for each chapter.

Nichols, John. THE PROGRESSES AND PUBLIC PROCESSIONS OF QUEEN ELIZABETH. AMONG WHICH ARE INTERSPERSED OTHER SOLEMNITIES, PUBLIC EXPENDITURES, AND REMARKABLE EVENTS, DURING THE REIGN OF THAT ILLUSTRIOUS PRINCESS. COLLECTED FROM ORIGINAL MANUSCRIPTS,

SCARCE PAMPHLETS, CORPORATION RECORDS, PAROCHIAL REGISTERS, &C. &C. ILLUSTRATED WITH HISTORICAL NOTES. New Edition. 3 vols. London: Printed by and for John Nichols and Son, Printers to the Society of Antiquaries, 1823.

____. THE PROGRESSES, PROCESSIONS, AND MAGNIFICENT FESTIVITIES, OF KING JAMES THE FIRST, HIS ROYAL CONSORT, FAMILY, AND COURT, COLLECTED FROM ORIGINAL MANUSCRIPTS, SCARCE PAMPHLETS, CORPORATION RECORDS, PAROCHIAL REGISTERS, &C. &C. COMPRISING FORTY MASQUES AND ENTERTAINMENTS; TEN CIVIC PAGEANTS; NUMEROUS ORIGINAL LETTERS; AND ANNOTATED LISTS OF PEERS, BARONETS, AND KNIGHTS, WHO RECEIVED THOSE HONOURS DURING THE REIGN OF KING JAMES. ILLUSTRATED WITH NOTES, HISTORICAL, TOPOGRAPHICAL, BIOGRAPHICAL, AND BIBLIOGRAPHICAL. 4 vols. London: Printed by and for J.B. Nichols, Printer to the Society of Antiquaries, 1828.

These titles annotate.

[Nichols, John Gough, ed.]. LONDON PAGEANTS. I. ACCOUNTS OF SIXTY ROYAL PROCESSIONS AND ENTERTAINMENTS IN THE CITY OF LONDON; CHIEFLY EXTRACTED FROM CONTEMPORARY WRITERS. II. A BIBLIOGRAPHICAL LIST OF LORD MAYORS' PAGEANTS. London: Printed by and for J.B. Nichols and Son; Sold by Simkin and Marshall, 1831.

Nichols describes the editing of the materials: "As [the book] is intended for general perusal, the orthography has been corrected, and the phraseology so far modernized that the reader need be no antiquary to unravel its obscurity; yet so far retained that he will not entirely lose that charm which dwells in the quaintness of our early Chronicles" (p. [3]). Unfortunately, what made the book accessible to Nichols's contemporaries rather diminishes its usefulness over the long run, but the accounts and the bibliography may still be of use.

Northbrooke, John. TREATISE AGAINST DICING, DANCING, PLAYS AND INTERLUDES.

See EARLY TREATISES ON THE STAGE.

Painter, William. THE PALACE OF PLEASURE. ELIZABETHAN VERSIONS OF ITALIAN AND FRENCH NOVELS FROM BOCCACCIO, BANDELLO, CINTHIO, STRAPAROLA, QUEEN MARGARET OF NAVARRE, AND OTHERS. NOW AGAIN EDITED FOR THE FOURTH TIME. [Ed. J. Jacobs]. 3 vols. London: David Nutt, 1890.

There are other earlier and later printings of Painter. An edition is in preparation by Jean R. Buchert. Painter is important as a source book for Elizabethan drama, and the new edition is needed.

Prynne, William. HISTRIO-MASTIX. THE PLAYERS SCOVRGE, OR, ACTORS TRAGAEDIE, DIVIDED INTO TWO PARTS. WHEREIN IT IS LARGELY EVI-

DENCED, BY DIVERS ARGUMENTS, BY THE CONCURRING AUTHORITIES AND RESOLUTIONS OF SUNDRY TEXTS OF SCRIPTURE; OF THE WHOLE PRIMITIVE CHURCH, BOTH UNDER THE LAW AND GOSPELL; OF 55 SYNODES AND COUNCELS: OF 71 FATHERS AND CHRISTIAN WRITERS, BEFORE THE YEARE OF OUR LORD 1200; OF ABOVE 150 FORAIGNE AND DOMESTIQUE PROTESTANT AND POPISH AUTHORS, SINCE; OF 40 HEATHEN PHILOSOPHERS, HISTORIANS, POETS; OF MANY HEATHEN, MANY CHRISTIAN NATIONS, REPUBLIQUES, EMPERORS, PRINCES, MAGISTRATES; OF SUNDRY APOSTOLICALL, CANONICALL, IMPERIALL CONSTITUSIONS; AND OF OUR OWNE ENGLISH STATUTES, MAGISTRATES, VNIVERSITIES, WRITERS, PREACHERS. THAT POPULAR STAGE PLAYES (THE VERY POMPES OF THE DIVELL WHICH WE RENOUNCE IN BAPTISME, IF WE BELEEVE THE FATHERS) ARE SINFULL, HEATHENISH, LEWDE, UNGODLY SPECTACLES, AND MOST PERNICIOUS CORRUPTIONS; CONDEMNED IN ALL AGES, AS INTOLERABLE MISCHIEFES TO CHURCHES, TO REPUBLICKES, TO THE MANNERS, MINDES, AND SOULES OF MEN. AND THAT THE PROFESSION OF PLAY-POETS, OF STAGE PLAYERS; TOGETHER WITH THE PENNING, ACTING, AND FREQUENTING OF STAGE-PLAYES, ARE UNLAWFULL, INFAMOUS AND MISBESEEMING CHRISTIANS. ALL PRETENCES TO THE CONTRARY ARE HERE LIKEWISE FULLY ANSWERED; AND THE UNLAWFULNES OF ACTING, OF BEHOLDING ACADEMICALL ENTERLUDES, BRIEFLY DISCUSSED; BESIDE SUNDRY OTHER PARTICULARS CONCERNING DANCING, DICING, HEALTH-DRINKING, &C. OF WHICH THE TABLE WILL INFORME YOU. London: Printed by E.A. and W.I. for Michael Sparke, 1633.

> The title annotates, except perhaps to say that the topic is developed at the length of 1006 pages, plus the "Table."

[Puttenham, George?]. THE ARTE OF ENGLISH POETRY. Ed. Gladys Doidge Willcock and Alice Walker. Cambridge: At the University Press, 1936; reprint ed. 1970.

> THE ARTE has been published a number of times since its first printing in 1589 and has been assigned to a number of authors. Willcock and Walker provide a modern edition which discusses the problem of assigning authorship--to George Puttenham, to his brother Richard, or to some other--and which supplies various appendices, including a bibliography of "The Sources of the Arte" (pp. 319-33) and a full index. Another recent edition, which I have not seen, is:
>
> > Puttenham, Richard. THE ARTE OF ENGLISH POESIE [BY] LORD LUMLEY? New York: Da Capo Press; Amsterdam: Theatrum Orbis, 1971.
>
> Whoever wrote THE ARTE, it is a substantial tract on English poesy, useful to the understanding of Renaissance theory, though not specifically oriented towards drama.

Rymer, Thomas. THE CRITICAL WORKS. Ed., with an introduction and notes, by Curt A. Zimansky. New Haven, Conn.: Yale University Press; London: Oxford University Press, 1956.

The "Appendix: The Canon of Rymer's Work" (pp. 277-88) constitutes a primary bibliography. The "References" (pp. 177-78) are in effect a secondary bibliography. The works of Rymer here edited are: "The Rapin Preface," THE TRAGEDIES OF THE LAST AGE, "Advertisement to EDGAR," "The Rochester Preface," and A SHORT VIEW OF TRAGEDY. Zimansky provides ample notes. Two facsimile reprints of A SHORT VIEW OF TRAGEDY, one from Augustus M. Kelley (New York, 1970) and one from AMS Press (New York, 1970), have appeared recently. Rymer's work is represented in the facsimile edition of various tracts edited by Freeman (see Freeman, Arthur, ed.). See also the next item.

_____. A DEFENCE OF DRAMATICK POETRY: BEING A REVIEW OF MR. COLLIER'S "VIEW OF THE IMMORALITY AND PROFANENESS OF THE STAGE." London: Printed for Eliz. Whitlock, 1698.

In A DEFENCE and the other pieces above, Rymer offers a fascinating defense of the stage.

SHAKESPEARE SOCIETY'S PAPERS, THE. London: Printed for the Shakespeare Society, 1853.

See main entry in Section 2 C: Editions--Serial and Multi-Volume Editions. The Shakespeare Society published editions of plays and various pieces related to the drama. Some instructive hours could be spent in browsing through the series. A few volumes are listed in this section under author or editor.

Sidney, Sir Philip. THE COMPLETE WORKS. Ed. Albert Feuillerat. 4 vols. Cambridge: At the University Press, 1912-26.

See Volume 3 for "The Defence of Poesie," originally published in 1595 and often given the title AN APOLOGY FOR POETRY. Recent separate editions of THE DEFENCE include:

> _____. AN APOLOGY FOR POETRY; OR, THE DEFENCE OF POESY. Ed. Geoffrey Shepherd. London: T. Nelson, 1967.
>
> _____. THE DEFENCE OF POETRY. Ed. Wolfgang H. Clemen. Heidelburg: Universitat Verlag, 1950.

In addition to these editions, THE DEFENCE may be found in many anthologies, sometimes excerpted. Sidney's subject, of course, is the whole of poetry, not specifically drama.

Smith, G. Gregory, ed. ELIZABETHAN CRITICAL ESSAYS. 2 vols. 1904; reprint ed. London: Oxford University Press, 1967.

The "Preface" to the 1967 edition describes the collection as "the writings of the Elizabethan age which are concerned with Literary Criticism" (p. [v]). Defining literary criticism "in its most comprehensive sense" and designing the collection to be "fairly complete," Smith includes both "academic treatises" and "tracts and prefaces which express contemporary taste." Volume I: Roger Ascham, Richard Willes, George Gascoigne, George Whetstone, Thomas Lodge, the "Spenser-Harvey Correspondence," "E.K.," Richard Stanyhurst, Sir Philip Sidney, James VI, William Webbe, Abraham Fraunce, and Thomas Nashe, with part of the Hoby translation of Coignet as an Appendix; Volume II: Puttenham, Sir John Harington, Nashe, Gabriel Harvey, Richard Carew, George Chapman, Francis Meres, William Vaughan, Thomas Campion, and Samuel Daniel, with selections from Jonson in the appendix.

Spingarn, J.E., ed. CRITICAL ESSAYS OF THE SEVENTEENTH CENTURY. 3 vols. Oxford: Clarendon Press, 1908-9.

The "Preface" states: "The aim of this work is to collect all the material (save the writings of Dryden) necessary for a thorough study of the development of English criticism in the seventeenth century, and to make this development more intelligible by annotation and comment" (p. [iii]). Volume I, 1605-50, contains the work of Bacon, Jonson, Webster, Chapman, Edmund Bolton, Henry Peacham, Michael Drayton, Henry Reynolds, Sir William Alexander, Suckling, Milton, and the Jonson-Drummond material; Volume II, 1650-85: Davenant, Hobbes, Cowley, Richard Flecknoe, Sir Robert Howard, Sprat, Shadwell, Rymer, E. Phillips, Glanvill, Butler, the Earl of Rochester, the Earl of Mulgrave, the Earl of Roscommon, and two letters by Evelyn; Volume III, 1685-1700: Robert Wolseley, Sir William Temple, Langbaine, Dennis, Gildon, Wotton, Blackmore, Congreve, Collier, and Granville. Many of the works are excerpts, not full texts, but the collection will point the reader to texts he may need to examine as wholes. Bibliography.

Stow, John. A SURVEY OF LONDON. 1603.

Stow does not comment extensively on the drama, but he tells too much about too many aspects of London to be passed by. His SURVEY in the 1603 edition has been reprinted; see, for instance, the edition by Charles Lethbridge Kingsford (2 vols., 1908; reprint ed. Oxford: Clarendon Press, 1971); and the edition by H.B. Wheatley (London and New York: Dent, Everyman's Library, 1912; rev. ed. 1956; reprint ed. 1965). There are also editions of Stow with continuations by Edmund Howe to 1614 (printed in London, 1615); continued, again by Howe, to 1631 (London, 1631); and by J. Strype to 1720 (London, 1754-55), among others.

THEATRE MISCELLANY: SIX PIECES CONNECTED WITH THE SEVENTEENTH-CENTURY STAGE. Luttrell Society Reprints, No. 14. Oxford: Published for the Luttrell Society by Basil Blackwell, 1953.

The six pieces are: "Two Pageants by Thomas Heywood"; SIR WIL-

LIAM DAVENANT'S VOYAGE TO THE OTHER WORLD, by R. Flecknoe; "Songs and Masques in THE TEMPEST," edited by J.G. McManaway; "Musical Entertainments in RINALDO AND ARMIDA," by John Dennis; "The Petition of the Actors," edited by C.H. Wilkinson; and "The Florentine Agent Goes to a Masque in 1613," by D.J. Gordon.

Van Lennep, William, Emmett L. Avery, Arthur H. Scouten, George Winchester Stone, Jr., and Charles Beecher Hogan, eds. LONDON STAGE 1660-1800: A CALENDAR OF PLAYS, ENTERTAINMENTS & AFTERPIECES TOGETHER WITH CASTS, BOX-RECEIPTS AND CONTEMPORARY COMMENT COMPILED FROM THE PLAYBILLS, NEWSPAPERS AND THEATRICAL DIARIES OF THE PERIOD. Parts 1-5. Carbondale: Southern Illinois University Press, 1965-68.

The volumes yield something of the story of late seventeenth- and eighteenth-century revivals of Renaissance plays, though these figure rather less in the account than one might expect. Because of Van Lennep's death before the material was in print, the various parts are often more easily found under the names of the other editors.

Webbe, William. A DISCOURSE OF ENGLISH POETRIE, 1586. Ed. Edward Arber. 1870; reprint ed. Freeport, N.Y.: Books for Libraries Press, 1970.

Webbe's DISCOURSE is directed towards poetry.

Wells, Staring B., ed. A COMPARISON BETWEEN THE TWO STAGES. A LATE RESTORATION BOOK OF THE THEATRE. Princeton Studies in English, No. 26. Princeton, N.J.: Princeton University Press; London: Oxford University Press, 1942.

Charles Gildon has been suggested as the author of this anonymous piece, but Wells (pp. xii-xiii, n.5) expresses doubt about the correctness of the attribution. Wells suggests that it is the work of some "critickin" who "decided to present a brief survey of the two theatres, with some comments on actors and playwrights and a more detailed examination of a few current productions" (p. xii). Wells has edited the text, providing introduction, notes, and bibliography. The subject is Restoration, but there are references to Renaissance plays on the Restoration stage.

11. THE THEATRE AND STAGECRAFT

The materials in this section deal particularly with the relation of play and playwright to the stage, rather than to belles lettres. Knowledge and theory in this field have come a long way in our century.

Many of the studies cited here concern Medieval and Renaissance stage practices--not only in the production of plays but in the organization of companies of actors--and branch off into the lives of actors themselves. Others focus on the production of old plays for modern audiences. Discussions of the theatre and stagecraft are to be found in books in various other categories of this bibliography, in Section 6: General Studies of the Drama, in particular, and also in Section 4: Festschriften and Other Collections of Essays. Some of the primary materials are in Section 10: Contemporary and Other Early Records, Allusions, Criticism, Etc. Collected here are some specialized studies.

Acheson, Arthur. SHAKESPEARE, CHAPMAN, AND "SIR THOMAS MORE": PROVIDING A MORE DEFINITE BASIS FOR BIOGRAPHY AND CRITICISM. 1931; reprint ed. New York: AMS Press, 1970.

> Although a good deal of the book is about Shakespeare, Acheson regards it as necessary to have a "knowledge of his relations with his jealous academic competitors" (p. 8). Acheson also attempts to show that Burbage, as a theatre manager, maintained a policy of retaining "within his own organization . . . a producing playwright of his own technical training," a post held, according to Acheson, successively by Kyd, Marlowe, and Shakespeare (p. 10). The book, therefore, ranges over much of the Renaissance stage and presents a vast amount of deduction.

Adams, John Cranford. THE GLOBE PLAYHOUSE: ITS DESIGN AND EQUIPMENT. Cambridge, Mass.: Harvard University Press, 1942. 2nd ed. New York: Barnes & Noble, 1961.

> While time has realized Adams's expectation that the book would be "doubtless still subject in many ways to correction," this "first attempt at a complete and unified reconstruction of the Globe Playhouse" (p. vi) is clearly organized and suitably illustrated. In its

preparation, Adams "examined all available contemporary records bearing upon the subject--plays, dramatic entertainments, playhouse documents, legal cases, letters, maps, pamphlets, poems, and other material" and buttressed this evidence "by consulting stage historians" (p. vi), as the extensive bibliography in the notes records. Various appendices.

Adams, Joseph Quincy. SHAKESPEAREAN PLAYHOUSES: A HISTORY OF ENGLISH THEATRES FROM THE BEGINNINGS TO THE RESTORATION. Boston, New York, Chicago: Houghton Mifflin Co.; Cambridge, Mass.: Riverside Press, 1917.

Attempting for the first time a "history of playhouses" as distinct from the "method of dramatic representation," Adams "records the history of seventeen regular, and five temporary or projected, theatres" on the basis of "a first-hand examination of original sources" (pp. [vii]-viii). In addition to the usual sort of bibliography, Adams provides a three-page bibliography of "Maps and Views of London."

Albright, Victor E. THE SHAKSPERIAN STAGE. New York: Columbia University Press, 1909.

Albright proposes to make "an investigation of the structure of a typical stage and of the general method of play-production in the Elizabethan period." The early chapters deal with "Miracles and Longer Moralities" and "Interludes and Shorter Moralities." Fourteen plates.

Baldwin, T.W. THE ORGANIZATION AND PERSONNEL OF THE SHAKESPEAREAN COMPANY. Princeton, N.J.: Princeton University Press, 1927.

Baldwin undertakes to study the acting company as its "organization and personnel" affected the development of the drama.

Bentley, Gerald Eades. THE JACOBEAN AND CAROLINE STAGE.

See the main entry in Section 8: Studies of the Tudor and Stuart Drama. Bentley presents an enormous body of judiciously assembled fact.

_____. THE PROFESSION OF DRAMATIST IN SHAKESPEARE'S TIME, 1590-1642. Princeton, N.J.: Princeton University Press, 1971.

The "Preface" (p. vii) announces the book as "an explication of the normal working environment" of the London playwright. It treats such topics as the amateur and professional dramatists, their pay, "Contractual Obligations," "Regulation and Censorship," "Collaboration," "Revision," and "Publication." Bentley has drawn on both the usual printed sources and on "contemporary lawsuits, contracts, and agreements, the front matter of seventeenth-century editions of plays, miscellaneous publications of the time, and . . . remarks of dramatic characters making obvious allusions to customs or attitudes familiar to their audiences" (p. viii).

Bradbrook, M[uriel] C[lara]. THE RISE OF THE COMMON PLAYER: A STUDY OF ACTOR AND SOCIETY IN SHAKESPEARE'S ENGLAND. London: Chatto & Windus, 1962.

The book, designed for "students of drama and students of social history," examines "the social envelope within which [the plays] were made" (p. v). It is developed in four parts, concerned with "the public theatres," "typical individuals," "the one attempt by fully incorporated household players to establish on a commercial basis the old noble Theatre of the Hall," and "the general dramatic sports of the age" (pp. v-vi).

Brook, Donald. A PAGEANT OF ENGLISH ACTORS. New York: Macmillan; London: Rockliff Publishing Corp., 1950.

Brief biographies of fifteen actors, not all Renaissance, but including Richard Burbage, Richard Tarlton, William Kemp, and Edward Alleyn. Bibliography.

Burton, E.J. THE BRITISH THEATRE: ITS REPERTORY AND PRACTICE, 1100-1900 A.D. London: Herbert Jenkins, 1960.

The book is designed as a practical aid to the staging of plays. Bibliography.

Campbell, Lily B. SCENES AND MACHINES ON THE ENGLISH STAGE DURING THE RENAISSANCE: A CLASSICAL REVIVAL. 1923; reprint ed. New York: Barnes & Noble, 1960.

Campbell's now-classic book argues that the Renaissance stage made a "conscious and imitative re-creation of the classical stage" which was scholarly and aristocratic and that in "matters of spectacle, at least, the public stage followed after the academic stage and the court stage" (p. 293). Pages 1-5 provide a convenient review of earlier studies of staging.

Chambers, E[dmund] K[erchever]. THE ELIZABETHAN STAGE.

See the main entry in Section 8: Studies of Tudor and Stuart Drama. See also next item.

______. THE MEDIAEVAL STAGE.

See the main entry in Section 7 A: Studies of Medieval Drama--Broad Approaches. Chambers's two major studies, THE MEDIAEVAL STAGE and THE ELIZABETHAN STAGE, together with Bentley, Gerald Eades, THE JACOBEAN AND CAROLINE STAGE, above, provide a body of fact for the whole of the period under consideration here.

_____. NOTES ON THE HISTORY OF THE REVELS OFFICE UNDER THE TUDORS. London: A.H. Bullen, 1906.

This is an eighty-page analysis of materials on the Revels Office.

Collins, Fletcher, Jr. THE PRODUCTION OF MEDIEVAL CHURCH MUSIC-DRAMA. Charlottesville: University Press of Virginia, 1972.

A consideration of the repertory of surviving church music-drama, 1100-1275, and of the evidence concerning its production, with extended commentary on how this music-drama might be produced now and with a number of illustrations from Medieval art. Collins himself produces Medieval plays.

De Banke, Cecile. SHAKESPEAREAN STAGE PRODUCTION: THEN AND NOW. A MANUAL FOR THE SCHOLAR-PLAYER. New York, London, Toronto: McGraw-Hill, 1953.

Designed to give the "scholar-player"--the key word being player--the information he needs in a manageable bulk, the volume supplies bibliography and other such apparatus as a list of "Recordings Available for Use in Elizabethan Stage Production."

Goodman, Randolph, ed. DRAMA ON STAGE. New York: Holt, Rinehart & Winston, 1961.

The book is designed "to help the reader catch 'the meaning of the business of the stage'" (p. v). Among the six plays analyzed are EVERYMAN and MACBETH. For EVERYMAN, there are these materials: Various essays and interviews concerning Medieval stagecraft, productions of the play, the portrayal of certain roles, the music, choreography, scenery, and costumes, and a modernized text of the play.

Gurr, Andrew. THE SHAKESPEAREAN STAGE, 1574-1642. Cambridge: At the University Press, 1970.

Gurr claims for his book only that it is "primarily a summary of such books" as Chambers and Bentley (p. vii). There are chapters on "The Companies," "The Players," "The Playhouses," "The Staging," and "The Audiences."

Harbage, Alfred. THEATRE FOR SHAKESPEARE. The Alexander Lectures, 1954-55. Toronto: University of Toronto Press, 1955.

Asserting (pp. 1-3) that contemporary Shakespeare productions tend to be a bore and that the fault is in the style of the productions, Harbage seeks "to propose a theatre for Shakespeare" by exploring the Elizabethan stage. He argues that Elizabethan acting was formal rather than natural, and profited therefrom.

Hillebrand, H.N. THE CHILD ACTORS: A CHAPTER IN ELIZABETHAN STAGE HISTORY. University of Illinois Studies in Language and Literature, Vol. 11, Nos. 1-2. Urbana: University of Illinois, 1926.

Hillebrand's aim is to collect in one place the scattered material on child actors. Appendix II offers "A Chronological List of Children's Plays" and Appendix III, "Documents Illustrative of the History of Children's Companies and the Stage."

Hodges, C[yril] Walter. THE GLOBE RESTORED. A STUDY OF THE ELIZABETHAN THEATRE. 1953. 2nd ed. New York: Coward-McCann, 1968, 1970.

Hodges points out that the uncertainty "about the actual stagecraft employed . . . at the Globe" is greater than the uncertainty surrounding "any other event of comparable importance in the whole history of the theatre." Part of the cause, he argues, is that "conjectures, like old friends, have grown to be received without question." Hodges sets about rectifying the situation, providing extensive illustrations and a bibliography.

Hotson, Leslie. SHAKESPEARE'S WOODEN O. London: Rupert Hart-Davis; New York: Macmillan, 1960.

Hotson declares that he has "followed the trail of Shakespeare's theatre and of his stage-practice in it . . . not only recovering lost features of that Elizabethan staging in detail, but also tracing them to their sources. Now for the first time we can understand and visualize the stage of the Globe" (p. 13).

Hyde, Mary Crapo. PLAYWRITING FOR ELIZABETHANS, 1600-1605. Columbia University Studies in English and Comparative Literature, No. 167. New York: Columbia University Press, 1949.

Hyde suggests that "it is . . . possible to deduce an Elizabethan dramaturgy from a study of the plays that are extant" (p. [vii]). Although the dramatists have said little or nothing about their dramaturgy, Hyde suggests that they would have accepted about themselves the conclusion: "Elizabethan playwrights bowed to the authority of the ancients in dramatic principles, but in dramatic conventions they followed the dictates of public taste" (p. [5]). Bibliography.

Joseph, B[ertram] L. ELIZABETHAN ACTING. London: Oxford University Press, 1951; 2nd ed. 1964.

There are chapters on "Acting and Rhetoric," "Rhetorical Delivery in the Scheme of Humanist Learning," "All the Parts of an Excellent Orator," "The Rhetorical Pronunciation and Gesture Fit for Every Word, Sentence, and Affection," "Decorum and Characterization," "The Grounds of Criticism in Elizabethan Drama," and "The Poem and the Theatre."

Kernodle, George R. FROM ART TO THEATRE: FORM AND CONVENTION IN THE RENAISSANCE. Chicago: University of Chicago Press, 1944.

Kernodle argues that in our endeavors to visualize "the Shakespearean stage" we have overlooked "the traditions of the visual arts which shaped that theatre" and "the other theatres of the time" (p. 1). He studies continental as well as English stages and concludes that the modern stage is "an entirely logical development in the history of the visual arts--the realization in three dimensions of the forms and conventions of painting, sculpture, and the tableaux vivants" (p. 216). Extensive bibliography; sixty-two illustrations.

King, T[homas] J. SHAKESPEAREAN STAGING, 1599-1642. Cambridge, Mass.: Harvard University Press, 1971.

King provides "a systematic survey of theatrical requirements for 276 plays first performed by professional actors in the period between the autumn of 1599 . . . and 2 September 1642" in order to suggest "how the plays of Shakespeare were acted by his contemporaries" (p. 1). Appendix A offers "An appraisal . . . of fourteen books on Shakespearean stagecraft published since 1940" (p. 119).

Laver, James. DRAMA, ITS COSTUME & DECOR. London: Studio Publications, 1951.

The text runs from "Greeks and Romans" to "since 1914," but pages 32-102 contain chapters on "The Medieval Stage," "Pageants and Triumphs," "The Shakespearean and other Platform Stages," "The Pioneers of Perspective Scenery," and "The English Court Masques," with many illustrations and bibliography.

Lawrence, W[illiam] J. THE ELIZABETHAN PLAYHOUSE AND OTHER STUDIES. First Series, 1912; Second Series, 1913; reprint ed., in 2 vols. New York: Russell & Russell, 1963.

Each series contains essays on a number of specific problems: "Proscenium Doors: An Elizabethan Heritage," "Light and Darkness in the Elizabethan Theatre," "Early Systems of Admissions," and so on. Illustrations.

______. OLD THEATRE DAYS AND WAYS. London: G.G. Harrap & Co., 1935.

Declaring that the "whole theatre has been my province," Lawrence calls his book "an easy discussion of certain new aspects of an old but inexhaustible theme" (p. 5).

_____. THE PHYSICAL CONDITIONS OF THE ELIZABETHAN PUBLIC PLAYHOUSE. Cambridge, Mass.: Harvard University Press; London: Oxford University Press, 1927.

Lawrence describes the book as "a fusion of several lectures forming part of an undergraduate course" at Harvard and Radcliffe in 1925-26 (p. [vii]).

_____. PRE-RESTORATION STAGE STUDIES. Cambridge, Mass.: Harvard University Press, 1927.

The volume provides a collection of essays on a variety of problems: "The Inn-Yard Play," "Illusion of Sounds in the Elizabethan Theatre," and so on.

Linthicum, M[arie] Channing. COSTUME IN THE DRAMA OF SHAKESPEARE AND HIS CONTEMPORARIES. 1936; reprint ed. New York: Russell & Russell, 1963.

A thoroughgoing account of colors, textiles, garments, and details of garments referred to in the plays, with dates of their earliest recorded appearance, symbolism, and so on, with quotations drawn "from drama and contemporary accounts" to support the data. (See the "Preface" for details of what is included.)

Mander, Raymond, and Joe Mitchenson. A PICTURE HISTORY OF THE BRITISH THEATRE. London: Hulton Press, 1957.

Largely pictures, with a little explanatory text. Part 1 deals with "Elizabethan and Jacobean to the Closing of the Theatres (1576-1642)" with twenty-seven pictures.

Mantzius, Karl. A HISTORY OF THEATRICAL ART IN ANCIENT AND MODERN TIMES. Introduction by William Archer. Trans. Louise von Cossel. Vols. 2 and 3. London: Duckworth & Co., 1903-4.

Archer calls Mantzius "one of the few actors of note who have also won distinction in the field of serious scholarship" (Vol. 1, p. xi). Volume 2 deals with THE MIDDLE AGES AND THE RENAISSANCE; Volume 3 with THE SHAKESPEAREAN PERIOD IN ENGLAND.

Murray, John Tucker. ENGLISH DRAMATIC COMPANIES, 1558-1642. 2 vols. 1910; reprint ed. New York: Russell & Russell, 1963.

Volume I deals with LONDON COMPANIES, Volume II with PROVINCIAL COMPANIES, providing factual records in a convenient format, with extensive appendices, notes, and index.

Nagler, A[lois] M[aria]. SOURCES OF THEATRICAL HISTORY.

See the main entry in Section 10: Contemporary and Other Early Records, Allusions, Criticism, Etc.

Ordish, T. Fairman. THE EARLY LONDON THEATRES [IN THE FIELDS]. London: Elliott Stock, 1894.

As long ago as 1917, Joseph Quincy Adams, in his SHAKESPEAREAN PLAYHOUSES (see above), page vii, could quite fairly call Ordish's book "good for its time" but point to the number of documents recovered since Ordish wrote which need to be considered. Ordish remains worth remembering, however.

Reynolds, George Fullmer. SOME PRINCIPLES OF ELIZABETHAN STAGING. 1905; reprint ed. New York: AMS Press, 1970.

The reprint makes this University of Chicago thesis readily accessible.

_____. THE STAGING OF ELIZABETHAN PLAYS AT THE RED BULL THEATER, 1605-1625. New York: Modern Language Association of America; London: Oxford University Press, 1940.

The book is "a study of the basic details and principles of Elizabethan staging" (p. [1]). Among other useful apparatus, it provides a "Chronological List of Plays Given at the Red Bull, ca. 1605 to ca. 1625" (pp. 15-29).

Sisson, C[harles] J. THE BOAR'S HEAD THEATRE: AN INN-YARD THEATRE OF THE ELIZABETHAN AGE. Ed. Stanley Wells. London and Boston: Routledge & Kegan Paul, 1972.

The "Introduction" (pp. xvii-xviii) argues for a totally new view of the Boar's Head and for the position that there was "a continuous link between inn-yard theatres and other public theatres." After developing his own case, Sisson concludes with an appendix, "The Inn-yard Theatre in Chambers, Lawrence and Hotson" (pp. 78-83), reviewing the position Sisson wishes to refute. Bibliography.

Smith, Irwin. SHAKESPEARE'S BLACKFRIARS PLAYHOUSE: ITS HISTORY AND ITS DESIGN. New York: New York University Press, 1964.

Smith studies the King's Men at Blackfriars and also the children's companies there, with twenty-five figures, eight plates, forty-six documents, full documentation at all points, and a bibliography.

_____. SHAKESPEARE'S GLOBE PLAYHOUSE: A MODERN RECONSTRUCTION IN TEXT AND SCALE DRAWING, BASED UPON THE RECONSTRUCTION OF THE GLOBE BY JOHN CRANFORD ADAMS. Introduction by James G. McManaway. New York: Charles Scribner's Sons, 1956.

The "Preface" points out that our century has seen a burgeoning of interest in stage technique (p. xi). This study is a graphic manifestation of that interest. Bibliography.

Smith, Roy. THREE MODEL THEATRES: ELIZABETHAN, EIGHTEENTH CENTURY, MODERN. Edinburgh: T. Nelson, 1960.

Detailed instructions on how to build small models.

Southern, Richard. CHANGEABLE SCENERY: ITS ORIGIN AND DEVELOPMENT IN THE BRITISH THEATRE. London: Faber and Faber, 1952.

Part 1, "The Rise of Changeable Scenery at Court" (pp. 17-106) discusses in particular the masque as performed at court, "the nursery of changeable scenery" (p. 109). Extensive illustration.

_____. THE MEDIEVAL THEATRE IN THE ROUND.

See the main entry in Section 7 D: Studies of Medieval Drama--Morality Plays.

_____. THE OPEN STAGE AND THE MODERN THEATRE IN RESEARCH AND PRACTICE. London: Faber and Faber, 1953.

Southern says his book results from "a conviction . . . that whenever you put on any sort of theatrical show the thing which matters most (on the material side) is . . . the stage--its shape, its nature, and its relation to the audience" (p. 9). Beginning with the "simplest form of stage [which] I may call 'the booth stage'" (p. 15), he develops the idea of a stage, suggesting that the theatre grows up to enclose the stage. The Elizabethan stage is a frequent point of reference.

_____. THE SEVEN AGES OF THE THEATRE. New York: Hill and Wang, 1961.

Southern attempts to trace the development of the theatre from its earliest forms and to reduce theatre to its minimum essentials. In a section called "Stripping the Onion," he says that if one peels away accretions--scenery, auditorium, stage, down finally to the player's "Costume and Mask"--the removal of these last will result in a "fall[ing] apart [of] two separate pieces, leaving nothing inside; those two pieces would be the Player and the Audience. Take these apart and you can have no theatre" (p. 21). Hence his argument that at the center of dramatic art is "the living player, and his one indispensable technical adjunct--his costume" (p. 18). Southern is a scene designer-critic who can be counted upon to offer provocative insights. Bibliography.

Speaight, Robert. WILLIAM POEL AND THE ELIZABETHAN REVIVAL. Cambridge, Mass.: Harvard University Press, 1954.

Poel, or Pole, born 1852, founded the "Elizabethan Stage Society, whose long list of performances [1895-1905] gives Poel his title to fame" (p. 90).

Stopes, [Mrs.] C[harlotte] C[armichael]. BURBAGE AND SHAKESPEARE'S STAGE. London: Alexander Moring Ltd., The De La More Press, 1913.

The account begins: "The story of James Burbage is a wonderful record, not only for the work he did, but for its results. . . . Through his courageous struggle . . . he became the founder of the modern British Stage, the teacher as well as father of its greatest actor, and the discoverer of its greatest Dramatist" (p. 1). Beginning on page 145, Stopes supplies "Authorities," that is, texts or translations of a wide variety of materials relevant to the stage.

Venesky, Alice S. PAGEANTRY ON THE SHAKESPEAREAN STAGE. New York: Twayne Publishers, 1951.

Venesky "attempts to analyze the influence on the Elizabethan drama of the most popular forms of public display--the procession, pageant, and progress entertainment." She supplies an appendix which "lists the events . . . referred to in the text and gives the most accessible printed sources" (pp. 13-14). Bibliography.

Wallace, Charles William. THE CHILDREN OF THE CHAPEL AT BLACKFRIARS, 1597-1603. University of Nebraska Studies, Vol. 8, Nos. 2-3. Lincoln: University of Nebraska, 1908.

Wallace provides a meticulously documented study, though it is of necessity somewhat dated now.

_____. THE EVOLUTION OF THE ENGLISH DRAMA UP TO SHAKESPEARE WITH A HISTORY OF THE FIRST BLACKFRIARS THEATRE; A SURVEY BASED UPON ORIGINAL RECORDS NOW FOR THE FIRST TIME COLLECTED AND PUBLISHED. Schriften der Deutschen Shakspeare-Gesellschaft, Vol. 4. Berlin: Georg Reimer, 1912.

Wallace describes his intention as "to gather and present reliable historical data concerning the drama and the circumstances and conditions under which it flourished" (p. xi). He prints a large collection of documents and discusses their import.

_____. THE FIRST LONDON THEATRE: MATERIALS FOR A HISTORY. University of Nebraska Studies, Vol. 13, Nos. 1-3. Lincoln: University of Nebraska, 1913.

Wallace has assembled an extensive collection of materials about "the first London Theatre, from the date of its inception by James Burbage in 1576 to the full Florescence of Shakespeare in 1599" (p. 1).

_____. THREE LONDON THEATRES OF SHAKESPEARE'S TIME. University of Nebraska Studies, Vol. 9, No. 4. Lincoln: University of Nebraska, 1909.

Wallace has here assembled documents from "the Court of Requests, of the reign of James I" (p. 4) concerning the Red Bull, the Fortune, and the Bear Garden.

Wickham, Glynne. EARLY ENGLISH STAGES, 1300 TO 1660. Vol. 1: 1300 TO 1576; Vol. 2: 1576 TO 1660. London: Routledge and Kegan Paul; New York: Columbia University Press, 1959-63.

Wickham says of the two volumes: "Broadly speaking, [the] first volume is devoted to the Elizabethan theatrical inheritance and the second to the substitution of a new kind of stagecraft for the old . . . on the public stages built in London between 1576 and 1614" (Vol. I, pp. vii-viii). Wickham supplies extensive illustrations and documentation, bibliography, and appendices to support an argument which deals with basic questions concerning the nature and origins of drama.

Wright, Louis B. SHAKESPEARE'S THEATRE AND THE DRAMATIC TRADITION. Folger Booklets on Tudor and Stuart Civilization. Washington, D.C.: Folger Shakespeare Library, 1958.

Wright provides a thirty-six-page survey, proceeding from the liturgical drama forward, with seventeen plates.

Yates, Frances A. THEATRE OF THE WORLD. London: Routledge and Kegan Paul; Chicago: University of Chicago Press, 1969.

Through the study of "John Dee and Robert Fludd as representatives of Renaissance philosophy in England, with particular reference to the evidence in their works of the influence of the Renaissance revival of Vitruvious . . . one is enabled to take a new way through the vexed question of English theatre history" (p. xi). Among topics discussed at some length is the work of Inigo Jones. Fully documented; useful appendices.

12. BIOGRAPHICAL NOTES AND STUDIES: MULTI-FIGURE

Included in this section are books which are basically dictionaries of authors or studies focused in biographical accounts of several authors. Many of the materials in Section 6: General Studies of the Drama, include similar biographical information, as do a number of the books listed in Section 9: Playlists, Records of Early Publication, Etc. On the other hand, entries here will often give critical evaluations as well as biographical information. Biographical studies focused in single authors appear in the various sections on individual playwrights in Part 2.

Adams, W[illiam] Davenport. A DICTIONARY OF THE DRAMA: A GUIDE TO THE PLAYS, PLAYWRIGHTS, PLAYERS, AND PLAYHOUSES OF THE UNITED KINGDOM AND AMERICA, FROM THE EARLIEST TIMES TO THE PRESENT. Vol. I: A-G. London: Chatto & Windus, 1904.

> Intended as a compendium of "the leading facts of the history of the theatre" with "information about playhouses and their designers, the writers of plays, plays themselves, performers in them, their critics, their scenic and musical illustrators, theatrical terms, and stage literature generally," Adams's DICTIONARY was never published beyond the first volume. It is, however, a concise source of a good deal of information through the letter G.

Aubrey, John. "BRIEF LIVES." CHIEFLY OF CONTEMPORARIES, SET DOWN BY JOHN AUBREY, BETWEEN THE YEARS 1669 & 1696. EDITED FROM THE AUTHOR'S MSS. 2 vols. Ed. Andrew Clark. Oxford: Clarendon Press, 1898.

> Aubrey was a seventeenth-century gentleman who set down short accounts of many persons, many dramatists among them. Two abridgements of Aubrey are:
>
> > AUBREY'S BRIEF LIVES. Ed. Oliver Lawson Dick. Ann Arbor: University of Michigan Press, 1957.
> >
> > THE SCANDAL AND CREDULITIES OF JOHN AUBREY. Ed. John Collier. New York: D. Appleton, 1931.
> >
> > > Collier's title suggests the proper attitude for reading Aubrey, with a mixture of caution and delight.

Baker, David Erskine, Isaac Reed, and Stephen Jones. BIOGRAPHIA DRAMATICA.

See the main entry in Section 9: Playlists, Records of Early Publication, Etc.

BIBLIOGRAPHIA POETICA.

See [Ritson, Joseph].

BIOGRAPHIA BRITANNICA: OR, THE LIVES OF THE MOST EMINENT PERSONS WHO HAVE FLOURISHED IN GREAT BRITAIN AND IRELAND, FROM THE EARLIEST AGES, DOWN TO THE PRESENT TIMES: COLLECTED FROM THE BEST AUTHORITIES, BOTH PRINTED AND MANUSCRIPT, AND DIGESTED IN THE MANNER OF MR. BAYLE'S HISTORICAL AND CRITICAL DICTIONARY. 6 vols. in 7. London: Printed for W. Innys, 1747-66.

Not so many dramatists qualify as "Eminent" as one might expect.

Birch, Thomas. THE HEADS OF ILLUSTRIOUS PERSONS OF GREAT BRITAIN, ENGRAVEN BY MR. HOUBRAKEN, AND MR. VERTUE. WITH THEIR LIVES AND CHARACTERS BY THOMAS BIRCH. 2 vols. in 1. London: Printed for John and Paul Knapton, 1747.

Sackville, Jonson, Otway, and Shakespeare appear among the heads and lives.

Blount, Sir Thomas Pope. DE RE POETICA: OR, REMARKS UPON POETRY. WITH CHARACTERS AND CENSURES OF THE MOST CONSIDERABLE POETS, WHETHER ANCIENT OR MODERN. EXTRACTED OUT OF THE BEST AND CHOICEST CRITICKS. London: Printed by Ric. Everingham, for R. Bently, 1694.

Pages 1-129 contain the "Remarks upon Poetry," including "Concerning Tragedy" and "Concerning Comedy." The section on "Characters and Censures" is separately numbered. Among dramatists considered are Beaumont and Fletcher, Cowley, Davenant, Jonson, Shakespeare, and Suckling. The early date of the volume contributes to its interest.

Bullen, A.H. ELIZABETHANS. London: Chapman and Hall, 1924.

Bullen is famous as an editor of Elizabethan dramatists--see the various editions listed under individual playwrights in Part 2. The unsigned "Preface" to this volume of essays says of Bullen as an editor that he "may be said to hold a unique place. He worked on broad lines, and his method stands a little apart alike from the meticulous research of later scholars and the rhapsodical eulogies of earlier commentators" (p. ix). Of these essays, originally delivered as lectures at Oxford, the "Preface" says that in 1889, when first delivered, "(before his anthologies had made, of Elizabethan poetry, common knowledge)" they "must have come almost as a revelation" (p. vii). The essays are on Michael Drayton, Samuel Daniel, George Chapman, Thomas Dekker, Nicholas Breton, Dr. Thomas Campion, William Bullein, Dr. George Hakewill, Fulke Greville, Lord Brooke, and Shakespeare--not all dramatists, of course.

Chalmers, Alexander, ed. THE WORKS OF THE ENGLISH POETS, FROM CHAUCER TO COWPER; INCLUDING THE SERIES EDITED, WITH PREFACES, BIOGRAPHICAL AND CRITICAL, BY DR. SAMUEL JOHNSON: AND THE MOST APPROVED TRANSLATIONS. THE ADDITIONAL LIVES BY ALEXANDER CHALMERS. 21 vols. London: Printed for J. Johnson and Others, 1810.

The works are poems, but since dramatists may also write poems, LIVES of various dramatists are to be found throughout the set. The work is of such historic fame that it must be mentioned, though for general purposes more recent studies will usually be more helpful.

Chambers, Robert, ed. CYCLOPEDIA OF ENGLISH LITERATURE: A HISTORY, CRITICAL AND BIOGRAPHICAL, OF BRITISH AUTHORS, FROM THE EARLIEST TO THE PRESENT TIME. 2 vols. 1844; rev. ed., edited by D. Patrick and J.L. Geddie in 3 vols., London: Chambers, [1922-38].

There have been various editions of Chambers's CYCLOPEDIA. Chambers offers a general treatment of Renaissance dramatists. The entries supply miscellaneous information about each author considered and offer "Extracts" from his work, making up an interesting period piece.

Cibber, Theophilus. THE LIVES OF THE POETS OF GREAT BRITAIN AND IRELAND, TO THE TIME OF DEAN SWIFT. COMPILED FROM AMPLE MATERIALS SCATTERED IN A VARIETY OF BOOKS, AND ESPECIALLY FROM THE MS. NOTES OF THE LATE INGENIOUS MR. COXETER AND OTHERS, COLLECTED FOR THIS DESIGN, BY MR. CIBBER. 5 vols. London: Printed for R. Griffiths, 1753.

The title page of Volume I says "In Four Volumes," but there are five. The title pages of Volumes II, III, IV, and V differ slightly from that of Volume I and read "By Mr. Cibber, and other Hands." Among the array of lives are those of a number of playwrights, treated in the style promised by the title page.

Collier, J[ohn] Payne. THE POETICAL DECAMERON, OR TEN CONVERSATIONS ON ENGLISH POETS AND POETRY, PARTICULARLY OF THE REIGNS OF ELIZABETH AND JAMES I. 2 vols. Edinburgh: Archibald Constable; London: Hurst, Robinson, 1820.

The book contains ten dialogues, in which three friends converse on miscellaneous literary topics, indexed so that one may locate an author with whom one is concerned. The book provides another interesting period piece.

Cooper, Charles Henry, and Thompson Cooper. ATHENAE CANTABRIGIENSES. 2 vols. Cambridge: Deighton, Bell, & Co., and Macmillan & Co.; London: Bell & Daldy, 1858-61. With a third volume, WITH ADDITIONS AND CORRECTIONS TO THE PREVIOUS VOLUMES BY HENRY BRADSHAW, PROF. JOHN E.B. MAYOR, JOHN GOUGH NICHOLS, AND OTHERS, AND FROM THE UNIVERSITY GRACE BOOKS, &C. AND ALSO A NEW AND COMPLETE INDEX TO THE WHOLE WORK BY GEORGE J. GRAY. Cambridge: Bowes & Bowes, 1913.

Volume I is for 1500-85; Volume II, 1586-1609; Volume III, 1609-11. The "Introduction" (Vol. I, p. iii) indicates that the work is intended to do for Cambridge what Anthony a Wood did for Oxford (see Wood, Anthony a, and Philip Bliss). Consult the index for the wanted entry.

Crawford, Charles. COLLECTANEA. FIRST SERIES. Stratford-on-Avon: Shakespeare Head Press, 1906; SECOND SERIES. Stratford-on-Avon: Shakespeare Head Press, 1907.

The FIRST SERIES contains essays largely reprinted from NOTES AND QUERIES: "Richard Barnfield, Marlowe, and Shakespeare," "Ben Jonson's Method of Composing Verse," "John Webster and Sir Philip Sidney," "Edmund Spenser, 'Selimus,' and 'Locrine,'" and "The Authorship of 'Arden of Feversham.'" The SECOND SERIES contains two essays reprinted from NOTES AND QUERIES: "Montaigne, Webster, and Marston: Donne and Webster" and "The Bacon-Shakespeare Question."

Davies, Thomas. DRAMATIC MICELLANIES: CONSISTING OF CRITICAL OBSERVATIONS ON SEVERAL PLAYS OF SHAKESPEARE: WITH A REVIEW OF HIS PRINCIPAL CHARACTERS, AND THOSE OF VARIOUS EMINENT WRITERS, AS REPRESENTED BY MR. GARRICK, AND OTHER CELEBRATED COMEDIANS. WITH ANECDOTES OF DRAMATIC POETS, ACTORS, &C. 3 vols. 1784; reprint ed. New York: AMS Press, 1973.

The title annotates.

DICTIONARY OF NATIONAL BIOGRAPHY, THE. Ed. Sir Leslie Stephen and Sir Sidney Lee, with others. 28 vols. London: Oxford University Press, 1949-71.

The DNB was "Founded in 1882 by George Smith," as its title page still records. It was first published in 1885-1901, in sixty-six volumes. In the current edition, Stephen and Lee, or Lee alone, edited Volumes 1-23, with various editors responsible for the subsequent volumes. Volume 28 covers the years 1951-60. Volumes 1-21 constitute one alphabetical list through 1900. The volumes thereafter are alphabetical within certain year-groups. The DNB provides brief but generally reliable sketches of notable Britons. The user should notice, however, that some of the information is now out of date. Two related publications are:

THE DICTIONARY OF NATIONAL BIOGRAPHY . . .

THE CONCISE DICTIONARY FROM THE BEGINNINGS TO 1921, BEING AN EPITOME OF THE MAIN WORK AND ITS SUPPLEMENT, TO WHICH IS ADDED AN EPITOME OF THE TWENTIETH CENTURY VOLUMES, COVERING 1901-1921. London: Oxford University Press, 1903; 2nd ed. 1906, with various reprintings and the addition of the 1901-11 and 1912-21 EPITOMES.

CORRECTIONS AND ADDITIONS TO THE DICTIONARY OF NATIONAL BIOGRAPHY, CUMULATED FROM THE BULLETIN OF THE INSTITUTE OF HISTORICAL RESEARCH, UNIVERSITY OF LONDON, COVERING THE YEARS 1923-1963. Boston: G.K. Hall & Co., 1966.

Fleay, Frederick Gard.

See the two main entries under Fleay, Frederick Gard, in Section 8: Studies of Tudor and Stuart Drama.

Fletcher, C[harles] R[obert] L[eslie]. HISTORICAL PORTRAITS. VOL. I: RICHARD II TO HENRY WRIOTHESLEY, 1400-1600. THE LIVES BY C.R.L. FLETCHER, THE PORTRAITS CHOSEN BY EMERY WALKER. Vol. II: 1600-1700, THE LIVES BY H.B. BUTLER AND C.R.L. FLETCHER, THE PORTRAITS CHOSEN BY EMERY WALKER, WITH AN INTRODUCTION BY C.F. BELL. Oxford: Clarendon Press, 1909-11.

A few dramatists appear, particularly in Volume II.

Foster, Joseph. ALUMNI OXONIENSES: THE MEMBERS OF THE UNIVERSITY OF OXFORD, 1500-1714: THEIR PARENTAGE, BIRTHPLACE, AND YEAR OF BIRTH, WITH A RECORD OF THEIR DEGREES, BEING THE MATRICULATION REGISTER OF THE UNIVERSITY, ALPHABETICALLY ARRANGED, REVISED, AND ANNOTATED. WITH ILLUSTRATIONS. 4 vols. Oxford and London: James Parker, 1891-92.

Small bits of information about dramatists can be found here.

[Fuller, Thomas]. ANGLORUM SPECULUM, OR THE WORTHIES OF ENGLAND. IN CHURCH AND STATE. ALPHABETICALLY DIGESTED INTO THE SEVERAL SHIRES AND COUNTIES THEREIN CONTAINED; WHEREIN ARE ILLUSTRATED THE LIVES AND CHARACTERS OF THE MOST EMINENT PERSONS SINCE THE CONQUEST TO THIS PRESENT AGE. ALSO AN ACCOUNT OF THE COMMODITIES AND TRADE OF EACH RESPECTIVE COUNTY, AND THE MOST FLOURISHING CITIES AND TOWNS THEREIN. London: Thomas Passinger, William Thackary, and John Wright, 1684.

Fuller tells brief but entertaining stories. Whether a particular writer is sufficiently worthy to appear can be learned from the index. See the New Edition, edited by P. Austin Nuttall in three volumes (London: Thomas Tegg, 1840), and an edition of selections, edited by John Freeman (London: Allen & Unwin, 1952).

Garvin, Katharine, ed. THE GREAT TUDORS. New York: E.P. Dutton and Co., 1935.

The essays, by various hands, include: W.H. Auden, "John Skelton"; Alfred Noyes, "Christopher Marlowe"; H.J. Massingham, "John Lyly"; Alfred W. Pollard and J. Dover Wilson, "William Shakespeare"; Nigel Playfair, "Richard Burbage"; Enid Glen, "Ben Jonson." A 1956 edition omits Skelton, Lyly, Burbage, and Jonson.

Gildon, Charles.

See main entry under [Langbaine, Gerard, and Charles Gildon] in Section 6: General Studies of the Drama.

Gosse, Edmund, SEVENTEENTH CENTURY STUDIES: A CONTRIBUTION TO THE HISTORY OF ENGLISH POETRY. 3rd ed. London: Heinemann; New York: Dodd, Mead, 1897.

The volume contains essays on Thomas Lodge and John Webster, among the dramatists.

Granger, J[ames]. A BIOGRAPHICAL HISTORY OF ENGLAND, FROM EGBERT THE GREAT TO THE REVOLUTION: CONSISTING OF CHARACTERS DISPOSED IN DIFFERENT CLASSES, AND ADAPTED TO A METHODICAL CATALOGUE OF ENGRAVED BRITISH HEADS. INTENDED AS AN ESSAY TOWARDS REDUCING OUR BIOGRAPHY TO SYSTEM, AND A HELP TO THE KNOWLEDGE OF PORTRAITS. INTERSPERSED WITH VARIETY OF ANECDOTES, AND MEMOIRS OF A GREAT NUMBER OF PERSONS NOT TO BE FOUND IN ANY OTHER BIOGRAPHICAL WORK. WITH A PREFACE, SHEWING THE UTILITY OF A COLLECTION OF ENGRAVED PORTRAITS TO SUPPLY THE DEFECT, AND ANSWER THE VARIOUS PURPOSES, OF MEDALS. 2 Vols. London: Printed for T. Davies, 1769.

Class IX is made up of "Physicians, Poets, and other ingenious Persons, who have distinguished themselves by their Writings." The set I examined, interestingly, lacks the engravings. (Sets of portraits for Granger were engraved and published later.) Other editions have appeared, through the fifth, "Carefully Revised and Corrected" in six volumes (London: W. Baynes, 1824).

Grinsted, T.P. RELICS OF GENIUS: VISITS TO THE LAST HOMES OF POETS, PAINTERS, AND PLAYERS, WITH BIOGRAPHICAL SKETCHES. London: W. Kent, 1859.

The "Preface" declares: "Pilgrimages to the birthplaces and last homes [i.e., graves] of men of genius have ever been sources of refined interest, as well to the general wayfarer as to the visitor of a more reflective turn of mind" (p. [v]). Not much is to be learned here in the usual way of critical or scholarly perception, but the book is whimsically charming.

Hamilton, Walter. THE POETS LAUREATE OF ENGLAND; BEING A HISTORY OF THE OFFICE OF POET LAUREATE, BIOGRAPHICAL NOTICES OF ITS HOLD-

ERS, AND A COLLECTION OF THE SATIRES, EPIGRAMS, AND LAMPOONS DIRECTED AGAINST THEM. 1879; reprint ed. Detroit: Gale Research Co., 1968.

In the opening section, "The Volunteer Laureates (to the Reign of James I)," John Skelton, Richard Edwards, and Samuel Daniel appear. Then come Ben Jonson and Sir William Davenant.

Hazlitt, William. JOHNSON'S LIVES OF THE BRITISH POETS COMPLETED BY WILLIAM HAZLITT. 4 vols. London: Nathaniel Cooke, 1854.

Hazlitt says in the "Preface": "The number of Lives contained in the present volumes is ten times greater than those given by Dr. Johnson" (Vol. I, pp. ix-x). Hazlitt has included authors on a generous scale, so that something may be found about many dramatists, though as he further notes, his lives are necessarily brief.

Inglis, Ralston. THE DRAMATIC WRITERS OF SCOTLAND. Glasgow: G.D. Mackellar, 1868.

Inglis offers an alphabetical list with brief sketches in the "attempt towards the compilation of a Scottish Biographia Dramatica, i.e., a Biographical and Bibliographical Catalogue of Scottish Authors who have written any dramatic pieces which have been either printed or acted" (p. [3]).

[Jacob, Giles]. THE POETICAL REGISTER.

See the main entry in Section 10: Contemporary and Other Early Records, Allusions, Criticism, Etc.

Langbaine, Gerard.

See various entries in Section 6: General Studies of the Drama.

[Neve, Philip]. CURSORY REMARKS ON SOME OF THE ANCIENT ENGLISH POETS, PARTICULARLY MILTON. London: [Privately Printed], 1789.

Neve comments on Skelton, Shakespeare, Beaumont and Fletcher, Jonson, and others. His remarks are both cursory and candid, if not profoundly discerning. Of Jonson, for example, he observes: "[T]here are not many pieces, among all the volumes he has left, that can be pointed out to a reader of taste, for his amusement or approbation" (p. [39]).

Nungezer, Edwin. A DICTIONARY OF ACTORS AND OTHER PERSONS ASSOCIATED WITH THE PUBLIC REPRESENTATION OF PLAYS IN ENGLAND BEFORE 1642. New Haven, Conn.: Yale University Press; London: Oxford University Press, 1929.

Nungezer says he has "attempted to assemble all the available information regarding actors, theatrical proprietors, stage attendants, and other persons known to have been associated with the representation of plays in England before the year 1642" (see the "Preface"). How thorough Nungezer has tried to make the list is indicated by its inclusion of such entries as "Alleyn's Boy."

Phillips, Edward. THEATRUM POETARUM, OR A COMPLEAT COLLECTION OF THE POETS, ESPECIALLY THE MOST EMINENT, OF ALL AGES. THE ANTIENTS DISTINGUISH'T FROM THE MODERNS IN THEIR SEVERAL ALPHABETS. WITH SOME OBSERVATIONS AND REFLECTIONS UPON MANY OF THEM, PARTICULARLY THOSE OF OUR OWN NATION. TOGETHER WITH A PREFATORY DISCOURSE OF THE POETS AND POETRY IN GENERALL. London: Charles Smith, 1675. Facsimile reprint, Hildesheim and New York: Georg Olms, 1970.

The title annotates.

[Procter, B.W.]. EFFIGIES POETICAE: OR THE PORTRAITS OF THE BRITISH POETS ILLUSTRATED BY NOTES BIOGRAPHICAL, CRITICAL, AND POETICAL. London: James Carpenter and Son, 1824.

These are verbal portraits, in prose, from Chaucer to Charlotte Smith, designed "to introduce the public, personally as it were, to the most eminent of their countrymen; and to illustrate at once faithfully and with becoming spirit the poetical literature of England." Interesting as a period piece.

[Ritson, Joseph]. BIBLIOGRAPHIA POETICA: A CATALOGUE OF ENGLISH POETS, OF THE TWELFTH, THIRTEENTH, FOURTEENTH, FIFTEENTH, AND SIXTEENTH CENTURYS, WITH A SHORT ACCOUNT OF THEIR WORKS. London: G. and W. Nicol, 1802.

The "accounts" are brief but unrestrained; John Bale, for example, is identified as "a foul-mouth'd railer against, and bitter enemy to the papists" (p. 123).

Stephen, Sir Leslie, and Sir Sidney Lee, eds.

See DICTIONARY OF NATIONAL BIOGRAPHY, THE.

Tegg, William. SHAKESPEARE AND HIS CONTEMPORARIES: TOGETHER WITH THE PLOTS OF HIS PLAYS, THEATRES AND ACTORS. London: William Tegg & Co., 1879.

Tegg says his book is "principally intended for the use of youthful students of Shakespeare" but that he sees no need "to warn off maturer admirers of the genius of our mighty poet, to whom it may not have occurred that their appreciation and enjoyment of his works might be materially enhanced by an acquaintance with the general character of the other dramatic authors of his day" (p. [iii]). The book is an interesting product of its time.

Venn, John, and J.A. Venn, comps. ALUMNI CANTABRIGIENSES: A BIOGRAPHICAL LIST OF ALL KNOWN STUDENTS, GRADUATES, AND HOLDERS OF OFFICE AT THE UNIVERSITY OF CAMBRIDGE, FROM THE EARLIEST TIMES TO 1900. Part I: FROM THE EARLIEST TIMES TO 1751. 4 vols. Cambridge: At the University Press, 1922-27.

The entries are brief indeed.

Winstanley, William. ENGLAND'S WORTHIES. SELECT LIVES OF THE MOST EMINENT PERSONS FROM CONSTANTINE THE GREAT, TO THE DEATH OF OLIVER CROMWELL LATE PROTECTOR. London: Nath. Brooke, 1660.

See next item.

_____. THE LIVES OF THE MOST FAMOUS ENGLISH POETS, OR THE HONOUR OF PARNASSUS; IN A BRIEF ESSAY OF THE WORKS AND WRITINGS OF ABOVE TWO HUNDRED OF THEM, FROM THE TIME OF K. WILLIAM THE CONQUEROR. TO THE REIGN OF HIS PRESENT MAJESTY KING JAMES II. London: Printed for Samuel Manship, 1687.

"The Preface to the Reader" declares: "As we account those Books best written which mix Profit with Delight, so, in my opinion, none more profitable nor delightful than those of Lives, especially them of Poets, who have laid out themselves for the publick Good; and under the Notion of Fables, delivered unto us the highest Mysteries of Learning. These are the Men who in their Heroick Poems have made mens Fames live to eternity; therefore it were pity (saith Plutarch) that those who write to Eternity should not live so too." Winstanley accordingly offers brief notes on a large number of writers.

Wood, Anthony a, and Philip Bliss. ATHENAE OXONIENSIS. AN EXACT HISTORY OF ALL THE WRITERS AND BISHOPS WHO HAVE HAD THEIR EDUCATION IN THE UNIVERSITY OF OXFORD. TO WHICH ARE ADDED THE FASTI, OR ANNALS OF THE SAID UNIVERSITY. A NEW EDITION, WITH ADDITIONS, AND A CONTINUATION BY PHILIP BLISS. 5 vols. London: F.C. and J. Rivington, 1813-20.

Part 1 covers the years 1500-1640; Part 2, the period from 1641 to 1691.

[Wrangham, F.]. THE BRITISH PLUTARCH, CONTAINING THE LIVES OF THE MOST EMINENT STATESMEN, PATRIOTS, DIVINES, WARRIORS, PHILOSOPHERS, POETS, AND ARTISTS, OF GREAT BRITAIN AND IRELAND, FROM THE ACCESSION OF HENRY VIII. TO THE PRESENT TIME. INCLUDING A COMPENDIOUS VIEW OF THE HISTORY OF ENGLAND, DURING THAT PERIOD. A New Edition, Corrected and Considerably Enlarged. 8 vols. Perth: R. Morison & Son, 1795.

Finding the poet one seeks may be time consuming, since there is no table of contents or index and the arrangement is chronological rather than alphabetical.

Part 2

INDIVIDUAL AUTHORS
(WITH SOME ANONYMOUS PLAYS)

1. INTRODUCTION

Part 2 is made up basically of sections concerned with individual authors. Most Medieval plays being anonymous, they do not figure here very largely. Out of the enormous number of Renaissance playwrights, only a group of the more significant can be shown. Lesser figures are treated in the general studies shown in Part I, however. For each author cited below, the arrangement is as follows: first, reasonably current, separately published bibliographies (if any) on the author; second, selected editions of his work; third, concordances (if any); and fourth, selected secondary works. Bibliographies and editions are arranged chronologically, secondary works alphabetically. When secondary works of fairly recent date contain bibliographies, the fact is noted in the annotation. If there is no individual bibliography of the author shown, those contained in secondary works will help to remedy the lack. A general bibliography of an author and one on the subject of a book about a special aspect of the author's work will serve somewhat different purposes, however.

Editing Renaissance plays presents staggering difficulties of several kinds. Punctuation, spelling, canon--every detail, small and large--must be resolved in some way. An editorial practice which solves a problem satisfactorily for one audience is likely to leave it unresolved for another. Many of the editions offer some discussion of the editing problems and the approach towards solution chosen by the editor. Studies in Part 1 touch on the topic of editions; see especially Section 2 C: Editions--Serial and Multi-Volume Editions, for brief analyses of some current series of editions of one or more plays. A scholar who has worked extensively with the problem of the critical edition is Fredson Bowers. See especially:

Bowers, Fredson. ON EDITING SHAKESPEARE AND THE ELIZABETHAN DRAMATISTS. Richmond, Va.: William Byrd Press, for the Philip H. and A.S.W. Rosenbach Foundation of the University of Pennsylvania Library; London: Oxford University Press, 1955.

The volume contains three essays originally delivered at the University of Pennsylvania under the sponsorship of the A.S.W. Rosenbach Fellowship in Bibliography in

1954: "The Texts and Their Manuscripts," "The Function of Textual Criticism and Bibliography," and "The Method for a Critical Edition."

The problem of canon is a large one indeed. There are (1) anonymous plays which it might be possible to assign to the proper author(s) if one could discover the right technique or the right evidence; (2) plays which have been assigned to a particular author but which might in fact belong to someone else; (3) plays by more than one person--either persons working in collaboration or in layers, one hand revising what another had earlier written. Again, many of the secondary materials cited under individual authors deal with these problems--see especially Beaumont and Fletcher and Marlowe. A few studies, several of them having to do with Shakespeare's possible role in some play and having a more general than a specific focus, may be mentioned here, however. They offer examples of various periods of scholarship, one being nearly a hundred years old, several about a half century old, and some recent.

Maxwell, Baldwin. STUDIES IN THE SHAKESPEARE APOCRYPHA. New York: King's Crown Press, Columbia University, 1956.

The plays studied are THE LAMENTABLE TRAGEDY OF LOCRINE; THE TRUE CHRONICLE HISTORY OF THOMAS LORD CROMWELL; THE PURITAN, OR THE WIDOW OF WATLING STREET; and A YORKSHIRE TRAGEDY. Maxwell argues that the initials W.S. on a title page might have been intended to point to someone other than Shakespeare. He probes each of the four plays rather carefully.

Muir, Kenneth. SHAKESPEARE AS COLLABORATOR. London: Methuen & Co.; New York: Barnes & Noble, 1960.

Muir deals specifically with EDWARD III, PERICLES, and THE TWO NOBLE KINSMEN, which he identifies as "those plays which, though excluded from the First Folio, show unmistakable traces of [Shakespeare's] hand," together with the lost CARDENIO (p. ix).

Schoenbaum, S[amuel]. INTERNAL EVIDENCE AND ELIZABETHAN DRAMATIC AUTHORSHIP: AN ESSAY IN LITERARY HISTORY AND METHOD. Evanston, Ill.: Northwestern University Press, 1966.

Schoenbaum says: "The first two parts . . . deal in roughly chronological fashion with the origins and curious history of inquiries into Elizabethan dramatic authorship. The third is concerned largely with methodology" (p. vii). Bibliography.

Spalding, William. A LETTER ON SHAKSPERE'S AUTHORSHIP OF "THE TWO NOBLE KINSMEN" AND ON THE CHARACTERISTICS

OF SHAKSPERE'S STYLE AND THE SECRET OF HIS SUPREMACY. New Edition, ed. John Hill Burton. New Shakspere Society, Series 8, No. 1. London: Published for the New Shakspere Society by N. Trubner & Co., 1876.

See also the entry under Spalding in Section 3: Francis Beaumont and John Fletcher.

Sykes, H. Dugdale. THE AUTHORSHIP OF "THE TAMING OF A SHREW," "THE FAMOUS VICTORIES OF HENRY V," AND THE ADDITIONS TO MARLOWE'S "FAUSTUS." Shakespeare Association Papers, No. 4. London: Chatto & Windus, 1920.

Sykes argues for Samuel Rowley's authorship of, or collaboration in, THE FAMOUS VICTORIES, THE TAMING OF A SHREW, WILY BEGUILD, JUDAS (lost), JOSHUA (lost), and WHEN YOU SEE ME YOU KNOW ME, and credits him with additions to ORLANDO FURIOSO and DR. FAUSTUS.

_____. SIDELIGHTS ON ELIZABETHAN DRAMA: A SERIES OF STUDIES DEALING WITH THE AUTHORSHIP OF SIXTEENTH AND SEVENTEENTH CENTURY PLAYS. London: Oxford University Press, 1924.

Essays, largely reprinted from NOTES AND QUERIES, on Peele, Webster, Massinger, Middleton, Ford, Field, and others.

_____. SIDELIGHTS ON SHAKESPEARE: BEING STUDIES OF "THE TWO NOBLE KINSMEN," "HENRY VIII," "ARDEN OF FEVERSHAM," "A YORKSHIRE TRAGEDY," "THE TROUBLESOME REIGN OF KING JOHN," "KING LEIR," "PERICLES PRINCE OF TYRE." Stratford-upon-Avon: Shakespeare Head Press, 1919.

Sykes attributes THE TWO NOBLE KINSMEN and HENRY VIII to Massinger and Fletcher. He sees no real reason to attribute ARDEN to Shakespeare and suggests it may be Kyd's. Sykes hypothesizes that George Wilkins wrote YORKSHIRE and PERICLES, possibly with revisions of both by Shakespeare, takes THE TROUBLESOME REIGN to be Peele's, and sees "Peele's hand" in the old KING LEIR.

Tannenbaum, S[amuel] A[aron]. "THE BOOKE OF SIR THOMAS MOORE": (A BIBLIOTIC STUDY). New York: The Tenny Press, 1927.

Tannenbaum points out among other curiosities in connection with the play that "[o]f the three thousand plays which it has been estimated were written during the reigns of Elizabeth and James, this is the only one that is known to have been written by six authors" (p. v). In addition to Munday and Dekker, Tannenbaum argues for Kyd, Henry Chettle, Thomas Heywood, and possibly Shakespeare as authors. He dates the play early in 1593 and attributes its never being acted to "Kyd's arrest on a charge of being involved in the publication of seditious libels" (p. 101).

_____. SHAKSPERIAN SCRAPS AND OTHER ELIZABETHAN FRAGMENTS. New York: Columbia University Press, 1933.

Tannenbaum says that his "main purpose has been to demonstrate . . . the value of a knowledge of paleography and bibliotics" as these may help "to determine the genuineness or the spuriousness of a literary document" and also "to determine whether a literary manuscript was or was not written by the person alleged, or supposed, to have written it" (p. [xv]). The essays focus on John Payne Collier's editorial practices and include studies of LOCRINE, GEORGE A GREENE, MISOGONUS, Chapman, and Marlowe.

Wells, William. THE AUTHORSHIP OF "JULIUS CAESAR." London: G. Routledge & Sons; New York: E.P. Dutton & Co., 1923.

Wells argues for Marlowe as the original author, with Shakespeare and Beaumont as revisers.

Note: See also Part 1, Section 8: Studies of Tudor and Stuart Drama, for the series SALZBURG STUDIES IN ENGLISH LITERATURE, which includes studies of individual playwrights in both the series ELIZABETHAN STUDIES and in the series JACOBEAN DRAMA STUDIES.

2. JOHN BALE

BIBLIOGRAPHIES

Davies, W.T. "A Bibliography of John Bale." OXFORD BIBLIOGRAPHICAL SOCIETY, PROCEEDINGS & PAPERS, 5 (1940), 201-79. Oxford: Printed for the Society at the Oxford University Press, 1940.

Useful preliminary matter: "Introduction: John Bale's Life and Work," "Catalogues of Bale's Work," "Bale's Handwriting," followed by a bibliography of primary materials, with careful descriptions of each item.

EDITIONS

THE DRAMATIC WRITINGS OF JOHN BALE, BISHOP OF OSSORY. Ed. John S. Farmer. 1907; facsimile reprint ed. Guildford: Charles W. Traylen; New York: Barnes & Noble, 1966.

The critical apparatus in the Farmer editions is limited largely to a few notes and word lists, but he was a diligent editor.

KING JOHAN. Ed. Barry B. Adams. San Marino, Calif.: Huntington Library, 1969.

An admirable, scholarly edition, with a full introduction, a faithful text, and a list of books (pp. vii-ix), especially useful in pointing out materials on the historical King John which Bale follows or which he might have known and does not follow.

SECONDARY WORKS

Blatt, Thora B. THE PLAYS OF JOHN BALE: A STUDY OF IDEAS, TECHNIQUE AND STYLE. Copenhagen: G.E.C. Gad, 1968.

The book works from the broad background "of the political and religious turbulence of his day," through Bale's ideas, to the "structure and content of the individual plays" and to narrower matters such as costumes, props, and style (see p. 233). Bibliography.

Harris, Jesse W. JOHN BALE: A STUDY IN THE MINOR LITERATURE OF THE REFORMATION. Illinois Studies in Language and Literature, Vol. 25, No. 4. Urbana: University of Illinois Press, 1940.

The text has two parts, "Bale's Life" and "Bale's Works in General," stressing the work as "transitional" (p. 130). There are two appendices: a "Facsimile of Bale's Autobiography, 1536" and "Excerpts from Contemporary Letters on Bale." Bibliography.

McCusker, Honor [Cecilia]. JOHN BALE, DRAMATIST AND ANTIQUARY. 1942; reprint ed. Freeport, N.Y.: Books for Libraries, 1971.

In this Bryn Mawr dissertation, McCusker pictures the man and his plays as "links between an old world and a new" (p. 72; page references are to the 1942 edition) but regards Bale as having "little influence on the playwrights who followed him" (p. 96). McCusker argues that Bale uses the morality play in a new way, "not merely as a sermon but as a weapon" (p. 78).

3. FRANCIS BEAUMONT AND JOHN FLETCHER

BIBLIOGRAPHIES

Tannenbaum, Samuel A[aron], and Dorothy R. Tannenbaum, comps. ELIZABETHAN BIBLIOGRAPHIES. Vol. I. Port Washington, N.Y.: Kennikat Press, 1967.

Reprints the 1938 Tannenbaum bibliography of Beaumont and Fletcher and the 1950 supplement. Designed as an exhaustive, unannotated listing.

Pennel, Charles A., and William P. Williams, comps. ELIZABETHAN BIBLIOGRAPHIES SUPPLEMENTS. Vol. VIII. London: Nether Press, 1968.

Includes Beaumont and Fletcher, 1937-65. Less inclusive than the Tannenbaum, which it supplements. Entries arranged by year of publication.

EDITIONS

COMEDIES AND TRAGEDIES WRITTEN BY FRANCIS BEAVMONT AND IOHN FLETCHER, GENTLEMEN. NEVER PRINTED BEFORE. AND NOW PUBLISHED BY THE AUTHOURS ORIGINALL COPIES. London: For Humphrey Robinson and Humphrey Moseley, 1647.

This is the "First Folio" of Beaumont and Fletcher. Moseley says that he has printed all the plays of Beaumont and Fletcher not heretofore printed, except THE WILD-GOOSE CHASE. His preface deserves quotation at some length: "[A]s it is all New, so here is not any thing Spurious or impos'd; I had the Originalls from such as received them from the Authours themselves . . . .

"And as here's nothing but what is genuine and Theirs, so you will finde here are no Omissions; you have not onely All I could get but All that you must ever expect. For (besides those which were formerly printed) there is not any Piece written by these Authours, either Joyntly or Severally, but what are now publish'd to the

World in this Volume. One only Play I must except (for I meane to deale openly) 'tis a COMEDY called the Wilde-goose Chase, which hath beene long lost, and I feare Irrecoverable; for a Person of quality borrowed it from the Actours many yeares since, and (by the Negligence of a Servant) it was never return'd; therefore now I put up this Si quis, that whosoever hereafter happily meetes with it, shall be thankfully satisfied if he please to send it home" [signature A 4, recto]. On this edition, see Bald, R.C., in Secondary Works.

FIFTY COMEDIES AND TRAGEDIES. WRITTEN BY FRANCIS BEAUMONT AND JOHN FLETCHER, GENTLEMEN. ALL IN ONE VOLUME. PUBLISHED BY THE AUTHORS ORIGINAL COPIES, THE SONGS TO EACH PLAY BEING ADDED. London: Printed by J. Macock, for John Martyn, Henry Herringman, Richard Marriot, 1679.

An essay, "The Book-Sellers to the Readers," declares this edition (the "Second Folio") to have been emended in many details on the advice of a person who "had an intimacy with both our Authors, and had been a Spectator of most of them when they were Acted" (signature A [1], verso). The booksellers point to the addition of seventeen plays "which we have taken the pains and care to Collect, and Print out of 4to in this volume, which for distinction sake are markt with a Star in the Catalogue of them facing the first Page of the Book" (signature A [1], recto). In addition to these seventeen, the Second Folio contains THE WILD-GOOSE CHASE that Moseley had been unable to discover.

THE WORKS OF MR. FRANCIS BEAUMONT, AND MR. JOHN FLETCHER; IN SEVEN VOLUMES, ADORN'D WITH CUTS. REVIS'D AND CORRECTED; WITH SOME ACCOUNT OF THE LIFE AND WRITINGS OF THE AUTHORS. London: Jacob Tonson, 1711.

Notable as the work of the eighteenth-century publisher Jacob Tonson.

THE DRAMATICK WORKS OF BEAUMONT AND FLETCHER; COLLATED WITH ALL THE FORMER EDITIONS, AND CORRECTED; WITH NOTES, CRITICAL AND EXPLANATORY, BY VARIOUS COMMENTATORS; AND ADORNED WITH FIFTY-FOUR ORIGINAL ENGRAVINGS. 10 vols. London: Printed by T. Sherlock, for T. Evans and P. Elmsley, 1778.

The 1778 edition reprints various prefaces from the 1647 and 1679 folios, the 1711 Tonson octavo, and the 1750 (Seward) octavo.

THE WORKS OF BEAUMONT AND FLETCHER: THE TEXT FORMED FROM A NEW COLLATION OF THE EARLY EDITIONS, WITH NOTES AND BIOGRAPHICAL MEMOIR. Ed. Alexander Dyce. 11 vols. 1843-46; reprint ed. Freeport, N.Y.: Books for Libraries, 1970.

Dyce, one of the very assiduous editors of the nineteenth century, supplies an introduction and notes.

THE WORKS OF FRANCIS BEAUMONT AND JOHN FLETCHER. Ed. [A.H. Bullen]. Variorum Edition. 4 vols. London: G. Bell and Sons and A.H. Bullen, 1904-12.

Bullen and various other hands have provided an introduction and notes, including extensive textual notes, for each play printed, but Bullen prints just twenty of the plays.

THE WORKS OF FRANCIS BEAUMONT AND JOHN FLETCHER. Ed. Arnold Glover and A.R. Waller. 10 vols. 1905-12; reprint ed. New York: Octagon Books, 1969.

The texts are based on the second folio. The proposed volume or two of notes were never printed.

THE DRAMATIC WORKS IN THE BEAUMONT AND FLETCHER CANON. General ed. Fredson Bowers. Cambridge: At the University Press, 1966--.

Volume I of this edition-in-progress appeared in 1966, Volume II in 1970. Volume III is expected in 1975. The individual plays are edited by various scholars. The edition is designed to provide "a critical old-spelling text" of "the plays conventionally assigned to the Beaumont and Fletcher canon," including those on which "Fletcher collaborated with dramatists other than Beaumont" and those for which "the preserved texts . . . represent revision at a later date by various hands" (Vol. I, pp. ix, vii). The edition provides full scholarly apparatus.

SECONDARY WORKS

Appleton, William W. BEAUMONT AND FLETCHER: A CRITICAL STUDY. London: Allen & Unwin, 1956.

In view of the popularity of Beaumont and Fletcher with their contemporaries and with Restoration audiences on the one hand and their "current neglect" on the other, Appleton proposes to study the plays in such a way as to make them relevant to "the general reader's interest" (p. [5]). Bibliography.

Bald, R.C. BIBLIOGRAPHICAL STUDIES IN THE BEAUMONT AND FLETCHER FOLIO OF 1647. Supplement to Bibliographical Society Transactions No. 13 for 1937. Oxford: At the University Press for the Bibliographical Society, 1938.

Bald studies Moseley's work as a publisher and the "light [thrown] on various points of theatrical practice and history during the decade immediately preceding the closing of the theatre" by his First Folio of Beaumont and Fletcher, concluding that "an examination of the texts . . . shows the extent to which Moseley's preface is to be relied upon, and vindicates his reputation for fair and just dealing as a publisher" (p. 114). (See the Moseley edition under Editions.)

Bertram, Paul Benjamin. SHAKESPEARE AND "THE TWO NOBLE KINSMEN." New Brunswick, N.J.: Rutgers University Press, 1965.

Bertram's study "seeks to show . . . that the play must have been entirely the work of Shakespeare" (p. vi). Appendix: "Checklist of Editions," pages 297-99.

Brody, Ervin C. THE DEMETRIUS LEGEND AND ITS LITERARY TREATMENT IN THE AGE OF THE BAROQUE. Rutherford, N.J.: Fairleigh Dickinson University Press, 1972.

Brody examines the legends concerning a young man who claimed to be a presumably dead son of Ivan the Terrible. The chapter "John Fletcher's THE LOYAL SUBJECT" (pp. 141-216) discusses the relation of the play to the legend.

Chelli, Maurice. ETUDE SUR LA COLLABORATION DE MASSINGER AVEC FLETCHER ET SON GROUPE. Universite de Paris: Bibliotheque de la Faculte des Lettres, Deuxieme Serie, VI. Paris: University of Paris, 1926.

A contribution to the untangling of the maze of hands in the "Fletcher" plays. On the problem of collaboration, see the 1956-62 papers by Hoy, Cyrus, below.

Danby, John F. POETS ON FORTUNE'S HILL: STUDIES IN SIDNEY, SHAKESPEARE, BEAUMONT & FLETCHER. 1952; reprint ed. Port Washington, N.Y.: Kennikat Press, 1966.

Also published in 1964 with the title ELIZABETHAN AND JACOBEAN POETS, Danby's study attempts a reassessment of Beaumont and Fletcher, arguing that they "are dramatic opportunists" (p. 179) fundamentally different from Shakespeare, to whom they are often compared. Danby characterizes their work as "Petrarchan" (p. 189ff) and says they wrote with a "two-level" aim, to please the mass audience and the aristocracy (p. 180). Detailed analysis of PHILASTER and THE MAID'S TRAGEDY.

Fellowes, E.H., ed. SONGS & LYRICS FROM THE PLAYS OF BEAUMONT & FLETCHER. WITH CONTEMPORARY MUSICAL SETTINGS. London: Frederick Etchells & Hugh Macdonald, 1928.

The book contains "a few typical settings . . . for the purpose of illustrating the methods of the seventeenth-century musicians in dealing with the songs of the dramatists, and particularly those of Fletcher" (p. 44). Only six settings are given.

Fletcher, Ian. BEAUMONT AND FLETCHER. Writers and Their Work, No. 199. London: Published for the British Council and the National Book League by Longmans, Green, 1967.

Brief critical study with a useful annotated, selected bibliography.

Gayley, Charles Mills. BEAUMONT, THE DRAMATIST: A PORTRAIT, WITH SOME ACCOUNT OF HIS CIRCLE, ELIZABETHAN AND JACOBEAN, AND OF HIS ASSOCIATION WITH JOHN FLETCHER. New York: Century Co., 1914.

Gayley proposes to distinguish and evaluate the respective work of Beaumont and Fletcher (see also Hoy, Cyrus) and to study the questions of Beaumont's influence on Shakespeare and of his contribution to the "decadence" of the stage (concluding that he contributed to neither).

Hatcher, Orie Latham. JOHN FLETCHER: A STUDY IN DRAMATIC METHOD. Chicago: Scott, Foresman, 1905.

Attacks the problems of distinguishing the "hands" of Beaumont and Fletcher in their collaborations and of characterizing Fletcher as a dramatist (see also next item).

Hoy, Cyrus. "The Shares of Fletcher and his Collaborators in the Beaumont and Fletcher Canon." STUDIES IN BIBLIOGRAPHY, PAPERS OF THE BIBLIOGRAPHICAL SOCIETY OF THE UNIVERSITY OF VIRGINIA, 8 (1956), [129]-46; 9 (1957), [142]-62; 11 (1958), [85]-106; 12 (1959), [91]-116; 13 (1960), [77]-108; 14 (1961), [45]-67; 15 (1962), [71]-90.

Hoy identifies the problem thus: "The Beaumont and Fletcher canon consists traditionally of fifty-two plays, but it has been recognized that of these only a small number represent the work of the two dramatists in collaboration" (8 [1956], p. [129]). He sets out to determine which plays are the work of Beaumont and Fletcher jointly and to investigate what other hands are to be found in the plays, for there have been arguments for assigning them to "virtually every dramatist known to have been plying his trade in Jacobean London" (p. [129]). Hoy's arguments are accepted to such an extent as to constitute the basis on which Pennel and Williams, in ELIZABETHAN BIBLIOGRAPHIES SUPPLEMENTS (see main entry under Bibliographies) rest their attributions, to cite one evidence of acceptance.

Leech, Clifford. THE JOHN FLETCHER PLAYS. London: Chatto & Windus; Cambridge, Mass.: Harvard University Press, 1962.

Leech considers Fletcher "the man who exercised perhaps the largest influence on English drama for three-quarters of a century" (p. 3), yet says that Fletcher cannot be classed with Shakespeare, Jonson, Marlowe, Chapman, Webster, and Ford: "He simply does not illuminate life enough for us to have the sense of a major experience in reading his plays. But that does not mean that he offers no illumination" (p. 5). Leech proposes to search for Fletcher's "individual qualities" (p. 6).

Macaulay, George Campbell. FRANCIS BEAUMONT: A CRITICAL STUDY. 1883; reprint ed. New York: Lemma, 1972.

The reprint makes Macaulay's old study again available.

McKeithan, Daniel Morley. THE DEBT TO SHAKESPEARE IN THE BEAUMONT-AND-FLETCHER PLAYS. 1938; reprint ed. New York: AMS Press, 1970.

Argues for a debt to Shakespeare, particularly on the part of Fletcher, rather than of Shakespeare to Beaumont and Fletcher.

Makkink, Henri Jacob. PHILIP MASSINGER AND JOHN FLETCHER, A COMPARISON. 1927; reprint ed. New York: Haskell House, 1966.

Makkink proposes to attack the problem of separating the work of Fletcher and Massinger by metrical tests and also by the examination of such further internal evidence as "Attitude towards woman," "Religious belief and superstitions," and the like (see also Hoy, Cyrus).

Mason, J[ohn] Monck. COMMENTS ON THE PLAYS OF BEAUMONT AND FLETCHER, WITH AN APPENDIX CONTAINING SOME FURTHER OBSERVATIONS ON SHAKESPEARE, EXTENDED TO THE LATE EDITIONS OF MALONE AND STEEVENS. London: Printed by V. Griffiths for E. Harding, 1798.

Finding the plays of Beaumont and Fletcher in a state of eclipse and proposing that "many of theirs will be found superior to [Shakespeare's], though none of them equal in excellence to his best," Mason undertakes to "redeem" the plays of Beaumont and Fletcher "from this state of unmerited oblivion" (p. v). Mason's text is made up of brief quotations and his comments on them.

Maxwell, Baldwin. STUDIES IN BEAUMONT, FLETCHER, AND MASSINGER. 1939; reprint ed. New York: Octagon Books; London: Frank Cass & Co., 1966.

Seventeen essays, all by Maxwell, nine of them reprinted, with various revisions--a collection which combines the convenience of book form with the incisiveness of the essay as it can be directed to the exploration of individual problems.

Muir, Kenneth. SHAKESPEARE AS COLLABORATOR. London: Methuen & Co.; New York: Barnes & Noble, 1960.

See the main entry in Section 1: Introduction.

Oliphant, E[rnest] H[enry] C[lark]. THE PLAYS OF BEAUMONT AND FLETCHER: AN ATTEMPT TO DETERMINE THEIR RESPECTIVE SHARES AND THE SHARES OF OTHERS. New Haven, Conn.: Yale University Press; London: Oxford University Press, 1927.

Another essay on one of the most debated Beaumont and Fletcher issues (see also, Hoy, Cyrus).

Spalding, William. A LETTER ON SHAKSPERE'S AUTHORSHIP OF "THE TWO NOBLE KINSMEN" AND ON THE CHARACTERISTICS OF SHAKSPERE'S STYLE AND THE SECRET OF HIS SUPREMACY. New Edition, ed. John Hill Burton.

New Shakspere Society, Series 8, No. 1. London: Published for the New Shakspere Society by N. Trubner & Co., 1876.

In the longstanding debate about who wrote what, or what part of what, Spalding leans towards attributing a great deal to Shakespeare (see also, Hoy, Cyrus).

Sprague, Arthur Colby. BEAUMONT AND FLETCHER ON THE RESTORATION STAGE. 1926; reprint ed. New York: Benjamin Blom, 1965.

In two parts, "The Stage History of the Plays," a carefully detailed, factual, stage history; and "The Alterations and Adaptations," an essay on "the contrasting dramatic ideals of the Jacobean and Restoration eras" (p. xv). Sprague provides the kind of fact one needs access to, in a readily manageable format.

Thorndike, Ashley H. THE INFLUENCE OF BEAUMONT AND FLETCHER ON SHAKSPERE. 1901; reprint ed. New York: Russell & Russell, 1965; AMS Press, 1966.

Thorndike argues "two main hypotheses: first, that Shakspere's change from tragedies to romances is to be accounted for by the contemporaneous production of the Beaumont-Fletcher romances; and second, that these latter definitely influenced CYMBELINE, a WINTER'S TALE, and the TEMPEST" (p. 169).

Waith, Eugene M. THE PATTERN OF TRAGICOMEDY IN BEAUMONT AND FLETCHER. New Haven, Conn.: Yale University Press; London: Oxford University Press, 1952.

Waith believes that "the ancient practice of declamation and . . . a theory of rhetoric current in Augustan Rome and still operative in Jacobean England" offer a key to the Beaumont and Fletcher tragicomedies. He proposes to analyze the plays "in the light of certain contemporary literary forms and, ultimately, of the rhetorical tradition" (p. [ix]).

Wallis, Lawrence B. FLETCHER, BEAUMONT & COMPANY, ENTERTAINERS TO THE JACOBEAN GENTRY. Morningside Heights, N.Y.: King's Crown Press, 1947.

A two-part study, a "history of the reputation of 'Beaumont and Fletcher' from Stuart times until nearly the present day" and a reinterpretation of their whole careers as playwrights in light of the world in which they moved (pp. [vii]-viii). Bibliography.

Wilson, John Harold. THE INFLUENCE OF BEAUMONT AND FLETCHER ON RESTORATION DRAMA. 1928; reprint ed. New York: Benjamin Blom, 1968.

The study attempts to demonstrate that the Beaumont and Fletcher plays were known and liked by Restoration dramatists, audiences, and critics, and further that they were revised, drawn upon, and imitated by the dramatists. The appendix supplies various useful lists of plays which were revived in the Restoration.

4. RICHARD BROME

EDITIONS

THE DRAMATIC WORKS OF RICHARD BROME, CONTAINING FIFTEEN COMEDIES, NOW FIRST COLLECTED IN THREE VOLUMES. Ed. [John Pearson]. London: John Pearson, 1873.

Volume I reprints FIVE NEW PLAYES (London: Printed for Humphrey Moseley, Richard Marriot, and Thomas Dring, 1653). Volume II reprints FIVE NEVV PLAYES (London: Printed for A. Crook and H. Brome, 1659). Volume III adds the last five plays. There is very little critical apparatus.

SECONDARY WORKS

Allen, Herbert F. A STUDY OF THE COMEDIES OF RICHARD BROME, ESPECIALLY AS REPRESENTATIVE OF DRAMATIC DECADENCE. Ann Arbor: University of Michigan, 1912.

In this sixty-one-page dissertation, Allen argues that Brome's plays are characterized by an "essential emptiness" which "shows that the dramatic time is out of joint." He finds this emptiness "true of Brome" and "true of his contemporaries" to the extent that Brome's plays have their chief significance from "the fact that they show this fact so fully" (p. 61).

Andrews, Clarence E. RICHARD BROME: A STUDY OF HIS LIFE AND WORKS. Yale Studies in English, Vol. 46. New York: Henry Holt, 1913.

Andrews has assembled the available data about Brome and "made a study of his position with relation to his contemporaries, the structure of his plays, and the influences exerted upon him" (p. [v]). He provides a chronology and bibliography of Brome's work, an analysis of the plays, and an analysis of such influences as Jonson, Shakespeare, and Dekker on Brome's work.

Kaufmann, R.J. RICHARD BROME, CAROLINE PLAYWRIGHT. New York and

London: Columbia University Press, 1961.

Kaufmann aims at "mak[ing] Brome's work as accessible to modern readers as possible" through a biographical and critical study. He believes that Brome "achieved a very coherent body of work" through a "talent for transporting an internally consistent set of moral convictions into effective dramatic statement" (see the "Preface"). Kaufmann provides two appendices: "Undigested Records" and a "Chronology of Brome's Plays," and a slender bibliography.

5. GEORGE CHAPMAN

BIBLIOGRAPHIES

Tannenbaum, Samuel A[aron], and Dorothy R. Tannenbaum, comps. ELIZABETHAN BIBLIOGRAPHIES. Vol. I. Port Washington, N.Y.: Kennikat Press, 1967.

Reprints the 1938 Tannenbaum bibliography of Chapman and the 1946 supplement. Designed as an exhaustive, unannotated listing.

Yamada, Akihiro, comp. "George Chapman: A Checklist of Editions, Biography, and Criticism 1946-1965." RESEARCH OPPORTUNITIES IN RENAISSANCE DRAMA, 10 (1967), 75-86.

Bibliography, unannotated, grouped under "Collected Works," "Individual Plays," and "Biography and Criticism."

Pennel, Charles A., and William P. Williams, comps. ELIZABETHAN BIBLIOGRAPHIES SUPPLEMENTS. Vol. IV. London: Nether Press, 1968.

Includes a bibliography of Chapman for 1937-65. Less inclusive than the Tannenbaum, which it supplements. Entries arranged in annual groups.

EDITIONS

THE COMEDIES AND TRAGEDIES OF GEORGE CHAPMAN. NOW FIRST COLLECTED WITH ILLUSTRATIVE NOTES AND A MEMOIR OF THE AUTHOR. Ed. [R(ichard) Herne Shepherd]. London: John Pearson, 1873.

The edition has sometimes been attributed to Pearson as editor as well as publisher; see Edmund Gosse's "Prefatory Note" to Swinburne, Algernon Charles, LETTERS ON THE WORKS OF GEORGE CHAPMAN (in Secondary Works) on the evidence that this and several other editions formerly attributed to Pearson are in fact Shepherd's work. Notes in the edition are not abundant.

THE WORKS OF GEORGE CHAPMAN. Ed. Algernon C. Swinburne and R.H. Shepherd. 3 vols. London: Chatto and Windus, 1875.

Herne Shepherd edited Volumes I and III, containing the plays and THE ILIAD and THE ODYSSEY. Swinburne edited Volume II, POEMS AND MINOR TRANSLATIONS. Swinburne's essay on Chapman, also published separately (see Secondary Works) constitutes the introduction to the edition.

THE PLAYS AND POEMS OF GEORGE CHAPMAN. Ed. Thomas Marc Parrott. 2 vols. 1910-14; reprint ed. New York: Russell & Russell, 1961.

Volume I contains THE TRAGEDIES; Volume II, THE COMEDIES. The third volume, designed to contain the poems, together with "a general introduction, a glossary, and a bibliography" (Vol. I, p. vii), never appeared. Holaday (see next item) says of Parrott's editing that it was good for its time but has "serious limitations."

THE PLAYS OF GEORGE CHAPMAN: THE COMEDIES, A CRITICAL EDITION. General ed. Allan Holaday, assisted by Michael Kiernan. Urbana, Chicago, and London: University of Illinois Press, 1970.

In addition to a "General Introduction," the edition provides for each play a "Textual Introduction" and a "four-part apparatus: a table of press-variants; two 'collations,' and textual notes" (p. 2). A fine example of scholarly editing so arranged that the general reader is not impeded by the critical apparatus and the scholar can readily find what he needs.

SECONDARY WORKS

Acheson, Arthur. SHAKESPEARE AND THE RIVAL POET: DISPLAYING SHAKESPEARE AS A SATIRIST AND PROVING THE IDENTITY OF THE PATRON AND THE RIVAL OF THE SONNETS, WITH A REPRINT OF SUNDRY POETICAL PIECES BY GEORGE CHAPMAN BEARING ON THE SUBJECT. London and New York: John Lane, The Bodley Head, 1903.

Acheson suggests Chapman's role as both the object of satire and the writer of satires. Acheson's account of Shakespeare is interesting, and not the less so for being debatable. He reprints from Chapman's works, pages 221-360.

Allen, Percy. THE PLAYS OF SHAKESPEARE & CHAPMAN IN RELATION TO FRENCH HISTORY. London: Denis Archer, 1933.

Arguing from the assumption that Edward de Vere wrote the plays, Allen sees a parallel between de Vere (Oxford) and Lear and interprets "KING LEAR as French History." Chapman rather frequently appears in connection with some other topic, as here.

_____. SHAKESPEARE AND CHAPMAN AS TOPICAL DRAMATISTS, BEING A

FURTHER STUDY OF ELIZABETHAN DRAMATIC ORIGINS AND IMITATIONS. London: Cecil Palmer, 1929.

Allen asserts that in his plays Chapman "deliberately imitated, and criticized, Shakespeare" and in so doing displayed considerable recall of Shakespeare's plays (p. vii). Having presented evidence in an earlier book, SHAKESPEARE, JONSON, AND WILKINS AS BORROWERS (see under Section 15: Jonson), that Elizabethan drama "was the newspaper and debating platform of the day, upon which topical themes, and contemporary celebrities, were discussed" (p. 2), Allen here explores the "topicality" of Shakespeare and Chapman.

Ellis, Havelock. CHAPMAN, WITH ILLUSTRATIVE PASSAGES. 1934; reprint ed. Folcroft, Pa.: Folcroft Library Editions, 1971.

Ellis provides an "Essay" on Chapman which concludes: "[H]e was sometimes a great poet, he was always a great Englishman" (p. 82). The remainder of the volume (pp. 85-[147]) is made up of the "Illustrative Passages."

Jacquot, Jean. GEORGE CHAPMAN (1554-1634): SA VIE, SA POESIE, SON THEATRE, SA PENSEE. Annales de l'Universite de Lyon, Troisieme Serie, Lettres, Fascicule 19. Paris: Les Belles Lettres, 1951.

A study of the life in two parts, the Elizabethan and Jacobean periods; a study of the work, divided into poetry and drama; and a study of Chapman's thought, considering Platonism, Stoicism, and Christianity in the context of Chapman's "Poetic Doctrine" and his "Ethic." Bibliography.

Kreider, Paul V. ELIZABETHAN COMIC CHARACTER CONVENTIONS AS REVEALED IN THE COMEDIES OF GEORGE CHAPMAN. University of Michigan Publications, Language and Literature, Vol. 17. Ann Arbor: University of Michigan Press, 1935.

Kreider characterizes Chapman's work as displaying an "almost complete lack of originality," making him "an excellent playwright" through whom to study "the influence of convention in drama" (p. 5). Kreider discusses conventional figures and also conventions drawn from psychology and "the Comedy of Humours" as these affect characterization. Bibliography.

MacLure, Millar. GEORGE CHAPMAN: A CRITICAL STUDY. Toronto: University of Toronto Press, 1966, 1969.

MacLure states: "At this writing, there exists no book-length study of Chapman in English, and no study in any language which provides a detailed discussion of all his work: poems, plays, translations" (p. [vii]). MacLure's well-documented study initiates the remedy.

Rees, Ennis. THE TRAGEDIES OF GEORGE CHAPMAN: RENAISSANCE ETHICS IN ACTION. Cambridge, Mass.: Harvard University Press, 1954.

Rees ("Preface") proposes that "poet and moralist are, in Chapman, one. . . . [W]e see an inherited and profoundly held moral philosophy as a mode of imagination." Bibliography.

Robertson, J.M. SHAKESPEARE AND CHAPMAN: A THESIS OF CHAPMAN'S AUTHORSHIP OF "A LOVER'S COMPLAINT," AND HIS ORIGINATION OF "TIMON OF ATHENS." WITH INDICATIONS OF FURTHER PROBLEMS. London: T.F. Unwin; New York: E.P. Dutton, 1917.

The tone of the discussion is perhaps suggested in Robertson's statement that the removal of certain plays or parts of plays "from the Shakespeare Canon" does not constitute "a diminution of Shakespeare's glory. . . . So far as I know, no attempt at such elimination has ever touched any save inferior or second-rate work." He identifies as the "immediate issue . . . whether Chapman does enter into certain of the inferior plays" (p. 291).

Solve, Norma Dobie. STUART POLITICS IN CHAPMAN'S "TRAGEDY OF CHABOT." University of Michigan Publications, Language and Literature, Vol. 4. Ann Arbor: University of Michigan Press, 1928.

The discussion assumes that the play is basically of Chapman's composition, with revisions by James Shirley, and wrestles with problems of source and date among other topics.

Spivack, Charlotte [Kesler]. GEORGE CHAPMAN. Twayne's English Authors Series, No. 60. New York: Twayne Publishers, 1967.

Brief evaluations of the plays, one by one, in the context of a general life and works study, with a final chapter reviewing Chapman criticism since the seventeenth century. Bibliography.

Stagg, Louis C. AN INDEX TO THE FIGURATIVE LANGUAGE OF GEORGE CHAPMAN'S TRAGEDIES. Charlottesville: Bibliographical Society of the University of Virginia, 1970.

One of a series of such indexes.

Swinburne, Algernon Charles. GEORGE CHAPMAN: A CRITICAL ESSAY. 1875; reprint ed. New York: Lemma Publishing Corp., 1972.

The essay also appears as the introduction to the Swinburne and Shepherd edition of THE WORKS OF GEORGE CHAPMAN (see Editions).

_____. LETTERS ON THE WORKS OF GEORGE CHAPMAN. WITH A PREFATORY NOTE BY EDMUND GOSSE. London: Printed for Private Circulation, 1909.

See Gosse's "Note" on the evidence these letters offer of its having been Richard Herne Shepherd who edited the works of Dekker, Chapman, Heywood, and Glapthorne published in the 1870s by John Pearson and earlier thought to have been edited as well as published by Pearson.

Wieler, John W. GEORGE CHAPMAN--THE EFFECT OF STOICISM UPON HIS TRAGEDIES. 1949; reprint ed. New York: Octagon Books, 1969.

Wieler points out that his is the first study to consider the Stoicism in all the Chapman tragedies, not just in those strongly marked by Stoicism. He suggests that the study casts "new light . . . upon the playwright's treatment of character and situation, particularly upon those provocative issues: why Chapman's development as a Stoic contributed to his failure as a dramatist and why the possibilities of so great a dramatist as Chapman were never realized" (p. [vii]). Bibliography.

6. SAMUEL DANIEL

BIBLIOGRAPHIES

Sellers, H. "A Bibliography of the Works of Samuel Daniel, 1585-1623, With an Appendix of Daniel's Letters." OXFORD BIBLIOGRAPHICAL SOCIETY, PROCEEDINGS & PAPERS, 2 (1930), 29-54.

Includes both printed editions and manuscripts.

Tannenbaum, Samuel A[aron], and Dorothy R. Tannenbaum, comps. ELIZABETHAN BIBLIOGRAPHIES. Vol. II. Port Washington, N.Y.: Kennikat Press, 1967.

Includes a reprinting of the 1942 Tannenbaum bibliography of Daniel, designed as an exhaustive, unannotated listing.

Guffey, George Robert, comp. ELIZABETHAN BIBLIOGRAPHIES SUPPLEMENTS. Vol. VII. London: Nether Press, 1967.

Includes a bibliography of Daniel, 1942-65. Less inclusive than the Tannenbaum, which it supplements. Entries are grouped annually. No annotation.

EDITIONS

THE COMPLETE WORKS IN VERSE AND PROSE OF SAMUEL DANIEL. Ed. Alexander Grosart. 5 vols. London: Printed for Private Circulation Only, by Hazell, Watson, and Viney, 1885-96.

The apparatus is slight: a five-page "Preliminary Note" by George Saintsbury "On the Position of Daniel's Tragedies in English Literature," and a few notes.

SECONDARY WORKS

Rees, Joan. SAMUEL DANIEL: A CRITICAL AND BIOGRAPHICAL STUDY.

Liverpool English Texts and Studies, No. 9. Liverpool: Liverpool University Press, 1964.

Sympathetic though not adulatory, the study treats the plays to some extent but emphasizes the poetry. Bibliography.

Seronsky, Cecil. SAMUEL DANIEL. Twayne's English Authors Series, No. 49. New York: Twayne Publishers, 1967.

A general consideration of the life and works. Bibliography.

Spriet, Pierre. SAMUEL DANIEL, 1563-1619, SA VIE, SON OEUVRE. Paris: Didier, 1968.

Within a general life and works study, Spriet has a long chapter, "Daniel et le Theatre" (pp. [344]-450). Exceptionally useful bibliography.

7. WILLIAM DAVENANT

EDITIONS

THE WORKS OF Sr WILLIAM D'AVENANT K^t CONSISTING OF THOSE WHICH WERE FORMERLY PRINTED, AND THOSE WHICH HE DESIGN'D FOR THE PRESS: NOW PUBLISHED OUT OF THE AUTHORS ORIGINALL COPIES. 1673; reprint ed. in 2 vols., New York and London: Benjamin Blom, 1968.

Historically interesting. No critical apparatus, of course.

THE DRAMATIC WORKS OF SIR WILLIAM D'AVENANT, WITH PREFATORY MEMOIR AND NOTES. Ed. James Maidment and W.H. Logan. 5 vols. 1872-74; reprint ed. New York: Russell & Russell, 1964.

Critical apparatus is rather slight.

SECONDARY WORKS

Collins, Howard Stuart. THE COMEDY OF SIR WILLIAM DAVENANT. The Hague, Paris: Mouton, 1967.

Because Davenant was "the only important playwright to span the Stuart, Caroline, Interregnum, and Restoration periods" (p. [7]), Collins sees him as a valuable medium for the study of "the Comic Spirit [as it] operates on certain permanent principles" but "is subject to the fluctuations of fashion" (p. 171). Bibliography.

Harbage, Alfred. SIR WILLIAM DAVENANT: POET VENTURER, 1606-1668. Philadelphia: University of Pennsylvania Press; London: Oxford University Press, 1935.

A general biographical study which stresses Davenant's "key position as chief link between the common and courtly schools of play-writing, and between the old seventeenth-century drama and the new" (see the "Preface").

Nethercot, Arthur H. SIR WILLIAM D'AVENANT; POET LAUREATE AND PLAY-

WRIGHT-MANAGER. 1938; reprint ed. New York: Russell & Russell, 1967.

A general biographical study, with various appendices; further notes in the reprinted edition.

8. THOMAS DEKKER

BIBLIOGRAPHIES

Tannenbaum, Samuel A[aron], and Dorothy R. Tannenbaum, comps. ELIZABETHAN BIBLIOGRAPHIES. Vol. II. Port Washington, N.Y.: Kennikat Press, 1967.

Reprints the 1939 Tannenbaum bibliography of Dekker and the 1945 supplement. Designed as an exhaustive, unannotated listing.

Donovan, Dennis, comp. ELIZABETHAN BIBLIOGRAPHIES SUPPLEMENTS. Vol. II. London: Nether Press, 1967.

Includes a bibliography of Dekker, 1945-65. Less inclusive than the Tannenbaum, which it supplements. Material arranged in annual groupings.

Allison, A[ntony] F[rancis], comp. THOMAS DEKKER, C. 1572-1632, A BIBLIOGRAPHICAL CATALOGUE OF THE EARLY EDITIONS (TO THE END OF THE 17TH CENTURY). Pall Mall Bibliographies, No. 1. Folkestone & London: Dawsons of Pall Mall, 1972.

In addition to bibliographical entries, there are an introductory essay, title page facsimiles, and various indexes. The arrangement is clear and convenient.

EDITIONS

Note: The canon of Dekker's work is quite difficult to establish. See E.K. Chambers, THE ELIZABETHAN STAGE, III, 289-305, concerning lost and doubtful plays, and Gerald Eades Bentley, THE JACOBEAN AND CAROLINE STAGE, III, 241-75. (For the main entries for Chambers and Bentley, see Part 1, Section 8: Studies of Tudor and Stuart Drama.)

THE DRAMATIC WORKS OF THOMAS DEKKER, NOW FIRST COLLECTED, WITH ILLUSTRATIVE NOTES AND A MEMOIR OF THE AUTHOR. Ed. R[ichard]

H[erne] Shepherd. 4 vols. London: John Pearson, 1873.

One of the several editions of dramatists edited by Shepherd and published by Pearson.

THE DRAMATIC WORKS OF THOMAS DEKKER. Ed. Fredson Bowers. 4 vols. Cambridge: At the University Press, 1953-61.

The "Foreword" describes the edition as "a critical old-spelling text" (Vol. I, p. ix) using the canon proposed by E.K. Chambers (see note at the beginning of this section and also Part 1, Section 8: Studies of Tudor and Stuart Drama). There are full "Textual Introductions" and "Textual Notes" in this scholarly text with an attractive format.

See also, Dekker, Thomas, in Part 1, Section 10: Contemporary and Other Early Records, Allusions, Criticism, Etc.

SECONDARY WORKS

Conover, James H[arrington]. THOMAS DEKKER. AN ANALYSIS OF DRAMATIC STRUCTURE. Studies in English Literature, The Hague, No. 38. The Hague: Mouton Publishers, 1969.

In this endeavor "to re-evaluate Thomas Dekker as a play-craftsman," Conover hopes to raise Dekker in modern critical esteem but makes no pretense that he is flawless. Bibliography.

Hunt, Mary Leland. THOMAS DEKKER. Columbia University Studies in English. 1911; reprint ed. New York: Russell & Russell, 1964.

The "Preface" describes the study concisely: "The object . . . has been to collect scattered material, including that furnished by Dekker himself, which has been much neglected, to arrange that material in chronological order, and to arrive at an understanding of the man" (p. ix).

Jones-Davies, Marie Therese. UN PEINTRE DE LA VIE LONDONIENNE: THOMAS DEKKER (CIRCA 1572-1632). Collection des Etudes Anglaises, No. 6. 2 vols. Paris: Didier, 1958.

A full study, focused in Dekker's response to contemporary London. Volume II, pages [339]-416, provides a chronological, annotated list of original editions of Dekker's works. The bibliography lists other editions of Dekker as well as secondary material.

Pierce, Frederick Erastus. THE COLLABORATION OF WEBSTER AND DEKKER. Yale Studies in English, Vol. 37. 1909; reprint ed. Hamden, Conn.: Archon Books, 1972.

The "collaborated plays" are WESTWARD HO, NORTHWARD HO, and THE FAMOUS HISTORY OF SIR THOMAS WYATT, of which

Pierce says that "at the time of this collaboration Dekker was a mature writer, with a long list of successful plays behind him; Webster was only a beginner" (p. [1]). Pierce endeavors by various tests to determine "hands," with charts displaying the evidence.

Price, George R. THOMAS DEKKER. Twayne's English Authors Series, No. 71. New York: Twayne Publishers, 1969.

Price deals with the plays as representative of various genres. The annotated bibliography divides the primary materials into "Authentic Works," "Works Wrongly Ascribed to Dekker," and "Some Conjectural Revision." There is also a bibliography of secondary materials.

9. NATHAN FIELD

EDITIONS

THE PLAYS OF NATHAN FIELD, EDITED FROM THE ORIGINAL QUARTOS. Ed. William Peery. Austin: University of Texas Press, 1950.

The "Preface" (p. [vii]) indicates that the editor has aimed at an audience "somewhere between" the "bibliographical specialist" and the "general reader" who wishes to be unimpeded by apparatus, providing "for Field's undoubted work the first critical text" (p. viii). Peery supplies his readers an introduction, explanatory and textual notes, and a bibliography, together with the texts of A WOMAN IS A WEATHER-COCKE and AMENDS FOR LADIES.

SECONDARY WORKS

Brinkley, Roberta Florence. NATHAN FIELD, THE ACTOR-PLAYWRIGHT. Yale Studies in English, Vol. 77. New Haven, Conn.: Yale University Press; London: Oxford University Press, 1928.

A sane, carefully reasoned discussion of Field as a man and as a playwright, considering both individually written plays and collaborations.

10. JOHN FORD

BIBLIOGRAPHIES

Tannenbaum, Samuel A[aron], and Dorothy R. Tannenbaum, comps. ELIZABETHAN BIBLIOGRAPHIES. Vol. II. Port Washington, N.Y.: Kennikat Press, 1967.

Reprints the 1941 Tannenbaum bibliography of Ford. Designed as an exhaustive, unannotated listing.

Pennel, Charles A., and William P. Williams, comps. ELIZABETHAN BIBLIOGRAPHIES SUPPLEMENTS. Vol. VIII. London: Nether Press, 1968.

Includes a bibliography of Ford, 1940-65. Less exhaustive than the Tannenbaum, which it supplements. Entries are grouped annually.

EDITIONS

THE DRAMATIC WORKS OF JOHN FORD. Ed. Henry Weber. 2 vols. Edinburgh: George Ramsay & Co. for Archibald Constable and Co; London: Longman, Hurst, Rees, Orme, and Brown, William Miller, and John Murray, 1811.

Weber provides an introduction and notes.

THE DRAMATIC WORKS OF JOHN FORD . . . WITH NOTES CRITICAL AND EXPLANATORY, TO WHICH ARE ADDED FAME'S MEMORIAL, AND VERSES TO THE MEMORY OF BEN JONSON. Ed. W[illiam] Gifford. 2 vols. London: John Murray, 1827.

The Gifford edition has been the basis of a number of other editions. It was revised by Alexander Dyce and published in three volumes by James Touvery (London, 1869). Then another three-volume edition "with Further Additions" was issued by Lawrence and Bullen (London, 1895). The end product is now available in the following reprint.

THE WORKS OF JOHN FORD, WITH NOTES CRITICAL AND EXPLANATORY BY WILLIAM GIFFORD, ESQ. A NEW EDITION, CAREFULLY REVISED, WITH ADDITIONS TO THE TEXT AND TO THE NOTES BY THE REV. ALEXANDER DYCE. 3 vols. 1895; reprint ed. New York: Russell & Russell, 1965.

The reprint carries on the title page the advice: "Reproduced from the edition of 1895 and Reissued."

JOHN FORD'S DRAMATIC WORKS. Ed. W. Bang and H[enry] de Vocht. 2 vols. (MATERIALIEN ZUR KUNDE DES ALTEREN ENGLISCHEN DRAMAS, ed. Bang, Vol. I; MATERIALS FOR THE STUDY OF THE OLD ENGLISH DRAMA, ed. De Vocht, New Series, Vol. I), 1908-27; reprint ed. in 2 vols. with the title JOHN FORDES DRAMATISCHE WERKES, Vaduz: Kraus Reprint, 1963.

For more on the Bang-De Vocht series, see Part 1, Section 2 C: Editions--Serial and Multi-Volume Editions.

The age of these editions and the fact of their having been reprinted indicates the state of Ford editing. Mark Stavig, in JOHN FORD, says: "No sound modern collected edition of either Ford's plays or his non-dramatic work exists" (p. vii). He cites editions of certain single plays as indicative of a forthcoming remedy and uses for his own study the microcards in Henry W. Wells, ed., THREE CENTURIES OF DRAMA (see Part 1, Section 2 C: Editions--Serial and Multi-Volume Editions, for the edition here referred to; see G. William Bergquist, ed., THREE CENTURIES OF ENGLISH AND AMERICAN PLAYS, A CHECKLIST, in Part 1, Section 1 C: Bibliographies of Drama, for an index to Wells). Stavig points to the easy interchangeability of the facsimiles printed by Bang and De Vocht and the microprint edition (pp. vii-viii). H.J. Oliver, in THE PROBLEM OF JOHN FORD, calls Bang and De Vocht "the best edition" (p. v). (See Secondary Works for Stavig and Oliver.) Brian Morris, in THE BROKEN HEART (p. [vii]), calls Gifford as revised by Dyce, 1869, "still the standard edition" (see next entry). Since the collected editions are subject to criticism and since Ford is a more important playwright than the delay of a collected edition brought up to modern editorial standards suggests, it will be well to list some of the recent editions of single plays and one selected edition here.

THE BROKEN HEART. Ed. Brian Morris. The New Mermaids. New York: Hill & Wang, 1966.

THE BROKEN HEART. Ed. Donald K. Anderson, Jr. Regents Renaissance Drama Series. Lincoln: University of Nebraska Press, 1968.

PERKIN WARBECK. Ed. Donald K. Anderson, Jr. Regents Renaissance Drama Series. Lincoln: University of Nebraska Press, 1965.

THE CHRONICLE HISTORY OF PERKIN WARBECK. Ed. Peter Ure. London: Methuen & Co., 1968.

'TIS PITY SHE'S A WHORE. Ed. N.W. Bawcutt. Regents Renaissance Drama Series. Lincoln: University of Nebraska Press, 1966.

'TIS PITY SHE'S A WHORE. Ed. Brian Morris. The New Mermaids. New York: Hill & Wang, 1969.

THREE PLAYS. Ed. Keith Sturgess. Harmondsworth: Penguin Books, 1970.

The "Penguin paperback" includes 'TIS PITY SHE'S A WHORE, THE BROKEN HEART, and PERKIN WARBECK, with introduction, commentary, notes, and a brief bibliography. See Part 1, Section 2 C: Editions--Serial and Multi-Volume Editions on the general editorial plan of the Regents Renaissance Drama and the New Mermaids series. One of the problems with small collections or single-title editions, illustrated here, is that the best-known plays are likely to receive multiple printings, while the less well-known plays must often await full collected editions.

SECONDARY WORKS

Anderson, Donald K., Jr. JOHN FORD. Twayne's English Authors Series, No. 129. New York: Twayne Publishers, 1972.

Anderson begins with a convenient brief review of major nineteenth- and twentieth-century critics. He challenges certain established labels for Ford, such as decadent (p. 137), attempts to establish the worth of the less studied plays, THE LOVER'S MELANCHOLY and PERKIN WARBECK, and claims as "[p]robably the chief contribution of the present book . . . its exposition of Ford's knowledgeable dramaturgy" (p. 139). Bibliography.

Davril, R. LE DRAME DE JOHN FORD. Bibliotheque des Langues Modernes, No. 5. Paris: Didier, 1954.

In annotating the bibliography of his own JOHN FORD (Writers and their Work, London, 1964; see below), Clifford Leech says Davril displays "wide learning, sympathy, and no narrow thesis," and Peter Ure, in a review (REVIEW OF ENGLISH STUDIES, 6 [1955], 201-2), points to the middle section as a "polite repudiation of the views of Mr. Sensabaugh" (see Sensabaugh, George F.).

Ewing, S. Blaine. BURTONIAN MELANCHOLY IN THE PLAYS OF JOHN FORD. Princeton Studies in English, No. 19. Princeton, N.J.: Princeton University Press, 1940.

Ewing describes the study as "not an application of the methods of the modern science of abnormal psychology to Ford's plays" but as an analysis of "THE ANATOMY as the greatest repository up to its time of case histories and learned opinion in the field which we should now call abnormal psychology" (p. viii) and of Ford as a playwright who had studied Burton closely. The study is in three parts: a review of Burton; a study of "Melancholy in the Plays," taken play by play; and, in "The Significance of Melancholy," a hazarding of guesses as to why Ford read Burton so thoroughly.

Leech, Clifford. JOHN FORD. Writers and Their Work, No. 170. London and New York: Published for the British Council and the National Book League by Longmans, Green & Co., 1964.

Brief but cogent discussion of the values to be found in Ford, the only man in "the Caroline private theater . . . touched by what we call 'genius'" (p. 80). Leech suggests that "in THE BROKEN HEART we have the nearest English approach to the pure form of French classical tragedy" (p. 35). Bibliography.

_____. JOHN FORD AND THE DRAMA OF HIS TIME. London: Chatto & Windus, 1957.

Leech says that characteristic of Ford is "a presentation of exalted human beings whose actions never come within the scope of censure" and who are dominated by "the suffering of melancholy or of deprivation" which "comes to life through the experience of a fugitive happiness" (p. 11). He stresses the view that "[a]bove all, [Ford] was a poet, not only in his conceptions but in his words" (p. 122).

Oliver, H[arold] J[ames]. THE PROBLEM OF JOHN FORD. Carlton, Victoria: Melbourne University Press, 1955.

Oliver sees Ford "as a constant experimenter with dramatic form, who . . . did not find the new form he was seeking" (p. 127) but also as a writer of "quite exceptional clarity and simplicity, even--or particularly--in moments of greatest emotional stress" (p. 129). Oliver judges that "[t]aking full advantage of the opportunities which drama offered him, he almost overcame its limitations" (p.130).

Sargeaunt, M. Joan. JOHN FORD. 1935; reprint ed. New York: Russell & Russell, 1966.

Not a general life-and-works biography but a close study of Ford as a playwright. Sargeaunt suggests that "in outlook" we may be "nearer to Ford than the generations of the intervening centuries." She recognizes Ford's humorless coarseness and melodramatic excesses, but says that "there yet remains a body of poetry direct in expression and of grave and passionate import penetrated by a knowledge of the motives that sway the actions of mankind" (p. 187). Appendix II provides a primary bibliography with full bibliographical descriptions. There are also a list of "Principal Nineteenth- and Twentieth-Century Editions to Which Reference Is Made" and a bibliography of secondary materials, though these are rather out of date now.

Sensabaugh, George F. THE TRAGIC MUSE OF JOHN FORD. 1944; reprint ed. New York: Benjamin Blom, 1965.

The "Preface" points up the focus of the study on the question of "how the age stamped Ford and what stamp Ford . . . put on his age" (p. vii). Sensabaugh stresses the modernity of Ford's "values and thought" and says that his "real distinction" is that "he foresaw the ethical impasse of a world not only challenging old custom and laws in the name of individual rights but also supporting that challenge by immutable scientific statutes" (p. 190).

Stavig, Mark. JOHN FORD AND THE TRADITIONAL MORAL ORDER. Madison, Milwaukee, and London: University of Wisconsin Press, 1968.

The "Introduction" reviews recent critical viewpoints on Ford. In a chapter called "Concord in Discord," Stavig formulates the thesis that Ford's work is governed by a "moral concern with stress on the efficacy of the sacramental and ritualistic traditions of the Anglican church" and that Ford is "a Christian neo-Stoic who conceives of true honor as combining noble thought with heroic action." He regards the plays as cast "in a traditional, symbolic mode in which the thematic is much more important than the psychological" (p. 188).

11. GEORGE GASCOIGNE

BIBLIOGRAPHIES

Tannenbaum, Samuel A[aron], and Dorothy R. Tannenbaum, comps. ELIZABETHAN BIBLIOGRAPHIES. Vol. II. Port Washington, N.Y.: Kennikat Press, 1967.

Reprints the 1942 Tannenbaum bibliography of Gascoigne. Designed as an exhaustive, unannotated listing.

Johnson, Robert Carl, comp. ELIZABETHAN BIBLIOGRAPHIES SUPPLEMENTS: MINOR ELIZABETHANS. Vol. IX. London: Nether Press, 1968.

Less exhaustive than the Tannenbaum, which it supplements, with material arranged in annual groupings. Includes Gascoigne, 1941-66.

Price, John E., comp. "A Secondary Bibliography of George Gascoigne with an Introduction Summarizing the Trend of Gascoigne Scholarship." BULLETIN OF BIBLIOGRAPHY, 25 (1968), 138-40.

Convenient brief review.

EDITIONS

THE COMPLETE POEMS OF GEORGE GASCOIGNE . . . NOW FIRST COLLECTED AND EDITED FROM THE EARLY PRINTED COPIES AND FROM MSS. WITH A MEMOIR AND NOTES BY WILLIAM CAREW HAZLITT. 2 vols. London: Printed for the Roxburghe Library, 1869-70.

In spite of the POEMS of the title, the edition includes plays and prose.

THE COMPLETE WORKS OF GEORGE GASCOIGNE. Ed. John W. Cunliffe. 2 vols. 1907-10; reprint ed. Grosse Pointe, Mich.: Scholarly Press, 1969.

Limited critical apparatus.

SECONDARY WORKS

Chalmers, Alexander, ed. THE WORKS OF THE ENGLISH POETS, FROM CHAUCER TO COWPER; INCLUDING THE SERIES EDITED, WITH PREFACES, BIOGRAPHICAL AND CRITICAL, BY DR. SAMUEL JOHNSON; AND THE MOST APPROVED TRANSLATIONS, THE ADDITIONAL LIVES BY ALEXANDER CHALMERS. London: J. Johnson, 1810.

> Volume II (pp. [447]-66) contains "The Life of George Gascoigne," followed by a reprint of Whetstone's "Remembravnce" (see Whetstone, George) and various other matters, chiefly "Commendatory Verses," and then by Gascoigne's poems.

Johnson, Ronald C[onant]. GEORGE GASCOIGNE. Twayne's English Authors Series, No. 133. New York: Twayne Publishers, 1972.

> Johnson, feeling that Gascoigne the poet is overshadowed by his own "historical position" (p. [5]), wants to study the works as pure literature. He emphasizes the poetry over other modes but gives a chapter to "The Three Plays" and in the "Conclusion" summarizes Gascoigne's contributions to the drama. Bibliography.

Kittle, William. EDWARD DE VERE, 17TH EARL OF OXFORD AND SHAKESPEARE: EXTERNAL AND CONTEMPORARY EVIDENCE CONNECTING THE SEVENTEENTH EARL OF OXFORD AND THE WRITER NAMED SHAKESPEARE; TOGETHER WITH THE BACKGROUND OF ELIZABETHAN HISTORY NEEDED FOR THIS INVESTIGATION; TOGETHER WITH THE WRITER SHAKESPEARE'S BURIAL IN WESTMINSTER ABBEY AND THE BURIAL OF SHAKESPEARE BENEATH THE CHANCEL OF THE CHURCH IN STRATFORD. Baltimore, Md.: The Monumental Printing Co., 1942.

> Kittle argues that the Earl of Oxford wrote the plays more usually attributed to Shakespeare and to Gascoigne, respectively. Another work of Kittle's, which I have not seen, is G. GASCOIGNE, APRIL 1562 TO JANUARY 1, 1578; OR, EDWARD DE VERE, SEVENTEENTH EARL OF OXFORD, 1550-1604 (Washington, D.C.: W.F. Roberts, 1930).

Prouty, C[harles] T. GEORGE GASCOIGNE, ELIZABETHAN COURTIER, SOLDIER, AND POET. 1942; reprint ed. New York: Benjamin Blom, 1966.

> Prouty believes that through Gascoigne we may "learn something tangible about the literature which Lyly, Marlowe, Shakespeare, Greene, and Nashe knew in their youth" (p. 4). Prouty does not overpraise Gascoigne, seeing him as marked by "vanity, levity, and a want of resolution" but also by "versatility" (p. 284).

Schelling, Felix E. THE LIFE AND WRITINGS OF GEORGE GASCOIGNE WITH THREE POEMS HERETOFORE NOT REPRINTED. Publications of the University of Pennsylvania, Series in Philology, Literature and Archaeology, Vol. 2, No. 4. Philadelphia: University of Pennsylvania Press; Boston: Ginn &

Co.; Halle: Max Niemeyer, Agents, 1893.

Schelling concentrates on the life. Chapter IV (pp. 36-49) deals with "Dramatic Writings." Bibliography of primary sources, pages 117-23.

Whetstone, George. A REMEMBRAVNCE OF THE WELL IMPLOYED LIFE, AND GODLY END OF GEORGE GASKOIGNE, ESQUIRE, WHO DECEASSED AT STALMFORD IN LINCOLNE SHIRE, THE 7 OF OCTOBER 1577. THE REPORTE OF GEOR. WHETSTONS, GENT. AN EYE WITNES OF HIS GODLY AND CHARITABLE END IN THIS WORLD. London: Edward Aggas, [1577].

Whetstone's REMEMBRAVNCE is reprinted in Chalmers (above) and in Edward Arber's ENGLISH REPRINTS, No. 11: GEORGE GASCOIGNE, ESQUIRE (London: A. Murray & Son, 1868).

12. ROBERT GREENE

BIBLIOGRAPHIES

Tannenbaum, Samuel A[aron], and Dorothy R. Tannenbaum, comps. ELIZABETHAN BIBLIOGRAPHIES. Vol. III. Port Washington, N.Y.: Kennikat Press, 1967.

> Reprints the 1939 Tannenbaum bibliography of Greene and the 1950 supplement. Designed as an exhaustive, unannotated listing.

Johnson, Robert C[arl], comp. ELIZABETHAN BIBLIOGRAPHIES SUPPLEMENTS. Vol. V. London: Nether Press, 1968.

> Bibliography of Greene, 1945-65. Less exhaustive than the Tannenbaum, which it supplements. Entries are grouped annually. No annotation.

Hayashi, Tetsumaro, comp. ROBERT GREENE CRITICISM: A COMPREHENSIVE BIBLIOGRAPHY, WITH AN INTRODUCTION BY LOUIS MARDER. Scarecrow Author Bibliographies Series, No. 6. Metuchen, N.J.: Scarecrow Press, 1971.

> Full listing. No annotation.

EDITIONS

THE DRAMATIC WORKS OF ROBERT GREENE, TO WHICH ARE ADDED HIS POEMS, WITH SOME ACCOUNT OF THE AUTHOR, AND NOTES. Ed. Alexander Dyce. 2 vols. London: William Pickering, 1831.

> Among materials supplied by the editor are a "Specimen of the Famous Historie of Fryer Bacon" in Volume I and a "Specimen of the History of George-a-Greene" and a "Ballad of the Jolly Pinder of Wakefield, with Robin Hood, Scarlet, and John" in Volume II.

THE LIFE AND COMPLETE WORKS IN PROSE AND VERSE OF ROBERT GREENE, M.A. CAMBRIDGE AND OXFORD. FOR THE FIRST TIME COLLECTED AND

EDITED, WITH NOTES AND ILLUSTRATIONS, ETC. Ed. Alexander Grosart. 15 vols. 1881-86; reprint ed. New York: Russell & Russell, 1964.

Volume I contains [Nicholas] Storojenko's ROBERT GREENE: HIS LIFE AND WORKS, A CRITICAL INVESTIGATION, MOSCOW, 1878, TRANS. E.A.B. HODGETTS, WITH INTRODUCTION AND NOTES BY THE EDITOR. See Volume XV for a number of indexes, lists, etc. See especially Volumes XIII and XIV for plays.

THE PLAYS AND POEMS OF ROBERT GREENE. Ed. J[ohn] Churton Collins. 2 vols. Oxford: Clarendon Press, 1905.

In addition to the "General Introduction," each play has an introduction and light notes. Accompanying ORLANDO FURIOSO (Vol. I) is an appendix, "The Alleyn Ms."

SECONDARY WORKS

Assarsson-Rizzi, Kerstin. FRIAR BACON AND FRIAR BUNGAY: A STRUCTURAL AND THEMATIC ANALYSIS OF ROBERT GREENE'S PLAY. Lund Studies in English, 44. Lund: Gleerup, 1972.

This detailed analysis of a single play argues the probability of "a strong unbroken native dramatic tradition in medieval England, of which the Elizabethan drama is a continuation and a culmination" (p. 144). Bibliography.

Austin, Warren B. A COMPUTER-AIDED TECHNIQUE FOR STYLISTIC DISCRIMINATION: THE AUTHORSHIP OF "GREEN'S GROATSWORTH OF WIT." Project No. 7-G-036, Grant No. OEG-I-7-070036-4593, U.S. Dept. of Health, Education, and Welfare. Washington, D.C.: Office of Education, Bureau of Research, 1969.

The opening "Summary" describes the object of the study as the development of "a computer-aided technique for distinguishing one writer's style from another's" (p. vii). The specific result of the project has been to lead Austin to the conclusion that "[t]his evidence points decisively to Chettle's having forged the GROATSWORTH OF WIT, including the letter to Greene's fellow-playwrights and the attack on Shakespeare, within three weeks after the death of the purported author" (p. xi).

Born, Hanspeter. THE RARE WIT AND THE RUDE GROOM: THE AUTHORSHIP OF "A KNACK TO KNOW A KNAVE" IN RELATION TO GREENE, NASHE & SHAKESPEARE. Swiss Studies in English, Vol. 64. Bern: Francke Verlag, 1971.

Born attributes the play in the main to Greene: "I have not only attempted to claim this particular masterless play for Robert Greene, but I have also presented a somewhat farfetched theory of revision" (p. 163). Born also sees some evidence of Shakespeare's hand, and therein an occasion for Greene's wrath at Shakespeare (see pp. 166-67, for example). The study is written with wit and with a full realization that much of what is said is speculation. Bibliography.

Castle, Edward James. SHAKESPEARE, BACON, JONSON, AND GREENE: A STUDY. 1897; reprint ed. Port Washington, N.Y.: Kennikat, 1970.

Basically about Shakespeare, the study draws upon Greene and Jonson for evidence that Shakespeare wrote "Shakespeare."

Harvey, Gabriel. FOUR LETTERS AND CERTAINE SONNETS . . . ESPECIALLY TOUCHING ROBERT GREENE. London: Iohn Wolfe, 1592.

FOUR LETTERS AND CERTAINE SONNETS is available in a number of reprintings. An easily obtainable one is in THE WORKS OF GABRIEL HARVEY, edited by Alexander B. Grosart in three volumes (1884-85; reprint ed. New York: AMS Press, 1966). See further under Harvey in Part 1, Section 10: Contemporary and Other Early Records, Allusions, Criticism, Etc.

Hayashi, Tetsumaro.

See main entry in Section 18: Thomas Lodge.

Jones, Gwyn. GARLAND OF BAYS. New York: Macmillan, 1938.

A full-fleshed story of Greene's life is created out of the available facts about him.

Jordan, John Clark. ROBERT GREENE. Columbia University Studies in English and Comparative Literature. 1915; reprint ed. New York: Octagon Books, 1965.

Jordan studies "the man [and] his attitude toward literature" (p. ix) without attempting to whitewash Greene or to make excessive claims about his literary achievements.

Sanders, C. ROBERT GREENE AND THE HARVEYS. Indiana University Studies, Vol. 18. Bloomington: University of Indiana, 1931.

A short exploration of a small but famous and rather cloudy literary quarrel. Bibliography.

Senn, Werner. STUDIES IN THE DRAMATIC CONSTRUCTION OF ROBERT GREENE AND GEORGE PEELE. Swiss Studies in English, Vol. 74. Bern: Francke Verlag, 1973.

A two-part study, "Theory and Methods" and "Analysis." Senn insists, perhaps too modestly (p. 207) that his study is "tentative and provisional" and that its chief contributions may be its "individual, limited glimpses and insights into the dramatic construction of single plays" (p. 211). Bibliography.

Storojenko, [Nicholas]. ROBERT GREENE: HIS LIFE AND WORKS.

See annotation of the Alexander Grosart edition of THE LIFE AND COMPLETE WORKS of Greene.

Perhaps one should not leave the subject of Greene without noticing a book by William Hall Chapman, SHAKESPEARE: THE PERSONAL PHASE ([Los Angeles: United Printing Co.], 1920), directed to the thesis that "William Shakespeare of Stratford" cannot be "the author of the works called 'Shakespeare'" (p. 11). In the section "Who Was Shake-Scene?--(The Object of Robert Greene's Censure)" Chapman asserts that Greene "was one of the very few poets and dramatic writers who in a licentious age,--'left scarce a line that dying he need have wished to blot'" (p. 281).

13. JOHN HEYWOOD

BIBLIOGRAPHIES

Tannenbaum, Samuel A[aron], and Dorothy R. Tannenbaum, comps. ELIZABETHAN BIBLIOGRAPHIES. Vol. III. Port Washington, N.Y.: Kennikat Press, 1967.

Reprints the 1946 Tannenbaum bibliography of Heywood. Designed as an exhaustive, unannotated listing.

Johnson, Robert Carl, comp. ELIZABETHAN BIBLIOGRAPHIES SUPPLEMENTS. Vol. IX: MINOR ELIZABETHANS. London: Nether Press, 1968.

Includes Heywood, 1944-66. Less inclusive than the Tannenbaum, which it supplements. Items arranged in annual groupings.

EDITIONS

THE DRAMATIC WRITINGS OF JOHN HEYWOOD, COMPRISING "THE PARDONER AND THE FRIAR"; "THE FOUR P.P."; "JOHN THE HUSBAND, TYB HIS WIFE, AND SIR JOHN THE PRIEST"; "PLAY OF THE WEATHER"; "PLAY OF LOVE"; "DIALOGUE CONCERNING WITTY AND WITLESS" [WITH A] NOTE-BOOK AND WORD-LIST. Ed. John S. Farmer. 1905; reprint ed. New York: Barnes & Noble, 1966.

See also the reprints of Farmer's editions of THE PROBERBS, EPIGRAMS, AND MISCELLANIES and of THE SPIDER AND THE FLY TOGETHER WITH AN ATTRIBUTED INTERLUDE ENTITLED GENTLENESS AND NOBILITY BY JOHN HEYWOOD, originally printed in 1906 and 1908, respectively, and both reprinted in 1966. Farmer does not provide extensive apparatus, and the editions are old.

A workmanly modern edition of Heywood is needed. A partial remedy can be found in the editions below; all, however, are limited in some way. (See also in Secondary Works, Cameron, K[enneth] W[alter], AUTHORSHIP AND SOURCES OF "GENTLENESS AND NOBILITY," which provides a text of the play.)

JOHN HEYWOOD, ENTERTAINER. Ed. R[upert] de la Bere. London: Allen & Unwin, 1937.

De la Bere offers the texts of four plays: A PLAY OF WYTTY AND WYTTLES, THE PARDONER AND THE FRERE, THE FOURE P.P., and JOHAN JOHAN. He analyzes these and the two additional plays, LOVE and THE WETHER, along with the remainder "of Heywood's undoubted works," considering sources, outlining the plots, and examining "all the internal evidence" (p. [47]).

JOHN HEYWOOD'S "WORKS" AND MISCELLANEOUS SHORT POEMS. Ed. Burton A. Milligan. Illinois Studies in Language and Literature, Vol. 41. Urbana: University of Illinois Press, 1956.

Milligan's edition is recent and scholarly, but WORKS here means pieces other than plays. There is no drama in the edition.

JOHN HEYWOOD'S "A DIALOGUE OF PROVERBS," EDITED, WITH INTRODUCTION, COMMENTARY, AND INDEXES. Ed. Rudolph E. Habenicht. University of California Publications, English Studies, No. 25. Berkeley and Los Angeles: University of California Press, 1963.

Again, the edition contains no drama, though the extensive apparatus includes material which may be peripherally useful to the study of the plays.

THE PLAY OF THE WEATHER BY JOHN HEYWOOD AND OTHER TUDOR COMEDIES ADAPTED INTO MODERN ENGLISH. WITH INTRODUCTION. Ed. Maurice Hussey and Surenda Agarwala. New York: Theatre Arts, 1968.

The five plays are THE PLAY OF THE WEATHER, THE PARDONER AND THE FRIAR, THE FOUR P'S, JACK JUGGLER, and JOHN JOHN, TIB AND FATHER JOHN. Except for JACK JUGGLER, the plays are regularly attributed to Heywood. The editing, designed to produce "a collection suitable for reading or acting today," has resulted in so much cutting as to make the edition unusable for scholarly purposes. (See the "Preface" for an explanation of intent and method in editing.)

SECONDARY WORKS

Bolwell, Robert G.W. THE LIFE AND WORKS OF JOHN HEYWOOD. Columbia University Studies in English and Comparative Literature. New York: Columbia University Press, 1921.

Bolwell provides a sketch of Heywood's life, with a chapter (pp. 80-122) on "Heywood's Dramatic Works." Bolwell sees Heywood's plays as turning "from the medieval habit of considering humanity as a whole into the modern attitude towards realism and specific fact. . . . His farces begin comedy proper in English drama" (p. 122).

Cameron, K[enneth] W[alter]. AUTHORSHIP AND SOURCES OF "GENTLENESS AND NOBILITY": A STUDY IN EARLY TUDOR DRAMA. TOGETHER WITH A TEXT OF THE PLAY BASED ON THE BLACK-LETTER ORIGINAL. Raleigh, N.C.: Thistle Press, 1941.

Cameron concludes that the evidence will not allow for an absolute identification of the author but that "the probabilities are in Heywood's favor." Another leading candidate is Rastell, but Cameron thinks "that the epilogue is probably Rastell's chief contribution" (p. 88).

_____. THE BACKGROUND OF JOHN HEYWOOD'S "WITTY AND WITLESS": A STUDY IN EARLY TUDOR DRAMA. TOGETHER WITH A SPECIALIZED BIBLIOGRAPHY OF HEYWOOD SCHOLARSHIP. Raleigh, N.C.: Thistle Press, 1941.

Brief discussion of source and date. Bibliography.

_____. JOHN HEYWOOD'S "PLAY OF THE WETHER": A STUDY IN EARLY TUDOR DRAMA. Raleigh, N.C.: Thistle Press, 1941.

A brief treatment in two sections: "The Principal Source of WETHER" and "Interpretation and Dating of WETHER."

Johnson, Robert Carl. JOHN HEYWOOD. Twayne's English Authors Series, No. 92. New York: Twayne Publishers, 1970.

Johnson proposes "to re-evaluate the position of John Heywood in the development of English drama and to demonstrate his importance as a minor adherent to and propagandist for Christian Humanism" (p. 7). He concludes that Heywood combines the roles of experimenter and traditionalist. Bibliography.

Maxwell, Ian. FRENCH FARCE & JOHN HEYWOOD. Melbourne and London: Melbourne University Press in Association with Oxford University Press, 1946.

Maxwell interprets Heywood as, paradoxically, a true homespun Englishman whose work is in a "curious isolation . . . due in some measure to foreign influence," JOHN, TYB AND SIR JOHN and the PARDONER AND FRIAR showing in various ways an indebtedness to the French (p. 11). Maxwell supplies three appendices: "List of Farces," "Dates of Certain Farces," and "Farce Plots in English Jest Books." Bibliography.

Reed, Arthur W. THE CANON OF JOHN HEYWOOD'S PLAYS. London: Alexander Moring, De La More Press, 1918.

Reed traces the story of the ascriptions of various plays to Heywood through the early play lists and argues for the establishment of the canon through both internal and external evidence. The book is slight--forty-eight pages--but it makes a clear and interesting statement.

____. JOHN HEYWOOD AND HIS FRIENDS. London: Alexander Moring, 1917.

A brief essay (fifty-seven pages) designed "to ascertain and extend the basis of fact as to [Heywood's] career" (p. [1]).

14. THOMAS HEYWOOD

BIBLIOGRAPHIES

Clark, Arthur Melville. "A Bibliography of Thomas Heywood." OXFORD BIBLIOGRAPHICAL SOCIETY, PROCEEDINGS & PAPERS, Vol. 1 (1925), [97]-153.

Clark divides the material into "Works," "Works Edited by Thomas Heywood," "Books for Which Heywood Wrote Verses," "Entries in Henslowe's 'Diary,' Court Accounts, and the 'Stationers' Register.'" He attributes "to Heywood, in whole or in part, over a dozen works not previously accepted as his," with a summary of "the evidence for the attributions" (p. [97]). Entries are given full descriptions.

Tannenbaum, Samuel A[aron], and Dorothy R. Tannenbaum, comps. ELIZABETHAN BIBLIOGRAPHIES. Vol. III. Port Washington, N.Y.: Kennikat Press, 1967.

Reprints the 1939 Tannenbaum bibliography of Heywood. Designed as an exhaustive, unannotated listing.

Donovan, Dennis, comp. ELIZABETHAN BIBLIOGRAPHIES SUPPLEMENTS. Vol. II. London: Nether Press, 1967.

Includes a bibliography of Heywood, 1938-65. Less inclusive than the Tannenbaum, which it supplements. Entries are grouped annually.

EDITIONS

THE DRAMATIC WORKS OF THOMAS HEYWOOD: WITH A LIFE OF THE POET, AND REMARKS ON HIS WRITINGS. Ed. J. Payne Collier. The Shakespeare Society's Papers. 2 vols. London: Printed for the Shakespeare Society, 1853.

See next item.

THE DRAMATIC WORKS OF THOMAS HEYWOOD NOW FIRST COLLECTED WITH ILLUSTRATIVE NOTES AND A MEMOIR OF THE AUTHOR. Ed. [Richard Herne Shepherd]. 6 vols. 1874; reprint ed. New York: Russell & Russell, 1964.

Time, if nothing else, has rendered both these editions less than fully satisfactory. Some remedy can be found in the editions of single plays now appearing. (See the general descriptions of certain series issuing volumes of single plays in Part 1, Section 2 C: Editions--Serial and Multi-Volume Editions.)

See Part 1, Section 10: Contemporary and Other Early Records, Allusions, Criticism, Etc., for editions of some of Heywood's works on but not for the stage.

SECONDARY WORKS

Boas, Frederick S. THOMAS HEYWOOD. London: Williams & Norgate, 1950.

Boas attempts to familiarize the reader with the lesser known of Heywood's works. He regards Heywood as particularly typical of his time, more typical than his great contemporaries.

Clark, Arthur Melville. THOMAS HEYWOOD: PLAYWRIGHT AND MISCELLANIST. 1931; reprint ed. New York: Russell & Russell, 1967.

Clark says that he has "tried to reconstruct the life of Thomas Heywood more fully than has been done before, and to correct many old errors about him or about his work" (p. [vii]). Various appendices, including "Plays Misattributed to Heywood," in which the plays are not merely listed but discussed.

Cromwell, Otelia. THOMAS HEYWOOD: A STUDY IN THE ELIZABETHAN DRAMA OF EVERYDAY LIFE. Yale Studies in English, Vol. 78. 1928; reprint ed. Hamden, Conn.: Archon Books, 1969.

Cromwell sees as Heywood's chief characteristic "the presentation of wholesome types of Elizabethan men and women in a rich and varied atmosphere of Elizabethan life" (p. 206). In Heywood's work one sees "the man in the ordinary walks of life raised to the dignity of a hero" in a way which "points forward to the realism of the social dramas of our own [i.e., 1928] day" (pp. 208-10).

Stagg, Louis C. AN INDEX TO THE FIGURATIVE LANGUAGE OF THOMAS HEYWOOD'S TRAGEDIES. Charlottesville: Bibliographical Society of the University of Virginia, 1967.

One in a series of seven such indexes by Stagg.

Velte, Mowbray. THE BOURGEOIS ELEMENTS IN THE DRAMAS OF THOMAS

HEYWOOD. 1924; reprint ed. New York: Haskell House, 1966.

A five-part study, with a section on each of four major types: chronicle histories, classical, romance and adventure, and contemporary life, studying "one thing only, the bourgeois elements," and strictly limited to plays, "the city pageants and 'Pleasant Dialogues and Dramma's' being regarded as non-dramatic" (p. [3]).

15. BEN JONSON

BIBLIOGRAPHIES

Steensma, Robert C., comp. "Ben Jonson: A Checklist of Editions, Biography, and Criticism, 1947-1964." RESEARCH OPPORTUNITIES IN RENAISSANCE DRAMA, 9 (1966), 26-46.

Title annotates.

Tannenbaum, Samuel A[aron], and Dorothy R. Tannenbaum, comps. ELIZABETHAN BIBLIOGRAPHIES. Vol. IV. Port Washington, N.Y.: Kennikat Press, 1967.

Reprints the 1938 Tannenbaum bibliography of Jonson and the 1947 supplement; designed as an exhaustive, unannotated listing.

Guffey, George Robert, comp. ELIZABETHAN BIBLIOGRAPHIES SUPPLEMENTS. Vol. III. London: Nether Press, 1968.

Supplement to Tannenbaum, but less exhaustive. Entries are arranged in annual groupings. Includes "Ben Jonson 1947-1965."

EDITIONS

THE WORKES OF BENIAMIN JONSON. 2 vols. London: William Stansby, 1616, and Richard Meighen, 1640.

Jonson's dates are 1572-1637. In 1616, he published a volume of WORKES which includes EUERY MAN IN HIS HVMOVR; EUERY MAN OVT OF HIS HVMOVR; CYNTHIAS REVELS; POETASTER; SEIANVS HIS FALL; VOLPONE; EPICOENE, OR THE SILENT VVOMAN; THE ALCHEMIST; CATILINE HIS CONSPIRACY; EPIGRAMMES 1. BOOKE; THE FORREST; PART OF THE KINGS ENTERTAINMENT IN PASSING TO HIS CORONATION; A PANEGYRE ON THE HAPPIE ENTRANCE OF IAMES, OVR SOVERAIGNE, TO HIS FIRST HIGH SESSION OF PARLIAMENT; A PARTICVLAR ENTERTAINMENT OF THE QVEENE AND PRINCE . . . AT AL-

THROPE; and MASQVES AT COVRT. There is ready access to this "First Folio" through University Microfilms No. 20248, Carton 756, and through the microprint edition in THREE CENTURIES OF DRAMA, edited by Henry W. Wells (see the main entry for Wells, Part 1, Section 2 C: Editions--Serial and Multi-Volume Editions). The second volume is rather more complex. The title page reads: THE WORKES OF BENJAMIN JONSON. THE SECOND VOLUME. CONTAINING THESE PLAYES, VIZ. 1. BARTHOLOMEW FAYRE. 2. THE STAPLE OF NEWES. 3. THE DIVELL IS AN ASSE. London: Printed for Richard Meighen, 1640. The plays named on the title page have separate title pages with the date 1631. In addition, the volume contains THE MAGNETICK LADY; A TALE OF A TUB; THE SAD SHEPHERD; UNDER-WOODS. CONSISTING OF DIVERS POEMS; MORTIMER HIS FALL; MASQUES; HORACE, HIS ART OF POETRIE, MADE ENGLISH; THE ENGLISH GRAMMAR; and TIMBER: OR DISCOVERIES. The MASQUES lacks a separate title page. The remainder have title pages dated 1640 or 1641 and giving no printer. This volume is also available on microfilm, University Microfilms, No. 17689, Carton 671, for the SHORT-TITLE CATALOGUE NO. 14754b; and No. 20250, Carton 756 for the SHORT-TITLE CATALOGUE NO. 14754, a variant edition.

See Ford, H[erbert] L., in Secondary Works, for a study of the folios, which imply a 1631 edition in some of the Volume II title pages and which offer a number of other problems.

See also Library of Congress, THE NATIONAL UNION CATALOG. PRE-1956 IMPRINTS (main entry in Part 1, Section 1 B: General Literary Bibliographies) for a convenient review of these and other early editions of Jonson. A few relatively recent editions follow.

THE WORKS OF BEN JONSON . . . . WITH NOTES CRITICAL AND EXPLANATORY, AND A BIOGRAPHICAL MEMOIR BY W. GIFFORD. 9 vols. London: Printed for G. and W. Nicol, by W. Bulmer and Co., 1816.

The Gifford edition has been reprinted, sometimes with further editing, several times. See the edition "with an Introduction and Appendices by Lieut.-Col. F. Cunningham" in nine volumes (London: Bickers and Son, Henry Southeran and Co., 1875).

BEN JONSON. Vol. 1-5, ed. C.H. Herford and Percy Simpson; vols. 6-11, ed. C.H. Herford and Percy and Evelyn Simpson. Oxford: Clarendon Press, 1925-52, with some volumes reprinted, 1952-61.

Volume I contains a "Life of Ben Jonson" with several appendices: "Contemporary Notes and Records," "Letters of Jonson," "Legal and Official Documents," and "Books in Jonson's Library." Volumes I and II contain the editors' introductions to the plays and other works. Volumes III-VII contain the plays; Volume VIII, poems and prose works. Volume IX contains "An Historical Survey of the Text" and "The Stage History of the Plays." Volume IX begins, and Volume X continues, the "Commentary on the Plays." Volume X also contains "Masque Commentary." Volume XI contains "Commentary," "Jonson's Literary Record," "Supplementary Notes," and the index. This fine example of scholarly editing remains an indispensable edition.

THE YALE BEN JONSON. General eds. Alvin B. Kernan and Richard B. Young. New Haven, Conn., and London: Yale University Press, 1962--.

The "Preface of the General Editors" (quoted here from the Orgel edition of THE COMPLETE MASQUES, p. ix) describes this edition of the plays, "based primarily" on the 1616 and 1640 folios, as designed to provide "the modern reader" with "a readily intelligible text which will convey . . . the life and movement which invests the plays on the stage" and "the critic and scholar" with "a readily available text which represents as accurately as possible, though it does not reproduce, the plays as Jonson printed them." Volumes now in print include Alvin B. Kernan, ed., VOLPONE, 1962; Eugene M. Waith, ed., BARTHOLOMEW FAIR, 1963; Jonas A. Barish, ed., SEJANUS, 1965; Stephen Orgel, ed., THE COMPLETE MASQUES, 1969; Gabriele B. Jackson, ed., EVERY MAN IN HIS HUMOUR, 1969; Edward Partridge, ed., EPICOENE, 1971. Orgel has also edited a volume of SELECTED MASQUES, 1970.

Jonson was a prolific critic as well as playwright. See also Part 1, Section 10: Contemporary and Other Early Records, Allusions, Criticism, Etc.

CONCORDANCES

Crawford, Charles, comp. A COMPLETE CONCORDANCE TO THE 1616 FOLIO OF BEN JONSON'S WORKS; ALSO TO THE QUARTO VERSIONS OF "EVERY MAN IN HIS HUMOUR," "EVERY MAN OUT OF HIS HUMOUR," "CYNTHIA'S REVELS," "THE POETASTER," "CATILINE," "THE FOX," AND "THE ALCHEMIST." London: 1923. [Not printed; the holograph MS.]

Crawford left a handwritten text, with an "Introduction" which explains why the CONCORDANCE is in manuscript: Prepared for Bang's MATERIALEN ZUR KUNDE DES ALTEREN ENGLISCHEN DRAMAS, its publication was prevented by the First World War. Seeing "little or no hope of its being put into print during my time" and wishing "to give it a chance of surviving me," Crawford copied the material "from my slips into these volumes, which will be more handy for reference; and of less bulk, besides being less liable to destruction" (p. 1). The CONCORDANCE is now available on microfilm (three reels; the film is identified as from the Micro Photo Division, Bell & Howell, Cleveland). The care with which the manuscript is executed makes it quite legible on microfilm, and its organization is clear and logical.

SECONDARY WORKS

Allen, Percy. SHAKESPEARE, JONSON, AND WILKINS AS BORROWERS: A STUDY IN ELIZABETHAN DRAMATIC ORIGINS AND IMITATIONS. With an Introduction by R.P. Cowl. [London]: Cecil Palmer, 1928.

Cowl identifies Allen as "a dramatic critic" knowledgeable in "the technique of stage-craft" (p. ix). Allen traces echoes of one play in another and draws various conclusions therefrom.

Arnold, Judd. A GRACE PECULIAR: BEN JONSON'S CAVALIER HEROES. The Pennsylvania State University Studies, No. 35. University Park: Pennsylvania State University, 1972.

Arnold challenges the view that "Jonson's fuming moralists and malcontents" speak for the author (p. 2). He argues that the "problem with Jonson's gallants is that they are not moralistic; they never take the folly and corruption they confront very seriously and have little interest in reforming it" (p. 3). He traces the "line" of development he discerns in Jonson into playwrights who follow.

Bamborough, J[ohn] B. BEN JONSON. Writers and Their Work, No. 112. London and New York: Published for the British Council and the National Book League by Longmans, Green & Co., 1959; reprint ed. with additions to the bibliography, 1965, 1971.

A brief sketch of the life and an analysis of the works, combining conciseness with authority in the usual manner of this series. Bibliography. This and the item immediately below, though they have the same author and title, are not the same texts.

______. BEN JONSON. London: Hutchinson, University Library, 1970.

The "Preface" calls attention to the fact that the book is "intended primarily for those approaching [Jonson] for the first time" (p. [7]). The study focuses on Jonson's works, chiefly the plays, rather than the life. Brief selective bibliography.

Barish, Jonas A. BEN JONSON AND THE LANGUAGE OF PROSE COMEDY. Cambridge, Mass.: Harvard University Press, 1960.

An analysis of Jonson's style and its utility for the stage. Sets Jonson in the context of what comes before and after.

______, ed. BEN JONSON: A COLLECTION OF CRITICAL ESSAYS. Twentieth Century Views. Englewood Cliffs, N.J.: Prentice-Hall, 1963.

Convenient collection of reprinted articles and parts of books by various hands. Chronological arrangement. Bibliography.

______, ed. JONSON: "VOLPONE": A CASEBOOK. London: Macmillan,

1972.

A collection of key essays, parts of books, introductions to editions, and so on, divided into three parts: "Comment from 1662 to 1920," "Articles and Essays from 1925 to the Present," and "Reviews of Productions, 1930 to the Present," with bibliography.

Baskervill, Charles Read. ENGLISH ELEMENTS IN JONSON'S EARLY COMEDY. Bulletin of the University of Texas, No. 178, Humanistic Series, No. 12, Studies in English, No. 1. Austin: University of Texas Press, 1911.

Baskervill makes a case for the view "that Jonson was a much more sympathetic student of English literature than has commonly been supposed" but "that his indebtedness was less to specific works . . . than to certain specific trends in English literature with which he was thoroughly in accord" (p. [iii]).

Baum, Helena Watts. THE SATIRIC & THE DIDACTIC IN BEN JONSON'S COMEDY. Chapel Hill: University of North Carolina Press, 1947.

A study of Jonson's achievement against the background of Renaissance and Jonsonian theories of poetic function, with an examination of the objects of Jonsonian satire.

Bayfield, M[atthew] A[lbert]. A STUDY OF SHAKESPEARE'S VERSIFICATION, WITH AN INQUIRY INTO THE TRUSTWORTHINESS OF THE EARLY TEXTS, AN EXAMINATION OF THE 1616 FOLIO OF BEN JONSON'S WORKS, AND APPENDICES INCLUDING A REVISED TEXT OF "ANTONY AND CLEOPATRA." Cambridge: At the University Press, 1920.

A now somewhat old study of an ever-current problem, how to edit a Renaissance text. Bayfield asserts that editors sometimes produce texts "clipped and trimmed to a featureless uniformity" but that the reprinting of "an Elizabethan text *ad litteram* may . . . misrepresent completely for modern readers the manner of utterance intended. The evidence afforded by Jonson's Folio and the Quarto of his *Sejanus* is decisive on the point" (pp. ix-x).

Bentley, Gerald Eades. SHAKESPEARE & JONSON: THEIR REPUTATIONS IN THE SEVENTEENTH CENTURY COMPARED. 2 vols. Chicago: University of Chicago Press, 1945.

By cataloging unnoticed allusions and reevaluating others, Bentley has reached a new conclusion about the relative popularity of Jonson and Shakespeare: "Jonson was evidently more popular than Shakespeare" (Vol. I, p. 132). Bentley concludes that Jonson himself "could perceive the genius of the artist who defied the rules. But for lesser minds the 'learned Jonson' was the man" (I, 140). Bentley argues the same position briefly in his Princeton University Inaugural Lecture of March 15, 1946, THE SWAN OF AVON AND THE BRICKLAYER OF WESTMINSTER, printed at Princeton in 1948.

Boughner, Daniel C. THE DEVIL'S DISCIPLE: BEN JONSON'S DEBT TO MACHIAVELLI. New York: Philosophical Library, 1968.

Broughner argues that THE DISCOVERIES reveal "an animadversion directed against . . . Machiavelli" (p. 139). He then shows how Machiavellianism appears in the Jonson plays, to provide a complex analysis of debt on the one hand and refutation on the other.

Bradley, Jesse Franklin, and Joseph Quincy Adams, eds. THE JONSON ALLUSION-BOOK: A COLLECTION OF ALLUSIONS TO BEN JONSON FROM 1597 TO 1700. Cornell Studies in English, Vol. 6. New Haven, Conn.: Yale University Press; London: Oxford University Press, 1922.

The allusions, as the editors note (p. v), illuminate "many poets of the Elizabethan and Jacobean ages" and provide "a body of seventeenth-century dramatic criticism." The mass of available material has required the exercise of editorial judgment in omission or abridgement.

Bryant, J[oseph] A[llen], Jr. THE COMPASSIONATE SATIRIST: BEN JONSON AND HIS IMPERFECT WORLD. Athens: University of Georgia Press, 1972.

Following up the recent interest in focusing critical concern in the study of Jonson on "the tone of the dramatic work--the attitude of the poet towards his characters and the play-world he has created for them, and the relation of both of these to the world outside" (p. 3), Bryant gives detailed consideration to VOLPONE, EPICOENE, THE ALCHEMIST, and BARTHOLOMEW FAIR, with an "Epilogue: A TALE OF A TUB."

Campbell, Oscar James. COMICALL SATYRE AND SHAKESPEARE'S "TROILUS AND CRESSIDA." San Marino, Calif.: The Huntington Library, 1938.

Jonas A. Barish, in BEN JONSON (Twentieth Century Views), above, calls this "[t]he most important study so far of Jonson's early comedy" (p. 179). See further in Part 1, Section 8: Studies of Tudor and Stuart Drama.

Castle, Edward James. SHAKESPEARE, BACON, JONSON, AND GREENE: A STUDY.

See the main entry in Section 12: Robert Greene.

Champion, Larry S. BEN JONSON'S "DOTAGES": A RECONSIDERATION OF THE LATE PLAYS. Lexington: University of Kentucky Press, 1967.

Studying THE DEVIL IS AN ASS, THE STAPLE OF NEWS, THE NEW INN, and THE MAGNETIC LADY, Champion finds "Jonson's comic intent, his theory of art, and his manipulation of material for both instruction and entertainment" in these plays to be "precisely that of his acknowledged masterpieces" (p. 8). Champion's term dotages comes from Dryden's assessment of the plays.

Chetwood, W[illiam] R[ufus]. MEMOIRS OF THE LIFE AND WRITINGS OF BEN JONSON, ESQ; POET LAUREAT TO KING JAMES THE FIRST, AND KING CHARLES THE FIRST, WITH AN ABSTRACT OF THE LIVES OF THEIR FAVOURITES, SOMERSET AND BUCKINGHAM. COLLECTED FROM THE WRITINGS OF THE MOST EMINENT HISTORIANS, AND INTERSPERSED WITH THE PASQUILS OF THOSE TIMES, TO WHICH ARE ADDED, TWO COMEDIES, (WROTE BY BEN JONSON, &C. AND NOT PRINTED IN HIS WORKS) CALLED "THE WIDOW" AND "EASTWARD HOE." Dublin: Printed for and Sold by, W.R. Chetwood, 1756.

Bradley and Adams, in THE JONSON ALLUSION-BOOK, above, comment on Chetwood's "numerous jingling rhymes" in these MEMOIRS as apparently "crude fabrications of his own Muse" (p. vi).

Chute, Marchette. BEN JONSON OF WESTMINSTER. New York: Dutton, 1953.

An effort to recreate the world of Jonson's time in an easy, readable style. Bibliography.

Cunningham, Peter. INIGO JONES. A LIFE OF THE ARCHITECT.

See Laing, David, ed.

Davis, Joe Lee. THE SONS OF BEN.

See the main entry in Part 1, Section 8: Studies of Tudor and Stuart Drama.

De Luna, B[arbara] N. JONSON'S ROMISH PLOT: A STUDY OF "CATILINE" AND ITS HISTORICAL CONTEXT. Oxford: Clarendon Press, 1967.

Arguing that the seventeenth century was "extraordinarily sensitive to coincidences" and "thoroughly analogical" (p. [1]), De Luna proposes "that Jonson's CATILINE of 1611 was both intended and in some circles understood" as having reference to the 1605 Gunpowder Plot (p. [360]). Bibliography.

Dessen, Alan C. JONSON'S MORAL COMEDY. Evanston, Ill.: Northwestern University Press, 1971.

Dessen argues that Jonson means to compel his viewer to confront truth: "Only by forcing the viewer to see himself in the glass of satire can moral comedy succeed" (p. 250).

Donaldson, Ian. THE WORLD-UPSIDE DOWN: COMEDY FROM JONSON TO FIELDING.

See the main entry in Part 1, Section 8: Studies of Tudor and Stuart Drama.

Dunn, Esther Cloudman. BEN JONSON'S ART: ELIZABETHAN LIFE AND

LITERATURE AS REFLECTED THEREIN. 1925; reprint ed. New York: Russell & Russell, 1963.

Dunn attacks a problem which she describes as "two-fold: to determine as accurately as possible [Jonson's] view of the time in which he lived; and to show how that time shines through his pages coloured by that view" (p. 4). Five appendices document Jonson's connections with various groups.

Enck, John J. JONSON AND THE COMIC TRUTH. Madison, Milwaukee, and London: University of Wisconsin Press, 1957, 1966.

Enck sees Jonson's plays as remaining vital because of their grounding in "the actual" and their "unfaltering craftsmanship"; he describes them as recording "discoveries in the partly uncharted and constantly expanding, if sometimes elliptical, circle of the true and comic art" (p. 253).

Evans, Willa McClung. BEN JONSON AND ELIZABETHAN MUSIC, WITH A NEW PREFACE TO THE SECOND PRINTING. 1929; reprint ed. New York: Da Capo Press, 1965, 1967.

A study of the relation of Jonson's plays and masques to music, concluding that he was the "supreme" writer of masques in his day because of "his power over both lyrical and dramatic poems" (p. 118).

Ford, H[erbert] L. COLLATION OF THE BEN JONSON FOLIOS, 1616-31-1640. Oxford: At the University Press, 1932.

A brief, technical essay on the state of the folios.

Fricker, Franz. BEN JONSON'S PLAYS IN PERFORMANCE AND THE JACOBEAN THEATRE. The Cooper Monographs of English and American Language and Literature, No. 17, Theatrical Physiognomy Series. Bern: Francke Verlag, 1972.

Fricker studies the stage directions, the "mirror passages" (those passages in which "the appearance of a character, a gesture, facial expression, stage-business, or a piece of property are mirrored in speech"), "gestic impulses" and "the reported scene" among the "elements which constitute the theatrical physiognomy of a play" (pp. 7-9). He suggests also "a possible influence of the different theatres, their methods of production and audiences, on the plays" (p. 138). Bibliography.

Furniss, W. Todd. "Ben Jonson's Masques," in THREE STUDIES IN THE RENAISSANCE: SIDNEY, JONSON, MILTON. Yale Studies in English, Vol. 138. 1958; reprint ed. Hamden, Conn.: Archon Books, 1969.

Discussions of "Masques in the Tradition of the Golden Age," "The Pastoral Tradition," "The Triumphs: Spectacle vs. Sense," and "Combats of Concepts." Bibliography.

Gilbert, Allan H. THE SYMBOLIC PERSONS IN THE MASQUES OF BEN JONSON. Durham, N.C.: Duke University Press, 1948.

Gilbert proposes "to show what the allegorical and mythological characters in Jonson's masques and entertainments looked like, in order to aid those who wish to understand his art and that of his age" (p. v). The characters are listed alphabetically, located in the masque or entertainment, and described. Seventy-one plates. Bibliographies of "Works Accessible to Jonson," "Works Published after 1637"; "Appendix: Authors, in Addition to Those Listed in the Bibliography, Mentioned or Quoted in the Masques and Entertainments."

Gilchrist, Octavius. AN EXAMINATION OF THE CHARGES MAINTAINED BY MESSRS. MALONE, CHALMERS, AND OTHERS, OF BEN JONSONS ENMITY, &C. TOWARDS SHAKESPEARE. London: Printed for Taylor and Hessey by J. Moyes, 1808.

Gilchrist says: "My motive has been, to rescue a venerable bard . . . from charges founded on error and fostered by misrepresentation" (p. 61).

Goldmark, Ruth Ingersoll. STUDIES IN THE INFLUENCE OF THE CLASSICS ON ENGLISH LITERATURE. 1918; reprint ed. Port Washington, N.Y.: Kennikat Press, 1965.

The three studies (Jonson, Landor, and Arnold) represent work begun as a doctoral dissertation and broken off by Mrs. Goldmark's early death.

Goldsworthy, W. Lansdown. BEN JONSON AND "THE FIRST FOLIO." London: Cecil Palmer, 1931.

Goldsworthy is concerned with the topical allusions possibly to be found in THE STAPLE OF NEWS.

Gottwald, Maria. SATIRICAL ELEMENTS IN BEN JONSON'S COMEDY. Prace Wroclawskiego Towarzystwa Naukowego. Travaux de la Societe des Sciences et des Lettres de Wroclaw, Series A., Nr. 137. Wroclaw: [Zaklad Narodowy im Ossolinskich], 1969.

Acknowledging a debt to the groundwork laid by Baskervill, Knights, Campbell, and Baum, Gottwald studies the satire of the comedies in the attempt to see how the comedy measures up to Jonson's own specifications and to reveal it in the context of "the economic, social, and political situation of the day" (p. 11). Bibliography.

Greenwood, [Granville] George. BEN JONSON AND SHAKESPEARE. London: Cecil Palmer, 1921.

Greenwood argues that Shakespeare was not a writer and that Jonson knew that he was not, "however much it may have suited his

[Jonson's] purpose and the purpose of those who were associated with him in the publication of the Folio, that he should 'camouflage' the immortal poet under the semblance of the player [Shakespeare]" (p. 40).

Gum, Coburn. THE ARISTOPHANIC COMEDIES OF BEN JONSON: A COMPARATIVE STUDY OF JONSON AND ARISTOPHANES. Studies in English Literature, The Hague, No. 40. The Hague and Paris: Mouton Publishers; New York: Humanities Press, 1969.

Believing that Jonson made a "determined effort to adapt Old Comedy to the English stage, Gum regards the imitations, except for BARTHOLOMEW FAIR, as inferior to Aristophanes and attributes the failure to Jonson's reservations in imitating and to his choice of PLUTUS as a principal model (see especially p. 187). Bibliography.

Hett, Francis Page. THE MEMOIRS OF SIR ROBERT SIBBALD, 1641-1722, EDITED WITH AN INTRODUCTION AND A REFUTATION OF THE CHARGE AGAINST SIR ROBERT SIBBALD OF FORGING BEN JONSON'S "CONVERSATIONS." London: Oxford University Press, 1932.

Hett refutes the argument of C.L. Stainer in JONSON AND DRUMMOND, THEIR CONVERSATIONS (see below), that Sir Robert Sibbald forged the CONVERSATIONS.

Jackson, Gabriele B. VISION AND JUDGMENT IN BEN JONSON'S DRAMA. Yale Studies in English, Vol. 166. New Haven, Conn., and London: Yale University Press, 1968.

Proposes the interesting thesis that "Jonson saw his structural principles as analogues of the metaphysical principles which regulate the universe. . . . The gap between the real and ideal action being caused, in his view, by ignorance of these principles, he had only to clarify them for his characters and audience in order to transform the situation" (pp. [1]-2). Bibliography.

Johansson, Bertil. LAW AND LAWYERS IN ELIZABETHAN ENGLAND AS EVIDENCED IN THE PLAYS OF BEN JONSON AND THOMAS MIDDLETON. Acta Universitatis Stockholmiensis. Stockholm Studies in English, No. 18. Stockholm: Almqvist & Wiksell ForLag AB, 1967.

Holding that the "Elizabethan drama reflects faithfully all the trends of the age," Johansson proposes "to present a picture of the law and the various officers of the law in Elizabethan England such as they appear in the plays of . . . Ben Jonson and Thomas Middleton" (pp. 5-6). Bibliography.

______. RELIGION AND SUPERSTITION IN THE PLAYS OF BEN JONSON AND THOMAS MIDDLETON. 1950; reprint ed. New York: Haskell House, 1966.

Johansson argues "that Jonson's and Middleton's plays give a fairly good idea of what aspects of religion and irreligion interested men most and were most talked of in Elizabethan and Jacobean England" (p. 317). Bibliography.

Johnston, George Burke. BEN JONSON: POET. Columbia University Studies in English and Comparative Literature, No. 162. 1945; reprint ed. New York: Octagon Books, 1970.

Johnston sees a trend towards evaluating Jonson for himself rather than "as a straw man to be knocked down in order to exhibit Shakespeare as the champion among them all" (p. 3). The study is focused on the poetry rather than the plays.

Jones-Davies, M[arie]-T[herese]. INIGO JONES, BEN JONSON ET LE MASQUE. Ouvrage publie avec le concours du Centre National de la Recherche Scientifique. Paris: M. Didier, 1967.

Jones-Davies holds that "Inigo Jones, l'architecte, et Ben Jonson, le poete, furent les deux hommes qui, sous les Stuarts, eleverent le divertissement royal appele 'masque' a l'apogee de sa gloire" (p. 11). Numerous illustrations, some in color. "Liste chronologique des divertissements de cour en Angleterre (1603-1631)" (pp. 165-68). Bibliography.

JONSONIUS VIRBIUS: OR, THE MEMORY OF BEN JONSON. REVIVED BY THE FRIENDS OF THE MUSES, 1638.

These poems by various hands--Lucius Cary, Lord Buckhurst, Edmund Waller, Shackerley Marmion, John Ford, and others--have been reprinted, most accessibly in the Herford and Simpson edition of Jonson, Volume XI, pages 428-81 (see main entry in Editions).

Kerr, Mina. INFLUENCE OF BEN JONSON ON ENGLISH COMEDY 1598-1642. New York: D. Appleton, Agents for the University of Pennsylvania, 1912.

See the main entry in Part 1, Section 8: Studies of Tudor and Stuart Drama.

King, Arthur H. THE LANGUAGE OF SATIRIZED CHARACTERS IN "POETASTER": A SOCIO-STYLISTIC ANALYSIS, 1597-1602. Lund Studies in English, 10. London: Williams & Norgate; Lund: C.W.K. Gleerup; Copenhagen: Ejnar Munksgaard, 1941.

Believing that Jonson's "moral and linguistic judgements are delicately interlocked" (p. [218]), King makes a close analysis of language as it relates to other aspects of the plays.

Kingman, Tracy. AN AUTHENTIC CONTEMPORARY PORTRAIT OF SHAKESPEARE. New York: William Edwin Rudge, 1932.

The portrait shows two men playing chess. Kingman quotes the opinion of Paul Wislicenus and Maximilian Toch that the portrait represents Shakespeare checkmating Jonson and therefore represents the part of Shakespeare's TROILUS AND CRESSIDA in the "Stage Quarrel."

Knights, L.C. DRAMA & SOCIETY IN THE AGE OF JONSON.

See the main entry in Part 1, Section 8: Studies of Tudor and Stuart Drama.

Knoll, Robert E. BEN JONSON'S PLAYS: AN INTRODUCTION. Lincoln: University of Nebraska Press, 1964.

Knoll urges the need to avoid letting Jonson's life overshadow his work. He examines the plays systematically, in chronological order, arguing the basic Englishness rather than classicalness of Jonson's work.

Laing, David, ed. INIGO JONES AND BEN JONSON: BEING THE LIFE OF INIGO JONES BY PETER CUNNINGHAM, ILLUSTRATED WITH NUMEROUS FAC-SIMILES OF HIS DESIGNS FOR MASQUES, AND BEN JONSON'S CONVERSATIONS WITH DRUMMOND OF HAWTHORNDEN. The Shakespeare Society's Papers. London: Printed for the Shakespeare Society, 1853.

The volume has a second title page with an earlier date and a fuller title: INIGO JONES. A LIFE OF THE ARCHITECT; BY PETER CUNNINGHAM, ESQ. REMARKS ON SOME OF HIS SKETCHES FOR MASQUES AND DRAMAS; BY J.R. PLANCHE, ESQ. AND FIVE COURT MASQUES; EDITED FROM THE ORIGINAL MSS. OF BEN JONSON, JOHN MARSTON, ETC. BY J. PAYNE COLLIER, ESQ. ACCOMPANIED BY FACSIMILES OF DRAWINGS BY INIGO JONES; AND BY A PORTRAIT FROM A PAINTING BY VANDYCK. London: Printed for the Shakespeare Society, 1848. As a theatrical designer and as a man with whom Jonson quarreled over aesthetic principles, Jones is important to the understanding of Jonson's life and work.

Linklater, Eric. BEN JONSON AND KING JAMES: BIOGRAPHY AND PORTRAIT. London: Jonathan Cape, 1931.

Linklater provides a general biographical study, without scholarly apparatus.

Lumley, Eleanor P[atience]. THE INFLUENCE OF PLAUTUS ON THE COMEDIES OF BEN JONSON. New York: Knickerbocker Press, 1901.

Originally a Ph.D. thesis, this study argues that Jonson, like Plautus, is now out of favor because each "put into his dramas . . . the manners of his age" but that Jonson "is one of the best, nay, the completest authority we have for ascertaining the manners of the age in which he lived" (p. 120).

Meagher, John C. METHOD AND MEANING IN JONSON'S MASQUES (COSTUME SKETCHES BY INIGO JONES). Notre Dame, Ind.: University of Notre Dame Press, 1966, 1969.

Meagher sees Jonson as having "unified the constituents of the masque . . . into a single whole" designed to reveal "a golden world" and cause his audience "to love and desire the virtuous life by which their brazen world may be alchemized to gold" (pp. 177-78). When Jonson ceased to write masques, the form "settled back . . . into the playful extravagence in which it died" (p. 178), not of inherent failure in the form, but from failure in the audience.

[Morris], Elisabeth Woodbridge. STUDIES IN JONSON'S COMEDIES. Yale Studies in English, Vol. 5. 1898; reprint ed. New York: Gordian Press, 1966.

Sees Jonson's theory and practice as consistent with one another and consistent throughout his life. Analyzes the plays to derive a theory of comedy.

Musgrove, S. SHAKESPEARE AND JONSON. The Macmillan Brown Lectures, 1957. Bulletin No. 51. English Series, No. 9. Auckland, N.Z.: Auckland University College, 1957.

Musgrove argues that "Shakespeare and Jonson enjoyed a closer companionship, as friends and as playwrights, than is often supposed" (p. 210).

Nason, Arthur Huntington. HERALDS AND HERALDRY IN BEN JONSON'S PLAYS, MASQUES AND ENTERTAINMENTS. University Heights: [New York University Press], 1907.

An explanation of the aspects of heraldry needed to understand Jonson's allusions and an annotation of the passages referring to heraldry, amplifying and correcting earlier explanations. Pages [143]-64 provide an "Index, In Which Is Included a Concordance of the Heraldic Terms in Jonson's Plays, Masques, and Entertainments."

Nichols, J[ohn] G[ordon]. THE POETRY OF BEN JONSON. New York: Barnes & Noble, 1969.

Characterizing Jonson as "foremost in the ranks of the great unread" (p. 1), Nichols attempts to redeem him thence as "a poet who deserves, if not love, at least great admiration" (p. 157). Focused chiefly in the poetry, the study touches on drama only incidentally. Bibliography.

Noyes, Robert Gale. BEN JONSON ON THE ENGLISH STAGE, 1660-1776. Harvard Studies in English, Vol. 17. Cambridge, Mass.: Harvard University Press; London: Oxford University Press, 1935.

Stating that "[n]o study of the fortunes of his plays on the stage, based on records which have become increasingly available, has been made since the . . . account of John Genest appeared more than a hundred years ago" (p. [vii]), Noyes analyzes "Main Currents in the Criticism of Ben Jonson, 1660-1776." Two appendices: "A Chronology of the Performances of Ben Jonson, 1660-1776" and "Editions of Ben Jonson's Plays, 1660-1777."

Orgel, Stephen. THE JONSONIAN MASQUE. Cambridge, Mass.: Harvard University Press, 1965.

Announcing as his topic "the changing relationship between the masque as spectacle or revel and the masque as literature" (p. [vii]), Orgel provides detailed discussions of six masques in terms of three important relationships: to tradition, audience, and theatre (p. [186]).

Palmer, John Leslie. BEN JONSON. London: Routledge; New York: Viking Press, 1934.

Declaring Jonson to be "perhaps the greatest of English worthies," Palmer praises the comedies, tragedies, lyrics, and masques, but says that "Jonson was even more important in life than in literature. . . . For forty years the poets and dramatists of England looked to him as their leader" (p. ix). The book builds a picture of Jonson through a series of contrasts.

Partridge, A[stley] C. THE ACCIDENCE OF BEN JONSON'S PLAYS, MASQUES, AND ENTERTAINMENTS, WITH AN APPENDIX OF COMPARABLE USES IN SHAKESPEARE. Cambridge, England: Bowes & Bowes, 1953.

Partridge states that the "object of this study" is "an historical account of the morphology of Ben Jonson's plays, masques and entertainments" (p. xii). He provides an appendix, "Dialect Forms," and a bibliography divided into the headings: "Dictionaries," "Grammars," "Histories of English Language," "Monographs and Special Studies," "Shakespearian Studies," and "Journals."

_____. STUDIES IN THE SYNTAX OF BEN JONSON'S PLAYS. Cambridge, England: Bowes & Bowes, 1953.

This study concerns particularly the verb do, nouns, pronouns, and definite articles. A bibliography similar to that in the preceding item is provided.

Partridge, Edward B. THE BROKEN COMPASS: A STUDY OF THE MAJOR COMEDIES OF BEN JONSON. London: Chatto & Windus; New York: Columbia University Press, 1958.

Having carefully defined what he feels are the limits of imagery as a critical tool, Partridge analyzes VOLPONE, THE ALCHEMIST,

EPICOENE, THE STAPLE OF NEWES, THE NEW INNE, and THE MAGNETIC LADY "to reveal how [Jonson's] imagination works in his major comedies" (p. 18). The study ends with an analysis of the broken compass image as a figure for the impossibility of earthly perfection. Bibliography.

Pennanen, Esko V. NOTES ON THE GRAMMAR IN BEN JONSON'S DRAMATIC WORKS. Acta Academiae Socialis Series A, Vol. 3. Tampere: Yhteiskunnallinen Korkeakoulu, 1966.

A detailed analysis of certain aspects of Jonson's grammar designed to "bring out the motive powers and salient features of the author's use of language." (See the "Preface" for a statement of the design of the book, followed by a brief bibliography, pp. [9]-11).

Sackton, Alexander H. RHETORIC AS A DRAMATIC LANGUAGE IN BEN JONSON. New York: Columbia University Press, 1948.

Sackton sees Jonson as "always a dramatist and a poet, never merely a rhetorician" (p. 167). The study "attempts to describe . . . certain values which Jonson created with rhetoric," especially with the use of "jargon and the language of hyperbole" (p. [vii]). Bibliography.

Savage, James E[dwin]. BEN JONSON'S BASIC COMIC CHARACTERS, AND OTHER ESSAYS. Hattiesburg: University and College Press of Mississippi, 1973.

The book contains five essays: "Ben Jonson's Basic Comic Characters," "Ben Jonson in Ben Jonson's Plays," "Some Antecedents of the Puppet Play in BARTHOLOMEW FAIR," "The Cloaks of THE DEVIL IS AN ASSE," and "Ben Jonson and Shakespeare: 1623-1626."

Small, Roscoe Addison. THE STAGE-QUARREL BETWEEN BEN JONSON AND THE SO-CALLED POETASTERS. Forschungen zur Englischen Sprache und Litteratur, Vol. 1. Breslau: M. & H. Marcus, 1899.

See the main entry in Part 1, Section 8, Studies of Tudor and Stuart Drama.

Smith, G. Gregory. BEN JONSON. English Men of Letters. 1919; reprint ed. St. Clair Shores, [Mich.]: Scholarly Press, 1972.

A general life and works study.

Stagg, Louis C. INDEX TO THE FIGURATIVE LANGUAGE OF BEN JONSON'S TRAGEDIES. Charlottesville: Bibliographical Society of the University of Virginia, 1967.

One of a series of seven such indexes prepared by Stagg.

Stainer, C.L. JONSON AND DRUMMOND, THEIR CONVERSATIONS: A

FEW REMARKS ON AN 18TH CENTURY FORGERY. Oxford: Basil Blackwell, Publisher to the Shakespeare Head Press, 1925.

Argues that Sir Robert Sibbald forged the CONVERSATIONS (see Hett, Francis Page, above).

Steegmuller, Francis [Byron Steel]. O RARE BEN JONSON. New York and London: Alfred A. Knopf, 1927.

The author expresses the belief that meditation on the facts has enabled him to produce a "poetically true conception" of "Jonson, his friends, and his surroundings" (p. 153).

Steel, Byron [pseud.].

See Steegmuller, Francis.

Swinburne, Algernon Charles. A STUDY OF BEN JONSON. New York: Worthington; London: Chatto & Windus, 1889.

Swinburne's opening premise is: "If poets may be divided into two exhaustive but not exclusive classes,--the gods of harmony and creation, the giants of energy and invention,--the supremacy of Shakespeare among the gods of English verse is not more unquestionable than the supremacy of Jonson among its giants" (p. [3]). About half the discussion concerns drama.

Symonds, John Addington. BEN JONSON. London: Longmans, Green & Co.; New York: Appleton, 1886.

The emphasis is on Jonson's life rather than on criticism.

Thayer, C.G. BEN JONSON: STUDIES IN THE PLAYS. Norman: University of Oklahoma Press, 1963.

Because he sees Jonson as "[s]trongly ethical in every bent, very much the moralist," Thayer deals "primarily with Jonson's arguments, secondarily with his art" (p. vii). The emphasis is on the comedies. Bibliography.

Thomas, Mary Olive, ed. "Ben Jonson: Quadricentennial Essays." STUDIES IN THE LITERARY IMAGINATION, 4 (April 1973), entire issue.

I have not seen this collection.

Thomson, James. BIOGRAPHICAL AND CRITICAL STUDIES. London: Reeves and Turner and Bertram Dobell, 1896.

The "Preface" (p. vii) points out that the Jonson essay (pp. 80-239) and others "are reprinted from COPE'S TOBACCO PLANT."

Townsend, Freda L. APOLOGIE FOR "BARTHOLOMEW FAYRE": THE ART OF

JONSON'S COMEDIES. New York: Modern Language Association of America; London: Oxford University Press, 1947.

A study of BARTHOLOMEW FAIR, not as "an abberation" but, by considering it together with others of his comedies, as evidence that "the classical portrait" of Jonson is a distortion. The study proposes that "Jonson, proponent of art and labor, is reconciled with Jonson, prodigal playwright, by taking new measure of his art" (p. vi).

Trimpi, Wesley. BEN JONSON'S POEMS: A STUDY OF THE PLAIN STYLE. Stanford, Calif.: Stanford University Press, 1962, 1969.

On poetry rather than drama but addressed to a central issue: the revelation of intention through style.

Venables, Morris. "VOLPONE" & "THE ALCHEMIST" (JONSON). Notes on English Literature, No. 47. Oxford: Basil Blackwell, 1970.

One of a series (chief adviser, John D. Jump; general editor, W.H. Mason) "designed primarily for the school, college, and university student" and intended to "indicate the main areas of critical interest, to suggest suitable critical approaches, and to point out possible critical difficulties . . . in as simple and lucid a manner as possible" (p. iv).

Vocht, H[enry] de. STUDIES ON THE TEXTS OF BEN JONSON'S "POETASTER" AND "SEJANUS." MATERIALS FOR THE STUDY OF THE OLD ENGLISH DRAMA, New Series, Vol. 27. 1958; reprint ed. Vaduz: Kraus Reprint, 1963.

The title annotates. See Bang, W., ed., in Part 1, Section 2 C: Editions--Serial and Multi-Volume Editions, for more on the Bang-De Vocht collection.

Wheeler, Charles Francis. CLASSICAL MYTHOLOGY IN THE PLAYS, MASQUES, AND POEMS OF BEN JONSON. Princeton, N.J.: Princeton University Press, for the University of Cincinnati; London: Oxford University Press, 1938.

Largely an alphabetical list of classical allusions, with brief explanations and references to classical sources.

Woodbridge, Elisabeth.

See [Morris], Elisabeth Woodbridge.

Young, Richard B., W. Todd Furniss, and William G. Madsen. THREE STUDIES IN THE RENAISSANCE.

See Furniss, W. Todd, above.

16. THOMAS KYD

BIBLIOGRAPHIES

Tannenbaum, Samuel A[aron], and Dorothy R. Tannenbaum, comps. ELIZABETHAN BIBLIOGRAPHIES. Vol. IV. Port Washington, N.Y.: Kennikat Press, 1967.

Reprints the 1941 Tannenbaum bibliography of Kyd. Designed as an exhaustive, unannotated listing.

Johnson, Robert Carl, comp. ELIZABETHAN BIBLIOGRAPHIES SUPPLEMENTS. Vol. IX: MINOR ELIZABETHANS. London: Nether Press, 1968.

Contains a bibliography of Kyd, 1940-66. Less inclusive than the Tannenbaum, which it supplements. Entries arranged in annual groups.

EDITIONS

THE WORKS OF THOMAS KYD, EDITED FROM THE ORIGINAL TEXTS WITH INTRODUCTION, NOTES, AND FACSIMILES. Ed. Frederick S. Boas. Oxford: Clarendon Press, 1901. Reprinted with SUPPLEMENT, 1955; reprint ed. 1962.

Boas has made a careful job of this edition. He includes THE SPANISH TRAGEDIE, CORNELIA, SOLIMAN AND PERSEDA, THE HOUSHOLDERS PHILOSOPHIE (prose), THE MURDER OF JOHN BREWEN (prose), fourteen lines from Robert Allott, ENGLAND'S PARNASSUS, representing otherwise lost work, and THE FIRST PART OF IERONIMO, though Boas himself rejects the IERONIMO from the Kyd canon. (On the subject of the canon, see Chambers, E[dmund] K[erchever], THE ELIZABETHAN STAGE, Vol. III, pp. 394-97. Main entry appears in Part 1, Section 8: Studies of Tudor and Stuart Drama.)

Since THE SPANISH TRAGEDY looms large in the surviving canon of plays which can or may be ascribed to Kyd, some recent editions of that troublesome text may be mentioned, in two groups--three facsimile editions and three editions for students and scholars needing something other than a facsimile. For facsimile editions see:

THE SPANISH TRAGEDY, WITH ADDITIONS, 1602. Ed. W.W. Greg in consultation with Frederick S. Boas. Malone Society Reprints. London: Printed for the Malone Society at the Oxford University Press, 1925.

THE SPANISH TRAGEDY, 1592. Ed. W.W. Greg and D. Nichol Smith. Malone Society Reprints. London: Printed for the Malone Society at the Oxford University Press, 1949.

THE SPANISH TRAGEDIE [1592]. A Scolar Press Facsimile. Leeds: Scolar Press, 1966.

For more general editions, see:

THE SPANISH TRAGEDY. Ed. Philip Edwards. Revels Plays. Cambridge, Mass.: Harvard University Press, 1959.

THE SPANISH TRAGEDY. Ed. Thomas W. Ross. Fountainwell Drama Series. Los Angeles and Berkeley: University of California Press, 1968.

THE SPANISH TRAGEDY. Ed. J.R. Mulryne. London: Benn, 1970.

CONCORDANCES

Crawford, Ch[arles]. A CONCORDANCE TO THE WORKS OF THOMAS KYD. MATERIALIEN ZUR KUNDE DES ALTEREN ENGLISCHEN DRAMAS, ed. W. Bang, Vol. XV. 1906-10; reprint ed. Vaduz: Kraus Reprint, 1963.

This is not a run-of-the-mill concordance. Crawford says of it: "My main object in compiling this concordance was to enable others to test the accuracy or otherwise of my conclusion that the anonymous play of ARDEN OF FEVERSHAM is a work by Thomas Kyd" (p. [1]). Including the "Hamlet Appendix," a concordance of HAMLET, the volume runs to 690 pages.

SECONDARY WORKS

Baker, Howard. INDUCTION TO TRAGEDY. A STUDY IN A DEVELOPMENT OF FORM IN "GORBODUC," "THE SPANISH TRAGEDY," AND "TITUS AN-

DRONICUS." 1939; reprint ed. New York: Russell & Russell, 1965.

See the main entry in Part 1, Section 8: Studies of Tudor and Stuart Drama.

Carrere, Felix. LA THEATRE DE THOMAS KYD: CONTRIBUTION A L'ETUDE DU DRAMA ELIZABETHAIN. Toulouse: Edouard Privat, 1951; new ed. 1956.

Carrere provides a biographical sketch, a discussion of the "Authentique" works: THE SPANISH TRAGEDY, the "Pre-Hamlet," and ARDEN OF FAVERSHAM; a discussion of attributed works; a discussion of "L'Ecrivain et le Penseur"; and finally of "Kyd et le theatre elizabethain." Ten appendices and a bibliography.

Edwards, Philip. THOMAS KYD AND EARLY ELIZABETHAN TRAGEDY. Writers and Their Work, No. 192. London and New York: Published for the British Council and the National Book League by Longmans, Green, & Co., 1966.

Edwards asserts: "Elizabethan tragedy was really created, in a year or two, by two men of extraordinary originality, Christopher Marlowe and Thomas Kyd. . . . [W]hat they themselves achieved, and what they were able to bequeath to Shakespeare, made what they inherited from the past seem almost unimportant" (p. 5). Edwards compares a number of plays with Kyd's to argue this thesis. Bibliography.

Freeman, Arthur. THOMAS KYD: FACTS AND PROBLEMS. Oxford: Clarendon Press, 1967.

Freeman tackles two problems: assembling the factual material--"matters of date, authorship, source, and stage history"--and providing an estimate of Kyd's achievement. Freeman does not claim too much for Kyd but suggests that he is "currently underestimated" (p. [vii]). Bibliography.

Murray, Peter B. THOMAS KYD. Twayne's English Authors Series, No. 88. New York: Twayne Publishers, 1970.

Murray treats THE SPANISH TRAGEDY as the one surviving play which can be certainly assigned to Kyd. He sees it as enormously influential, especially on "Shakespeare, John Marston, Cyril Tourneur, John Webster, Thomas Middleton, and John Ford" (p. 11). Bibliography.

17. DAVID LINDSAY

BIBLIOGRAPHIES

Hamer, Douglas. "The Bibliography of Sir David Lindsay (1490-1555)." LIBRARY, 4th Series, 10 (1929), [1]-42.

> Hamer describes the paper as a "preface" to a bibliography and the bibliography itself as "the introduction to a complete edition of [Lindsay's] work on which I have been engaged for the last four years." (See next item.) The essay describes various editions, errors made in earlier descriptions of them, failure to locate certain materials cited in earlier bibliographies, and other editorial and bibliographical problems.

EDITIONS

THE WORKS OF SIR DAVID LINDSAY OF THE MOUNT, 1490-1555. Ed. Douglas Hamer. 4 vols. Scottish Text Society, 3rd Series, Vols. 1-2, 6, 8. Edinburgh and London: Printed for the Society by William Blackwood and Sons, 1931-36.

> Volume II contains ANE SATYRE OF THE THRIE ESTAITIS. Volume IV contains critical apparatus: introduction, notes, appendices, indexes, bibliography, and glossary.

ANE SATYRE OF THE THRIE ESTAITS. Ed. James Kinsley, with a Critical Introduction by Agnes Mure Mackenzie and a Foreword by Ivor Brown. London: Cassell and Co., 1954.

> The Mackenzie introduction concerns "The Background and the Play"; Brown discusses "ANE SATYRE OF THE THRIE ESTAITS at the Edinburgh Festival." The text retains the old spelling and is based on the 1602 edition because, Kinsley says, "although published nearly half a century after Lindsay's death, [it] is the only full and reliable version of the play" (p. 36).

A SATIRE OF THE THREE ESTATES. A PLAY ADAPTED BY MATTHEW MCDIAR-

MID FROM THE ACTING TEXT MADE BY ROBERT KEMP FOR TYRONE GUTHRIE'S PRODUCTION AT THE EDINBURGH FESTIVAL 1948, WITH MUSIC BY CEDRIC THORPE-DAVIE. INTRODUCTION AND NOTES BY MATTHEW MCDIARMID. London: Heinemann Education Books, n.d.

Title annotates.

For a discussion of earlier editions, see Hamer, Douglas, in Bibliographies.

SECONDARY WORKS

Murison, W[illiam]. SIR DAVID LYNDSAY, POET, AND SATIRIST OF THE OLD CHURCH IN SCOTLAND. Cambridge: At the University Press, 1938.

Focused primarily in theological problems.

18. THOMAS LODGE

BIBLIOGRAPHIES

Tannenbaum, Samuel A[aron], and Dorothy R. Tannenbaum, comps. ELIZABETHAN BIBLIOGRAPHIES. Vol. IV. Port Washington, N.Y.: Kennikat Press, 1967.

Reprints the 1940 Tannenbaum bibliography of Lodge. Designed as an exhaustive, unannotated listing.

Johnson, Robert C[arl], comp. ELIZABETHAN BIBLIOGRAPHIES SUPPLEMENTS. Vol. V. London: Nether Press, 1968.

Includes Lodge, 1939-65. Less inclusive than the Tannenbaum, which it supplements. Entries are grouped annually.

EDITIONS

THE COMPLETE WORKS OF THOMAS LODGE, 1580-1623? NOW FIRST COLLECTED. 4 vols. 1883; reprint ed. New York: Russell & Russell, 1963.

THE COMPLETE WORKS of 1883 was preceded by various separate publications for the Hunterian Club in 1875, 1876, 1879, 1880, 1881, and 1882. Volume I contains a "Memoir of Thomas Lodge" by Edmund W. Gosse. The "Memoir" also appeared as a separate publication in 1882 and has been reprinted in the Gosse's SEVENTEENTH CENTURY STUDIES (1897; reprint ed. 1972. See Part 1, Section 12: Biographical Notes and Studies: Multi-Figure, for the main entry). The "Prefatory Note," Volume I, states: "The principle steadily kept in view in the reproduction of the several pieces now brought together has been to preserve the appearance and character of the original, so far as it could be done with a uniform type." The principle has been applied even to misprints.

See Part 1, Section 10: Contemporary and Other Early Records, Allusions, Criticism, Etc., for an edition of Lodge's DEFENCE OF POETRY, printed in EARLY TREATISES ON THE STAGE.

SECONDARY WORKS

Harman, Edward George. "THE COUNTESSE OF PEMBROKES ARCADIA," EXAMINED AND DISCUSSED . . . (WITH A CHAPTER ON THOMAS LODGE). London: Cecil Palmer, 1924.

In what he calls "the last contribution which I expect to make to the subject of Baconian authorship," Harman says that Lodge has no "connection with the 'Arcadia,' but he has, in my opinion, a very remarkable connection, never hitherto observed, with the real author (as I regard him) of that work" (p. 182).

Hayashi, Tetsumaro. A TEXTUAL STUDY OF "A LOOKING GLASS FOR LONDON AND ENGLAND" BY THOMAS LODGE AND ROBERT GREENE. Ball State Monograph No. 17, Publications in English, No. 11. Muncie, Ind.: Ball State University, 1969.

The study is designed "to present as comprehensive a textual background of the play as possible and then to make a bibliographical analysis of the four major quartos of the play" (p. vii). It includes "Bibliographical Descriptions of Early Editions," "Bibliographical Analysis of Early Editions," and a bibliography.

Paradise, N. Burton. THOMAS LODGE: THE HISTORY OF AN ELIZABETHAN. New Haven, Conn.: Yale University Press; London: Oxford University Press, 1931.

Paradise points out that Lodge is remembered "as the author of ROSALYNDE," although in fact "he summed up in his life and work . . . nearly all the most characteristic elements of the life and literature of the Elizabethan age" (pp. v-vi). Paradise avoids extravagant claims for Lodge, admitting that "he did not often reach the heights" (p. vi). In attempting to round out a portrait of the man and his works, Paradise gives over one of his six chapters to "The Dramatist." See pages 231-43 for "A Chronological List of the Writings of Thomas Lodge."

Rae, Wesley D. THOMAS LODGE. Twayne's English Authors Series, No. 59. New York: Twayne Publishers, 1967.

Rae sees Lodge as playing a secondary role in English letters during the Renaissance but also as "one of the most interesting and influential representatives of his age" (p. 110). Rae concentrates on the prose and poetry rather than the drama. Bibliography.

Ryan, Pat M., Jr. THOMAS LODGE, GENTLEMAN. Hamden, Conn.: Shoe String Press, 1958.

Ryan modestly asserts: "I venture no claim to the painstaking scholarship of others upon which THOMAS LODGE, GENTLEMAN is manifestly dependent; my function in its preparation has been largely an editorial one" (p. 7). Bibliography.

Sisson, Charles J. "Thomas Lodge and His Family," in THOMAS LODGE AND OTHER ELIZABETHANS.

See the main entry under Sisson, Charles J., ed., in Part 1, Section 4: Festschriften and Other Collections of Essays.

Tenney, Edward Andrew. THOMAS LODGE. Cornell Studies in English, Vol. 26. 1935; reprint ed. New York: Russell & Russell, 1969.

Tenney sees Lodge as "a typical figure," distinguished by "the length and picturesque variety of his career." The emphasis of the book is biographical, though Tenney laments, "Of this career, unhappily, we possess but the outline" (p. viii).

19. JOHN LYLY

BIBLIOGRAPHIES

Tannenbaum, Samuel A[aron], and Dorothy R. Tannenbaum, comps. ELIZABETHAN BIBLIOGRAPHIES. Vol. V. Port Washington, N.Y.: Kennikat Press, 1967.

Reprints the 1940 Tannenbaum bibliography of Lyly. Designed as an exhaustive, unannotated listing.

Johnson, Robert C[arl], comp. ELIZABETHAN BIBLIOGRAPHIES SUPPLEMENTS. Vol. V. London: Nether Press, 1968.

Includes a bibliography of Lyly, 1939-65. Less inclusive than the Tannenbaum, which it supplements. Not annotated. Arranges entries in annual groups.

EDITIONS

THE DRAMATIC WORKS OF JOHN LILLY (THE EUPHUIST) WITH NOTES AND SOME ACCOUNT OF HIS LIFE AND WRITINGS. Ed. F.W. Fairholt. 2 vols. London: John Russell Smith, 1858.

Little scholarly apparatus.

THE COMPLETE WORKS OF JOHN LYLY, NOW FOR THE FIRST TIME COLLECTED AND EDITED FROM THE EARLIEST QUARTOS WITH LIFE, BIBLIOGRAPHY, ESSAYS, NOTES AND INDEX. Ed. R. Warwick Bond. 3 vols. Oxford: Clarendon Press, 1902; reprint ed. 1967.

Bond provides a thorough piece of work, with extensive notes, though he declares himself "troubled by the sense that there is more yet to be discovered about Lyly" (Vol. I, p. xiii).

QUEEN ELIZABETH'S ENTERTAINMENT AT MITCHAM: POET, PAINTER, AND MUSICIAN. ATTRIBUTED TO JOHN LYLY. Ed. Leslie Hotson. New Haven, Conn.: Yale University Press, for the Yale Elizabethan Club; London: Oxford

University Press, 1953.

Hotson provides an edition of an "entertainment" which at the time of the printing had been recently discovered among the papers of "one of Queen Elizabeth's longest-lived and busiest judges, Dr. Julius Caesar" by Nellie McNeill O'Farrell (p. 3) and attributed to Lyly on internal evidence (p. 4). The "Poet, Painter, and Musician" of the title speak in the piece.

SECONDARY WORKS

Child, Clarence Griffin. JOHN LYLY AND EUPHUISM. Munchener Beitrage zur Romanischen und Englischen Philologie, Vol. 7. Erlanger and Leipzig: A. Deichert, 1894.

Detailed analysis (in English) of the characteristic devices of euphuism, with much of the evidence displayed in charts.

Colvile, K.N. FAME'S TWILIGHT: STUDIES OF NINE MEN OF LETTERS. London: Philip Allan, 1923.

Among the nine, Lyly is the subject of a short but pleasant informal essay, pages [65]-101.

Croll, Morris W. STYLE, RHETORIC, AND RHYTHM: ESSAYS BY MORRIS W. CROLL. Ed. J. Max Patrick et al. Princeton, N.J.: Princeton University Press, 1966.

Essay Six (pp. 237-95) is entitled "The Sources of the Euphuistic Rhetoric." R.J. Schoeck and J. Max Patrick, the editors who prepared the "Foreword" to this essay, call it "a standard reference in Renaissance studies for half a century" and say that although it now needs some revision, the "main thesis, that the important roots of the Euphuistic style are to be found in medieval rhetoric, remains unchallenged" (p. 237).

Feuillerat, Albert. JOHN LILY: CONTRIBUTION A L'HISTOIRE DE LA RENAISSANCE EN ANGLETERRE. Cambridge: At the University Press, 1910.

After a long consideration of Lyly and his influence as a prose writer and a dramatist, Feuillerat concludes: "Il avait toutes les qualites qui font un grand ecrivain. . . . Mais il a manque d'ideal; il n'a pas eu foi en la grandeur de sa mission" (p. 499).

Halpin, N[icholas] J[ohn]. OBERON'S VISION IN THE "MIDSUMMER-NIGHT'S DREAM," ILLUSTRATED BY A COMPARISON WITH LYLIE'S "ENDYMION." The Shakespeare Society's Papers. London: Printed for the Shakespeare Society, 1843.

Halpin interprets A MIDSUMMER NIGHT'S DREAM, Act II, Scene 2, as containing contemporary allusions, with the "true solution" to them being "a love-adventure of Queen Elizabeth's" (p. [1]). Lyly is used to support this reading of Shakespeare.

Hunter, G[eorge] K. JOHN LYLY: THE HUMANIST AS COURTIER. Cambridge, Mass.: Harvard University Press, 1962.

Hunter holds that an understanding of Lyly and of the Elizabethan age work together, each casting light upon the other. He devotes a long chapter, pages 159-256, to "The Plays."

_____. LYLY AND PEELE. Writers and Their Work, No. 206. London: Published for the British Council and the National Book League by Longmans, Green & Co., 1968.

Hunter sees Lyly and Peele as "the first writers to bring the full fruits of the new Humanist education to the service of popular commercial entertainment" (p. 7). He calls their work a "shotgun marriage of the Universities and the Folk" (p. 8) but a happy marriage for English drama. Bibliography.

Jeffrey, Violet M. JOHN LYLY AND THE ITALIAN RENAISSANCE. 1928; reprint ed. New York: Russell & Russell, 1968.

The study proposes the view (pp. v-vii) that the failure to perceive Lyly's debt to Italian literature stems from a failure to read the right Italians--i.e., not major writers but those read in Lyly's day and now neglected. It argues that Lyly's creative use of sources is the quality "that stamps him as an artist" (p. 137). The discussion ends, however, with the suggestion that Lyly is important, not so much in his own right, as in his "influence upon Shakespeare" (p. 140).

Jones, Deborah. "John Lyly at St. Bartholomew's, or Much Ado about Washing," in THOMAS LODGE AND OTHER ELIZABETHANS.

See the main entry under Sisson, Charles J., ed., in Part 1, Section 4: Festschriften and Other Collections of Essays.

LeComte, Edward Semple. ENDYMION IN ENGLAND: THE LITERARY HISTORY OF A GREEK MYTH. New York: King's Crown Press, 1944.

The "Introduction" states that an "original intention to confine this study to English nondramatic verse" (p. xi) gave way to a study of Lyly's ENDYMION and thence to other plays. The book is not focused primarily on drama, however.

Saccio, Peter. THE COURT COMEDIES OF JOHN LYLY: A STUDY IN ALLEGORICAL DRAMATURGY. Princeton, N.J.: Princeton University Press, 1969.

Centered directly in the analysis of the plays. An appendix (pp. 225-26) contains "what is known or reasonably conjectured about the dates, locations, and auspices of the first productions given the Court comedies."

Tilley, Morris Palmer. ELIZABETHAN PROVERB LORE IN LYLY'S "EUPHUES" AND IN PETTIE'S "PETITE PALLACE" WITH PARALLELS FROM SHAKESPEARE. University of Michigan Publications, Language and Literature, 2. New York and London: Macmillan, 1926.

The "Introduction" concerns "The Proverbial Element in EUPHUES." There are various appendices and an enormous "List of Proverbs."

Wilson, John Dover. JOHN LYLY. Cambridge: Macmillan and Bowes, 1905.

Wilson regards the plays as "greatly outweigh[ing] his novel both in aesthetic and historical importance" (p. [85]). He sees in Lyly the beginnings of a romanticism which manifests itself in Shakespeare, Goethe, and Hugo, and of "that classical tradition which even Shakespeare's 'purge' could do nothing to check, and which was eventually to lay its dead hand upon the art of the 18th century" (pp. 130-31).

20. CHRISTOPHER MARLOWE

BIBLIOGRAPHIES

Cole, Douglas. "Christopher Marlowe, 1564-1964, A Survey." SHAKESPEARE NEWSLETTER, 14 (1964), 44.

A brief survey and evaluation of primary and secondary materials.

Tannenbaum, Samuel A[aron], and Dorothy R. Tannenbaum, comps. ELIZABETHAN BIBLIOGRAPHIES. Vol. V. Port Washington, N.Y.: Kennikat Press, 1967.

Reprints the Tannenbaum bibliography of Marlowe of 1937 and the 1937 and 1947 supplements. Designed as an exhaustive, unannotated listing.

Johnson, Robert C[arl], comp. ELIZABETHAN BIBLIOGRAPHIES SUPPLEMENTS. Vol. VI. London: Nether Press, 1967.

Contains a bibliography of Marlowe, 1946-65. Less inclusive than the Tannenbaum, which it supplements. Not annotated. Entries grouped by years.

EDITIONS

THE WORKS OF CHRISTOPHER MARLOWE WITH NOTES AND SOME ACCOUNT OF HIS LIFE AND WRITINGS. Ed. Alexander Dyce. 3 vols. London: William Pickering, 1850.

The "Preface" (Vol. I, p. [viii]) calls this "a new text formed on a collation of the early copies." There is also a revised, one-volume edition by Dyce published by George Routledge and Sons (London and New York, 1876).

THE WORKS OF CHRISTOPHER MARLOWE. Ed. A.H. Bullen. 3 vols. London: John C. Nimmo, 1885.

Bullen says in the "Preface" (Vol. I, p. [v]): "The present volumes are the first instalment towards a collective edition of the dramatists who lived about the time of Shakespeare. As the series is intended neither for school-boys nor antiquarians, I have avoided discussions on grammatical usages, and I have not preserved the orthography of the old copies." Bullen did, in fact, edit many of the Renaissance dramatists. For the edition of Marlowe he supplies introduction, notes, and various appendices, among which is "a reprint of Mr. R.H. Horne's noble and pathetic tragedy, THE DEATH OF MARLOWE (originally published in 1837)" (III, [315]-53).

THE WORKS OF CHRISTOPHER MARLOWE. Ed. C.F. Tucker Brooke. Oxford: Clarendon Press, 1910; often reprinted.

The "Preface" (p. [iii]) describes the edition as "designed to furnish the student and the general reader with a serviceable edition of Marlowe's accepted writings." To that end, Brooke provides short introductions to the various pieces and notes. Brooke is, of course, an impressive figure amongst scholars of his generation.

THE WORKS AND LIFE OF CHRISTOPHER MARLOWE. General ed. R.H. Case. 6 vols. London: Methuen & Co., 1930-33.

Volume I, containing "The Life of Marlowe" and DIDO, was edited by C.F. Tucker Brooke; Volume II, TAMBURLAINE, by U[na] M. Ellis-Fermor; Volume III, THE JEW OF MALTA and THE MASSACRE AT PARIS, by H.S. Bennett. Volume IV, The POEMS, edited by L.C. Martin, includes "all the non-dramatic verse that can be attributed to Marlowe with reasonable certainty" and "Chapman's four completing sestiads" to HERO AND LEANDER (p. v). Volume V, DR. FAUSTUS, edited by Frederick S. Boas, uses the text of the 1616 quarto together with variants from the 1604 quarto "where the variants are considerable" (p. v), and provides extensive appendices of Faust material and other matters. Volume VI, edited by H.B. Charlton and R.D. Waller, contains EDWARD II. The edition is in modern spelling. There are extensive introductions and notes and some bibliography. The edition should be consulted.

THE PLAYS OF CHRISTOPHER MARLOWE. Ed. Leo Kirschbaum. Cleveland and New York: World Publishing Co., 1962, 1966.

Editors of Marlowe have usually been exercised by textual corruption. Kirschbaum, however, believes "that for all five major plays" the extant texts are "very close to what Marlowe wrote. The disintegrators . . . are, in short, wrong. The text of DOCTOR FAUSTUS which I present should, I believe, be considered both new and authentic" (p. [7]). Kirschbaum omits DIDO "because Marlowe's share is not clear" and MASSACRE AT PARIS "because the text is extremely corrupt" (p. 9).

THE COMPLETE PLAYS OF CHRISTOPHER MARLOWE . . . WITH AN INTRODUC-

TION AND NOTES. Ed. Irving Ribner. New York: Odyssey Press, 1963.

The "Preface" describes the edition as designed "to make the plays of Marlowe available to the modern student and the general reader in a form which preserves what the author wrote as closely as modern scholarship can determine, but which does not preserve the vagaries of the Elizabethan printing house, of orthography or pointing" (p. ix). Bibliography.

THE PLAYS OF CHRISTOPHER MARLOWE. Ed. Roma Gill. London, Oxford, and New York: Oxford University Press, 1971.

This paperback edition, with modern spelling, an introduction, light notes, and a short bibliography, is designed to make Marlowe readily available.

THE COMPLETE WORKS OF CHRISTOPHER MARLOWE. Ed. Fredson Bowers. 2 vols. London: Cambridge University Press, 1973.

The edition is so new that I have not been able to examine a copy. It has, however, Bowers's formidable reputation as an exacting editor to vouch for it.

DR. FAUSTUS has presented textual problems of singular difficulty. Two editions, both by W.W. Greg, must be mentioned because of their influence on modern textual studies:

MARLOWE'S "DOCTUR FAUSTUS," 1604-1616. PARALLEL TEXTS. Oxford: Clarendon Press, 1950.

Greg supplies the parallel-text edition and scholarly apparatus in plentitude.

THE TRAGICAL HISTORY OF THE LIFE AND DEATH OF DOCTOR FAUSTUS BY CHRISTOPHER MARLOWE, A CONJECTURAL RECONSTRUCTION. Oxford: Clarendon Press, 1950.

This is Greg's duly famous effort to reconstruct the text as Marlowe might have intended it to read.

See also, under Secondary Works the "casebook" editions of several plays, edited by Bates, Jump, and Ribner.

CONCORDANCES

Crawford, Charles. THE MARLOWE CONCORDANCE. 2 vols. 1911-32; reprint ed. New York: Burt Franklin, [1964].

The Crawford CONCORDANCE originally appeared in MATERIALIEN ZUR KUNDE DES ALTEREN ENGLISCHEN DRAMAS, edited by W.

Bang (Vol. 34), and MATERIALS FOR THE STUDY OF THE OLD ENGLISH DRAMA, edited by H. de Vocht (New Series, Vols. 2, 3, 6 [1928-32]). It is reprinted in the Burt Franklin Bibliography & Reference Series 105. The entire Bang-De Vocht series has been reprinted by Kraus Reprint Ltd. (Vaduz, 1963).

SECONDARY WORKS

Bakeless, John. CHRISTOPHER MARLOWE: THE MAN IN HIS TIME. New York: William Morrow, 1937.

Bakeless announces the intention to include a review of "all that is really important in three hundred years' discussion of Marlowe and his writings," to verify "everything from original sources; and, where possible, to add new and previously undiscovered material" (p. vii). He evaluates the evidence as adding up to "a curiously consistent picture of a man" (p. 4). The book represents a valiant attempt to recreate a little-known man, and also supplies critical evaluations of his works.

_____. THE TRAGICALL HISTORY OF CHRISTOPHER MARLOWE. 2 vols. Cambridge, Mass.: Harvard University Press; London: Oxford University Press, 1942.

A full treatment of the life and works, with a very full bibliography.

Bates, Paul A., ed. FAUST: SOURCES, WORKS, CRITICISM. Harbrace Sourcebooks. New York, Chicago, San Francisco, Atlanta: Harcourt, Brace, & World, 1969.

An introductory book of the Faust materials, with an English translation of the Johann Spies FAUSTBUCH in the section of "Sources"; Marlowe in the "Works"; and various essays in the "Criticism." Bibliography.

Battenhouse, Roy W. MARLOWE'S "TAMBURLAINE": A STUDY IN RENAISSANCE MORAL PHILOSOPHY. Nashville, Tenn.: Vanderbilt University Press, 1941; reprint ed. 1964.

The "Preface" outlines the three concerns of the book: with TAMBURLAINE as a study in the dictator type; with Marlowe's own thought (including the theory that the "atheist" documents may represent Marlowe's efforts as a government spy to provoke criminal statements in others); and with the general intellectual currents of the time.

Beard Th[omas]. THE THEATRE OF GODS IUDGEMENTS: OR, A COLLECTION OF HISTORIES OUT OF SACRED, ECCLESIASTICALL, AND PROPHANE AUTHOURS, CONCERNING THE ADMIRABLE IUDGEMENTS OF GOD VPON THE TRANGRESSOURS OF HIS COMMANDEMENTS. TRANSLATED OVT OF FRENCH

AND AVGMENTED BY MORE THAN THREE HUNDRED EXAMPLES. London: Printed by Adam Islip, 1597.

Chapter 25, "Of Epicures & Atheists," includes Marlowe. C.F. Tucker Brooke, in THE LIFE OF MARLOWE (see Volume I of THE WORKS AND LIFE, edited by R.H. Case, in Editions, above), reprints "Thomas Beard's Account of Marlowe's Death."

Bevington, David M. FROM "MANKIND" TO MARLOWE.

See the main entry in Part 1, Section 7 D: Studies of Medieval Drama--Morality Plays.

Boas, Frederick S. CHRISTOPHER MARLOWE: A BIOGRAPHICAL AND CRITICAL STUDY. Oxford: Clarendon Press, 1940; reprint eds., with corrections, 1946, 1954, 1960, 1964, 1966.

A basic work on Marlowe as man and playwright, making a high evaluation of Marlowe's accomplishments.

______ MARLOWE AND HIS CIRCLE: A BIOGRAPHICAL SURVEY. 1929; reprint ed. New York: Russell & Russell, 1968.

Boas works from the documentary evidence available to him, deliberately eschewing the endeavor to synthesize "documentary materials" with "impressions . . . drawn from [Marlowe's] plays and poems" (p. 8). Two useful appendices, "Allegations against Marlowe in Thomas Kyd's Letters" and "A List of Principal Documents."

Brockbank, J.P. MARLOWE: "DR. FAUSTUS." Studies in English Literature, No. 6. London: Edward Arnold; Great Neck, N.Y.: Barron's Educational Series, 1962.

Designed to provide general assistance to students early in their approach to the play. Bibliography.

Brooke, C[harles] F[rederick] Tucker. "The Authorship of the Second and Third Parts of 'King Henry VI.'" TRANSACTIONS OF THE CONNECTICUT ACADEMY OF ARTS AND SCIENCES, 17 (1912-13), 141-211.

Brooke sees the CONTENTION OF THE TWOO FAMOUS HOUSES OF YORK AND LANCASTER and THE TRUE TRAGEDIE OF RICHARD DUKE OF YORKE as Marlowe's, revised by Shakespeare as 2 & 3 HENRY VI. He sees "the Marlovian versions preserved in the CONTENTION and TRUE TRAGEDY" as "intrinsically better plays than those which resulted from the Shakespearean alteration" because, he argues, "between 1590 and 1592--Marlowe was undoubtedly a maturer and more effective dramatist than Shakespeare" (pp. 210-11).

______. "The Reputation of Christopher Marlowe." TRANSACTIONS OF THE

CONNECTICUT ACADEMY OF ARTS AND SCIENCES, 25 (1922), 347-408.

A detailed, factual survey of various reactions to Marlowe, divided chronologically into three sections, "To the Closing of the Theatres (1642)," "From the Closing of the Theatres to the Appearance of Dodsley's SELECT COLLECTION OF OLD PLAYS (1642-1744)," and "From Dodsley's SELECT COLLECTION OF OLD PLAYS (1744) to the Present."

Churchill, R.C. SHAKESPEARE AND HIS BETTERS: A HISTORY AND CRITICISM OF ATTEMPTS WHICH HAVE BEEN MADE TO PROVE THAT SHAKESPEARE'S WORKS WERE WRITTEN BY OTHERS. Bibliography and research by Churchill and Maurice Hussey. Foreword by Ivor Brown. London: Max Reinhardt, 1958.

The nominees for the role of the true Shakespeare are numerous but rather often not dramatists; Marlowe is among those whom Churchill discounts as the author of the Shakespeare canon.

Clark, Eleanor Grace. THE PEMBROKE PLAYS: A STUDY IN THE MARLOWE CANON. Bryn Mawr, Pa.: Bryn Mawr College, 1928.

A study of the problem of whether five plays probably acted by the Earl of Pembroke's Company are Marlowe's. The plays are THE TAMING OF A SHREW (not Shakespeare's THE SHREW), THE FIRST PART OF THE CONTENTION, THE TRUE TRAGEDY OF RICHARD DUKE OF YORK, EDWARD II, and TITUS ANDRONICUS. Clark considers internal and external evidence and argues, not "that Marlowe was sole author," but that one can detect "the presence of Marlowe's own hand" (p. 51).

______. RALEGH AND MARLOWE: A STUDY IN ELIZABETHAN FUSTIAN. 1941; reprint ed. New York: Russell & Russell, 1965.

What is now Part I of the book was originally published separately as ELIZABETHAN FUSTIAN: A STUDY IN THE SOCIAL AND POLITICAL BACKGROUNDS OF THE ELIZABETHAN DRAMA, somewhat revised for inclusion here (see the "Preface," p. v, of RALEGH AND MARLOWE). Part I concludes (p. 219) that Elizabethan drama was typically "topical" and that "contemporary issues were normally presented under a mask or prosopopoiea of fancy or historical parallel. Fustian was . . . the normal device for avoiding prosecution for political propoganda or personal libel." Part II then offers evidence that the Marlowe plays can be read as such a "fustian" presentation of "Ralegh-issues" (p. 461).

Cole, Douglas. SUFFERING AND EVIL IN THE PLAYS OF CHRISTOPHER MARLOWE. Princeton, N.J.: Princeton University Press, 1962.

Cole examines the influence of various native dramatic traditions and of Seneca on Marlowe, concluding that it is the native English tradition which has the chief impact. Cole also argues that the beliefs concerning suffering and evil which emerge from the plays are essentially Christian. He uses the plays as evidence about themselves, not as a means to construct a view of Marlowe's convictions.

Dean, Leonard, Michael Bristol, and Neil Kleinman. MARLOWE'S "THE JEW OF MALTA": GRAMMAR OF POLICY. Midwest Monographs, Series 1, No. 2. Urbana: University of Illinois, Department of English, 1967.

Three brief notes (totalling six pages).

Eccles, Mark. CHRISTOPHER MARLOWE IN LONDON. Harvard Studies in English, Vol. 10. Cambridge, Mass.: Harvard University Press, 1934.

Eccles explores the evidence for a friendship with Thomas Watson, using what, in 1934, was new evidence. The book has an introduction by Leslie Hotson.

Ellis-Fermor, U[na] M. CHRISTOPHER MARLOWE. 1927; reprint ed. Hamden, Conn.: Archon Books, 1967.

The study, "an attempt to trace the development of Marlowe's mind and art as these are revealed in the surviving parts of his work and to portray the personality thus perceived" (p. [v]), emphasizes the plays.

Fanta, Christopher G. MARLOWE'S "AGONISTS": AN APPROACH TO THE AMBIGUITY OF HIS PLAYS. The Le Baron Russell Briggs Prize Honors Essays in English, 1970. Cambridge, Mass.: Harvard University Press, 1970.

A short treatment of the problem in Marlowe's plays of conflicts which "involve two morally corrupt positions" and of agonists who "achieve salvation in their virtuous lives" but "fail to bring their goodness into the world" (pp. 40-41). Bibliography.

Farnham, Willard, ed. TWENTIETH CENTURY INTERPRETATIONS OF "DOCTOR FAUSTUS": A COLLECTION OF CRITICAL ESSAYS. Englewood Cliffs, N.J.: Prentice-Hall, 1969.

A useful collection of reprinted materials. Chronology. Bibliography.

Fieler, Frank B. "TAMBURLAINE," PART I, AND ITS AUDIENCE. University of Florida Monographs, Humanities Series, No. 8. Gainesville: University of Florida Press, 1962.

A study focused on the special problem of Marlowe's "conscious manipulation of audience reaction to his main character" (p. [iii]), arguing that Marlowe was "an artist . . . sensitive at all times to the inevitable interaction between his material and his audience and capable of manipulating the one to control the other" (p. 1).

Gibson, H.N. THE SHAKESPEARE CLAIMANTS: A CRITICAL SURVEY OF THE FOUR PRINCIPAL THEORIES CONCERNING THE AUTHORSHIP OF THE SHAKESPEAREAN PLAYS. 1962; reprint ed. New York: Barnes & Noble; London: Methuen & Co., 1971.

The claimants are Bacon, the Earl of Derby, the Earl of Oxford, and Marlowe. Bibliography.

Haile, H.G., ed. DAS FAUSTBUCH NACH DER WOLFENBUTTLER HANDSCHRIFT. Philologische Studien und Quellen, Vol. 14. Berlin: Erich Schmidt, 1963.

_____, ed. and trans. THE HISTORY OF DOCTOR JOHANN FAUSTUS, RECOVERED FROM THE GERMAN. Urbana: University of Illinois Press, 1965.

Haile's works are useful to the total history of the Faust legend.

Heller, Otto. FAUST AND FAUSTUS: A STUDY OF GOETHE'S RELATION TO MARLOWE. Washington University Studies, New Series, Language and Literature, No. 2. St. Louis, Mo.: Washington University Press, 1931.

Heller argues that Goethe made use of Marlowe (that he did not is sometimes argued).

Henderson, Philip. AND MORNING IN HIS EYES: A BOOK ABOUT CHRISTOPHER MARLOWE. London: Boriswood, 1937.

A general biographical study, beginning with the modest assertion that "[f]or experts on the period it will be found to contain little that is new" (p. 15). The two parts, "The Man and His World" and "The Dramatist," interpret Marlowe as a man of his times: "The intense individualism of the Renaissance found in Christopher Marlowe one of its most daring exponents" (p. 342).

_____. CHRISTOPHER MARLOWE. London, New York, Toronto: Longmans, Green & Co., 1952.

Henderson sees Marlowe, "the one English poet in whom is most fully incarnated the spirit of the Italian Renaissance" (p. 1), as reaching for more than he could grasp: "Intoxicated by the celestial vistas opened by the 'new philosophy,' he attempted more than he, or anyone else, could achieve" (p. 157). Bibliography.

_____. CHRISTOPHER MARLOWE. Writers and Their Work, No. 81. London, New York, and Toronto: Published for the British Council and the National Book League by Longmans, Green & Co., 1956; rev. ed. 1962.

Brief review of life, works, criticism. Bibliography.

Hoffman, Calvin. THE MURDER OF THE MAN WHO WAS "SHAKESPEARE."

1955; reprint ed. New York: Grosset & Dunlap, 1960.

Hoffman is the man who hoped to find "Shakespeare" in the Walsingham tomb. The "Postscript" to the 1960 edition ends with these words: "[W]hatever ensues, I pledge that the passion for the drive to vindicate Christopher Marlowe as author is a goal from which I shall never swerve. Is it a worthwhile goal? I leave it to my readers to judge" (p. 260).

Honey, William. THE SHAKESPEARE EPITAPH DECIPHERED. London: Mitre Press, 1969.

Fascinated by Hoffman's view but unconvinced by its details and finding it lacking in scholarship, Honey has made his own investigation and concludes that "[i]t was not William Shakespeare the actor from Stratford-upon-Avon who wrote the plays, but the poet-dramatist Christopher Marlowe" (p. 213). Honey deciphers the Shakespeare epitaph as reading, in code: "Entombed here . . . Christopher Marlowe's bones," and argues that the manuscripts are in the tomb, that Shakespeare died at Deptford (p. 214). Bibliography.

Hotson, Leslie. THE DEATH OF CHRISTOPHER MARLOWE. London: Nonesuch Press; Cambridge, Mass.: Harvard University Press, 1925.

"The Introduction" by G.L. Kittredge offers the judgment: "The mystery of Marlowe's death . . . is now cleared up for good and all on the authority of public records of complete authenticity and gratifying fulness" (p. 7). Nothing is ever quite so settled as Professor Kittredge here hopes, but Hotson's book, though brief (seventy-six pages), is a major contribution to Marlowe studies.

Ingram, John H. CHRISTOPHER MARLOWE AND HIS ASSOCIATES. London: Grant Richards, 1904.

Ingram asserts: "For upwards of three centuries the brightness of Marlowe's name has been dimmed by libel and slander. . . . The following pages will show that the remembrance and references of every one who knew Marlowe personally were favourable to his character" (p. vii). Ingram concentrates on the life rather than the works. Some discoveries of important material have been made since Ingram's day, of course; part of these would gratify Ingram.

_____. MARLOWE & HIS POETRY. 1914; reprint ed. New York: AMS Press, 1972.

The "General Preface," signed William Henry Hudson (p. 5), argues that most "young students" can be made interested in poetry through a knowledge of "the character and career of the poet himself." Much of the small volume is made up of quotations from Marlowe discussed and analyzed.

Jump, John D., ed. MARLOWE: "DOCTOR FAUSTUS": A CASEBOOK. London: Macmillan, 1969.

The basic divisions of the material are "Extracts from Earlier Critics" and "Recent Studies." There are also an introduction and a bibliography. The material is reprinted and generally emphasizes the modern.

Knoll, Robert E. CHRISTOPHER MARLOWE. Twayne's English Authors Series, No. 74. New York: Twayne Publishers, 1969.

The "Preface" describes the book as "a general, critical introduction to the works of Christopher Marlowe." It provides a study of the life and writings and gives bibliography.

Kocher, Paul Harold. CHRISTOPHER MARLOWE: A STUDY OF HIS THOUGHT, LEARNING, AND CHARACTER. 1946; reprint ed. New York: Russell & Russell, 1962.

Kocher proposes that "[t]he biographical evidence harmonizes with that of his plays to make it plain that, out of conscious rational disbelief overlying unconscious need and fear, controversy about religion was the ruling passion of his soul" (p. 137). Kocher argues that Marlowe sought a religious creed but rejected and even sought to destroy Christianity, a faith with "more of significance and beauty than he knew" (p. 334).

Leech, Clifford. "WHEN WRITING BECOMES ABSURD" AND "THE ACTING OF SHAKESPEARE AND MARLOWE." George Fullmer Reynolds Lectures for 1963. Boulder: University of Colorado Press, 1964.

The two essays are reprinted from THE COLORADO QUARTERLY, Summer, 1964. The first refers, among other titles, to TAMBURLAINE. The second deduces from the plays "the acting-manner that the playwrights seem to have envisaged" (p. 20).

_____, ed. MARLOWE: A COLLECTION OF CRITICAL ESSAYS. Twentieth Century Views. Englewood Cliffs, N.J.: Prentice-Hall, 1964.

Reprints of articles, sections of books. Brief bibliography. Well-chosen materials throughout.

Levin, Harry. THE OVERREACHER: A STUDY OF CHRISTOPHER MARLOWE. Cambridge, Mass.: Harvard University Press, 1952.

Levin undertakes to study Marlowe's "'poetic' . . . personality" so as to "explicate his poetry and his dramaturgy," using <u>hyperbole</u> as "a unifying key" (p. xi). Bibliography.

Lewis, J.G. CHRISTOPHER MARLOWE: OUTLINES OF HIS LIFE AND WORKS. 1891; reprint ed. Folcroft, Pa.: Folcroft Press, 1969.

The "Prefatory Note" (p. [2]) indicates that the essay (twenty-eight pages) was largely written "with the view of stimulating the inhabitants of Marlowe's birthplace to take an interest in the poet's writing and to do themselves the honour of helping on the Memorial which was then under discussion."

McMichael, George, and Edgar M. Glenn. SHAKESPEARE AND HIS RIVALS: A CASEBOOK ON THE AUTHORSHIP QUESTION. New York: Odyssey Press, 1962.

There is a section on "Marlowe as Shakespeare," with materials from various sources, pro and con.

Mahood, M[olly] M. POETRY AND HUMANISM. 1950; reprint eds. Port Washington, N.Y.: Kennikat Press, 1967; New York: W.W. Norton & Co., 1970.

The book is chiefly concerned with poetry, but it contains a chapter, "Marlowe's Heroes" (pp. 54-86), which opens with the assertion: "The whole story of Renaissance humanism is told in four Elizabethan tragedies: the two parts of TAMBURLAINE THE GREAT, DOCTOR FAUSTUS, THE JEW OF MALTA, and EDWARD II."

Masinton, Charles G. CHRISTOPHER MARLOWE'S TRAGIC VISION: A STUDY IN DAMNATION. Athens: Ohio University Press, 1972.

Masinton offers as his thesis "the central importance of the theme of damnation in Christopher Marlowe's five major plays." He believes Marlowe's "overriding concern" to be "to represent the diabolical and rebellious in man and to portray the intense, hopeless agony of souls who have damned themselves" (p. ix). Bibliography.

Morris, Brian, ed. CHRISTOPHER MARLOWE. Mermaid Critical Commentaries. London: Benn, 1968; New York: Hill & Wang, 1969.

The "Introduction" identifies the book as "the record of the first York Symposium, held at Langwith College, in the University of York, from 19 to 21 April 1968" and says that its publication represents a decision "to enlarge the scope of the [New Mermaid] series by publishing collections of critical essays on the major dramatists, to accompany the editions" (p. v). The volume contains an introduction by Morris and these essays: James L. Smith, "THE JEW OF MALTA in the Theatre"; Brian Gibbons, "'Unstable Proteus': THE TRAGEDY OF DIDO QUEEN OF CARTHAGE"; J.R. Mulryne and Stephen Fender, "Marlowe and the 'Comic Distance'"; Harold F. Brooks, "Marlowe and Early Shakespeare"; Michael Hattaway, "Marlowe and Brecht"; Brian Morris, "Comic Method in HERO AND LEANDER"; Roma Gill, "'Snakes Leape by Verse'"; D.J. Palmer, "Marlowe's Naturalism"; and W. Moelwyn Merchant, "Marlowe the Orthodox." It should be stressed that this is not a volume of reprinted materials.

Norman, Charles. THE MUSES'S DARLING: THE LIFE OF CHRISTOPHER MAR-

LOWE. New York and Toronto: Rinehart & Co., 1946; new ed. Drexel Hill, Pa.: Bell Publishing Co., 1950; Macmillan paperback, 1960; reprint ed. with additions, Indianapolis: Bobbs-Merrill, 1971.

Norman describes his intention as "to bring [Marlowe] and his friends and enemies into focus--first as men; second, as Elizabethans." He provides the caution that "while I have scrupulously adhered to the story found in the records and documents, occasionally, in the accompanying dramatic reconstructions, it has been necessary to go beyond them," though never "without warrant from the records" (pp. xv-xvi).

O'Neill, Judith, ed. CRITICS ON MARLOWE. Readings in Literary Criticism, No. 4. London: Allen and Unwin, 1969; Coral Gables, Fla.: University of Miami Press, 1970.

Reprints materials from periodicals and books, organized into two groups, "Critics on Marlowe: 1592-1930" and "Modern Critics on Marlowe," with an introduction and a bibliography.

Palmer, Philip Mason, and Robert Pattison More, eds. and trans. THE SOURCES OF THE FAUST TRADITION FROM SIMON MAGUS TO LESSING. 1936; reprint ed. New York: Octagon Books, 1966.

The material was compiled specifically as background to Goethe, but it serves as background for Marlowe, too. Among other useful materials, it contains a reprinting of the 1592 English FAUSTBOOK, with original spelling and so on retained.

Poirier, Michel. CHRISTOPHER MARLOWE. 1951; reprint ed. Hamden, Conn.: Archon Books, 1968.

Poirier describes the book as "a general introduction to the man and his work" with "a psychological portrait" and an assessment "of the aesthetic value of his writings" (p. viii). Bibliography.

Ribner, Irving, ed. DOCTOR FAUSTUS: TEXT AND MAJOR CRITICISM. New York: Odyssey Press, 1966.

See next two items.

______, ed. EDWARD II: TEXT AND MAJOR CRITICISM. New York: Odyssey Press, 1970.

See next item.

______, ed. THE JEW OF MALTA: TEXT AND MAJOR CRITICISM. New York: Odyssey Press, 1970.

The "casebook," usually bringing together a primary text and selected critical materials, is a phenomenon of relatively recent origin. When well executed, these volumes can be useful in the classroom, particularly where library resources are limited. The Marlowe casebooks mentioned here--these three by Ribner and two above by Bates and Jump--are all edited by scholars with considerable experience in Marloviana.

Richards, Alfred E., ed. STUDIES IN ENGLISH FAUST LITERATURE: 1. THE ENGLISH WAGNER BOOK OF 1594, EDITED, WITH INTRODUCTION AND NOTES. Literarhistorische Forschungen, Vol. 35. Berlin: Felber, 1907.

Among other materials, the volume contains a reprint of part of THE SECOND REPORT OF DOCTOR JOHN FAUSTUS, CONTAINING HIS APPEARANCES AND THE DEEDES OF WAGNER. WRITTEN BY AN ENGLISH GENTLEMAN STUDENT AT WITTENBERG AN VNIUERSITY OF GERMANY IN SAXONY (London: Printed by Abell Jeffes, for Cuthbert Burby, 1594).

Robertson, J.M. MARLOWE: A CONSPECTUS. London: Routledge, 1931.

Philip Henderson, in CHRISTOPHER MARLOWE (Writers and Their Work; p. 45; see above), labels this study "unreliable." The "Epilogue" contains an imaginary twentieth-century interview with "the shade of Marlowe" (pp. 181-82).

Rohrman, H. MARLOWE AND SHAKESPEARE: A THEMATIC EXPOSITION OF THEIR PLAYS. Arnhem: Van Loghum Slaterus, 1952.

A discussion of Elizabethan and Jacobean drama through "what," the author says, "I believe, may be looked upon as its five most representative plays," that is, TAMBURLAINE, FAUSTUS, HAMLET, TROILUS AND CRESSIDA, and MACBETH (p. 3). Bibliography.

Rose, William, ed. THE HISTORIE OF THE DAMNABLE LIFE AND DESERVED DEATH OF DOCTOR JOHN FAUSTUS, 1592. MODERNIZED, EDITED, AND INTRODUCED BY WILLIAM ROSE. FOREWORD TO THE AMERICAN EDITION BY WILLIAM KARL PFEILER. 1925; reprint ed. Notre Dame, Ind.: University of Notre Dame Press, 1963.

An accessible text of the 1592 version of the legend.

Rowse, A.L. CHRISTOPHER MARLOWE: HIS LIFE AND WORKS. New York: Harper & Row, 1964.

Also printed with the title CHRISTOPHER MARLOWE: A BIOGRAPHY (London: Macmillan, 1964). Rowse reads the life through the works. For example, he sees DR. FAUSTUS as yielding its meaning if read with "acute psychological perceptions" (p. 148).

Sanders, Wilbur. THE DRAMATIST AND THE RECEIVED IDEA: STUDIES IN THE PLAYS OF MARLOWE & SHAKESPEARE. London: Cambridge University Press, 1968.

Sanders endeavors to relate "artist and culture" (p. 1), past and present.

Sims, James H. DRAMATIC USES OF BIBLICAL ALLUSIONS IN MARLOWE AND SHAKESPEARE. University of Florida Monographs, Humanities Series, No. 24. Gainesville: University of Florida Press, 1966.

Sims describes the study as not "exhaustive" but "illustrative," designed to show how Biblical allusions generally "add depth and breadth" and to point out "a discernible continuity in the uses made by English dramatists of Biblical allusion" (p. 77). Bibliography.

Smith, Marion Bodwell. CHRISTOPHER MARLOWE'S IMAGERY AND THE MARLOWE CANON. Philadelphia: University of Pennsylvania Press, 1940.

Patterned on Caroline F.E. Spurgeon's SHAKESPEARE'S IMAGERY AND WHAT IT TELLS US (originally printed New York: Macmillan; Cambridge, England: University Press, 1936; see Smith, p. iii), the book contains two main parts, "Marlowe's Imagery," a catalog and discussion; and "The Marlowe Canon: A discussion, in the light of their imagery, of the authorship of doubtful plays within the canon and of plays attributed to Marlowe." The conclusions are supported by various charts.

Steane, J.B. MARLOWE: A CRITICAL STUDY. Cambridge: At the University Press, 1964; reprint ed., cloth, 1965, paper, 1970.

Steane stresses the impossibility of making a final assessment of Marlowe, "partly because great writers tend to exceed our grasp" and also because factual information is sketchy (p. 361). Bibliography.

Tannenbaum, Samuel A[aron]. THE ASSASSINATION OF CHRISTOPHER MARLOWE (A NEW VIEW). New York: The Tenny Press, 1928.

Tannenbaum, acknowledging a debt to Hotson's discovery of documents related to Marlowe's death, argues from the nature of the wounds, the quality of the witnesses, and so on, that Frizer deliberately murdered Marlowe while he slept, "that the Coroner was influenced by certain powers not to inquire too curiously" and further that Ralegh could have gained by "the removal by assassination of a dangerous foe" (see pp. 37-51 for Tannenbaum's conclusions).

Verity, Arthur Wilson. THE INFLUENCE OF CHRISTOPHER MARLOWE ON SHAKSPERE'S EARLIER STYLE. Cambridge, England: Macmillan and Bowes, 1886.

Verity says: "To estimate exactly the obligations of one writer to another is always a difficult, if not altogether impossible task" (p. 101), but he sees Marlowe in himself as having both historical and intrinsic merit (p. 103).

Wells, William. THE AUTHORSHIP OF JULIUS CAESAR.

Wells argues that JULIUS CAESAR was written by Marlowe and revised by Beaumont, with Shakespeare having "contributed . . . the first fifty-seven lines of the opening scene" (p. 190). The argument is supported by style and parallel passages. See the main entry in Section 1: Introduction.

Williams, David Rhys. SHAKESPEARE, THY NAME IS MARLOWE. New York: Philosophical Library; London: Vision Press, 1966.

Williams argues that Marlowe did not die at twenty-nine but lived on to write Shakespeare's plays, protected by Thomas Walsingham. Bibliography.

Williamson, Hugh Ross. KIND KIT: AN INFORMAL BIOGRAPHY OF CHRISTOPHER MARLOWE. London: Michael Joseph, 1972.

As the title states, informal, with little scholarly apparatus, but quite readable.

Wilson, F[rank] P[ercy]. MARLOWE AND THE EARLY SHAKESPEARE. Clark Lectures, Trinity College, Cambridge, 1951. Oxford: Clarendon Press, 1953; reprint eds., 1954, 1963, 1967.

A brief and somewhat general book but with good critical observations. Wilson addresses himself to two basic problems: biographical material that leads to questions more than to answers, and corrupt texts. He says that the question "What produced the sudden flowering of the Renaissance stage?" cannot be answered.

Wraight, A.D. IN SEARCH OF CHRISTOPHER MARLOWE: A PICTORIAL BIOGRAPHY. Photography by Virginia F. Stern. London: Macdonald & Co., 1965.

A visually attractive book, with many illustrations of persons, places, manuscripts, books, and the like. Full text in support of the pictures. Bibliography.

Zeigler, Wilbur Gleason. IT WAS MARLOWE: A STORY OF THE SECRET OF THREE CENTURIES. Chicago: Donohue, Henneberry & Co., 1895.

Zeigler argues that Marlowe lived and wrote after 1593. Of his own work, Zeigler says (p. xi): "Upon these conjectural answers to the question of who was the author, and why did he conceal his identity, I have built the story of 'It Was Marlowe,' and I trust that in its narration I have made my theory plausible." It is the Shakespeare plays which are again in question, of course.

21. JOHN MARSTON

BIBLIOGRAPHIES

Tannenbaum, Samuel A[aron], and Dorothy R. Tannenbaum, comps. ELIZABETHAN BIBLIOGRAPHIES. Vol. V. Port Washington, N.Y.: Kennikat Press, 1967.

Reprints the 1940 Tannenbaum bibliography of Marston. Designed as an exhaustive, unannotated listing.

Pennel, Charles A., and William P. Williams, comps. ELIZABETHAN BIBLIOGRAPHIES SUPPLEMENTS. Vol. IV. London: Nether Press, 1968.

Includes a bibliography of Marston, 1939-65. Less inclusive than the Tannenbaum, which it supplements. Groups entries annually.

EDITIONS

THE WORKS OF JOHN MARSTON. REPRINTED FROM THE ORIGINAL EDITIONS. WITH NOTES, AND SOME ACCOUNT OF HIS LIFE AND WRITINGS. Ed. J.O. Halliwell [-Phillipps]. 3 vols. London: John Russell Smith, 1856.

Apparatus is not extensive.

THE WORKS OF JOHN MARSTON. Ed. A.H. Bullen. 3 vols. London: Bullen; Boston: Houghton Mifflin; Cambridge, Mass.: Riverside Press, 1887.

Introduction and a few notes. Concerning the text Bullen says: "I have done my best to regulate the text, which is frequently very corrupt; but I am painfully conscious that I have left plenty of work for future editors" (Vol. I, p. vii).

THE PLAYS OF JOHN MARSTON, EDITED FROM THE EARLIEST TEXTS WITH INTRODUCTION AND NOTES. Ed. H[enry] Harvey Wood. 3 vols. Edinburgh and London: Oliver and Boyd, 1934-39.

Readable text. Light notes. Bibliography.

SECONDARY WORKS

Allen, Morse S. THE SATIRE OF JOHN MARSTON. Columbus: Ohio State University Press, 1920.

Allen discusses Marston's life, his involvement in the "Stage-Quarrel," and his satires, dramatic and nondramatic. He concludes: "Marston's satire began in wrangling, and ended in failure" (p. 161). Although Allen thinks Marston unlikely ever to "have been a great writer" (p. 161), he suggests that Marston might have done better in the novel as a form.

Axelrad, A. Jose. UN MALCONTENT ELIZABETHAIN: JOHN MARSTON (1576-1634). Paris: Didier, 1955.

Extensive treatment of the plays and of "La Technique dramatic." Axelrad reviews the critical reception of Marston from his own times, in an effort not "de rehabiliter, mais de comprendre" (p. 327).

Caputi, Anthony. JOHN MARSTON, SATIRIST. Ithaca, N.Y.: Cornell University Press, 1961.

Caputi sees Marston as unusual because of "the unusual integrity of his canon" which was "produced in a single decade" and which was limited strictly "to satire and satiricomic forms" (p. viii). Bibliography.

Finkelpearl, Philip J. JOHN MARSTON OF THE MIDDLE TEMPLE: AN ELIZABETHAN DRAMATIST IN HIS SOCIAL SETTING. Cambridge, Mass.: Harvard University Press, 1969.

Finkelpearl's study is focused on Marston in the context of the Inns of Court, particularly the Middle Temple. He concludes that Marston's literary achievement is somewhat limited but that his "visions of the dark but comic battle between a corrupt world and the integrity of the individual still convey an urgent power" (p. 259).

Lyon, John Henry Hobart. A STUDY OF "THE NEWE METAMORPHOSIS" WRITTEN BY J.M. GENT., 1600. Columbia University Studies in English and Comparative Literature. New York: Columbia University Press, 1919.

THE NEWE METAMORPHOSIS, sometimes thought to be Marston's, is here credited to Jervase Markham. The question is germaine to the total Marston canon, but THE NEWE METAMORPHOSIS, whoever wrote it, is not a play.

Lyons, Bridget Gellert. VOICES OF MELANCHOLY: STUDIES IN LITERARY TREATMENTS OF MELANCHOLY IN RENAISSANCE ENGLAND. London: Routledge & Kegan Paul, 1971.

There is a chapter, pages 58-76, on "Marston and Melancholy." Bibliography.

Stagg, Louis C. AN INDEX TO THE FIGURATIVE LANGUAGE OF JOHN MARSTON'S TRAGEDIES. Charlottesville: Bibliographical Society of the University of Virginia, 1970.

The last in Stagg's series of seven such indexes.

22. PHILIP MASSINGER

BIBLIOGRAPHIES

Tannenbaum, Samuel A[aron], and Dorothy R. Tannenbaum, comps. ELIZABETHAN BIBLIOGRAPHIES. Vol. VI. Port Washington, N.Y.: Kennikat Press, 1967.

Reprints the 1938 Tannenbaum bibliography of Massinger. Designed as an exhaustive, unannotated listing.

Pennel, Charles A., and William P. Williams, comps. ELIZABETHAN BIBLIOGRAPHIES SUPPLEMENTS. Vol. VIII. London: Nether Press, 1968.

Includes Massinger (in a set with Beaumont and Fletcher), 1937-65. Less inclusive than the Tannenbaum, which it supplements. Groups entries annually. No annotation.

EDITIONS

THE DRAMATICK WORKS OF PHILIP MASSINGER, COMPLETE . . . REVISED AND CORRECTED, WITH NOTES CRITICAL AND EXPLANATORY, BY JOHN MONCK MASON, ESQ., TO WHICH ARE ADDED, REMARKS AND OBSERVATIONS OF VARIOUS AUTHORS. CRITICAL REFLECTIONS ON THE OLD ENGLISH DRAMATICK WRITERS; A SHORT ESSAY ON THE LIFE AND WRITINGS OF MASSINGER, INSCRIBED TO DR. S. JOHNSON. 4 vols. London: Printed for T. Davies and Others. 1779.

Title (and date) annotate.

THE PLAYS OF PHILIP MASSINGER . . ., WITH NOTES CRITICAL AND EXPLANATORY. Ed. W. Gifford. 4 vols. London: Printed by W. Bulmer and Co., for G. & W. Nicol and Others, 1805; 2nd ed. 1813; 3rd ed. in 1 vol., London: John Templeman and John Russell Smith, 1840.

Gifford is the basis for the Cunningham edition (see next item). In spite of their age, these are the complete editions which one must use. A few plays have appeared as single titles (see, for instance, the Princeton Studies in English, the Regents Renaissance Drama Series, and the Fountainwell Drama Series).

THE PLAYS OF PHILIP MASSINGER, FROM THE TEXT OF WILLIAM GIFFORD, WITH THE ADDITION OF THE TRAGEDY "BELIEVE AS YOU LIST." Ed. Francis Cunningham. New ed. in 1 vol., London: John Camden Hotten, n.d.; new ed. London: Chatto & Windus, 1897.

See the Gifford edition, immediately above.

SECONDARY WORKS

Ball, Robert Hamilton. THE AMAZING CAREER OF SIR GILES OVERREACH, BEING THE LIFE AND ADVENTURES OF A NEFARIOUS SCOUNDREL WHO FOR THREE CENTURIES PURSUED HIS SINISTER DESIGNS IN ALMOST ALL THE THEATRES OF THE BRITISH ISLES AND AMERICA, THE WHOLE COMPRISING A HISTORY OF THE STAGE. Princeton, N.J.: Princeton University Press; London: Oxford University Press, 1939.

Though the approach is whimsical, treating Massinger's Overreach (from A NEW WAY TO PAY OLD DEBTS) as a person (p. 3: "This book is the biography of a character who actually never lived"), the book is fully researched and documented. It uses the stage history of A NEW WAY TO PAY OLD DEBTS as an approach to evaluating the play and to characterizing the stage in England and America.

Chelli, Maurice. LE DRAME DE MASSINGER. Lyon: M. Audin, 1923; Paris: Societe d'Editions Les Belles Lettres, 1924.

A consideration of Massinger's life, reputation, collaboration, and dramatic technique.

_____. ETUDE SUR LA COLLABORATION DE MASSINGER AVEC FLETCHER ET SON GROUPE.

See the main entry in Section 3: Beaumont and Fletcher.

Cruickshank, A.H. PHILIP MASSINGER. New York: Frederick A. Stokes, n.d.; Oxford: Basil Blackwell, 1920.

Largely concerned with the plays, Cruickshank sees Massinger as classical: "sober, well balanced, dignified, and lucid . . . the most Greek of his generation" (p. 142). Various appendices.

Dunn, T.A. PHILIP MASSINGER: THE MAN AND THE PLAYWRIGHT. London: Thomas Nelson and Sons for the University College of Ghana, 1957.

Dunn asserts that Massinger cannot be considered "a great or even always a very good dramatist" but that his work is significant because he "was the principal writer for the public theatres from 1625 to 1640" (p. v). Bibliography.

Lawless, Donald S. PHILIP MASSINGER AND HIS ASSOCIATES. Ball State Monograph No. 10, Publications in English, No. 6. Muncie, Ind.: Ball State University Press, 1967.

Focused on Massinger's life and his "relation to his patrons and other members of his circle" (p. v). Bibliography.

Makkink, Henri Jacob. PHILIP MASSINGER AND JOHN FLETCHER, A COMPARISON.

See the main entry in Section 3: Beaumont and Fletcher.

Maxwell, Baldwin. STUDIES IN BEAUMONT, FLETCHER, AND MASSINGER.

See the main entry in Section 3: Beaumont and Fletcher.

Peterson, J.M. THE DOROTHEA LEGEND: ITS EARLIEST RECORDS, MIDDLE ENGLISH VERSIONS, AND INFLUENCE ON PHILIP MASSINGER'S "VIRGIN MARTYR." Heidelberg: Rossler & Herbert, 1910.

Peterson argues that "two versions of the Dorothea legend" and "the Agnes legend" influenced Massinger's play (see, for example, p. 108).

23. THOMAS MIDDLETON

BIBLIOGRAPHIES

Tannenbaum, Samuel A[aron], and Dorothy R. Tannenbaum, comps. ELIZABETHAN BIBLIOGRAPHIES. Vol. V. Port Washington, N.Y.: Kennikat Press, 1967.

Reprints the 1940 Tannenbaum bibliography of Middleton. Designed as an exhaustive, unannotated listing.

Donovan, Dennis, comp. ELIZABETHAN BIBLIOGRAPHIES SUPPLEMENTS. Vol. I. London: Nether Press, 1967.

Includes a bibliography of Middleton, 1939-65. Less inclusive than the Tannenbaum, which it supplements. Groups entries annually. No annotation.

EDITIONS

THE WORKS OF THOMAS MIDDLETON. NOW FIRST COLLECTED, WITH SOME ACCOUNT OF THE AUTHOR, AND NOTES. Ed. Alexander Dyce. 5 vols. London: Edward Lumley, 1840.

As described by title.

THE WORKS OF THOMAS MIDDLETON. Ed. A.H. Bullen. 8 vols. London: John C. Nimmo, 1885-86.

Bullen supplies an introduction and notes.

THOMAS MIDDLETON. Ed. Martin W. Sampson. New York, Cincinnati, Chicago: American Book Co., 1915.

Introduction, some notes.

Because editions of Middleton's works are old and not extensively annotated, the student will want to see editions of single plays. Consult such series as the New Mermaids, the Regents Renaissance Drama Series, the Fountainwell Drama Series, and the Revels Plays, for example. See Part 1, Section 2 C: Editions--Serial and Multi-Volume Editions, on the general editorial policies of these various series.

SECONDARY WORKS

Barker, Richard Hindry. THOMAS MIDDLETON. New York: Columbia University Press, 1958.

Barker's concern is to establish Middleton's place as a playwright, which he considers rather high: "He is not indeed another Shakespeare or another Jonson, but he stands above his other contemporaries. He is the third great dramatist of the Jacobean stage" (p. 153). Bibliography.

Brittin, Norman A. THOMAS MIDDLETON. Twayne's English Authors Series, No. 139. New York: Twayne Publishers, 1972.

Brittin proposes "to provide a guide to the whole body of Middleton's work in the light of contemporary scholarship," considering him as a representative Jacobean writer of comedy and tragedy and emphasizing his "powers of construction, his psychological penetration, his realistic social settings, the appropriateness of his style at its best, and his almost-modern intelligence" (p. [5]). Bibliography.

Dunkel, Wilbur Dwight. THE DRAMATIC TECHNIQUE OF MIDDLETON IN HIS COMEDIES OF LONDON LIFE. 1926; reprint ed. New York: Russell & Russell, 1967.

Based on a selected group of plays, the discussion deals with "Action," "Character," "Devices and Conventions," "Emotional Values," and "Dialogue."

Farr, Dorothy M. THOMAS MIDDLETON AND THE DRAMA OF REALISM: A STUDY OF SOME REPRESENTATIVE PLAYS. Edinburgh: Oliver & Boyd, 1973.

The study sees "Middleton's 'message'" as "contained in . . . an irony born of the equivocal view of life which for Middleton was basic to the human comedy" (p. 1). The conclusion conjectures that "in the play he did not write he could have anticipated the moderns" (p. 124). Bibliography.

Holmes, David M. THE ART OF THOMAS MIDDLETON: A CRITICAL STUDY. Oxford: Clarendon Press, 1970.

In a discussion oriented towards the analysis of form and theme,

Holmes argues that "[i]n Middleton's dramatic microcosm success as a human being" involves the development of some knowledge of self, while "tragedy lies in ignorance of self and the world, moral incompetence, and the perversion of the human spirit" (p. 200). Bibliography.

Johansson, Bertil. LAW AND LAWYERS IN ELIZABETHAN ENGLAND AS EVIDENCED IN THE PLAYS OF BEN JONSON AND THOMAS MIDDLETON.

See the main entry in Section 15: Ben Jonson.

_____. RELIGION AND SUPERSTITION IN THE PLAYS OF BEN JONSON AND THOMAS MIDDLETON.

See the main entry in Section 15: Ben Jonson.

[Leonard], Pauline Gertrude Wiggin. AN INQUIRY INTO THE AUTHORSHIP OF THE MIDDLETON-ROWLEY PLAYS. Radcliffe College Monographs, No. 9. Boston: Ginn & Co., 1897.

A fifty-nine-page monograph which attempts the hazardous task of identifying the "hands" of collaborators. (Schoenbaum, in MIDDLETON'S TRAGEDIES, p. 204, immediately below, refers to "the high quality of the Wiggin monograph"; however, Brittin, in THOMAS MIDDLETON, p. 171, above, calls Schoenbaum's early view--i.e., that of the comment here noted--a "radical" notion of the Middleton canon.)

Schoenbaum, Samuel. MIDDLETON'S TRAGEDIES: A CRITICAL STUDY. Columbia University Studies in English and Comparative Literature, No. 168. New York: Columbia University Press, 1955.

Schoenbaum proposes to study canon, sources, influences, and the plays themselves, to reveal Middleton's "special contribution" and "to call attention to the moral order which seems so clearly to underlie the action of the plays" (p. [vii]). Schoenbaum sees Middleton as a flawed but significant dramatist, next after Shakespeare and before Ford, Chapman, and Webster "in the hierarchy of Jacobean writers of tragedy" (p. 150). Bibliography.

Stagg, Louis C. AN INDEX TO THE FIGURATIVE LANGUAGE OF THOMAS MIDDLETON'S TRAGEDIES. Charlottesville: Bibliographical Society of the University of Virginia, 1970.

One of a series of seven such indexes prepared by Stagg.

Wiggin, Pauline Gertrude.

See [Leonard], Pauline Gertrude Wiggin.

24. THOMAS NASHE

BIBLIOGRAPHIES

Tannenbaum, Samuel A[aron], and Dorothy R. Tannenbaum, comps. ELIZABETHAN BIBLIOGRAPHIES. Vol. VI. Port Washington, N.Y.: Kennikat Press, 1967.

> Reprints the 1941 Tannenbaum bibliography of Nashe. Designed as an exhaustive, unannotated listing.

Johnson, Robert C[arl], comp. ELIZABETHAN BIBLIOGRAPHIES SUPPLEMENTS. Vol. V. London: Nether Press, 1968.

> Includes a bibliography of Nashe, 1941-65. Less inclusive than the Tannenbaum, which it supplements. Arranges entries in annual groups.

EDITIONS

THE WORKS OF THOMAS NASHE, EDITED FROM THE ORIGINAL TEXTS. Ed. Ronald B. McKerrow. 5 vols. London: A.H. Bullen, 1904-8; Sidgwick and Jackson, 1910.

> See the edition immediately below.

THE WORKS OF THOMAS NASHE, EDITED FROM THE ORIGINAL TEXTS BY RONALD B. MCKERROW, REPRINTED FROM THE ORIGINAL EDITION WITH CORRECTIONS AND SUPPLEMENTARY NOTES BY F.P. WILSON. 5 vols. Oxford: Basil Blackwell, 1958.

> McKerrow and Wilson provide an old-spelling text with extensive apparatus.

SECONDARY WORKS

Born, Hanspeter. THE RARE WIT AND THE RUDE GROOM: THE AUTHOR-

SHIP OF "A KNACK TO KNOW A KNAVE" IN RELATION TO GREENE, NASHE & SHAKESPEARE.

See the main entry in Section 12: Robert Greene.

Harman, Edward George. GABRIEL HARVEY AND THOMAS NASHE. London: J.M. Ouseley & Son, 1923.

Harman attempts to elucidate the "so-called Harvey-Nashe 'Controversy,'" arguing a position which he does not expect to "meet with universal acceptance": that "under the various supposed personalities on the anti-Harvey side . . . lay concealed one individuality," Francis Bacon. Harman argues that Bacon "flood[ed] the country anonymously--or rather through assumed names--with writings by which English literature, then practically non-existent, was to be formed" (pp. [1]-5).

Harvey, Gabriel. THE WORKS.

See the main entry in Part 1, Section 10: Contemporary and Other Early Records, Allusions, Criticism, Etc. Nashe is one of Harvey's subjects.

Hibbard, G.R. THOMAS NASHE: A CRITICAL INTRODUCTION. Cambridge, Mass.: Harvard University Press, 1962.

Although Hibbard's "Introduction" urges that Nashe receive "the recognition he deserves as a literary artist" (p. xi), the "Conclusion" concedes that "[t]here is a tantalizing gap between the talents that were his and what he actually achieved with them" (p. 250). Hibbard suggests that Nashe lacked the gift for drama which would have enabled him to succeed in his times, while the times did not offer the form for which he might have been best suited, the novel.

Schrickx, W. SHAKESPEARE'S EARLY CONTEMPORARIES: THE BACKGROUND OF THE HARVEY-NASHE POLEMIC AND "LOVE'S LABOUR'S LOST." Antwerpen: Nederlandsche Boekhandel, 1956.

Schrickx's "Preface" (p. vi) asserts that "many mythological terms came to have strong topical and personal meanings," a possibility which he studies in Chapman's poem, "The Shadow of Night," and in works by Nashe, Fraunce, Greene, Harvey, and others, "with a view to determining the matrix from which Shakespeare's LOVE'S LABOUR'S LOST seems to have issued." Bibliography.

25. THOMAS NORTON AND THOMAS SACKVILLE

EDITIONS

THE WORKS OF THOMAS SACKVILLE, LORD BUCKHURST, AFTERWARDS LORD TREASURER TO QUEEN ELIZABETH AND EARL OF DORSET. Ed. Reginald W. Sackville-West. London: John Russell Smith, 1859.

The edition provides a "Biographical Memoir" with an appendix of Sackville's letters and the texts of FERREX AND PORREX and THE LAST PART OF THE MIRROUR FOR MAGISTRATES.

THE DRAMATIC WRITINGS OF RICHARD EDWARDS, THOMAS NORTON, AND THOMAS SACKVILLE, COMPRISING "DAMON AND PITHIAS"--"PALAMON AND ARCYTE" (NOTE)--"GORBODUC" (OR "FERREX AND PORREX")--NOTE-BOOK AND WORD-LIST. Ed. John Stephen Farmer. 1906; reprint ed. Guildford, England: Charles W. Traylen, 1966.

The 1966 edition is a facsimile of the 1906. It provides rather slight critical apparatus.

GORBODUC: OR, FERREX AND PORREX. Ed. Irby B. Cauthen, Jr. Regents Renaissance Drama Series. Lincoln: University of Nebraska Press, 1970.

A scholarly edition with various useful materials, including an appendix, "The Reply of Elizabeth to the House of Commons Touching the Succession" and another giving a chronology of Norton and Sackville.

GORBODUC is frequently reprinted in anthologies. See Part 1, Section 2 B: Editions--Miscellaneous Medieval and Tudor Plays.

SECONDARY WORKS

Bacquet, Paul. UN CONTEMPORAIN D'ELISABETH I: THOMAS SACKVILLE: L'HOMME ET L'OEUVRE. Travaux d'Humanisme et Renaissance, No. 76. Geneve: Librairie Droz, 1966.

Bacquet studies Sackville's life and works, giving three chapters to GORBODUC. Extensive bibliography.

Swart, J. THOMAS SACKVILLE: A STUDY IN SIXTEENTH-CENTURY POETRY. Groningen Studies in English, I. Batavia: J.B. Wolters, 1949.

Swart tries to see Sackville as his contemporaries did. Because he has used "the earliest sources for Sackville's life, and . . . sources that would have been available to Sackville" (p. [136]), his bibliography is rich in early materials.

Watt, Homer Andrew. GORBODUC; OR, FERREX AND PORREX. Bulletin of the University of Wisconsin, No. 351. Philology and Literature Series, Vol. 5, No. 1. Madison: University of Wisconsin, 1910.

Watt studies the play's "genesis," "authorship," "political import," "sources," and the like, to conclude that while the play has limitations and while "its classical spirit did not permanently affect the later drama," it "is important as furnishing a first example of certain very definite innovations in English dramatic art" (p. 92).

Whole titles devoted to Norton and Sackville are scarce, but they are regularly discussed in the context of their historical importance; see Part 1, Section 5: General Literary Histories; Section 6: General Studies of the Drama; Section 8: Studies of Tudor and Stuart Drama.

26. THE PARNASSUS PLAYS

EDITIONS

"THE PILGRIMAGE TO PARNASSUS" WITH THE TWO PARTS OF "THE RETURN FROM PARNASSUS." THREE COMEDIES PERFORMED IN ST. JOHN'S COLLEGE CAMBRIDGE A.D. MDXCVII-MDCI. EDITED FROM MSS. Ed. W.D. Macray. Oxford: Clarendon Press, 1886.

Although the critical apparatus is slight, Macray performed a useful act in making available this anonymous "trilogy of dramas which, although known to have once existed, has lain _perdu_ to the world from the time of its composition, except with regard to the third part" ("Preface"). The texts are slightly modernized.

THE RETURN FROM PARNASSUS OR THE SCOURGE OF SIMONY. Ed. [William Henry] Oliphant Smeaton. The Temple Dramatists. London: J.M. Dent, 1905.

Smeaton has edited one of the Parnassus group, with introduction, glossary, and notes.

THE THREE PARNASSUS PLAYS (1598-1601). Ed. J.B. Leishman. London: Ivor Nicholson & Watson, 1949.

An old spelling edition with extensive apparatus.

27. GEORGE PEELE

BIBLIOGRAPHIES

Larsen, Thorlief. "A Bibliography of the Writings of George Peele." MODERN PHILOLOGY, 32 (1934), 143-56.

Full descriptions. Larsen omits "the doubtful plays as well as the spurious pieces" (p. 143).

Tannenbaum, Samuel A[aron], and Dorothy R. Tannenbaum, comps. ELIZABETHAN BIBLIOGRAPHIES. Vol. VI. Port Washington, N.Y.: Kennikat Press, 1967.

Reprints the 1940 Tannenbaum bibliography of Peele, which is designed as an exhaustive, unannotated listing.

Johnson, Robert C[arl], comp. ELIZABETHAN BIBLIOGRAPHIES SUPPLEMENTS. Vol. V. London: Nether Press, 1968.

Includes a bibliography of Peele, 1939-65. Less inclusive than the Tannenbaum, which it supplements. Entries grouped annually. No annotation.

EDITIONS

THE WORKS OF GEORGE PEELE: NOW FIRST COLLECTED, WITH SOME ACCOUNT OF HIS WRITINGS, AND NOTES. Ed. Alexander Dyce. 2 vols. London: William Pickering, 1828, with various reprintings and revisions, 1829, 1839, 1881.

THE WORKS OF GEORGE PEELE. Ed. A.H. Bullen. 2 vols. London: John C. Nimmo, 1888.

The editor's comments on the preparation of the text indicate the care with which he has attended to it. He provides a preface, an introduction, and light notes.

THE LIFE AND WORKS OF GEORGE PEELE. General ed., Charles T. Prouty. 3 vols. New Haven, Conn.: Yale University Press, 1952-70.

The materials have individual editors. Volume I, edited by David H. Horne, contains a LIFE of Peele and the MINOR WORKS. Volume II contains plays edited by Frank S. Hook and John Yoklavich; Volume III, plays edited by R. Mark Benlow, Elmer Blistein, and Frank S. Hook. The texts adhere closely to the originals.

SECONDARY WORKS

Ashley, Leonard R.N. AUTHORSHIP AND EVIDENCE: A STUDY OF ATTRIBUTION AND THE RENAISSANCE DRAMA ILLUSTRATED BY THE CASE OF GEORGE PEELE (1556-1596). Etudes de Philologie et d'Histoire, No. 6. Geneve: Librairie Droz, 1968.

Ashley states as his objective, not so much the determination of the Peele canon, as the exploration of a methodology which will be reliable. He provides two appendices, "Plays of Unknown or Uncertain Authorship 1556-1660" and "Lost Plays of Unknown or Disputed Authorship 1556-1660," and a bibliography.

_____. GEORGE PEELE. New York: Twayne Publishers, 1970.

Ashley provides a review of Peele's life and of his general position as an author, then gives a chapter to each of these pieces by Peele: THE ARRAIGNMENT OF PARIS, THE BATTLE OF ALCAZAR, THE FAMOUS CHRONICLE OF KING EDWARD THE FIRST, THE OLD WIVES' TALE, and THE LOVE OF KING DAVID AND FAIR BETHSABE, with a final chapter on "Pageants, Poems, Lost Plays, and Attributions." Extensive bibliography, especially important for periodical and other essay-length materials.

Cheffaud, P.H. GEORGE PEELE (1558-1596?). Paris: F. Alcan, 1913.

A life-and-works study, in French. Johnson, in ELIZABETHAN BIBLIOGRAPHIES SUPPLEMENTS (above), mentions a translation by Leslie Tomlinson Longwell ("Unpublished doctoral dissertation, University of Washington, 1942").

Hunter, G[eorge] K. LYLY AND PEELE.

See the main entry in Section 19: John Lyly.

Senn, Werner. STUDIES IN THE DRAMATIC CONSTRUCTION OF ROBERT GREENE AND GEORGE PEELE.

See the main entry in Section 12: Robert Greene.

28. JAMES SHIRLEY

BIBLIOGRAPHIES

Tannenbaum, Samuel A[aron], and Dorothy R. Tannenbaum, comps. ELIZABETHAN BIBLIOGRAPHIES. Vol. IX. Port Washington, N.Y.: Kennikat Press, 1967.

Reprints the 1946 Tannenbaum bibliography of Shirley, which is designed as an exhaustive, unannotated listing.

Pennel, Charles A., and William P. Williams, comps. ELIZABETHAN BIBLIOGRAPHIES SUPPLEMENTS. Vol. VIII. London: Nether Press, 1968.

Includes a bibliography of Shirley, 1945-65. Less inclusive than the Tannenbaum, which it supplements. Entries arranged in annual groups. No annotation.

EDITIONS

THE DRAMATIC WORKS AND POEMS OF JAMES SHIRLEY, NOW FIRST COLLECTED; WITH NOTES BY THE LATE WILLIAM GIFFORD, ESQ. AND ADDITIONAL NOTES, AND SOME ACCOUNT OF SHIRLEY AND HIS WRITINGS, BY THE REV. ALEXANDER DYCE. 6 vols. London: John Murray, 1833.

As described by title.

SECONDARY WORKS

Forsythe, Robert Stanley. THE RELATIONS OF SHIRLEY'S PLAYS TO THE ELIZABETHAN DRAMA. 1914; reprint ed. New York: Benjamin Blom, 1965.

An exploration of Shirley's sources, arranged so as to offer information about Shirley and to provide "lists of stock incidents, situations, devices, and characters" (p. ix). The format does not lend itself to continuous reading, but the material is displayed so that one can discover quickly the details of a given topic.

Gregory, George MacKendricks. TWO STUDIES IN JAMES SHIRLEY. I. SHIRLEY'S AUTHORSHIP OF "THE TRAYTOR"; II. SHIRLEY'S HEADMASTERSHIP OF THE FREE GRAMMAR SCHOOL OF ST. ALBANS. Durham, N.C.: Duke University, 1935.

> The title page carries the information that the studies are "[a] digest of matter selected from a dissertation entitled 'James Shirley's THE TRAYTOR,' accepted by the Graduate School of Arts and Sciences, Duke University, in 1932."

Nason, Arthur Huntington. JAMES SHIRLEY, DRAMATIST: A BIOGRAPHICAL AND CRITICAL STUDY. New York: A.H. Nason, Publisher, 1915.

> A two-part study of the "Life" and the "Plays."

Parlin, Hanson T. A STUDY IN SHIRLEY'S COMEDIES OF LONDON LIFE. Bulletin of the University of Texas No. 371, Humanistic Series, No. 17, Studies in English, No. 2. Austin: University of Texas, 1914.

> A sixty-eight page study originally designed as the introduction to an abandoned edition of THE BALL.

Radtke, Stephen J. JAMES SHIRLEY: HIS CATHOLIC PHILOSOPHY OF LIFE. Washington, D.C.: The Catholic University of America, 1929.

> A study designed "to demonstrate the fact of a practical Catholicism in the works of James Shirley, and the effects of this in his maturer dramas" (p. 98).

29. JOHN SKELTON

BIBLIOGRAPHIES

Kinsman, Robert S., and Theodore Yonge, comps. JOHN SKELTON: CANON AND CENSUS. Renaissance Society of America, Bibliographies and Indexes, No. 4. Darien, Conn.: Monographic Press, for the Renaissance Society of America, 1967.

Kinsman and Yonge write: "We have compiled this book in an effort to supply satisfactory accounts of the writings of John Skelton, and of early printed editions of his works to 1600" (p. ix).

EDITIONS

MAGNYFYCENCE, A MORAL PLAY. Ed. Robert Lee Ramsay. Early English Text Society, Extra Series, No. 98. London: Published for the Early English Text Society by Kegan Paul, Trench, Trubner & Co., 1906.

The edition has a long and thorough introduction--though William O. Harris, in SKELTON'S "MAGNYFYCENCE" (p. 12; see Secondary Works), cautions against ready acceptance of some of Ramsay's political interpretations.

SECONDARY WORKS

Carpenter, Nan Cooke. JOHN SKELTON. Twayne's English Authors Series, No. 61. New York: Twayne Publishers, 1967.

In a general review of the life and works, the author provides a discussion of MAGNIFICENCE. Bibliography.

Edwards, H.L.R. SKELTON: THE LIFE AND TIMES OF AN EARLY TUDOR POET. London: Jonathan Cape, 1949.

A broad biographical study, with a chapter devoted to Skelton as a playwright. Bibliography.

Fish, Stanley Eugene. JOHN SKELTON'S POETRY. Yale Studies in English, Vol. 157. New Haven, Conn., and London: Yale University Press, 1965.

Fish does not discuss Skelton as a playwright, but his reassessment of the poetry provides a useful background for reading MAGNIFICENCE.

Gordon, Ian A. JOHN SKELTON, POET LAUREATE. 1943; reprint ed. New York: Octagon Books, 1970.

Gordon says little about the play, thinks of Skelton as far more the poet than the playwright.

Green, Peter. JOHN SKELTON. Writers and Their Work, No. 128. London and New York: Published for the British Council and the National Book League by Longmans, Green & Co., 1960.

Green sees Skelton as "the last wholly authentic utterance of the Middle Ages" (p. 39). Bibliography.

Harris, William O. SKELTON'S "MAGNYFYCENCE" AND THE CARDINAL VIRTUE TRADITION. Chapel Hill: University of North Carolina Press, 1965.

In a valuable study, Harris interprets MAGNIFICENCE through the evidence offered by the play, by other Skelton pieces, and by contemporary moral treatises. He argues that "magnificence" is the cardinal virtue of _fortitudo_, not an Aristotelean magnificence, and that the play so interpreted is an organic, self-consistent whole. Bibliography.

Heiserman, Arthur R. SKELTON AND SATIRE. Chicago: University of Chicago Press, 1961.

In this "historical critique of John Skelton's satires and a critical history of the traditions of medieval satire with which they worked" (see the "Preface"), Heiserman discusses MAGNIFICENCE, particularly in Chapter 3. Bibliography.

Lloyd, L.J. JOHN SKELTON: A SKETCH OF HIS LIFE AND WRITINGS. Oxford: Basil Blackwell, 1938.

The "Preface" modestly asserts: "This little book does not claim to be anything more than an introduction to its subject." Lloyd provides a chapter on MAGNIFICENCE.

Nelson, William. JOHN SKELTON, LAUREATE. Columbia University Studies in English and Comparative Literature, No. 139. 1939; reprint ed. New York: Russell & Russell, 1964.

More concerned with the man and the poetry than with the play, but a useful study.

Pollet, Maurice. JOHN SKELTON: POET OF TUDOR ENGLAND. Trans. John Warrington. London: J.M. Dent & Sons, 1971.

Pollet's study was published in France in 1962. In the "Foreword" Pollet says that Skelton is so surrounded by controversy and opinion, hostile and friendly, as to require a severe, new critical evaluation of "every document we possess" (pp. xi-xii). He concludes his evaluation by ranking Skelton among "the most rugged minds of English literature. . . . recognized as a master" and by suggesting that Skelton "is indeed quaintly in tune with modern times inasmuch as he finally preferred vigour to beauty" (p. 202). Bibliography.

30. [WILLIAM STEVENSON?]

EDITIONS

GAMMER GURTON'S NEEDLE. Ed. John S. Farmer. The Museum Dramatists. London: Published by Gibbings & Co. for the Early English Drama Society, 1906.

Farmer supplies a brief introduction, notes, and a "Word-List."

GAMMER GVRTON'S NEDLE BY MR. S. MR. OF ART. Ed. H.F.B. Brett-Smith. Percy Reprints, No. 2. Boston and New York: Houghton Mifflin, 1920.

Whether the play is by Stevenson or not, he is, as Brett-Smith remarks, the "most likely" candidate, having "the right initial" and the proper degree ("Introduction," pp. v-vi). GAMMER GURTON'S NEEDLE has both historic and intrinsic significance. Brett-Smith supplies a few notes.

See also: reprints of the play in various anthologies (see Part 1, Section 2 B: Editions--Miscellaneous Medieval and Tudor Plays).

SECONDARY WORKS

Consult Part 1, Section 5: General Literary Histories; Section 6: General Studies of the Drama; Section 8: Studies of Tudor and Stuart Drama, for books which discuss GAMMER GURTON.

31. JOHN SUCKLING

EDITIONS

FRAGMENTA AVREA. A COLLECTION OF ALL THE INCOMPARABLE PEECES WRITTEN BY SIR JOHN SVCKLING AND PUBLISHED BY A FRIEND TO PERPETUATE HIS MEMORY. PRINTED BY HIS OWNE COPIES. London: Humphrey Moseley, 1646.

The edition contains poems, letters, AN ACCOUNT OF RELIGION BY REASON, and the plays AGLAVRA, THE GOBLINS, and BRENNORALT. It lacks the incomplete play THE SAD ONE.

THE POEMS, PLAYS, AND OTHER REMAINS OF SIR JOHN SUCKLING, WITH A COPIOUS ACCOUNT OF THE AUTHOR, NOTES, AND AN APPENDIX OF ILLUSTRATIVE PIECES. Ed. W. Carew Hazlitt. 2nd ed. 2 vols. London: Reeves and Turner, 1892.

Hazlitt provides a long introduction but less other apparatus than the title page might lead one to expect. In addition to the plays in the Moseley edition, he includes THE SAD ONE.

THE WORKS OF SIR JOHN SUCKLING IN PROSE AND VERSE. Ed. A. Hamilton Thompson. 1910; reprint ed. New York: Russell & Russell, 1964.

Thompson offers the same plays as does Hazlitt. He provides a short introduction and rather extensive notes. The text is in modern spelling.

THE WORKS OF SIR JOHN SUCKLING. Ed. Thomas Clayton and L.A. Beaurline. 2 vols. Oxford: Clarendon Press, 1971.

Volume I, THE NON-DRAMATIC WORKS, edited by Clayton, contains a "General Introduction" in two parts, "Suckling's Life" and "Suckling's Reputation," as well as such other material as letters. Volume II, edited by Beaurline, contains the plays (the same titles as in Hazlitt and Thompson) in a meticulous "old spelling, critical edition"--see Volume II, page [xl], "The Treatment of the Text," on editorial practices.

SECONDARY WORKS

Suckling has faired better in editions of the plays than in studies of his work as a playwright. He is referred to in books on the general history of drama and in studies directed more explicitly to poetry than to drama. References to Suckling will be found in some of the books in Part 1, Section 5: General Literary Histories; Section 6: General Studies of the Drama; and Section 8: Studies of Tudor and Stuart Drama.

32. CYRIL TOURNEUR

BIBLIOGRAPHIES

Tannenbaum, Samuel A[aron], and Dorothy R. Tannenbaum, comps. ELIZABETHAN BIBLIOGRAPHIES. Vol. X. Port Washington, N.Y.: Kennikat Press, 1967.

Reprints the 1946 Tannenbaum bibliography of Tourneur, which is intended as an exhaustive, unannotated listing.

Donovan, Dennis, comp. ELIZABETHAN BIBLIOGRAPHIES SUPPLEMENTS. Vol. II. London: Nether Press, 1967.

Includes a bibliography of Tourneur for 1945-65. Less inclusive than the Tannenbaum, which it supplements. Groups entries annually. No annotation.

EDITIONS

THE PLAYS AND POEMS OF CYRIL TOURNEUR, . . . WITH CRITICAL INTRODUCTION AND NOTES. Ed. John Churton Collins. 2 vols. London: Chatto and Windus, 1878.

Title describes.

THE WORKS OF CYRIL TOURNEUR. Ed. Allardyce Nicoll. 1930; reprint ed. New York: Russell & Russell, 1963.

Nicoll states two basic editorial principles: "[T]he first, to present a text which remains as faithful as possible to the original editions; and the second, to make the volume a complete record of Tourneur's literary activities" (p. vii). The "Introduction" (pp. 1-46) reviews Tourneur's life and literary achievement. Among the plays, Nicoll includes "Music for THE NOBLEMAN," which he indicates is probably not Tourneur's. See pages 47-49 on his decision not to include THE SECOND MAYDEN'S TRAGEDY, THE HONEST MAN'S FORTUNE, and CHARLEMAGNE, OR THE DISTRACTED EMPEROR. The plays are suitably annotated.

SECONDARY WORKS

Murray, Peter B. A STUDY OF CYRIL TOURNEUR. Philadelphia: University of Pennsylvania Press; London: Oxford University Press, 1964.

Concerned to rectify the problem of Tourneur's current neglect, Murray provides a detailed study of THE TRANSFORMED METAMORPHOSIS, THE ATHEIST'S TRAGEDY, and THE REVENGER'S TRAGEDY and argues that there is "conclusive internal evidence" that THE REVENGER'S TRAGEDY is Middleton's, not Tourneur's. Bibliography.

Stagg, Louis C. AN INDEX TO THE FIGURATIVE LANGUAGE OF CYRIL TOURNEUR'S TRAGEDIES. Charlottesville: Bibliographical Society of the University of Virginia, 1970.

One of a series of seven such indexes prepared by Stagg.

33. NICHOLAS UDALL

EDITIONS

ROISTER DOISTER, WRITTEN, PROBABLY ALSO REPRESENTED, BEFORE 1533. Ed. Edward Arber. English Reprints No. 17. Westminster: A. Constable, 1899.

Arber retains the old spelling and supplies a brief preface.

THE DRAMATIC WRITINGS OF NICHOLAS UDALL, COMPRISING "RALPH ROISTER DOISTER"--A NOTE ON UDALL'S LOST PLAYS--NOTE-BOOK AND WORD-LIST. Ed. John S. Farmer. 1906; reprint ed. Guildford, England: Charles W. Traylen; New York: Barnes & Noble, 1966.

The apparatus is confined to that indicated in the title.

RALPH ROISTER DOISTER. THE FIRST REGULAR ENGLISH COMEDY. Ed. W.H. Williams and P.A. Robin. Temple Dramatists. London: J.M. Dent, Aldine House, 1911.

The editors provide preface, notes, and glossary in a modern-spelling text.

ROISTER DOISTER. Ed. W.W. Greg. Malone Society Reprints. London: Oxford University Press, 1935.

A faithful reprint.

RESPUBLICA: AN INTERLUDE FOR CHRISTMAS 1553, ATTRIBUTED TO NICHOLAS UDALL. Re-edited, W.W. Greg. Early English Text Society, Original Series, No. 226. London: Published for the Early English Text Society by Oxford University Press, 1952.

Introduction, notes, glossary.

RALPH ROISTER DOISTER is often printed in collections. See Part 1, Section 2 B: Editions--Miscellaneous Medieval and Tudor Plays.

SECONDARY WORKS

Edgerton, William L. NICHOLAS UDALL. Twayne's English Authors Series, No. 30. New York: Twayne Publishers, 1966.

Edgerton states his purposes as "to spell out Udall's achievements so that his ROISTER DOISTER will be seen to be the work of a scholar with a background that fitted him especially well for writing the first regular English Comedy" and "to see in focus what a typical Protestant humanist contributed to Tudor literature" (pp. [7]-8). Bibliography.

Udall is regularly discussed in histories of the drama. See Part 1, Section 5: General Literary Histories; Section 6: General Studies of the Drama; Section 8: Studies of Tudor and Stuart Drama.

34. JOHN WEBSTER

BIBLIOGRAPHIES

Tannenbaum, Samuel A[aron], and Dorothy R. Tannenbaum, comps. ELIZABETHAN BIBLIOGRAPHIES. Vol. X. Port Washington, N.Y.: Kennikat Press, 1967.

Reprints the 1941 Tannenbaum bibliography of Webster, which is designed as an exhaustive, unannotated listing.

Donovan, Dennis, comp. ELIZABETHAN BIBLIOGRAPHIES SUPPLEMENTS. Vol. I. London: Nether Press, 1967.

Includes a bibliography of Webster, 1940-65. Less exhaustive than the Tannenbaum, which it supplements. Entries are grouped annually. No annotation.

EDITIONS

THE WORKS OF JOHN WEBSTER: WITH SOME ACCOUNT OF THE AUTHOR AND NOTES. Ed. Alexander Dyce. Rev. ed. London: Edward Moxon, 1857.

The editor's "Notice" (p. [v]) says of the revised edition: "I have considerably altered both the Text and Notes throughout, and made some slight additions to the Memoir of the Poet. I have also excluded from the present edition a worthless drama, which I too hastily admitted into the former one,--THE TRACIAN WONDER." This is a one-volume edition; the edition of 1830 is in four volumes.

THE DRAMATIC WORKS OF JOHN WEBSTER. Ed. William Hazlitt. 4 vols. London: Reeves & Turner, 1897.

Brief introduction, light notes.

THE COMPLETE WORKS OF JOHN WEBSTER. Ed. F[rank] L. Lucas. 4 vols. 1927; reprint ed. London: Chatto & Windus; New York: Gordian Press, 1966.

Lucas retains the original spelling and for the most part the original punctuation. He writes: "My rule has been--'As little alteration as possible: but no ambiguity'" (Vol. I, p. xi). Lucas provides a fine edition, readable, thoroughly annotated and documented, with a life of Webster in Volume I.

SECONDARY WORKS

Ansari, K.H. JOHN WEBSTER: IMAGE PATTERNS & CANON. Kerala, India: Jalaluddin Rumi; Delhi: Sterling Publishers; Mystic, Conn.: Verry, 1969.

Ansari asserts (p. [vii]) that the study provides a means "to explain [Webster's] poetic vision and to qualify the traditional impression of Webster as a melodramatist" and also to restore "the classic play APPIUS AND VIRGINIA to Webster on the basis of its structural imagery and image clusters."

Berry, Ralph. THE ART OF JOHN WEBSTER. Oxford: Clarendon Press, 1972.

The "Preface" indicates the confines of the study: an analysis of "the three surviving plays . . . known to be solely [Webster's] work" analyzed "through the simple categories of form and content" (pp. [vii]-viii). Berry proposes that the form is baroque and that in content "[e]ach play displays a profound apprehension of evil . . . [and] hinges on the central concept of the Law--the moralist's metaphor, whereby every manifestation of evil is tested and rebuked by the sanctions of time" (p. [168]).

Bogard, Travis. THE TRAGIC SATIRE OF JOHN WEBSTER. 1955; reprint ed. New York: Russell & Russell, 1965.

Bogard (pp. vii-viii) declares the intention to read Webster "historically," in terms of Jacobean traditions, and "critically, without detailed reference to any period." He considers Webster "a great dramatist because, seeing the world with both pity and contempt, he remained faithful to his vision by blending two almost incompatible genres, tragedy and satire" (p. ix).

Boklund, Gunnar. "THE DUCHESS OF MALFI": SOURCES, THEMES, CHARACTERS. Cambridge, Mass.: Harvard University Press, 1962.

Boklund directs the study to the problems of sources, meaning, and dramatic value. He analyzes both confirmed sources and, in Chapter II, "Potential Secondary Sources."

______. THE SOURCES OF "THE WHITE DEVIL." Universitat Engelska Seminaret: Essays and Studies in English Language and Literature, No. 17. Uppsala: A.B. Lundequistska; Copenhagen: Ejnar Munksgaard; Cambridge, Mass.: Harvard University Press, 1957.

Boklund (p. 11) describes the study as "a survey of the early accounts of Vittoria Accoramboni's life that have been available to me," which, he says, at least makes it "obvious which documents need not be investigated." Boklund offers a reading of the play and provides an extensive bibliography of manuscript and printed materials (pp. 201-18). Although he points out (p. 11) that the problem is not solved, he has done much of the essential spade work.

Brooke, Rupert. JOHN WEBSTER AND THE ELIZABETHAN DRAMA. New York: John Lane; London: Sidgwick & Jackson, 1916.

Brooke lays the groundwork for his study with several chapters on the early and Elizabethan drama and theatre, then analyzes Webster's work.

Dent, R[obert] W. JOHN WEBSTER'S BORROWING. Berkeley and Los Angeles: University of California Press, 1960.

Dent is not concerned with Webster's sources for what he calls "the basic plots" but with those "for the detail in Webster's plays--for dialogue, for subordinate episodes, for what Jonson called the 'furniture'" (p. 5). He provides an extensive catalog of parallels.

Gunby, D.C. WEBSTER: "THE WHITE DEVIL." Studies in English Literature, No. 45. London: Edward Arnold, 1971.

One of a series of literary guides designed for "the advanced sixth-former and the university student" and focused in "critical discussion" ("General Preface," p. [5]). Bibliography.

Hunter, G[eorge] K., and S.K. Hunter, eds. JOHN WEBSTER: A CRITICAL ANTHOLOGY (WITH INTRODUCTION). Baltimore, Md.: Penguin, 1969.

Reprints of criticism from the seventeenth century through the twentieth. Gunby, in WEBSTER (immediately above), calls the collection "a perceptive commentary on the development of present state of Webster criticism" (p. [58]).

Koskenniemi, Inna. JOHN WEBSTER'S "THE WHITE DEVIL" AND LUDWIG TIECK'S "VITTORIA ACCOROMBONA": A STUDY OF TWO RELATED WORKS. Turun Yliopiston Julkaisuja Series B, No. 97. Turku: Turun Yliopisto, 1966.

A short study, more concerned with Tieck's novel than with the Webster play.

Lagarde, Fernand. JOHN WEBSTER. 2 vols. Publications de la Faculte des Lettres et Sciences Humaines de Toulouse. Serie A, Tome 7. Toulouse: Association des Publications de la Faculte des Lettres et Sciences Humaines de Toulouse, 1968.

The two enormous volumes--1308 pages--study Webster in the Elizabethan and Jacobean theatre, his collaborations, his nondramatic work, his independent plays, his relations to Machiavellianism, his world, his dramatic technique, his relation to posterity. Bibliography.

Leech, Clifford. JOHN WEBSTER: A CRITICAL STUDY. Hogarth Lectures on Literature. London: Hogarth Press, 1951.

Leech discusses various plays but explores THE WHITE DEVIL and THE DUCHESS OF MALFI in particular. He evaluates Webster as a major dramatist: "[W]hen the fit was on him, his intuitions were sure and deep"; but as a flawed one, for "the vision of suffering humanity" came to him "in fits and starts" (p. 119).

_____. WEBSTER: "THE DUCHESS OF MALFI." Studies in English Literature, No. 8. London: Edward Arnold, 1963.

One of a series of small volumes designed for "sixth form" and university students, providing a study of the play and a brief bibliography.

Moore, Don D. JOHN WEBSTER AND HIS CRITICS, 1617-1964. Louisiana State University Studies, Humanities Series, No. 17. Baton Rouge: Louisiana State University Press, 1966.

The "Preface" announces the intention "to examine the varying, sometimes violent, responses to Webster's art" (pp. ix-x). In the "Conclusion" Moore ventures some generalizations about the criticism and also about Webster's work. Bibliography, including "Selected Reviews of Webster Productions, 1850-1960."

Morris, Brian, ed. JOHN WEBSTER. Mermaid Critical Commentaries. London: Benn, 1970.

The essays in the volume are the product of a "York Symposium on the Plays of John Webster" held in April, 1969. Morris provides the "Introduction." The essays are: Elizabeth M. Brennan, "'An Understanding Auditory': An Audience for John Webster"; Peter Thomson, "Webster and the Actor"; Roger Warren, "THE DUCHESS OF MALFI on the Stage"; A.J. Smith, "The Power of THE WHITE DEVIL"; Nigel Alexander, "Intelligence in THE DUCHESS OF MALFI"; Gunnar Boklund, "THE DEVIL'S LAW-CASE--An End or a Beginning?"; J.R. Mulryne, "Webster and the Uses of Tragicomedy"; Inga-Stina Ewbank, "Webster's Realism or 'A Cunning Piece Wrought Perspective'"; D.C. Gunby, "THE DUCHESS OF MALFI: A Theological Approach"; and Dominic Baker-Smith, "Religion and John Webster."

Murray, Peter B. A STUDY OF JOHN WEBSTER. Studies in English Literature, The Hague, 50. The Hague and Paris: Mouton Publishers, 1969.

The study focuses on "two questions: What did Webster actually write? What is the artistic value and the significance of his work?"

(p. 8). In offering an interpretation of Webster's tragic vision, Murray sees Webster as asking: "What is humanity to do and to believe in a world governed by evil?" (p. [253]). There are four appendices concerned with the authorship of various plays.

Pierce, Frederick Erastus. THE COLLABORATION OF WEBSTER AND DEKKER.

See the main entry in Section 8: Thomas Dekker.

Rabkin, Norman, ed. TWENTIETH CENTURY INTERPRETATIONS OF "THE DUCHESS OF MALFI": A COLLECTION OF CRITICAL ESSAYS. Englewood Cliffs, N.J.: Prentice-Hall, 1968.

Reprints of articles and parts of books; a convenient cross-section within one cover. Bibliography.

Scott-Kilvert, Ian. JOHN WEBSTER. Writers and Their Work, No. 175. London: Published for the British Council and the National Book League by Longmans, Green & Co., 1964.

A brief essay sets Webster's life in the context of his times and addresses the question: What is tragedy? Bibliography.

Stagg, Louis C. AN INDEX TO THE FIGURATIVE LANGUAGE OF JOHN WEBSTER'S TRAGEDIES. Charlottesville: Bibliographical Society of the University of Virginia, 1967.

One of a series of seven such indexes prepared by Stagg.

Stoll, Elmer Edgar. JOHN WEBSTER: THE PERIODS OF HIS WORK AS DETERMINED BY HIS RELATIONS TO THE DRAMA OF HIS DAY. Boston: Alfred Mudge & Son, 1905.

Stoll's "Preface" describes the study as "merely for the Elizabethan scholar. . . . I have suffered footnotes, appendices, and index of plays and authors to swell to more than half of the whole. And I have deliberately omitted to give the stories . . . or summaries of my own argument" (p. [5]). For the scholar, Stoll has provided exactly the useful study indicated by the title.

INDEX

Indexed are authors, editors, and compilers cited in the text; illustrators are in general omitted. Underlined numbers indicate main entries in the text. Titles are indexed if they appear in isolation from authors or editors, or if they seem likely to be sought in themselves rather than by editor (e.g., SHORT-TITLE CATALOGUE). If a play title is given without the playwright's name, it is indexed only under the title. Further, since Shakespeare is not properly the subject of this bibliography, references to him and his plays are not indexed except as he relates to another dramatist of the period.

Only a few selected topics are entered; the reader should therefore be aware that the index can limit if relied upon too exclusively. Section 4 of Part I, "Festschriften and Other Collections," should in particular be studied directly and in detail for subjects which the index cannot show.

A

Index

C

D

M

N

U

V

Y

Z